THE UNITED STATES IN THE TWENTIETH CENTURY

EMPIRE

CONTRIBUTORS TO THIS VOLUME

Kathleen Burk, Reader in History, University College London

Michael Cox, Reader in Politics, Queen's University of Belfast

Michael Foley, Professor of International Politics, University College Aberystwyth

Stephen Gill, Professor of International Relations, York University Toronto

Brian Hocking, Principal Lecturer in International Relations, University of Coventry

Anthony McGrew, Professor of International Relations, University of Southampton

Michael Smith, Professor of European Politics, Loughborough University

Cover

Vietnam Veterans Memorial, Washington, DC

Photo: R. Morley/PhotoLink

THE UNITED STATES IN THE TWENTIETH CENTURY

EMPIRE

Edited by
Anthony McGrew

SECOND EDITION

Hodder & Stoughton
in association with

The Open University

This text forms part of an Open University course D214 *The United States in the Twentieth Century*. The list of texts that make up the course can be found on the back cover. Details of this and other Open University courses can be obtained from the Course Reservations Centre, PO Box 724, The Open University, Milton Keynes MK7 6ZS, United Kingdom: tel. (00 44) 1908 653231. Alternatively, much useful information can be obtained from The Open University's website http://www.open.ac.uk

Published in Great Britain by Hodder & Stoughton Educational, a division of Hodder Headline Plc, 338 Euston Road, London NW1 3BH; written and produced by The Open University.

Orders: please contact Bookpoint Ltd, 39 Milton Park, Abingdon, Oxon OX14 4TD. Telephone: (44) 01235 400414, Fax: (44) 01235 400454. Lines are open from 9.00 – 6.00, Monday to Saturday, with a 24 hour message answering service. Email address: orders@bookpoint.co.uk

British Library Cataloguing in Publication Data

A catalogue record for this title is available from The British Library

ISBN 0 340 75826 0

First published 1994

Second edition published 2000

Impression number   10 9 8 7 6 5 4 3 2 1
Year   2005 2004 2003 2002 2001 2000

Copyright © 2000 The Open University

All rights reserved. No part of this publication may be reproduced or transmitted in any form or by any means, electronic or mechanical, including photocopy, recording, or any information storage and retrieval system, without permission in writing from the publisher or under licence from the Copyright Licensing Agency Limited. Further details of such licences (for reprographic reproduction) may be obtained from the Copyright Licensing Agency Limited, of 90 Tottenham Court Road, London W1P 0LP.

Edited, designed and typeset by The Open University.

Printed in the United Kingdom by Bath Press, Bath

10613C/D214b4prelimsi2.1

CONTENTS

Preface vii

Introduction: Anthony McGrew 1

Chapter 1 The lineaments of foreign policy: the United States and a 'New World Order' 1919–1939: Kathleen Burk 5

1 Introduction 5
2 American perceptions and approaches to world affairs 6
3 The new diplomacy 9
4 Foreign policy ideals 11
5 Foreign policy of the 1920s 14
6 Isolationism and multilateralism 17
7 Assessing US foreign policy in the inter-war period 20

Chapter 2 American power and the Soviet threat: US foreign policy and the Cold War: Michael Cox 23

1 Introduction 23
2 The emergent superpower: 1941–1945 25
3 The origins of the Cold War: 1945–1950 28
4 Dilemmas of US foreign policy 40
5 The Cold War system: 1947–1968 45
6 The Nixon–Kissinger 'grand design': 1968–1975 51
7 Carter and the liberal alternative: 1976–1980 56
8 Reagan and the revitalization of containment: 1980–1988 59
9 Bush and the end of the Cold War: 1989–1992 66
10 Conclusion: the United States, the Cold War and beyond 68

Chapter 3 *Pax Americana*: multilateralism and the global economic order: Stephen Gill 71

1 Introduction 71
2 The construction of the *Pax Americana* and the 'Grand Area' strategy 71
3 Welfare-nationalism and post-war reconstruction 76
4 Hegemony, civil society and Fordism in the post-war order 78
5 Multilateralism and the international economic order 82
6 Global finance and the problems of economic multilateralism 88
7 The renewed centrality of the USA, its limits and contradictions 92
8 Conclusion 96

Chapter 4   The United States and Western Europe: empire, alliance and interdependence: Michael Smith   101

1   Introduction   101
2   The foundations of the transatlantic system: 1946–1949   103
3   Consolidation and conflict: 1950–1960   109
4   Partnership and rivalry: 1960–1971   112
5   European–American relations in a changing world: 1971–1981   116
6   The Reagan challenge   122
7   From change to transformation   124
8   Reassessment and conclusions   135

Chapter 5   Globalization and the foreign–domestic policy nexus: Brian Hocking   145

1   Introduction   145
2   The changing nature of foreign policy   146
3   Managing foreign and domestic policy   149
4   Globalization and localization   150
5   The foreign–domestic nexus and the policy process   158
6   Conclusion   170

Chapter 6   The democratic imperative: Michael Foley   175

1   Introduction   175
2   The USA and the external world   176
3   The USA and its internal democracy   179
4   American democracy and the world: cause and effect   183
5   The world and American democracy: cause and effect   188
6   American foreign policy and the democratic conscience   193
7   Conclusion: primacy versus democracy   203

Chapter 7   A second American century?: the United States and the new world order: Anthony McGrew   211

1   Introduction   211
2   Endings and new beginnings   212
3   The return of history   219
4   Planning for peace   226
5   Struggle for the turf   234
6   A new covenant with power   244

Index   251

Acknowledgements   260

PREFACE

The five volumes in this series are part of an Open University, Faculty of Social Sciences course *The United States in the Twentieth Century*. In many respects the course has been a new venture — it is the first time that the Open University has entered the field of American Studies and it did so at a time when resources were not abundant. So the development of this course is due, in no small part, to the enthusiasm and support of many colleagues in the Faculty of Social Sciences. There are too many people to thank individually, but my appreciation must be recorded for some of them.

The United States in the Twentieth Century would not have been made without my academic colleagues, Anthony McGrew, Jeremy Mitchell and Grahame Thompson. Their role was central to the conception and planning of the course and their presence made the production of it an intellectually stimulating as well as an enjoyable experience. Mike Dawson, the Course Manager, took all the tension out of a process that is normally fraught and difficult. His calm efficiency, common sense and good humour got the rest of us through the production process with few anxieties. Jeremy Cooper of the BBC not only ensured that the course has an excellent audio-visual component, but made a very important contribution to its overall development. The Course Team owes a substantial debt to the editorial work of Stephen Clift and Tom Hunter who did all that was asked of them plus a great deal more. The designs for the covers, and indeed for the entire course, by Sarah Crompton were immediately and enthusiastically welcomed by everybody. David Wilson of the Book Trade Department was always available and his advice was both appreciated and heeded. Our colleagues in Project Control and in the Operations Division of the university were unfailingly supportive and helpful. However, none of these books would have seen the light of day without Anne Hunt who, along with her colleagues Mary Dicker and Carole Kershaw, typed successive drafts of the manuscripts of all five volumes without complaint and with remarkable accuracy and speed.

These books owe an enormous debt to our Americanist colleagues in institutions other than the Open University. This series has drawn on their scholarship and expertise, and above all on their generosity in being willing to participate in this project. The Course Team owes a particular debt to Professor David Adams, Director of the David Bruce Centre at the University of Keele, the external assessor of *The United States in the Twentieth Century*. His tough advice and wise counsel assisted us greatly. We incurred a similar obligation to Professor Ian Bell, also of the University of Keele, who helped us far beyond the call of duty. Doctor Ronald Clifton, who has done so much for American Studies in Britain, was enormously helpful and supportive in making sure this course came to fruition.

Finally there were moments when it might have been easier for Margaret Kiloh, the Dean of the Faculty of Social Sciences, to have been less than enthusiastic about *The United States in the Twentieth Century* but her support never wavered.

Richard Maidment, Course Chair
Milton Keynes, December 1993

I would like to thank all the contributors to this volume who produced such fine essays to a tight schedule, making the job of Editor such a relatively easy task. Without their enthusiasm and co-operation this volume would not have been completed. Tom Hunter has provided excellent editorial support and ensured the very professional and timely completion of the manuscript. Anne Hunt and Mary Dicker have coped with their ususal good humour in typing numerous drafts to extremely tight timescales and even interpreting (correctly) my illegible handwriting. My colleagues on the D214 Course Team have also provided invaluable comments and criticism on drafts at every stage of the project. Finally, I wish to record my gratitude to Christine, Francesca, Naomi and Kathryn for all their support throughout the duration of this project.

Anthony G. McGrew
Milton Keynes, April 1994

PREFACE TO THE SECOND EDITION

In preparing this second edition thanks are due to the individual contributors, who worked to a tight schedule. In addition, Anne Hunt dealt with complicated manuscripts and Annabel Caulfield kept the production on track.

Anthony G. McGrew
Southampton, May 2000

INTRODUCTION

Anthony McGrew ★

Since 1945, the USA has exercised enormous power on a global scale arguably far surpassing that of any imperial state in previous historical epochs. In this respect, at least, the United States can be regarded, as so many Americans continue to see it, as an exceptional nation: exceptional not just in terms of its status as a truly global power, but also in its outlook as an imperial state that 'is so desperately anxious not to be an empire' (Niebuhr, 1959, p.28). The essays in this volume interrogate the notion of empire as a convincing description of America's global role in the twentieth century. As the American historian Arthur Schlesinger has observed, it is impossible to deny the almost imperial role of the United States in designing and constructing the post-Second World War liberal world order (Schlesinger, 1986, p.141).

To describe the United States as an imperial state is to draw an admittedly fine distinction between the notion of 'empire' and the notion of 'imperial power'. Nevertheless, such fine distinctions are analytically important. But to equate the USA's rise to global power with the emergence of an 'American empire' remains a somewhat controversial conclusion. Among diplomatic historians there is little sympathy for the view of William Appleman Williams that, since the founding of the republic, empire has been, like consumerism, a necessary adjunct to the 'American way of life' (Williams, 1980). According to Williams, the innate expansionist energies of American capitalism combined with the messianic political ideology of exceptionalism created a peculiarly American condition in which 'Empire became so intrinsically our American way of life that we rationalized ... the realities of expansionism, conquering and intervention into pious rhetoric about virtue, wealth and democracy [which] reached its culmination in the decades after World War Two' (Williams, 1980, p.ix). For Williams, the history of post-war American foreign policy is the story of the consolidation of the 'American empire' on a global scale. But an 'empire' in what sense?

Raymond Aron once commented that 'all those who use the term "American empire" promptly qualify it by adding that this empire does not in any way resemble any other empire' (Aron, 1973, p.279). The strict notion of 'empire' embraces 'a relationship, formal or informal, in which one state controls the effective political sovereignty of another political society' (Doyle, 1986, p.345). Defined in this way, 'empire' may describe the US's relations with its Central American client states, but it significantly misrepresents the form and nature of US power in other contexts, such as US–European relations. Indeed, as Lundestad observed, what distinguished the US from the Soviet Union during the Cold War was the fact that the US embraced its global role with some diffidence, becoming an 'empire by invitation' (Lundestad, 1986). However, an 'empire by invitation' is quite different in kind from the strict notion of 'empire' proposed by Williams. Indeed, abandoning the strict definition of 'empire' for the looser term 'empire by invitation' suggests that the word 'empire' is nothing more than a synonym for a hegemonic or great power.

Instead of using the vocabulary of 'empire', it is perhaps more fruitful to view the USA in the post-war period as a 'hegemonic' (dominant) or 'imperial' power. As Aron suggests, an imperial diplomacy is 'a diplomacy which intervenes all over the world without aiming at constructing an "empire" in the legal or practical sense of the term' (Aron, 1973, pp.255–6). It is a diplomacy through which a dominant or hegemonic state attempts to fashion the global economic and political order in ways that are consonant with its own interests and values. It is a diplomacy energized by the desire to construct a stable world order, as opposed to the diplomacy of empire building which seeks control of the political sovereignty of subordinate states. In short, the hegemonic or imperial state seeks to define the international order and political context within which other sovereign states operate. In this sense the United States can be considered a hegemonic or 'imperial' state, for the historical evidence betrays 'a country concerned to dominate the conduct of weaker peoples … in the name of an international order conforming to its design' (Smith, 1981, p.183). Twentieth-century American diplomacy, and more particularly post-war American diplomacy, is perhaps more convincingly accounted for in terms of the exercise of 'imperial' or hegemonic power than in terms of the unfolding logic of 'empire' (Keohane, 1991, p.437). Moreover, although 'imperial diplomacy' is closely associated with the Cold War era, some observers believe the end of the 'great contest' has not diminished this 'imperial temptation': on the contrary, the architects of post-Cold War American diplomacy have begun to devote their energies and American power to the task of constructing a 'new world order'. The twenty-first century, some argue, will be the second American century (Valladao, 1996; Zuckerman, 1998).

In this book considerable attention is devoted to analysing the changing global role and imperial power of the United States from the early days of the twentieth century through to the new millennium. In charting the emergence of the USA as a great power, and its subsequent role in constructing the post-war global economic and political orders, the chapters provide insights into the USA's decisive impact on global affairs in the twentieth century. There is a special emphasis on the relationship between domestic political conditions and processes, as key factors in any systematic attempt to account for the origins and dynamics of US foreign policy. In addition, the chapters reflect (to varying degrees) a concern with the present: they examine how the demise of the Cold War and the emergence of an increasingly globalized political economy have transformed the foundations of both the US's global role and its global power. Accordingly, the authors of these essays not only deliver valuable insights into how the exercise of US power has influenced the trajectory of world history, but they also deal with the increasingly salient issue of how the USA's deepening interdependence with the rest of humanity has transformed the conditions of its own economic and political existence. In a world of flows and connections – of migrants, footloose capital, the international narcotics trade, and so on – the distinction between the foreign and the domestic has become increasingly blurred. This has brought about what might be termed the 'end of foreign policy' as it is conventionally understood and, at the same time, transformed the instrumentalities of American power. As the twenty-first century beckons, the USA confronts new national vulnerabilities and critical policy choices driven by the growing intensity of the processes of globalization – a 'shrinking world'. In their quite different ways, the chapters reflect on the contemporary challenges confronting the guardians of American power as they attempt to fashion an appropriate role for the nation in the new millennium.

In Chapter 1, Kathleen Burk examines American foreign policy in the early part of the American century. It is a story of idealistic engagement and rapid disengagement from world affairs, expressing the underlying diffidence with which, since the dawning of the twentieth century, the United States has attempted to construct a 'covenant with power'. This coming to terms with power and global responsibilities is analysed further in Chapters 2 and 3, both of which concentrate on the construction of the post-war global order. In Chapter 2, Michael Cox describes the emergence of the USA as a global superpower and the forces shaping its role in the 'great contest' with the Soviet Union, a contest that dominated American foreign policy and domestic politics from 1947 to 1990. In Chapter 3, Stephen Gill analyses the critical role of the USA in constructing the post-war liberal international economic order. Because of its military supremacy and economic primacy, the USA was able to establish a global economic and political order that reflected its core interests. But as its relative power has been eroded with the emergence of new centres of power, especially Europe, the US's ability to sustain that order unilaterally has been called into question. This issue is discussed by Michael Smith in Chapter 4, which examines the US's relations with Europe in the post-war era in terms of the dynamics of empire, alliance and interdependence. Questions of interdependence figure prominently in subsequent chapters, which concentrate less on the USA's impact on the world and more on the domestic impact of its global role. In Chapter 5, Brian Hocking discusses the transformation of American foreign policy in the late twentieth century, as the growing globalization of economic affairs restructured the domestic political economy. Similarly, but taking a longer historical and political perspective, Chapter 6 by Michael Foley explains how the democratic imperative has shaped, and in turn been shaped by, the nation's entanglement in world affairs. Chapter 7 examines the crisis in American foreign policy, as the nation's political leaders attempt to redefine its national purpose and fashion a new global role in the wake of the ending of the Cold War. This chapter ends by questioning whether the end of the American century is at hand or a new American century is dawning.

Clearly, no collection of essays can aim to be comprehensive in its coverage, and this collection is no exception. By design, it is organized on an essentially thematic basis rather than constructed around a conventional geopolitical categorization of American foreign policy, that is, policy towards the Middle East, Asia and so on. Moreover, it is concerned almost exclusively with the US's post-war role within the East–West and Western axes of global politics. Despite this selective bias, the collection provides a novel and distinctive interpretation of US power in twentieth-century global politics while offering a historically grounded analysis of the key determinants of post-war, as well as contemporary, American foreign policy.

REFERENCES

Aron, R. (1973) *The Imperial Republic*, London, Weidenfeld and Nicolson.

Doyle, M.W. (1986) *Empires*, New York, Cornell University Press.

Keohane, R. (1991) 'The United States and the post-war order: empire or hegemony?', *Journal of Peace Research*, vol.28, no.4, pp.435–9.

Lundestad, G. (1986) 'Empire by invitation? The United States and Western Europe, 1945–1952', *Journal of Peace Research*, vol.23, pp.263–77.

Niebuhr, R. (1959) *Nations and Empires*, London, Faber and Faber.

Schlesinger, A. (1986) *The Cycles of American History*, Boston, Houghton Mifflin.

Smith, T. (1981) *The Pattern of Imperialism*, Cambridge, Cambridge University Press.

Valladao, A. (1996) *The Twenty First Century will be American*, London, Verso.

Williams, W.A. (1980) *Empire is a Way of Life*, Oxford, Oxford University Press.

Zuckerman, M. (1998) 'A second American Century', *Foreign Affairs*, vol.77, no.3, pp.18–31.

THE LINEAMENTS OF FOREIGN POLICY: THE UNITED STATES AND A 'NEW WORLD ORDER' 1919–1939

Kathleen Burk ★

1 INTRODUCTION

The end of the 1980s saw the break-up of the Soviet Union into a number of independent republics and the consequent breakdown of the Soviet Empire. With the self-inflicted defeat of the enemy, the United States proclaimed the end of the Cold War, with itself the winner. For the USA, all sorts of new possibilities beckoned, and the idea of a 'new world order', of an American opportunity to remake a broken world into a more liberal and democratic place, was very much in the air. It is analogous, in fact, to the period immediately after the First World War, when the United States, led by President Woodrow Wilson, consciously attempted to build a new world order on the ruins of the old.

The whole idea of mounting an attempt to build a new world order has a very positive ring to it. At the very least it appears to assume there is a plan, and an active personality or two as its architects; it also assumes a global reach on the part of the state at the centre. If these are indeed the necessary requirements, then the USA during the inter-war period fulfilled them only partially and erratically. Certainly, if one looks for a strong, cohesive pattern in US foreign policy at this time, the culmination of many smaller plans and patterns, then one can be found. This is a drive to convince the rest of the world that it should adopt policies which would lead to an international economy characterized by free trade, convertible currencies and open markets, together with a drive to convince the other world powers that they should disarm. All American Administrations from 1919 to 1939 would have agreed with these policy imperatives. But what is undeniable is that they varied in their emphases, in the efforts which US governments themselves made to get these policies accepted. Only Woodrow Wilson, President of the USA from 1912 to 1920, had a plan, and only he sought to involve the US government permanently in its implementation, to the extent of tying it down to future responsibilities: all others preferred, when feasible, to leave it to the private sector, bankers and businessmen, and merely to give indicative guidance.

This chapter begins by looking at US perceptions of the world and approaches to foreign relations. It continues with a look at the Wilsonian approach to diplomacy and its policy outcomes, and then at the foreign policy of the 1920s. The dominant trends of the 1930s, isolationism and multilateralism, are considered next, and the chapter ends with an overall assessment of US foreign policy during the inter-war period.

2 AMERICAN PERCEPTIONS AND APPROACHES TO WORLD AFFAIRS

Two points should be made at the outset. First of all, European and US policy makers viewed foreign policy from very different perspectives. The Europeans, for example, assumed that after the First World War the USA would continue to involve itself in international matters, particularly by helping to reconstruct Europe and to help keep the balance of power. When instead the USA showed a marked disinclination to become involved, this was taken as evidence of selfishness and immaturity. But it is worth pointing out that for most Americans during most of the inter-war period, there was no earthly reason why they (in the form of the US government) should become involved in what they considered to be the affairs of other nations. After all, they did not feel particularly threatened, and there were more important activities to which they wanted to devote their time and money. Secondly, when Americans did look abroad, the country to which they turned their eyes most often was Great Britain. This was true whether it was as a rival — either from an economic standpoint or as a naval power — or as ally and partner — in the financial diplomacy of the period or, for example, in the attempt of Henry L. Stimson, the Secretary of War, to have the two countries stand together against Japan in 1931 when she invaded China. The United States measured itself against Britain.

Foreign policy has seldom interested many Americans, except in times of crisis, and the inter-war period was no exception. Many Americans shared the European sense of disillusionment with the war and its aftermath, but they also believed that their involvement had been both unnecessary and a grave mistake. Thus, they were doubly certain that they did not wish to be involved in international affairs, their contrary enthusiasm only being aroused by conferences to limit armaments or to outlaw war. In this case, enthusiastic peace groups sometimes drove reluctant policy makers along — one example of this is Secretary of State Frank Kellogg's agreement to the Kellogg-Briand Pact in 1928, which solemnly committed the signatory nations to renounce war (see Section 4 and Ferrell 1952).

Certain presidents shared this general American reluctance to foster foreign relations, and in this period one thinks particularly of Warren G. Harding and Calvin Coolidge, neither of whom had much knowledge of or interest in foreign policy and both of whom tended to leave foreign affairs to their secretaries of state. It is worth noting that presidents are sometimes attracted to the conduct of foreign affairs because in this field they have more independent power, thanks to the Constitution, than in domestic affairs.

Woodrow Wilson, sometimes Herbert Hoover and almost certainly Franklin Roosevelt were internationalists, but for the latter two, the episode of Wilson and the Versailles Treaty was an awful example of what could happen to a president if he got ahead of his public and particularly of his Congress. Wilson's main goal at the Versailles Conference had been to commit the signatories of the Treaty to a League of Nations, intended to go some way towards committing member nations to come to the aid of states who were attacked. (The hope, of course, was that this threat would deter the attacker and thus prevent war.) Many senators and congressmen believed that the treaty took away Congress' constitutional power to declare war, and opposed it. Largely because of Wilson's insistence upon the inclusion of the League of Nations in the Versailles Treaty, Congress refused to ratify it (Ambrosius, 1987). Indeed, while the executive leader of no western industrial nation with a legislature took the possibility of its objections lightly, in no country was the legislature as powerful, and as uncontrollable by the Executive, as in the United States. Therefore while the president had the leading responsibility for making and conducting foreign policy, he worked within the boundaries set by his abilities to cajole Congress into following his lead.

President Wilson (right) at Versailles for the peace conference in 1919 with (from left to right) Italian Premier Orlando, British Prime Minister Lloyd George and French Premier Clemenceau

When presidents looked abroad, where did they look? What were the boundaries of their world? It is possible to argue that for Americans, there were two geographical areas, Latin America and everywhere else. The USA was deeply involved in Latin American affairs, in particular to ensure access to markets and raw materials, and to safeguard American property, a situation more akin to informal empire than political relations with perceived equals. As far as relations with European countries were concerned, involvement should be kept to a minimum.

When Americans thought at all about relations with other countries, they frequently thought in economic terms and spoke in categories of trade and finance. They spoke as though they believed — and perhaps did believe —

that there was little need for political involvement with other countries, and thus a refusal to become so involved was not a shirking of responsibility. These same men could profess to believe that questions of trade and finance belonged in the private sector, not in the public, and indeed, that even admitting that they were political questions could be disadvantageous to the USA, by opening up the question of providing American aid in, for example, reconstructing Europe (Leffler, 1979).

In short, the American approach to the world during the inter-war period was confused. Public opinion, and the Congress, appeared to be predominantly isolationist, and presidents and policy makers who wished to be more active had to take this into account (Adler, 1957; Cole, 1983). It is clear, for example, that the US government was quite active 'in the world' during the 1920s, but in certain categories of activity, for example, European reconstruction, trade and finance, they worked through surrogates. This was the age of bankers' diplomacy, when the private expert actually negotiated on behalf of the USA: an example of this was the involvement of the banker Charles Gates Dawes in the negotiations with Germany over reparation payments in 1924 (the Dawes Plan), which involved the rescheduling of that nation's debts (Schuker, 1976). Of course, when questions of high politics did move on to centre stage — that is, questions about reductions in arms or disarmament, or about the outlawing of war — the US government became directly involved. But it is also notable that these agreements committed the USA, basically, to nothing.

During the 1930s, on the other hand, the US State and Treasury Departments saw questions of trade and finance as political questions, and both on high moral and low political grounds, attempted to convince other countries to adopt certain policies which would transform the international economic system. For Secretary of State Cordell Hull and his department, it was imperative to return to an international system based on free trade and non-discrimination: Hull's particular *bête noire* was the British system of Imperial Preference, as negotiated and signed at the Imperial Conference at Ottawa in 1932. Under this system, members of the British Empire and Commonwealth gave preference to each other in terms of trade tariffs over outsiders — such as the USA. Henry Morgenthau, the Secretary of the Treasury, concentrated more on convertible currencies, with his goal being a general return to the gold standard. Neither was successful during this period.

Questions of international politics and particularly of security were a different matter, however: the country was isolationist, and Congress ensured, with the passage of a series of Neutrality Acts in 1935, 1936, 1937 and 1939, that the world knew it. Briefly, the Neutrality Act of 1935 placed a mandatory embargo on 'arms, ammunition, or implements of war', the last-named to be defined by the president; it prohibited US ships from carrying munitions to belligerent states; and it gave the president discretion to withhold protection from Americans travelling on belligerent ships. The Neutrality Act of 1936 in addition forbade loans to belligerents and made mandatory an arms embargo on states entering a war in progress. The Neutrality Act of 1937 gave the president discretion to withhold raw materials from belligerents and to apply the arms embargo to civil wars. Finally, the Neutrality Act of 1939 repealed the arms embargo and instituted the sale of goods on a cash-and-carry basis. The intention was to make it impossible for the USA to be dragged into another war merely to save the interests of bankers and munitions makers, as many professed to believe had been the case in 1917.

> *SUMMARY:*
>
> American foreign relations during the inter-war period were dominated by isolationism as apparently supported by public opinion and enforced by Congress. Foreign relations concentrated upon questions of trade and finance, but politicians and officials saw these as private sector interests with which government should not officially become involved.

3 THE NEW DIPLOMACY

The only president during the inter-war period who had a plan for a new world order was, as we have seen, Woodrow Wilson, and even he had been driven to such a plan by war. Wilson had not wanted the USA to fight in the First World War, and had kept the country out of it, until driven to join by the unrestricted use of submarines by the Germans. Rather than fight, Wilson's prime aim during the war had been to bring the belligerents to the peace table, where he, Wilson, would mediate a peace without victors. In other words, his concern was with structures to impose and to keep the peace, not structures with which to fight wars — such as alliances — and he was so horrified by the war that he decided that it should not be wasted. Therefore, almost before Congress had decided that the USA was at war, Wilson had his aides at work designing a new world order and an organization to support it (Knock, 1993).

Wilson believed that a major cause of war was the 'Old Diplomacy', with its secret negotiations, alliances and arms races. In its place he argued, in his Fourteen Points address to a joint session of Congress on 8 January 1918, for the adoption of a 'New Diplomacy', with its ideals of open diplomacy — or open covenants openly arrived at — absolute freedom of the seas in peace and war (unless closed by international agreement), general disarmament, the removal of barriers to trade between nations, an impartial settlement of colonial claims, and the establishment of a League of Nations. Most of these points were either ignored — for example, open diplomacy — or whittled down during the Versailles Peace Conference; but Wilson held on to the proposal for a League of Nations in some form, believing that with its establishment, there would be a forum for the re-consideration of the other problems (Egerton, 1991).

The League of Nations building in Geneva

In due course a League of Nations was set up, whose duty was to enforce the collective security of its member nations: that is, rather than an individual state reacting to aggression by another state, the members of the League agreed that together they would face down the aggressor, thereby, it was hoped, avoiding the need to fight. It was set up for two reasons: firstly, it had substantial support in other belligerent countries, such as Britain — and indeed, it was first suggested to Wilson by Sir Edward Grey, the British Secretary of State for Foreign Affairs, in a letter sent to Wilson's adviser, Colonel E.M. House, on 22 September 1915, which House passed on to the president; and secondly, Wilson made it clear that without the inclusion of such a League, he would not sign the Versailles Treaty. But in the end, Wilson could not carry the US Senate with him, and by its refusal to approve the treaty, the Senate ensured that the USA would join Germany and the USSR as non-members. This was ignominious company: Germany, saddled with responsibility for the war by the treaty, was prevented from joining, as was the Soviet Union, which had not only gone Bolshevik in 1917 and thereby become a pariah nation, but had also made a separate peace treaty with Germany in the same year.

Wilson and his liberal internationalist supporters, who included bankers such as Thomas Lamont of J.P. Morgan and Company, former President William Howard Taft and Colonel House, failed to ensure that the institutional structures of a new world order enjoyed the active support of the US government. Generally speaking, the term 'liberal internationalist' is used by historians to connote those who urged the co-operation of the great powers within a framework of world law and open world trade. Many, although not all, also supported the following Wilsonian tenets: an end to the system of entangling alliances, secret diplomacy and balances of power; a reduction in armaments by all countries until armies were only large enough to maintain internal security; and the creation of an international agency, based on collective security, which was strong enough to protect its members against aggression (Link, 1957; Ambrosius, 1991). In short, the set of ideas informing this world view remained influential during the inter-war period, encouraging active American involvement in the search for ways to limit armaments and wars. In this political involvement, the government enjoyed the backing of public opinion, which was apparently pro-peace and anti-war. 'Apparently', because it is unclear just how accurately public opinion can be assessed, before the period of even rudimentary opinion polls. It was measured by a combination of pressure by interest groups, newspaper comments, the reaction to politicians when they spoke at rallies, letters to the president, congressmen and senators, and electoral results. Certainly it was taken as a consensus against involvement by the US government in foreign affairs, except in attempts to limit armaments or war.

SUMMARY

The 'new diplomacy' was the term used to describe attempts to substitute open negotiations (based on international law and free trade, and supported by informed public opinion) for the world of secret negotiations and alliances. Woodrow Wilson was the major proponent of this.

4 FOREIGN POLICY IDEALS

How did American policy makers during this period work within the limits set by the pervasive isolationist policy? First of all, on the whole they shared certain notions. For one thing, they believed that the USA was a great power, and in the eyes of some, the most important of the great powers. This was based primarily on US economic and industrial strength, rather than on her military strength, which lagged behind that of the European great powers. In any case, the Republican presidents of the 1920s wanted to cut down on stockpiles of armaments, rather than build them up. The Europeans suspected that for the USA, encouraging or forcing the European nations to cut their levels of arms, rather than herself building up her stocks of arms to European levels, was primarily a cheap way for the USA to reach arms parity with the Europeans.

Indeed, it should be noted that US admirals, who certainly believed that the USA was a great power and ought to act like one, happily caught this wave in order to limit the size of their great rival, the Royal Navy. The Washington Conference of 1921-1922 limited the number of capital ships which participating countries would be allowed to sail to a ratio, and in this ratio the navies of the USA and the United Kingdom were to be equal. This conference worked because: (1) the USA threatened to enter into an arms race with Britain and bankrupt her if the United Kingdom did not agree; and (2) important elements in the British Cabinet believed that it was by no means certain that the USA would actually get round to building the required number of ships. The second conference, called by President Coolidge in Geneva in 1927, did not end so satisfactorily. The USA wanted land armies on the Continent to be limited, but refused to give any security guarantees. She also wanted the number of naval cruisers to be limited, but here Britain refused: she needed cruisers in order to protect her trade routes. Britain remembered that the USA had not in fact built up to her allowed ratio of capital ships after 1922, and decided to call the Americans' bluff in 1927: the conference broke up acrimoniously (Ferris, 1984).

The third conference, the London Naval Conference of 1930, took place after a change both of British Prime Minister — from Stanley Baldwin to Ramsay MacDonald — and of President — from Calvin Coolidge to Herbert Hoover; it was also the subject of better preparation. The 1922 ratio of 5:5:3 for British, American and Japanese capital ships — the so-called Rolls-Royce: Rolls-Royce: Ford ratio — was extended from capital ships to cruisers, which satisfied the Americans. Britain had now agreed that the USA had the right to a navy as big as her own, even if this were not yet the case. The aggrieved party was Japan, who, angry at the restrictions still imposed on her, and anxious to become a great power in her own right, turned her attention to China.

Even better than limiting armaments would be to eliminate the need to use them by outlawing war. France wanted to entice the USA into some sort of commitment to her existence, be it ever so tenuous, and so the French Foreign Minister, Aristide Briand, suggested a bilateral Franco-American agreement, in which the two countries would foreswear the use of war against each other. Naturally the US Secretary of State, Frank Kellogg, thought this was suspicious, but American pacifist groups were numerous and noisy. Ordinarily they were split over specific proposals, but they could at least agree upon the hatefulness of war, and therefore they united behind a treaty to renounce its use. Kellogg, to appease these groups while refraining from giving France any hook on which to hang a future claim for American support, substituted a multilateral pact amongst the principal powers, later extended to others, and on 27 August 1928 the Kellogg-Briand Pact for the Renunciation of War as an Instrument of National Policy was signed.

It was an empty document, but ordinary people found it heartening; policy makers, however, sneered at it (Ferrell, 1952). Indeed, it might almost be said to have been the ideal treaty for the US to sign: only two paragraphs long, strongly against sin, but with no commitment or enforcement clauses. To give American policy makers their due, they knew it was useless, one senator referring to it as an 'international kiss' (Marks, 1976). But the American public greeted it with enthusiasm, and the whole episode certainly made it clear that there were votes in peace and non-commitment. Other countries thought that the signing of the Pact might harbour the

1 THE LINEAMENTS OF FOREIGN POLICY

President Calvin Coolidge signing the anti-war treaty in the East Room of the White House, 17 January 1929

return of the USA to an active interest in world affairs, but this would not be the case, with the exception of financial and economic affairs.

And in fact, if one is looking for an active foreign policy at the service of a coherent concept during the inter-war period, this is the place to look. A strong isolationist movement, as well as many ordinary Americans, believed that military intervention in Europe had been a mistake, and that the way to lessen the chances of such a mistake being made again was to refuse to become involved in any negotiations or agreements which might compromise American freedom of action in the future. This was the negative side of things. But there was a positive side to this revulsion against the First World War, and this was an attempt to remove the causes of war by eliminating barriers to trade and economic growth. This had constituted one of Wilson's Fourteen Points, but its pedigree went even further back, at least to American Secretary of State John Hay and the Open Door Notes of the early years of the century. This was something on which virtually all American policy makers could agree.

SUMMARY

Most Americans agreed on certain foreign policy ideals: limitation of armaments, isolationism from foreign affairs, and the elimination of barriers to international trade — particularly if the barriers were imposed by other countries.

5 FOREIGN POLICY OF THE 1920s

During the 1920s the major international task was the reconstruction of Europe. Most currencies were inconvertible, many countries had tariffs, and a number of states, particularly the newer ones, had to rebuild their economies. A Republican Administration would be particularly prone to respond to such a challenge, since businessmen and business interest groups were amongst their strongest supporters. Europe was an increasingly important market, particularly in view of the fact that overproduction in the USA was not matched by an increasing ability of American consumers to buy. Large American businesses had their own means of getting around tariff barriers, and this included buying up native companies — 1927 saw General Motors buying Vauxhall Motors in the UK, for example (Burk, 1989) — but for most American businesses this would not work. Many Republican policy makers wanted the Europeans to integrate their economies by means of convertible currencies and multilateral free trade because the result would be enhanced opportunities for American business (Leffler, 1979).

But there was an altruistic side to this as well. Many, and not only Americans, believed that economic conflict was a fundamental cause of war, and the hope was that removing barriers would conduce the peoples to peace. American pressure for disarmament fitted in very well here, since if governments stopped spending so much on arms, their economies would be in much better shape and their peoples happier. They could also repay their war debts to the USA, which would make the Americans happier. Indeed, one reason American policy makers adduced for not forgiving the Europeans their war debts was the fear that they would just spend the money on armaments, which would lead to war. Much better to give it to the US government.

For whatever congeries of reasons, the USA became very involved in the reconstruction of Europe. American money was instrumental in the stabilization of the German mark, the British pound, the Belgian franc and the Italian lira, in the commercialization of the German reparations debt by means of the Dawes and Young Plans, and in supplying funds to most of the old and new European states in order to build or rebuild railways, utilities, factories, housing and even swimming baths. American negotiators were also instrumental in establishing the Bank for International Settlements, an organization established in 1930 to facilitate the payment of reparations (Costigliola, 1972).

This is not unimpressive, but it is important to understand that the US government was not directly involved in any of this. Because of the massive amount of war debts owed by the European nations to the US government, the USA always feared that if she became involved in negotiations over loans, debts, reconstruction or anything connected, she would be met by a phalanx of debtors, with support, perhaps, only from Britain, who was also a creditor nation with regard to the continental European nations, although a large debtor to the USA. Therefore the US government refused to attend some of the various international conferences called to discuss and possibly to sort out the political and economic imbroglio. One such was the Genoa Conference, held in April-May 1922, whose purpose was to re-establish ties between the Soviet Union and the West, and to promote the economic reconstruction of Europe. Its unexpected outcome was the Soviet-German Treaty of Rapallo, the publication of which destroyed the possibility of any wider agreement (Orde, 1990; Fink, 1984).

The US government also refused to become officially involved in the negotiations necessary to help individual countries. First of all, no US government money could be used, since Congress would never have countenanced it, and it never really occurred to any responsible policy maker to suggest it. But money was needed, and the only place where it could be found in large enough quantities was in the New York money market. This meant private sector funding and so, the US government said, private sector funding required private sector 'diplomacy' and decisions. In other words, if Belgium required a large loan in order to stabilize her currency, she would have to turn to private bankers to raise it, and it was their responsibility, not the US government's, to decide whether the Belgian balance sheet was such as to deserve a loan.

Indeed, in all of the negotiations requiring expert advice, such as financial transactions, where other countries sent Treasury or Finance Ministry officials, the USA fielded private bankers or businessmen. One example was the Dawes negotiations in 1924. What was at stake, beyond the question of the German currency and reparations payments, was the geopolitical relationship between France and Germany, since it involved France's withdrawal from the Ruhr, which she had occupied to try to force Germany to pay reparations. Yet, because Germany would have to borrow private money in order to fund her obligations, the US government insisted that it had no desire to become entangled in such matters and kept in the background. The US delegation was headed by Charles G. Dawes, a Chicago banker, with private help from partners in the House of Morgan (Schuker, 1976).

The use of private experts, especially bankers and big businessmen, was a hallmark of Republican diplomacy during the period. But this does not mean that the US government was not involved at all. It was very much indirectly involved, in particular while Herbert Hoover was the Secretary of Commerce and in control of foreign economic policy, but behind the scenes. Hoover would have liked to have had the power to direct American finance where it would support American goals, but this was not seen as a legitimate power for government. Instead, he insisted on being notified about all proposed foreign loans, so that he could indicate to bankers when it would be inappropriate to lend. For example, Hoover wanted bankers to refuse to lend to countries which had not come to an agreement with the USA to begin repayment of their war debts. This meant that until 1926, he tried to discourage bankers from lending to France, with the result that good French loans were refused and weak German ones accepted. Bankers were encouraged to develop plans for European stabilization and for increased

Charles G. Dawes

trading links, but under no circumstances was the US government to become directly involved (Brandes, 1962).

The point is that Republican administrations had a vision of the world as it should develop, but it was an economic world, not a political one. This vision was, in part, a result of their belief that a world based on free trade, convertible currencies and free markets would encourage the growth of private initiatives, which would lead to economic growth and a better standard of living, and this would in turn reduce the chances of war. It was also in part because they believed that the USA was self-evidently more liberal, democratic and peaceful, and should remain aloof from too close links with European powers, which might serve to pull it into conflict. And finally in part the main weapon the USA possessed in the international arena was her economic power. After all, Britain's navy was larger, the American army did not approach in size those of the main European powers, and she had a public who were clearly isolationist and would not support foreign involvement. All she really had was her money. But it was private, not public, money and indicative guidance was the only power available. What gave the US government influence over the financiers was the fact that on the whole, they agreed with the Republican analysis and approach.

> **SUMMARY**
>
> US foreign policy during the 1920s, as designed and implemented by Republican Party administrations, had two main themes: the first was the reconstruction of Europe, in which, for ideological reasons, the US government took a back seat to the private sector; and the second was the backing of moves for the reduction of armaments and the limitation of war, in which the government itself took the lead.

6 ISOLATIONISM AND MULTILATERALISM

Once the Democratic Party came to power in 1933, foreign policy did not remain so clear cut. On the one hand, US policy became even more isolationist and nationalist, as Roosevelt's smashing of the 1933 World Economic and Monetary Conference made clear: called to consider plans for stabilizing currencies and for tackling 'beggar-thy-neighbour' policies developing in the face of the Depression, the Conference fell victim to Roosevelt's announcement that the USA would concentrate on domestic economic recovery, rather than on schemes for international co-operation which would return currencies to a fixed exchange rate (Clavin, 1992). And as the foreign horizon darkened during the 1930s, Congress, if not the president, fostered a series of neutrality acts (see above) which were intended to fence off the USA from future conflicts by ensuring that American businessmen and financiers could not do business with belligerents.

Indeed, it seemed for a period as though isolationism, the desire to isolate the United States from the contagion of foreign entanglements which seemed to lead ineluctably to foreign wars, would entirely control the Administration's foreign policy. Certainly Roosevelt, and his more internationally-minded advisors, had to take heed of isolationism's influence, as had presidents in the 1920s. Its immediate source was the popular revulsion against the First World War, and in particular what seemed to be the uselessness of the slaughter, and in this sense most nations during the period were isolationist: Neville Chamberlain himself would not have been entirely out of place in the US Senate, when he spoke of Czechoslovakia as 'a far-away place of which we know nothing'. Furthermore, thanks to the activities of the Nye Committee of the US Senate, which proclaimed in 1935 that the USA had been lured into the First World War by armaments manufacturers and by Wall Street bankers who wanted to save their fortunes, the American public were taught that it had been an unnecessary war. In addition, the severity of the Depression led many Americans to conclude that their efforts and attention ought to be focused on home affairs rather than abroad.

But isolationism had a historical source as well: it was embedded in the very founding and development of the USA. The USA was largely a land of immigrants, of people who had left Europe and its problems behind: the last thing many desired was continued involvement in European conflicts. However, it is also fair to say that the strength of isolationism varied from region to region: for example, it was much weaker on the Atlantic seaboard, the stronghold of the internationalist impulse amongst the political, social and intellectual elites, than in the Midwest, for example. The Midwestern states and the South, in fact, were the main locus of support for isolationist politicians — Senator William Borah of Idaho was an exemplar — since these were rural areas, covered with farms and small towns and the occasional city, the quintessence of provincial society (McKenna, 1961). Their interests and their purview were local, or at best state-wide; lacking interest even in Washington, why should they care about Paris? The answer is, they did not, and this meant that support for international co-operation, even for the League of Nations, was lacking (Adler, 1957). This latter point is ironic: although the USA had been the main proponent at the Versailles Conference for the establishment of the League of Nations, the consequence of the Senate's refusal to allow the USA to join was that US officials could only act as observers at the League throughout the inter-war period.

Roosevelt's one tentative effort to engage with Europe during the 1930s, his suggestion in January 1938 for a conference to discuss European problems, was strangled at birth by Neville Chamberlain, who believed that it would lead to nothing but talk, might disrupt negotiations then in train with Italy, and would in any case lead to American demands (Rock, 1988). After Chamberlain's rebuff, the president and the US government turned their attention back to domestic problems.

During the run-up to the war, and particularly once the European states were at war (which for Britain was 3 September 1939), the US government paid closer attention to events, but Congress remained a bastion of isolationism and refused to countenance overt aid to its future allies. Roosevelt attempted to convince Congress to amend the Neutrality Acts to allow Britain and her allies to purchase supplies, but his first attempt, in the summer of 1939, was a failure. Only in November 1939 was the amended Neutrality Act passed, which allowed belligerents to purchase goods in the USA — but only as long as they paid cash and carried them away in their own ships, thereby obeying the so-called 'cash and carry' act. Congress was determined that the USA would not be lured into war again through loans and torpedoed merchant ships.

Yet if the USA continued to stand apart politically during the 1930s, the State and Treasury Departments still had the vision of a multilateral and convertible world, and were trying to do what they could to implement this vision. Cordell Hull, the Secretary of State, shared the Wilsonian vision of a peaceful world without trade barriers. Indeed, he looked at Europe, in particular at Germany with its attempts at autarky or self-sufficiency, and decided that trade barriers were a positive cause of war. Britain's setting up of the Ottawa Agreements in 1932, with tariffs and Imperial Preference, and the subsequent growth of the sterling block (a group of countries all of which based the rates of exchange of their currencies on the value of sterling), especially angered Hull, and he decided that one of his missions was to tear down these walls. He was joined in this by Henry Morgenthau, the Secretary of the Treasury, whose own particular goal was a world of freely convertible currencies, something which had been in abeyance since the early 1930s.

Cordell Hull

Certainly crosscurrents flowed both through the country at large and through Congress: should the USA take a determinedly nationalistic stance over trade, utilizing protectionist tariffs and rules, or try to break down barriers through international agreements? The supporters of the former were numerous and strong — not surprising, given the depth of the Depression — and not until March 1934 could Hull convince the president to ask Congress for legal authority to negotiate reciprocal trade agreements. Supported by a pamphlet entitled *America Must Choose*, which had been written by Henry Wallace (a future Vice-President), Hull managed to build general support for the trade law and it was passed by Congress with a wide margin.

Morgenthau's concern was to return the international economy to a system of freely convertible currencies. This was an impossible goal for the moment, but there was co-operation in small things. Morgenthau in 1936 responded to French pleas of domestic political difficulty and negotiated the Tripartite Stabilization Agreement with France and Britain. This was an arrangement whereby the three central banks helped to manage their floating currencies in a sensible manner (Drummond, 1981).

At the same time, however, European countries, including Britain, were setting up cartels, raising tariff barriers and controlling their currencies: clearly the success of Hull and Morgenthau, who in any case lacked clear-cut political support for their policy, was bound to be limited. But as the world slid into war, Hull became more and more convinced that free trade and non-discrimination might have helped to prevent it, while Morgenthau and the Treasury department took the need for convertible currencies as an article of faith. Both departments, but especially the Treasury, were determined to impose such policies as soon as possible, and there is a clear line on this from the 1938 Anglo-American Trade Agreement, through Lend-Lease, Bretton Woods and the American Loan of 1945 to the United Kingdom: in all cases the USA was trying to convince the British to adopt a free trade regime. Indeed, in the cases of Bretton Woods and the Loan, the emphasis was rather more on insisting that she do so (Kreider, 1943; Woods, 1990). The post-war world, or at least the post-war international economy, was indeed intended to be a new order, and one very much imposed by the United States. It just came a bit late.

SUMMARY

In the 1930s isolationism continued to be a dominant strain in US politics and thus in US foreign policy, with the withdrawal from the World Economic Conference and the passing of the Neutrality Acts. However, in a small way this was modified by the Tripartite Stabilization Agreement. The Department of State and the Department of the Treasury plans for free trade and convertible currencies would bear fruit after 1945 with the Bretton Woods Agreement, which established the International Monetary Fund, and the GATT, the General Agreement on Tariffs and Trade.

7 ASSESSING US FOREIGN POLICY IN THE INTER-WAR PERIOD

My own short-cut definition of a great power is 'a country which possesses both great resources and the sustained will to use them', and by that definition the USA was still a potential rather than an actual great power during this period: strong enough to exact compliance with its wishes in certain fields, but without the will for continuous involvement or responsibility. In contrast, one American historian of US foreign policy in the 1920s, Frank Costigliola, begins his book with the statement that 'The United States emerged from the Great War as the world's leading nation' (Costigliola, 1984). This assessment cannot be based on military power: the USA had an army smaller than that of any of the European great powers, and its navy was smaller than that of Britain. Any such assessment, whether by contemporaries or by historians, must therefore be based on economic — that is, industrial and financial power.

The problem is that in assessing American power primarily with regard to economic questions, US historians can only celebrate little victories. It was praiseworthy to try and build a new international economy in which all nations could grow together, but concentrating on this means downplaying, as did American policy makers of the period, the big questions: the balance of power on the Continent, with the need to re-integrate Germany and the USSR while safeguarding the security of France and Poland, or the expansion of Japanese power. Financial power was of little avail, because it addressed the wrong questions. Therefore, the American attempts to build a new world order between 1919 and 1939 failed because the economic dimension, on which the USA concentrated, although important, was not the vital one. Furthermore, they failed because, by refusing to participate in the political or diplomatic arena, they lacked credibility with other countries: Chamberlain's arguments (as noted above) are germane to this discussion. By 1945 the lesson had been learned, and the Marshall Plan marched alongside NATO, both backed by a sustained will to power — or even domination.

(*An earlier version of this chapter appeared in the Journal of American Studies in 1993.*)

REFERENCES

Adler, S. (1957) *The Isolationist Impulse: Its Twentieth Century Reaction,* New York, Free Press.

Ambrosius, L. E. (1987) *Woodrow Wilson and the American Diplomatic Tradition: The Treaty Fight in Perspective*, Cambridge University Press, Cambridge.

Ambrosius, L. E. (1991) *Wilsonian Statecraft: Theory and Practice of Liberal Internationalism During World War I*, Wilmington, Del., SR Books.

Brandes, J. (1962) *Herbert Hoover and Economic Diplomacy,* Pittsburgh, University of Pittsburgh Press.

Burk, K. (1989) *Morgan Grenfell 1838–1988: The Biography of a Merchant Bank*, pp.92–3, Oxford, Oxford University Press.

Clavin, P. (1992) '"The fetishes of so-called international bankers": Central Bank Co-operation for the World Economic Conference, 1932–33', *Contemporary European History,* 1, pp.278–307.

Cole, W. (1983) *Roosevelt and the Isolationists, 1932–1945,* Lincoln, University of Nebraska Press.

Costigliola, F. C. (1972) 'The other side of isolation: the establishment of the first World Bank, 1929–1930', *Journal of American History,* 59, pp.602–20.

Costigliola, F. C. (1984) *Awkward Dominion: American Political, Economic and Cultural Relations with Europe, 1919–1933*, Ithaca, Cornell University Press.

Drummond, I. (1981) *The Floating Pound and the Sterling Area, 1931–1939*, Cambridge, Cambridge University Press.

Egerton, G. (1991) 'Ideology, diplomacy and international organization: Wilsonism and the League of Nations in Anglo-American relations, 1918–1920' in McKercher, B. (ed.)

Ferrell, R. H. (1952) *Peace in Their Time: The Origins of the Kellogg-Briand Pact*, New Haven, Yale University Press.

Ferris, J. (1984) 'The symbol and the substance of seapower: Great Britain, the United States and the one power standard, 1919–1921' in McKercher, B. (ed.) pp.55–80.

Fink, C. (1984) *The Genoa Conference: European Diplomacy, 1921–1922*, Chapel Hill, The University of North Carolina Press.

Knock, T. J. (1993) *To End All Wars: Woodrow Wilson and the Quest for a New World Order*, Oxford, Oxford University Press.

Kreider, C. (1943) *The Anglo-American Trade Agreement: A Study of British and American Commercial Policies, 1934–1939*, Princeton, Princeton University Press.

Leffler, M. P. (1979) *The Elusive Quest: America's Pursuit of European Stability and French Security, 1919–1933*, Chapel Hill, University of North Carolina Press.

Link, A. S. (1957) *Wilson the Diplomatist: A Look at His Major Foreign Policies*, Baltimore, The John Hopkins Press.

McKenna, M. C. (1961) *Borah*, Ann Arbor, The University of Michigan Press.

McKercher, B. (ed.) (1991) *Anglo-American Relations in the 1920s: The Struggle for Supremacy*, London, Macmillan.

Marks, S. (1976) *The Illusion of Peace: International Relations in Europe 1918–1933*, London, Macmillan.

Orde, A. (1990) *British Policy and European Reconstruction After the First World War*, Cambridge, Cambridge University Press.

Rock, W. (1988) *Chamberlain and Roosevelt: British Foreign Policy and the United States, 1937–1940*, Columbus, University of Ohio Press.

Rosenberg, E. S. (1982) *Spreading the American Dream: American Economic and Cultural Expansion 1890–1945*, New York, Free Press

Schuker, S. A. (1976) *The End of French Predominance in Europe: The Financial Crisis of 1924 and the Adoption of the Dawes Plan*, Chapel Hill, University of North Carolina Press.

Woods, R. B. (1990) *A Changing of the Guard: Anglo-American Relations, 1941–1946*, Chapel Hill, The University of North Carolina Press.

FURTHER READING

Knock, T. J. (1993) *To End All Wars: Woodrow Wilson and the Quest for a New World Order*, Oxford, Oxford University Press.

Rosenberg, E. S. (1982) *Spreading the American Dream: American Economic and Cultural Expansion 1890–1945*, New York, Free Press

AMERICAN POWER AND THE SOVIET THREAT: US FOREIGN POLICY AND THE COLD WAR

Michael Cox ★

1 INTRODUCTION

On the eve of the Second World War, the United States possessed the most productive economy in the world, had one of the world's largest navies, and maintained extensive interests in Central and Latin America. Moreover, if actions are deemed to speak louder than words, then US actions before 1941 helped shape the fate of humanity. It was American military intervention during the First World War that finally sealed the fate of Germany. In the twenties it was its sheer financial strength that brought a degree of stability to Europe. And it was to be its retreat into economic protectionism and political neutrality during the thirties that upset the international system by exacerbating the Depression, encouraging German and Japanese expansion and weakening the resolve of the liberal democracies to stand up to aggression. Manifestly, what the United States did (and sometimes did not do) abroad had an enormous impact on world politics in the inter-war years.

But it would be inaccurate to characterize the United States as a fully active or engaged world power during these years. It was, as Chapter 1 argued, a reluctant international actor before the outbreak of the Second World War. Indeed, for a budding world power, it was remarkably ill-prepared. When war broke out in Europe in 1939, it had an army of only 185,000 men, an annual military budget of less than $500 million, was involved in no military alliances and had none of its troops stationed overseas. Furthermore, as Europe and Asia hurtled towards disaster, Americans tried desperately to shield themselves from the fall-out by retreating into isolation. If anything, the tendency towards isolationism — the expression, ultimately, of a profound fear of political contagion from a world in turmoil and a lack of integration into the international economy — was probably stronger at the end of the 1930s than at any time since the beginning of the First World War. American interests, it was widely felt, were better served by not becoming involved in other people's troubles. That had been the single most important lesson Americans had drawn from the First World War. It was certainly the feeling at home before Japanese planes launched themselves against the US Pacific fleet at Pearl Harbor on 7 December 1941.

This chapter seeks to explore the transition of the United States from potential world power in the inter-war years to active superpower in the post-war period. And as the most obvious cause of this (apart from the Second World War itself) was the belief that American interests were threatened by the Soviet Union after the Second World War, this is primarily a story about the Cold War — as seen from the perspective of one of the main protagonists. In the process we shall examine: the complex reasons why the United States became involved in the Cold War in the first place; how it fought the Soviet Union; how the conflict shaped the United States; how superpower rivalry evolved; why it came to an end in the late eighties; and what role, if any, the United States played in bringing about its demise. This is a long story. But it is one that has to be told if we are to understand the growth and development — some have argued the rise and fall — of that most important of post-war international phenomena: the 'American empire' (McCormick, 1989, p.1).

Historically, the discussion falls into two parts. In the first part we shall examine the period between 1947 and 1968: the years of 'preponderance' that opened with the confident announcement by a feisty President Truman that the United States would defend the free world from totalitarian aggression, and ended with a tired President Johnson declaring, to a divided and demoralized nation, that because of the Vietnam War he would not be seeking his party's nomination in the forthcoming presidential election. This leads logically to the second part: the post-Vietnam years during which the American foreign policy elite attempted, with varying degrees of success, to respond to a loss of certainty by devising what seemed to them at least to be novel policies to preserve American influence in the world. Three such strategies were tried after 1968. The first was formulated by perhaps the most Machiavellian of post-war American presidents, Richard Nixon; the second by probably the most liberal, Jimmy Carter; and the last by undoubtedly the most conservative, Ronald Reagan. All three employed different rhetoric, seeking to distinguish their strategy from that of their immediate predecessor. But each in his own way was attempting to answer the same question: How should stability be secured in an international system in which the United States was no longer as capable of shaping events? In this very special sense all three could be characterized as the 'managers of American decline'.

But before turning to the Cold War, it is important, in fact vital, to look briefly at the Second World War. For out of that historic trauma emerged a very different, more powerful United States to the one which had existed before 1941.

SUMMARY

The aims of this chapter are:

- to explain the transition of the USA from a potential world power to a global superpower;

> - to explore the US role in the making and ending of the Cold War;
> - to examine the forces shaping American foreign policy in the period of US preponderance (1947–1968) and the era of its relative decline (1969–1993).

2 THE EMERGENT SUPERPOWER: 1941–1945

The Second World War was a conflagration of immense proportions causing the death of over 50 million people, fatally weakening Europe and leading to an enormous expansion of Soviet influence. But perhaps the single most important result of the Second World War was the impact it had on the United States' position in the wider international system. In 1941, the USA was a very reluctant world power. Four years later it had become a superpower in every sense of the word.

The alteration in the USA's status was, in the first instance, the direct result of total war upon the rhythm, size and structure of the US economy. The war broke the back of the American Depression in less than two years, doubled the US gross national product (GNP) in four (from just under $100 billion to over $200 billion), and either created, or accelerated, the development of a number of key industries that laid the foundation for American economic hegemony in the post-war period. The dominant position of the United States in the world capitalist system in 1945 almost beggars belief. Basically, at the end of the war, the USA controlled about one half of the world's industrial output; unprecedented in modern times, even surpassing the position that Great Britain held in the early years of the Industrial Revolution in the nineteenth century.

The figures tell their own extraordinary story. In 1945 the United States produced half of the world's steel, owned 70 per cent of the world's merchant marine, manufactured 75 per cent of the world's planes, refined 60 per cent of the world's oil, mined more coal than any other country, and produced 90 per cent of the world's natural gas. Moreover, while the USA boomed and prospered, other countries declined or collapsed. Thus in victory the British Empire was exhausted, most of Europe was in tatters, the USSR was shattered and a good deal of Germany and Japan was in rubble. By the end of the Second World War indeed, it was difficult to believe that a country like Britain, for instance, had been a serious industrial and financial power before the conflict began. Standing by itself in 1945 it could no longer function as a major, independent actor in the international system. To all intents and purposes, the superpower of the nineteenth century had become junior partner to its former colonial possession.

Yet the Second World War did not just lead to a redistribution of economic power. It also transformed the United States militarily. The practical experience of war, waged victoriously across two oceans and three continents, revealed America's true war-making potential. In 1945 the United States was the undisputed master of the universe. Its navy was the biggest in both tonnage and number of vessels. Its airforce was the world's strongest. And it alone possessed the atomic bomb; the weapon of mass destruction that had finally forced Japan to submit and would play such a crucial role in America's relations with the USSR in the post-war years. So powerful was the USA in fact that it was difficult to conceive of a nation that could threaten its interests in 1945. Britain still had a military capability, but basically was in decline. Japan and Germany were now under allied occupation. And although the USSR possessed a vast land army, as a nation it was exhausted. It also had no navy worth speaking of, no long-range bombing capability, and until 1949, no nuclear weapons either.

Finally, although the war was fought by a coalition of nations, the struggle against the Axis Powers was conducted on the basis of American political principles, first articulated in August 1941 in the famous Atlantic Charter.

Franklin D. Roosevelt addressing Congress on the USA's entry into the Second World War 8 December 1941

As the Charter made clear, the Second World War would, from the outset, be a war with a democratic purpose. Winning battles was simply not enough. The peace had to be fought for as well; but it would never be achieved unless it brought liberty and self-determination to the peoples of the world. Such ideas concerned the imperialist Churchill. They certainly disturbed Stalin. However this American vision of freedom was to be central to the way in which the war was fought, and according to Washington had to be fought, for without the promise of a better world, ordinary people would not be prepared to make the sacrifices necessary to ensure victory. Furthermore, if there was to be stability after victory, it could only be constructed on democratic foundations. Any other basis, it was argued in Washington, would only produce new conflicts and tensions. A lasting peace presupposed freedom: and the champion of freedom was the United States of America.

2.1 THE USA's PLANS FOR THE PEACE

The Second World War transformed the world and in the process elevated the United States to superpower status. It also led to something of an intellectual revolution in American official circles. Faced with an entirely new situation, those whose job it was to plan for the peace — particularly those in the State Department in Washington and at the influential private think-tank, the Council on Foreign Relations in New York — gave a great deal of thought to the possible structure of the emerging international system and the USA's place within it. As they planned for the future, they looked back to the past: to see what lessons might be learned, in the hope that the Allies would succeed in constructing in the post-war period the sort of world they had manifestly failed to build between 1918 and 1939.

The first lesson that was drawn by planners was particularly important. The USA's prosperity and security, it was argued, could not be disentangled from developments in other parts of the world. What happened elsewhere had a very direct bearing on what happened in the USA. Isolationism therefore was no longer an option. Nor, by definition, was economic nationalism. Indeed, the second lesson that officials drew from the past was that the USA would have to conduct its economic affairs after this war with much greater responsibility than it had shown after the last. Here, interestingly, policy makers not only sought to learn from the inter-war period, but from the history of the nineteenth century as well. For the greater part of that one hundred years peace, the British had successfully underwritten the international system by exporting its capital and guaranteeing a stable economic environment. Now, in the second half of the twentieth century, the United States — it was reasoned — would have to perform the same historic task as a hegemonic power. If it did not do so, global disorder would inevitably follow.

The view that the USA would have to become an integral part of the post-war economic system was linked to another argument — about the deeper causes of peace. International law and order it was assumed was not just a function of military power. It was also a reflection of material prosperity as well. But capitalist prosperity could not be built in one country alone. It presupposed an expanding and open world economy. Again, the past hung heavily over American thinking about the future. The formation of economic blocs had, according to US planners, caused the depression of the thirties, which had, in turn, led to the Second World War. To prevent future wars it was thus essential for nations to move away from autarchy and towards a more fully integrated international economic order. Indeed, to some State Department officials there was a very direct connection between free trade and military conflict. When goods crossed frontiers, they reasoned, armies stayed at home. But when goods were forced to stay at home, armies crossed frontiers instead.

The last lesson drawn from history concerned the USSR. In the eyes of a number of more liberal policy makers (like Harry Hopkins and Henry Morgenthau Jnr.) the West between the wars had forced the Soviet Union into a corner from which it had been unable to escape. The purpose of policy now therefore was to move beyond the politics of confrontation and draw the USSR into a closer relationship with the democracies. This was only common sense. The Soviet Union, after all, had played a vital role in the defeat of Germany — and would hopefully continue to act as an important counterweight to Germany in the post-war years. It also controlled an increasingly influential communist movement world-wide. And by 1945, it had become a significant European power in its own right. For all these reasons, the Soviet Union had to be pulled back into the world order and not allowed to drift away into sullen isolation. Otherwise the results might be disastrous and everything the United States had worked for would be lost.

SUMMARY

- In 1945 the USA controlled 50 per cent of world output, had a nuclear monopoly, and boasted military supremacy in the air and on the oceans.
- In planning for the peace US policy makers assumed an open world economy, the primacy of liberal democratic principles, and the benign use of hegemonic power to create a new world order.

3 THE ORIGINS OF THE COLD WAR: 1945–1950

The dream (or illusion) that the USSR could be drawn into a close relationship with the United States quickly foundered on the harsh shoals of post-war reality. Certainly within a year of Japan's defeat in August 1945, the original idea of creating a security partnership between the Soviet Union and America had become a distant hope. Yet the transition from wartime co-operation to all-out Cold War did not happen overnight. It occurred in stages.

Yalta 1945 meeting of the big three: (left to right, seated) Winston Churchill, Franklin D. Roosevelt and Joseph Stalin

3.1 THE COLD WAR BEGINS

The conflict began, in effect, with the sudden death of the more liberal Roosevelt in April 1945, and his replacement by the less compromising Harry S. Truman. Truman was determined to face the Russians down and the issue over which he chose to do this, not surprisingly, was Eastern Europe. Here, he claimed, the USSR was not living up to the promises it had made at the Yalta summit in February 1945 of holding free elections in the region. The Russians responded in kind by accusing the United States of refusing to recognize their legitimate interests in the area. Now that the atom bomb actually worked, Truman (the Russians suspected) was going back on previous guarantees and attempting to bring pressure to bear upon them — in the sure knowledge that the USA was in sole possession of the 'winning weapon' and thus neither needed nor required Soviet help to manage the post-war world.

In 1946 relations between the two powers took a decided turn for the worse. Iran was perhaps the most critical geographical focal point of the emerging East–West crisis. However, it was really in February, when Stalin formally launched the Soviet Union's post-war plan for economic recovery in a celebrated public address, that things finally came to a head. Inoffensive though his speech may have sounded to some, it was read by many (including the highly influential Secretary of the Navy, James Forrestal) as a virtual declaration of war on the West. Washington responded by taking advice, and the advice they decided to accept was that provided by a State Department official, George F. Kennan; then, but not for long, a junior figure in the

Moscow embassy. Hostile to communism and suspicious of all attempts to build bridges to the USSR, Kennan's famous 'Long Telegram' (dispatched to Washington only a few days after Stalin's speech) provided officials like Forrestal with exactly what they were looking for: intellectual confirmation of their own conservative instincts that the Soviet Union remained an intractable foe of the West. Though confident in its conclusions, the Kennan communication set the alarm bells ringing around the Washington bureaucracy. When his piece was followed (a month later) by Churchill's announcement at Fulton, Missouri, that 'from Stettin in the Baltic, to Trieste in the Adriatic, an iron curtain' had descended across the continent of Europe, it was clear that the Cold War had become a fact of life.

In early 1947 the storm finally broke. The crisis began on 21 February when the British declared they were no longer able to underwrite Greece and Turkey. There followed two of the most hectic weeks in Washington's political history. These culminated with Truman's famous speech (later referred to as the Truman Doctrine) to Congress on 12 March in which he pledged American support to all those resisting 'totalitarianism' around the world.

President Harry S. Truman addresses a joint session of Congress on 12 March 1947

This call to action was followed three months later with the announcement of a Marshall Plan for Europe embracing vast financial aid to support economic reconstruction. This in turn provoked the Russians who responded firstly by ordering their Czech and Polish allies not to participate in the Plan, thus sealing the division of Europe, and secondly by creating the Communist Information Bureau (or Cominform) to oppose what it claimed was the American 'imperialist' takeover of the continent.

1948 saw a further increase in tension. In February, democracy was extinguished in Czechoslovakia. In late spring, the Russians began their blockade of West Berlin. A few weeks later, US officials started working on a plan that would, within months, lead to the formation of the North Atlantic Treaty Organization (NATO). During 1949, relations deteriorated even further. In April, the NATO Treaty was finally ratified by the US Senate. In August, the first West German elections were held bringing the conservative Konrad Adenauer to power. The following month, Truman announced that Russia had exploded its first atomic bomb; thus breaking the US monopoly. And by the end of the year, the communists had secured China, so bringing the most populous country in the world into the anti-American camp.

Finally, in June 1950, the Cold War turned hot when North Korea unexpectedly invaded South Korea. The impact of the Korean War on world politics can hardly be overstated. In the short and medium term, it led to 3 million dead and wounded (including 54,000 American casualties), caused a direct military confrontation between the United States and China, and drew the United States more completely into South-East Asian affairs. Over the longer term, it led to the further militarization of the Cold War while appearing to confirm what many American officials had been saying for at least four years: that the 'free world' did indeed face a global communist threat led, orchestrated and almost certainly financed by Moscow — and that the only means of resisting this was by a massive mobilization of western resources. For all these reasons, the Korean War has to be regarded as one of the turning points, if not the critical turning point, in the development of the Cold War.

3.2 FROM THE NATIONAL SECURITY ACT TO NSC-68

The challenge of the Cold War clearly demanded an American response. In historical terms, this went through two distinct but not unconnected stages.

The first reached its climax in 1947 with the Truman Doctrine and the Marshall Plan: the former providing the emergent American empire with an ideological *raison d'être*; the latter doing more than any other single US action to force the communists onto the defensive in Western Europe. In the same year, Congress also passed the National Security Act, probably the most important piece of legislation ever enacted during the Cold War. Under its terms three key bodies were established — the National Security Council (NSC), whose main role was to advise the president on international affairs; the Central Intelligence Agency (CIA) whose primary purpose was to gather information (although it did a great deal more in the form of covert operations); and the newly united Department of Defense (DOD) which drew together the previously separate branches of the armed services. On 5 May, 1947, Secretary of State George Marshall also decided to create a Policy Planning Staff (PPS) within the State Department. This was given the express task of thinking long-term about American global objectives. Significantly, its first Director was George F. Kennan, the author of the 1946 'Long Telegram', and by now an important player in policy-making circles.

Paul Nitze

After 1947 however containment took what some, including Kennan, believed was an unfortunate turn, one that both globalized the Cold War and set it into an almost unbreakable mould. The document that formally legitimized this transition was National Security Council order number 68, or, as it became known, NSC-68. Drawn up in late 1949 by Kennan's successor at PPS — Paul Nitze — in close consultation with the formidable Dean Acheson (who had succeeded the respected George Marshall in the Department of State) the highly secret NSC-68 received final presidential approval in the autumn of the following year. Criticized by many officials at the time for its florid language and cost implications, NSC-68 was endorsed in the end because of the crisis occasioned by events in Korea. Once accepted, however, it became, in effect, the blueprint for American grand strategy in the Cold War. This is why it has to be analysed in some detail here.

The document, interestingly, did not begin with a discussion of the USSR, but rather with a relatively sophisticated, albeit deeply alarming assessment of the international situation. The world, it noted, had experienced — and was still passing through — a profound 'crisis', the result, in the last analysis, of 'two global wars of tremendous violence' which had led to the 'collapse of five empires and the drastic decline of two imperial systems'. Into this already unstable situation was inserted the Soviet Union: at one and the same time both symptom and further cause of the world's troubles. Economically and militarily less powerful than the United States, the USSR nevertheless constituted a real threat. A combination of Russian history and its own totalitarian nature indeed made it a particularly unpleasant adversary. Unlike many 'previous aspirants to hegemony' moreover, Stalinist Russia was 'animated by a new fanatic faith antithetical to our own'. This is what made it especially dangerous. The Soviet Union was no ordinary opponent in fact, but a deadly menace whose aim was nothing less than 'the complete subversion or forcible destruction of the machinery of government and structure of society in the countries of the non-Soviet world'.

Painted in brush-strokes that were clear, vivid and bold, NSC-68 left no room for doubt. The Kremlin's goal was nothing less than 'world domination'. But if the USSR had such a 'design', then the United States had (and had to have) a 'purpose'; and that purpose, quite simply, was both to defend and advance the cause of freedom around the world. This was the great defining conflict of the age; between one 'way of life' that valued diversity and choice, and another which aimed to subordinate the individual to the

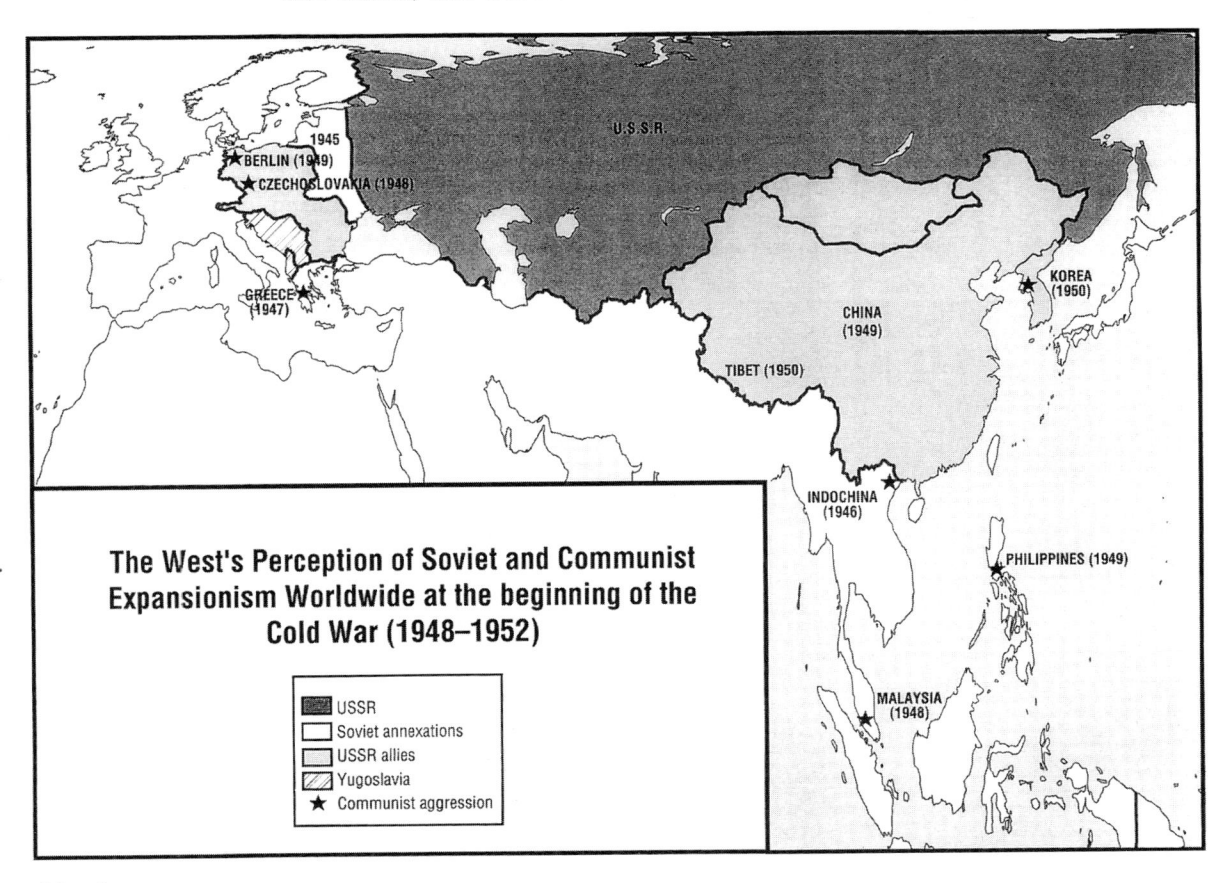

Map 1

new leviathan communist state. This was not a normal conflict, therefore, but a titanic moral struggle between the forces of light on the one hand and the powers of darkness on the other.

But how, specifically, was the United States to respond to this foreboding menace? NSC-68 rehearsed four possible alternatives. Three of these — preventative war, a retreat back into isolation and continuing with the sort of *ad hoc* policies the USA had been pursuing since 1947 — were all ruled out. War, because that would be a disaster; isolation, for that would effectively hand the world over to the Russians; and more of the same, because that would leave the initiative in the Kremlin's hands. There was only one alternative, and that was the 'rapid build-up of the political, economic and military strength' of the free world. This was the 'only course' consistent with 'progress toward achieving our fundamental purpose'.

But what in the end was the reason for building 'positions of strength?' Here, NSC-68 was remarkably explicit. A full-scale mobilization, it was argued, would restore and hopefully maintain American credibility. It would also allow the USA to take more risks abroad. It would reassure nervous allies. And finally, and perhaps crucially, it would force the USSR onto the defensive by impelling it 'to accommodate itself, with or without the conscious abandonment of its design, to co-existence on tolerable terms with the non-Soviet world'. In plain language, if the USSR opposed the United States, then it would have to be compelled to submit to superior force. The USA may not have been able to prevent the Kremlin from expanding, but it could bring maximum pressure to bear so as to make it pay the heaviest price possible (short of physical destruction) for upsetting world order. This was coercive diplomacy in its most explicit form (*Foreign Relations of the United States*, 1977, vol.1. pp.126–492).

3.3 THE POLITICS OF ANTI-COMMUNISM

NSC-68 was based upon one vital, seemingly irrefutable proposition: that the USSR had both the wherewithal and the desire to take over the world. This particular argument however has been subject to a good deal of criticism; both by later scholars of the Cold War, and, more significantly perhaps, by some of those actually involved in the formulation of American foreign policy at the time — including the important George Kennan. Kennan was, and remains, a key figure in the history of US-Soviet relations.

The intellectual author of containment in 1946, Kennan later went on to become one of the more influential critics of the Cold War. There were many dimensions to his critique, but at its heart was a consistent, and to some, persuasive attempt to show that the USSR was nowhere near as threatening as it was portrayed to be in NSC-68. It was certainly not some latter-day version of Nazi Germany. But his arguments fell on deaf ears, and by 1950 he found himself moving (and in some ways being moved) from the centre of the decision-making process to the periphery, from insider to outsider, and thereafter into the political wilderness; a respected but essentially irrelevant figure in the Washington game of high politics (Cox, 1991a).

George F. Kennan

Kennan's fate leads us, reasonably, to ask the important question: Why did the United States come to view the USSR in such alarming terms when much of its own intelligence suggested that the Soviet system was relatively weak? Was this tendency to exaggerate based on misperception? Was it a genuine error of judgement? Was it even a deliberate ploy used by a cynical elite to justify an emergent American Empire in the post-war years? There is no easy, or single answer to these questions. We cannot begin to answer them however unless we first examine the domestic and bureaucratic sources of anti-communism in the United States.

Domestic sources of anti-communism

To understand the way in which Americans in general, and the American state in particular, responded to the USSR, we have to be sensitive to, and take full account of the special, or 'exceptional' character of the United States. Constructed as an alternative to what existed in the class-based nations of the Old World, the USA always proved to be highly resistant to the appeal of socialism. The early development of 'bourgeois' democracy, the superabundance of cheap land, the deep insertion of religion into the fabric of society, the profound divisions between blacks and whites, the almost equally deep gulf between the different ethnic groups who made up the working class — not to mention the fierce repression of all dissident groups in American political life — all combined together to reduce the influence of collectivist ideas in the United States. Socialism was not merely unpopular in the country, but in a very real sense was perceived as being profoundly un-American as well.

In such an environment the Russian revolution, not surprisingly, was greeted with suspicion and antipathy. The Soviet Union's declared aim of building a godless, propertyless society was not one likely to elicit great sympathy from ordinary Americans. As a people, they were probably more hostile to the first worker's state than any other in the capitalist world. Significantly, the number of communists in the United States between the wars never rose above a few thousand. Symptomatically too, the last major state to recognize the USSR after 1917 was not imperial Britain — regarded by the Bolsheviks as their principle international antagonist — nor France (which lost more financially as a result of the Russian revolution than any other country) but the United States. Matters improved, it is true, during the Second World War. Indeed, for a short while, there were (as we have seen) high hopes in liberal circles that the struggle against fascism could be turned into an alliance for peace. But such hopes were misplaced, not just because of what the USSR was doing abroad, but because of the nature of American society. A nation whose core assumptions were so opposed to those of the other major power in the world was unlikely to be able to develop normal relations with it.

The very character of the United States thus worked against some form of 'peaceful co-existence' being established with the USSR. Political events on the American home front in the immediate post-war years further contributed to tensions. Marginalized for over a decade by Roosevelt and the New Deal, the Republicans after 1945 set about undermining the Democrats by deploying what they viewed as the main weapon in their political armoury: the liberalism of their opponents and their failure (according to the Republicans at least) to deal decisively enough with the communist threat. With this crude, but never-to-be underestimated ploy, the Republicans obviously hoped to regain the White House. In this endeavour they were supported by other key groups. These included the southern Democrats, who believed that the best means of protecting segregation was by red-baiting those who advocated civil rights; American employers, who saw anti-communism as a useful vehicle for weakening organized labour; sections of the powerful Roman Catholic church; and the FBI and J. Edgar Hoover whose antipathy to progressive politics was well known.

Now this anti-communist coalition did not in the end force Truman to abandon the politics of the New Deal. Nor of course did he lose the 1948 presidential elections. But to protect his flank he was impelled to implement tough anti-communist measures: at home in the shape of officially sponsored 'Loyalty' programmes, and abroad in the form of a progressively harder line against the Soviet Union. Moreover, if he had not taken these measures, it is doubtful whether he could have held onto power. It carried a price however measured in terms of an increasingly uncompromising American stance towards the USSR. In this way, US policy towards Russia became intertwined with — some have even argued was determined by — internal political factors, to such an extent that no American politician thereafter dared not repeat the traditional Cold War refrain that the Russians were coming. Those who failed to obey his simple political maxim soon found themselves being consigned to the dustbin of history.

The bureaucratic sources of anti-communism

The Cold War thus tapped and gave expression to a powerful undercurrent of anti-communism present in the American political culture. But in turn, one should not underestimate the degree to which policy makers themselves, including the wily and intelligent Secretary of State, Dean Acheson, used anti-communism as a means of selling the emerging American empire to an at times reluctant people. Indeed, if Kennan is historically interesting because he challenged the anti-communist consensus, Acheson is fascinating precisely because he — possibly more than any other policy maker at the time — manipulated it as a way of mobilizing support for US foreign policy. The interesting question, of course, is why did he feel it necessary to do so? Part of the answer lies in an appreciation of the post-war mood in the United States.

In 1945 the United States might accurately be characterized as a superpower without a mission. Immensely capable at one level, at another it had no obvious purpose other than to provide aid to a stricken world; and this was not a role with which many Americans felt particularly comfortable. Moreover, although the war had undermined the isolationist case, it had not done so entirely. As a matter of fact, only a rather narrow group of people were fully committed internationalists — notably liberal intellectuals, their allies in the eastern establishment, and those few economic interest groups dependent in some way or another on foreign markets. Amongst the majority of Americans however, the dominant inclination after 1945 was not to become more involved overseas, but rather of returning to base and getting back to 'normal'. Significantly, in 1946, the fiscally conservative Eightieth Congress was talking of reducing, or even cutting off American economic aid to Great Britain.

This, then, was the situation that confronted policy makers in 1947 as they contemplated economic disarray in western Europe and political chaos around the world. Acheson's 'solution', quite simply, was to shock the American people and Congress into action — and the most effective way of doing this, he believed, was by stressing the threatening nature of the USSR. In this way he convinced reluctant Congressional leaders to support American military aid to Greece and Turkey in 1947. By the same means he undercut any opposition there might have been for the expensive Marshall Plan. And using the same technique in 1949, and again in 1950, he sold NATO and then rearmament to an at first reluctant Congress.

This is not meant to imply that Acheson invented Soviet hostility to the West, but rather that he exploited it to the full in order to legitimize US actions abroad. Acheson admitted as much in his very revealing memoirs.

As he later confessed, getting public backing for expensive policies was not like writing a 'doctoral thesis'. Intellectual work involved looking for and explaining complexity; making foreign policy, on the other hand, was an education in what he termed the 'obvious'. Bold presentation may have led to oversimplification, but if it worked then, according to Acheson at least, it was justified. The 'task of the public officer' after all was not just to understand the world, but 'to explain and gain support for a major policy'. If, in the process this meant that 'qualification' gave way to 'simplicity of statement, nicety and nuance to bluntness, almost brutality in carrying home the point' then this was but a small price to pay. As Acheson put it in one of his more memorable phrases, if policy makers made their points somewhat 'clearer than the truth' (and stressed Soviet ambitions rather than Soviet weaknesses) this was entirely reasonable. Indeed, faced with an American public indifferent to, ignorant of, and none too happy about giving vast amounts of aid to other countries, there was probably no other way that the United States could have justified its new world role (Acheson, 1969).

3.4 THE SOVIET THREAT REVISITED

That there were powerful internal and bureaucratic factors inclining Americans, and American policy makers, to exaggerate the Soviet threat is self-evident. But this should not lead us to the opposite conclusion: that there was no real 'threat' at all. If we argued thus, the Cold War would be nothing but an invention; and this it most certainly was not. So what were the real causes for American concern?

The first was the new balance (or imbalance) of power in post-war Europe. The USSR may have been weak in relation to the United States, but in war-torn post-war Europe at least it was by far and away the most dominant nation. It had defeated Germany and secured Eastern Europe, and in spite of a rapid post-war demobilization, was still in possession of a large army. Faced with this situation the Americans — urged on by the British and the French it is true — felt they had to take necessary countermeasures; not because the USSR was about to launch a blitzkrieg (Stalin was certainly no Hitler), but because the sheer size of the Red Army and the new position of Russia in Central Europe made the West Europeans feel distinctly nervous. And so long as they remained nervous there was no possibility of economic recovery and political stability.

The second cause of American concern was the new strength of the communist movement in Western Europe. Marginal and unimportant before the Second World War, the communist parties were in a much stronger position after 1945. Admittedly, they were a good deal less revolutionary than most Americans believed. Indeed, some of their more left-wing critics later characterized them as being without a socialist goal. On the other hand, they now had a real presence and were prepared to mobilize this in defence of the Soviet Union — which they did on several occasions in the post-war period: first, in a half-hearted attempt to slow down West European recovery; then, in an effort to upset NATO; and finally, in a more serious campaign to arrest western rearmament. Clumsy and counterproductive though such moves were, they were further proof to policy makers in Washington that the USSR represented a serious political challenge after the war.

This brings us, then, to a third cause of American concern: the future political and economic orientation of the less developed countries. The war, we should recall, severely weakened the foundations of European rule in the colonies; something that many Americans, with their anti-colonial tradition, were bound to welcome. What concerned the United States however was the fact that many of those who assumed power in the post-colonial states did not always share western values. Many in fact were either opposed to the West, or believed that their countries would never become properly, as opposed to formally independent until they broke the bonds that tied them to the world market system. To make matters worse, some leaders in the emerging countries were even attracted to the Soviet model. The USSR, they reasoned, had once been a backward country subordinate to the more developed western capitalist states. It had then broken from imperialism, and having done so went on to achieve great economic feats. The lesson was obvious, or at least appeared to be so to many in the less developed nations. If they wanted to become independent they would have to develop; and to develop they would have to follow the Soviet example.

Anxiety about the orientation of the less developed countries was in turn linked to a more general concern about the free enterprise system as a whole. The USSR was in part the cause of this concern. With its apparently successful planned economy (which had laid the foundation for its historic victory over Germany) the Soviet economic system undoubtedly exerted a powerful attractive pull in 1945. However, it would not have represented a 'threat' as such, if capitalism had worked. The fact of the matter was that for nearly thirty years, the free enterprise system had manifestly failed to solve humanity's problems. Instead it had led to military conflict, economic stagnation and political repression. The old order thus seemed to be doomed. The future belonged to socialism; and the most extreme manifestation of this rising phenomenon after the war was the Soviet Union.

Finally, American fear of (and thus opposition to) the USSR, was the logical consequence of its vision of a more open world economy. The Soviet Union in US eyes was like some giant cuckoo in the international nest; the nest in this case being a multilateral free trade system within which all countries should operate, and outside of which there could be no reasonable existence. In 1945 many truly believed that this was the beginning of the American Century. Now complicating the whole picture was the USSR — a strange and peculiar entity that was economically different, made no pretence of being or ever becoming part of an American-led order, and, which in its own clumsy fashion, placed a limit on US global reach. This was not a system the United States could ever accept as being a legitimate member of the international community.

> **SUMMARY**
>
> - US hostility to the Soviet Union was stimulated initially by the perceived Soviet failure to abide by the Yalta accords.
>
> - US initiatives such as the Marshall plan, the formation of NATO, and the war in Korea confirmed the division of the world into two rival camps.
>
> - The essential basis of US national security strategy throughout the entire post-war period was laid down in NSC-68 which argued for a massive military build-up in order to contain the Soviet Union.
>
> - American policy responses to the Soviet Union in this period were conditioned by a deep ideological antipathy to communism and the desire of political elites to attract support for an internationalist foreign policy in the face of strong isolationist sentiments within the American polity.
>
> - The Soviet threat was real insofar as it was the only state which had the potential capability and motivation to challenge US power and interests in the post-war world.

4 DILEMMAS OF US FOREIGN POLICY

Situated outside the world order in a sullen and apparently uncompromising attitude towards it, the Soviet Union was bound to be viewed as some sort of 'threat'; and as such had to be dealt with. This of course was the ultimate reason for writing NSC-68: to lay down the basic rules of engagement with the enemy. What NSC-68 did not do however was to make clear what the ultimate American goal was in the Cold War. Was it, as some assumed, to contain the Soviet tide; or, as others insisted, to roll it back? On this the document was deeply ambiguous — as was the Truman administration itself. On the one hand, containment had much to recommend it, being both the safer and less dangerous of the two options. On the other hand, if Soviet power and influence could be undermined by all means short of war, this would remove the principle threat to peace, open up Eastern Europe to the West and lead to the fulfillment of that ultimate American dream: an open world system without let or hindrance to the free movement of goods and ideas.

4.1 BEYOND CONTAINMENT?

The struggle between these two different conceptions was never really resolved. Hence while containment remained the stated policy, roll back as such was never formally repudiated. Indeed, the urge to contest communism more forcefully tended to increase rather than diminish in the early fifties. The first clear confirmation of this was during the Korean War when US forces marched north over the 38th parallel in a bold attempt to destroy both the North Korean army and the North Korean regime. The next was in the run up to the 1952 presidential elections when the Republicans (now more desperate than ever to regain the White House) promised that if elected, they would go beyond the 'cowardly policy' of containment and force the Russians by political means out of Eastern Europe. In part an electoral ploy designed by Eisenhower and his soon-to-be Secretary of State, John Foster Dulles, to win emigré and Catholic votes away from their political opponents, the rhetoric about roll back nevertheless struck a chord — promising as it did the illusion of ultimate victory in the Cold War. For a nation mired down in Korea and beset by doubts at home, the idea was not without its appeal.

The attack upon containment certainly helped Eisenhower get into the White House. Yet significantly, once in office, he followed more or less the same strategy as his Democratic opponents. In fact, according to some of his more ardent academic admirers, he adopted an even more restrained policy than Truman himself.

Eisenhower (seated fourth from right at far side of table) at the 'Big Four' conference, Geneva 1955

Hence in 1953, Eisenhower negotiated an end to the Korean War. He then made every effort to reduce US military spending. And when confronted in 1956 with the first serious attempt by the Hungarian people to throw off the Soviet yoke, he made it abundantly clear to Soviet leaders that he had no intention of intervening. Roll back, it was evident, was a myth.

So, why were the Republicans so cautious? Why did they not go beyond the more limited objective of containment? Finding an answer to these questions takes us to the heart of understanding the paradox of the Cold War (Cox, 1990a).

The major problem with the roll back thesis was how, exactly, was it supposed to be achieved? The standard response provided by right-wing American gurus such as James Burnham was stunning in its simplicity: through a combination of economic, political and psychological pressure they asserted (Burnham, 1947, 1950). The flaw in this argument however was self-evident. Neither the United States nor its allies were ever able to mount enough pressure upon the USSR to bring about its surrender. This left the USA with one other possible option: war with the USSR itself. But this was a nonsense. The American 'purpose' in waging the Cold War after all was not actually to go to war with Russia, but rather to limit its capacity for exploiting contradiction in the wider world system; and this could be done by all means short of open hostility.

This brings us, logically, to the second flaw in the roll back argument. In terms of the balance of power and the requirements of an expanding international economy, there was really no need to push the Russians out of Eastern Europe or undermine the USSR. The reason, quite simply, was that the area within the Soviet orbit was not essential for the reconstruction of post-war western capitalism. The Soviet Union itself possessed little or nothing the West needed. Nor, it should be added, did the relatively backward nations of Eastern Europe. As American policy planners admitted (though none too loudly) countries like Romania, Poland, Bulgaria and Czechoslovakia were essentially insignificant. They were certainly not of vital interest to the United States.

Finally, so long as the USSR remained where it was, controlling the least important but most unruly part of the European continent, this had definite (but unspoken) advantages from the American point of view. Most obviously, it forced those outside of the Soviet sphere of influence in Europe into a dependency relationship on the United States. It also kept the formally ambitious and once united Germany under wraps. A Soviet presence in Europe moreover helped bind the NATO alliance together. And in its own rather brutal way, it put a lid on nationalism too. The Europe that emerged in the process may have been divided and one section of its people impelled to live under Soviet rule. But the new Europe was a good deal more stable than the one which had finally been laid to rest in 1945. And this is what really mattered to the Americans, who opposed communism, but seemed to dislike disorder even less. The new arrangement may not have been perfect, but it had much to recommend it to the United States (Deporte, 1978).

4.2 BEYOND THE COLD WAR?

If the USA under Eisenhower indicated no real interest in moving beyond containment, it showed even less of going beyond the Cold War. Indeed, by the late fifties, the Cold War began to assume the appearance of a building designed to endure. Neither the death of Stalin in 1953, the declaration by his successor (Khrushchev) that there could be peaceful co-existence between socialism and capitalism, nor the unexpected break between China and Russia in 1960, appeared to have much impact on this edifice. In the American view the Soviet Union remained what it had always been, and presumably would remain for ever: an enemy state whose ultimate design was the great globe itself.

This dogged refusal by US policy makers to rethink their policies was in part a function of their own intellectual rigidity, born of the belief that there could be no real change in a totalitarian state like the Soviet Union. But to be fair, there were other, intellectually defensible reasons for the USA remaining cautious. For in spite of certain modifications to the Soviet system during the fifties, these did not fundamentally alter its character nor its international posture. Indeed, many of the things it did — from the brutal suppression of Hungary in 1956, through supporting the Cuban revolution, to the building of the Berlin Wall in 1961 — all seemed to point to its persistently hostile character. And when Khrushchev prematurely declared in 1960 that within twenty years communism would bury capitalism, this only confirmed the official American view that there could be no escape from the Cold War. The only option, it seemed, was to remain strong in the vain hope that the USSR would one day see the error of its ways and rejoin the world community. Until that distant day arrived (if ever) the Great Contest would continue.

President John F. Kennedy taking the oath of office to become the thirty-fifth president of the USA

Now some may have hoped — and have argued since — that the election of the youthful John F. Kennedy in 1960 represented a new beginning. Some of his more ardent admirers (including the Hollywood director, Oliver Stone, in his controversial film *JFK*) have gone further. They have suggested that if Kennedy had lived, he would not only have avoided the Vietnam War, but would have tried to have drawn the USSR back into the international fold. His signing of the nuclear test ban treaty in particular and the establishment of a hot-line between the White House and the Kremlin (both in 1963), have even led some to conclude that Kennedy's death meant that one of the great opportunities of the post-war period was lost.

In the light of his unfulfilled promise, the desire to rehabilitate the dynamic Kennedy is perfectly understandable. But the attempt to recast him as a late convert to the anti-Cold War cause is both misplaced and misleading.

Kennedy, we need reminding, was no bleeding heart liberal nor a closet pacifist. An interested student of the thirties and a veteran of the Second World War, he took it as read that the USSR — like Nazi Germany before it — could not and should not be appeased. Less conservative than Eisenhower on domestic issues, in the area of foreign policy he was a confirmed anti-communist who, in the run up to his election, made it perfectly clear that he would be conducting the Cold War more, rather than less, aggressively than his Republican opponent. He even accused Eisenhower of not having waged the struggle effectively enough, vowing that once in office he would be far more active. Kennedy was true to his word. In 1961 he announced the biggest military build-up in over ten years. He then increased the number of US advisers on the ground in South-East Asia. He also did everything in his power (save committing American planes or ground troops) to get rid of the hated Castro regime in Cuba.

It is true that Kennedy had grave doubts about escalating the war in Vietnam. There is no doubt either that the Cuba missile crisis of 1962 forced him to curb his earlier rhetorical excesses. But we should not be misled into concluding that he was about to sue for peace. Part of that Cold War generation, Kennedy, like Truman and Eisenhower before him and Lyndon Johnson who followed, believed there could no compromise between the United States and the communist world. This was a struggle without end.

SUMMARY

- NSC-68 was deeply ambiguous since it appeared to commit the USA to a strategy of both containment and rolling back Soviet power. Despite the rhetoric policy makers never risked the latter.

- By the 1960s the Cold War had become a permanent feature of world politics and the dominant external reality shaping US foreign policy.

5 THE COLD WAR SYSTEM: 1947–1968

The vitality of the Cold War before Vietnam clearly owed a great deal to the fact that it reflected objective international realities. Once launched however it quickly embedded itself into the very sub-soil of America, shaping its institutions, moulding its citizens, and profoundly altering the structure of the American economy. In this sense we can legitimately talk of the United States after 1947 becoming, or being transformed into a Cold War system (Cox, 1986).

5.1 THE AMERICAN EMPIRE AT HOME

The most visible manifestation of the Cold War in the USA was at the level of 'high' politics; and the highest level of all was the office of the presidency. This changed in at least two important ways after 1947. First, its status was enhanced: in part because of the central role the president now played in the making of foreign policy, and partly because US presidents after 1947 were not simply leaders of one country, but symbolically and real, leaders of the 'free world' as a whole. The Cold War also shaped the way presidential elections were fought. In a number of cases it may have even influenced their outcome — in 1948 when Truman was seen to be tough on the Russians, then in 1952 when Eisenhower promised to free the peoples of Eastern Europe, and once again in 1960 when Kennedy pledged to rebuild American power. Elections may have been determined by economics, but foreign policy was not unimportant.

The Cold War moreover left an indelible mark on American society itself. In fact, for a decade or more, the United States was gripped by a hysteria which seemed to make no distinction between genuine communists, radicals and concerned liberals. This not only resulted in a political freeze on all serious discussion, but caused films to be censored, trade unions and universities to be purged, and even certain books to be removed from public libraries. Hostility to non-conformity was hardly a new phenomenon in America. After 1946 however it assumed a particularly virulent form with thousands being investigated, many hundreds losing their jobs and a few brave souls even being sent to prison. Fear and suspicion were the necessary outcome of all this, hardly surprising in a country where all critical thought seemed to have been driven underground.

The Cold War shaped the United States in a third crucial way: through the creation of an extensive military-industrial complex. While it would be absurd to imply that this 'complex' ran the country, there is little disputing its widespread influence. As President Eisenhower noted in his extraordinary Farewell Address to the nation in 1961, the military-industrial lobby had acquired great and 'unwarranted influence' in the corridors of power. It had also become a crucial part of the American economic system as well; so crucial in fact that many wondered whether the United States could ever afford peace. It is easy to understand why. In an average year between 1951 and 1971, defence spending took up 50 per cent of the annual budget, absorbed almost 10 per cent of American GNP, and employed about 10 per cent of the work force — approximately 7 million people in 1964 (Clayton, 1970).

Finally, with the growth of military spending during the Cold War, governments in the United States seemed to have found the perfect solution to the ever-present problem of the business cycle. It is true that in the five year period after the Second World War, America boomed while spending on arms fell. It is also the case that President Eisenhower tried to cut military expenditure on the good capitalist grounds that it represented a form of public spending. But this only tells one side of the story. Truman, after all, used rearmament in 1950 to counter the recession of the previous year. Ten years later Kennedy employed the same technique to stimulate economic activity after two years of sluggish growth. For Democrats at least, spending on arms seemed to be the quickest (and ideologically the most acceptable) way of generating full employment under conditions of modern American capitalism.

5.2   THE AMERICAN EMPIRE ABROAD

The American empire during its first two decades was not without its critics. Nor was it without its costs measured in terms of lives lost, money spent, risks taken and human rights denied to the peoples of the Third World. But in spite of all this, the United States was, by any measure, a highly effective imperial power in the twenty-one year period between the announcement of the Truman Doctrine in 1947 and the election of Richard Nixon in 1968.

Firstly, in terms of containing communism, America was extraordinarily successful. There were 'losses', China and Cuba being the most significant. But in the core areas of the world system — those deemed to be vital to the health of capitalism — communism was either forced on to the defensive or eliminated as a serious political challenge. Western Europe provides the best example of this. In 1947, the area appeared to be on the brink of collapse, but a decade later conservatism was in the ascendancy and the left was in retreat.

The United States also achieved a great deal in the Far East and Asia; possibly one of the most volatile areas of the world in the post-war period. Consider the record. By 1968 Japan was well on its way to becoming a prosperous (albeit an unloved) member of the international community. After a terrible and devastating war, South Korea had been rehabilitated; and by the late sixties was developing into an important economic actor in the region. Furthermore, revolutionary insurgencies had been contained in Malaya, the Philippines and Indonesia, albeit by highly repressive methods. A case might even be made for American policy in Vietnam. If history had taken its 'natural' course there, the communists would have almost certainly come to power earlier. But as a result of American efforts this was delayed for over twenty years; admittedly with dire consequences for both Vietnam and the USA.

But perhaps the most obvious measure of American success before Vietnam was economic. From being what it had once been between the two wars, that is a declining system with a powerful urge to disintegration, international capitalism after 1947 was transformed into a healthy and vibrant entity. And central to this transformation was the United States: dispensing huge amounts of aid, writing the economic rules of the game, forcing nations like Germany and France to bury their traditional enmities and securing the world from a variety of different threats. Whether the post-war system needed such a 'hegemon' is an open question. What is not in dispute is that under its guidance the world economy experienced a period of unprecedented expansion. Certainly when American policy makers compared the mess that passed for an international economy before the Cold War, with the dynamic order which emerged in the fifties and sixties, they had good reason to be satisfied.

5.3 THE CRISIS OF THE AMERICAN EMPIRE?

What has been characterized as the crisis of the American empire, has normally been explained in terms of the Vietnam War and the enormous strains this deeply divisive conflict imposed upon the United States. However although Vietnam did great damage to the United States, it was not the only reason for its malaise. Indeed, as Henry Kissinger later pointed out, Vietnam 'was not the cause' of the USA's difficulties, but a 'symptom' of something deeper: and that, he correctly surmised, was the transition from one period when America was virtually unassailable, to another when its power, though still 'vast' had reached a definite limit. The United States was not exactly becoming an ordinary country, but it had reached a certain point where it could no longer manage the world as easily as it had done before (Kissinger, 1981).

The first reason for this was straightforwardly economic. Although the USA still possessed the biggest and most productive economy in the capitalist world, its financial position was no longer as secure as it had once been. There were several reasons for this, but the strategically most significant one was that the USA was spending more by the late sixties policing the world than it was earning from its exports and foreign investments. The Cold War, in effect, was becoming a burden. What made this all the more difficult to bear were two additional financial strains: one imposed by increased spending on the 'Great Society' programme at home, and the other by the exponential costs involved in fighting the Vietnam War. The situation was made all the more problematic because the USA was now facing real competition on world markets from allies it had originally helped revive in the immediate post-war years.

This fiscal crisis of the American state was bound to force an alteration in its global posture, if for no other reason than that the USA could no longer afford to police the world, fight the war in Vietnam, underwrite the international financial system, compete internationally and support a welfare state at home. Something would have to give.

The second reason for the USA's problems was more political than economic, and arose, primarily, out of an understandable desire by its increasingly self-confident European allies to take a more independent line. This expressed itself in a number of ways, from the most extreme manifestation in 1965 when France finally withdrew from NATO's military command, to the less dramatic demand by nearly all West Europeans to establish better political and economic relations with their communist neighbours to the East. However, in 1969 this second, and ostensibly less threatening movement, assumed a more serious form when West Germany entered into direct negotiations with Moscow in an attempt to improve relations between the two German states. This set the alarm bells ringing in Washington; but the process could not be stopped. The United States thus had to follow its German ally as it opened up negotiations to the East, and hope to guide it along channels that did not threaten US interests.

The third reason for the United States revising its traditional Cold War policies was the changing military balance. Following its retreat over Cuba in 1962, the Soviet leadership resolved never to be humiliated again. Thereafter, it pursued a dual military strategy, the first aim of which was to allow it to project itself more forcefully around the world, and the second to acquire nuclear parity with the United States. By the late sixties it had achieved both ambitions. The implications were far-reaching. It now meant that the USSR had far greater international reach than ever before; of special significance in the Third World. It also undermined what most Americans regarded as the central prop of US strategy during the Cold War, namely, its nuclear edge over the USSR. A transformation of such dimensions was bound to bring about a policy review in Washington.

The final reason for the United States modifying its traditional Cold War policies were the alterations that had occurred (and were continuing to take place) in the enemy camp itself. For the greater part of the fifties the USA had worked on the simple, but then not unreasonable assumption that the communist world was unlikely to change to any great degree. By the end of the sixties this particular assessment (reassuring and threatening at one and the same time) no longer corresponded to reality. China by then had irrevocably broken from the USSR. In Eastern Europe there was a growing desire by sections of the elite to move beyond autarchy and associate their own increasingly stagnant economies with the more efficient West. Even in Russia there was talk of changing the way the planned economy worked and introducing elements of the market.

Once again the United States could hardly ignore these developments and continue as if the world was set in concrete. The opponent it had faced at the time of NSC-68 was not exactly the same opponent it faced in 1968. The nature of the challenge had changed and the American response, it was evident, would have to change too.

5.4 VIETNAM AND THE COLLAPSE OF CONSENSUS

Into this changing environment pregnant with potential was inserted the Vietnam War — one of the most analysed, most controversial and most significant events in American post-war history. Certainly as important as the Korean War in its wider implications, the impact of the Vietnam War on the United States can hardly be underestimated. It severely damaged the financial and competitive position of the US economy. It undermined the USA's moral and political credibility abroad. It produced what some believe was a near-civil war within the United States itself. It revived radical fortunes at home after over twenty years of Cold War conservatism. And it destroyed, or at least severely damaged, the national consensus about the purpose of American foreign policy. One might add that it also made inevitable what was already likely to happen anyway: that is, a change in the conduct of US policy abroad.

The impact of the Vietnam War on the national consensus can be detected at three distinct levels. The first and most significant of these was at the level of the foreign policy elite itself. Prior to the Vietnam War those involved in defining global objectives had generally been self-confident, reasonably cohesive and in broad agreement about procedures — believing that the ultimate authority in the making of foreign policy was the president. The Vietnam War changed all this and by the early seventies a quite different foreign policy elite had emerged: one which was measurably more cautious, intellectually less united and constitutionally now uncertain about the proper role of the presidency in the determination of grand strategy. Indeed, one of the reasons for the Vietnam debacle, it was now argued, was precisely because the president had become overly powerful (imperial even) during the Cold War. It was time therefore to alter the balance and give Congress a far greater share in the shaping of foreign policy.

The fragmentation of the foreign policy elite was the first important result of the Vietnam War. The second was the erosion of popular support for intervention. Americans might have remained patriotic, but after the Vietnam War they were no longer willing, in John F. Kennedy's immortal words, 'to pay any price and go anywhere' to defend US interests abroad. The trauma of South-East Asia made Americans extremely cautious. It also made some of them wonder if the United States should worry less about its global responsibilities and concentrate more instead on domestic issues. Though this new isolationism bore little resemblance to its inter-war predecessor, it did reflect the disenchantment many now felt towards world politics. Certainly after Vietnam, it would be increasingly difficult for American presidents to mobilize popular support for military adventures abroad.

Finally, Vietnam caused a profound ideological crisis in the United States. For twenty years it had been the accepted academic wisdom that the main cause of the superpower conflict had been Soviet expansion; a thesis that had the twin virtues of being both intellectually simple and ethically reassuring. Vietnam did a great deal to weaken the appeal of this standard argument, at least amongst intellectuals. In its wake emerged a very different, altogether more radical interpretation of the antagonism. Now, according to the so-called 'revisionists', the primary reason for the conflict was not Soviet aggression at all, but rather American imperialism. And the main American motive was not the defence of the free world, but the need by US capital for overseas markets. The main culprit in the Cold War therefore was not communism but capitalism; while the real threat to peace was not the USSR but the United States of America.

Last minute evacuation of personnel and civilians from the US Embassy in Saigon in 1975

It would be easy to dismiss the radical argument as a mere bubble that was bound to burst once subjected to serious academic scrutiny. But this misses the point. Whatever the rights and wrongs of the revisionist case (and here we have only presented the crudest version of it) for a time it carried the day amongst a large section of the American student and academic population. Consequently, it further accelerated the collapse of Cold War certainties in the United States. Certainly after the revisionist broadside against established truths, few historians would be prepared to repeat the traditional orthodoxy that American foreign policy after 1947 was merely a defensive response to Russian aggression (Melanson, 1991).

SUMMARY

- The Cold War involved a significant transformation in the domestic political, economic and cultural institutions of American life.

> - American power before 1968 was successful in containing communism, creating stability in Europe and Asia, and securing the future of the global capitalist order.
>
> - By 1968 the economic burdens of empire and the erosion of the USA's political and military primacy provoked a fundamental re-examination of the nation's foreign and national security policies.
>
> - The war in Vietnam was the critical catalyst in transforming US foreign policy in this period.

6 THE NIXON–KISSINGER 'GRAND DESIGN': 1968–1975

The controversial turn made by President Nixon towards the USSR after 1968 was attacked at the time, and has been criticized since, by different strands of American opinion: by liberals who approved his opening to the East, but disapproved of Nixon's disregard for human rights in the Soviet bloc; by conservatives who believed then (and still do) that his strategy made too many concessions to the USSR; and by traditional Cold War warriors who felt that Nixon and his foreign policy adviser, Henry Kissinger, simply ignored the lessons of history — and the most important lesson of all was that negotiating with the Russians was far less important than establishing one's own position of strength. Some critics have gone even further. The central weakness with the Nixon–Kissinger 'grand design', they maintain, was that it too readily accepted the inevitability of US decline. This, it is argued, was fatal. It demoralized the American people, weakened alliances and gave the green light to enemies to assert themselves more aggressively. This is why the seventies (the so-called decade of neglect) was such a disastrous one for the United States.

6.1 PRIMACY AND WORLD ORDER

The various attacks upon Kissinger and Nixon's diplomatic efforts should not however blind us to what they were trying to do and why. Confronted as the United States was in the late sixties with an enormous array of problems in a rapidly changing international environment, something had to be done. Deep divisions at home, the growth in Soviet military power, the desire to get out of Vietnam while maintaining US credibility, changes in the nature of the Atlantic alliance and the urgent need to reduce costs all necessitated a shift in policy. Novel circumstances required novel answers, and the new team in the White House tried to provide them under the double heading of superpower *détente* and the Nixon Doctrine. Though the two notions cannot be separated, they can be analysed separately (Cox, 1985).

Superpower *détente* neither implied friendship with the USSR nor an abandonment of containment. Rather it aimed to contain the USSR in an entirely different way. The question was how. The answer, according to Nixon and Kissinger, was to exploit Soviet fears, needs, desires and demands: and these were (in rough order) fear of closer ties between China and the United States, the need for better economic relations with the capitalist West, the desire to engage in arms control, and the demand to gain a tacit American acceptance of its control over Eastern Europe. Naturally, the USA sought a number of things in return. These were, in the short term, Russian help to allow America to gain 'peace with honour' in Vietnam; in the medium term, responsible Soviet behaviour in other regional disputes; and over the longer term, a co-operative Soviet attitude towards the West. Some even envisaged the USSR becoming increasingly tied down by a series of economic transactions with the capitalist world that would, over time, turn it from being an opponent into a partner, albeit a junior partner, of the United States.

Nixon and Kissinger thus presented the USSR with a simple choice. Moscow could, if it so wished, persist in making trouble for the West. But if it did so it would face continued military and economic competition. On the other hand, it could work with the West and enjoy the fruits of association in the form of increased trade, a serious American commitment to arms control, the promise not to tilt towards China and a *de facto* (if not *de jure*) recognition of its position in Eastern Europe. It was really up to the Soviet leadership.

While *détente* aimed to build a more constructive relationship with traditional enemies (and in the process create the foundation for a new global equilibrium) the purpose of the 'Nixon Doctrine' was to develop a more equitable partnership with old friends. This was to take two forms: a change in the distribution of costs so that its now more prosperous European allies would spend more, and the USA less, on defence; and the strengthening of a series of sub-regional powers, notably Iran, South Vietnam, South Korea and Brazil, who would be able to hold the line in their own area without direct American help. The United States, in Nixon's view, could no longer subsidize — and Americans were no longer willing to pay for — other people's security. It would provide them with military aid, train their soldiers and support them diplomatically. But it would not, and certainly after the Vietnam War could not afford to do all the fighting itself. That would be up to local forces.

But what was the connection between *détente* and the Nixon doctrine? On this point neither Kissinger nor Nixon were especially precise, but it is reasonably clear what they hoped to achieve. By drawing the USSR and China into a close relationship, this would, they assumed, reduce disturbance in the Third World. Less turbulence there would then stabilize the central core relationships between the USA and the two communist powers. This would sustain the momentum of *détente*, which in turn would ensure order along the periphery. In this way, each component part of the Nixon-Kissinger 'grand design' would serve as the instrumentality for the achievement of the other. The result it was hoped would be a more stable world achieved at a lower cost for the United States; or as some preferred to call it, containment on the cheap.

6.2 THE COLLAPSE OF THE 'GRAND DESIGN'

The most formal expression of the Nixon-Kissinger strategy was a series of agreements signed between Washington and the two communist powers in the early seventies. These included the Shanghai communiqué drawn up by Nixon and Mao in February 1972, the Anti-Ballistic Missile (ABM) Treaty, the Strategic Arms Limitation Talks (SALT) Treaty, the Basic Principles Governing Relations between the USSR and the United States, and finally several other accords defining trade relations, cultural exchanges, co-operation in science and technology and maritime matters. Taken together these all appeared to indicate that the Cold War had reached a terminal point (Lynch, 1992).

President Richard Nixon (on left) in discussion with Soviet President Leonid Brezhnev (centre) at the opening of the SALT on 23 May 1972

This perception was further reinforced by important modifications to the broader European landscape. Here too it seemed as if the East-West conflict was finally winding down. In August 1970 the Federal Republic of Germany and the Soviet Union signed a Treaty designed to strengthen peace and security on the continent. This was followed in September 1971 with a new four power agreement on Berlin. In November 1972 the two German governments decided to normalize relations. And finally, in August 1975, 35 nations signed the so-called Helsinki agreements. This, according to many observers at the time, put a formal lid on the conflict in Europe with both sides now having agreed not to disturb the status quo on the continent (Mayall and Navari, 1980).

So what went wrong? Why did this 'grand design' collapse? The simplest answer is that it did not collapse at all. At a pan-European level *détente* went from strength to strength. The two Germanys stabilized their relationship. So too did the United States and China. In fact, by the end of the decade, China and the US had virtually become allies. The real flaw in the new edifice was at the level of the superpower relationship. Here, after a promising beginning, the situation quickly turned sour. Thus by 1975 the new policy was in deep trouble. Two years later it had more or less been abandoned. And by the end of the decade, it had fallen apart completely. The question is why?

There is no simple, or agreed answer to this. Some insist that Nixon and Kissinger oversold their strategy. Hence when it could not deliver a new era of 'perpetual peace' as promised, it set off a wave of disillusionment that ended with the idea of *détente* being rejected altogether. Others believe it was a utopian project anyway, primarily because social systems as distinct (and antagonistic) as those of the Soviet Union and the United States simply could not co-operate. It has also been suggested that the two sides had diametrically opposed ideas of what *détente* meant, with the Americans seeing it as a means of disciplining the USSR, and the Russians as a way of increasing their influence in the wider world system. Given these differences there was probably little chance of the policy ever working. Finally, many conservatives maintain *détente* was bound to fail because it was premised on two flawed assumptions: that the United States could contain the Soviet Union from a position of weakness, and that the Soviet Union had abandoned its long-term goal of world domination. Given these design flaws, it was hardly surprising that the Kissinger-Nixon grand design soon came crashing to the ground.

There is perhaps some truth in nearly all of these arguments. But there were other factors — significantly all internal to the United States itself — that help explain the demise of superpower *détente* far better than abstract arguments about socio-economic differences between America and the Soviet Union, or the latter's continued desire to take over the world.

Building a new relationship with the USSR required two things: firm leadership and time. Unfortunately, Nixon did not get the breathing space he required. At the end of 1972 he stood at the pinnacle of his power. The Vietnam War was over. The Cold War, it seemed, was winding down too. The Democrats were in total disarray. Within three years however his political world had disintegrated; and it did so, quite simply, because of the Watergate scandal. Events simply overwhelmed Nixon. By the middle of 1973 he was in trouble. By the end of the year, he was on the slide. A year later he had been forced out of office. Now superpower *détente* was not dependent on Nixon alone. On the other hand, it was so closely identified with him personally that when he finally fell, his controversial strategy suffered a heavy blow.

Watergate alone would not have destroyed the 'grand design'. What further compromised it however was the fact that a number of powerful interest groups in the United States were deeply opposed to the strategy, albeit for different reasons. The Pentagon, for one, was worried (with good cause) that improved relations with the USSR would not only lead to smaller military budgets, but a diminished role for the military in the corridors of power. The well-connected Jewish lobby was equally concerned, fearing that a new opening to the Soviet Union might reduce American support for Israel. Organized labour had its doubts too fearing that improved trade access for goods from the communist East would mean fewer jobs for American workers.

This opposition need not have been fatal had the issue of *détente* not become intertwined with politics and the political ambitions of one particular man: Senator Henry 'Scoop' Jackson. Jackson, a powerful Democrat with his eyes on the White House — and with close ties to the military, the Jewish lobby and the American labour movement — conducted an extraordinarily successful rearguard action against Nixon. Accusing him of undermining American security by engaging in what he claimed was the 'one-way' street of arms control, Jackson severely compromised the American opening to the USSR: first, by making it appear as if it involved a series of unilateral concessions to Moscow; second, by suggesting that it was a betrayal of those fighting for freedom in the Soviet bloc; and then by implying that superpower *détente* was not so much a response to the USA's problems as a major cause of them. Possibly, without Jackson, superpower *détente* may just have survived.

Finally, superpower *détente* was undermined because of resistance it met from ordinary Americans. The Cold War, as we have argued, had sunk very deep roots in the USA. Institutions had been created, ideologies constructed, livelihoods shaped by, and a way of life defined in terms of a struggle with the Soviet Union. Suddenly it seemed as if Nixon and Kissinger were saying that the struggle was over and the USA could resume normal relations with a power previously regarded as illegitimate. This was asking a great deal. Herein perhaps was the biggest problem of all, for when the two men attempted to build what looked like a new type of relationship with the USSR, they encountered scepticism and suspicion. There was a great irony in this. Nixon after all had made his name in the late forties by playing the anti-communist card. The same anti-communism now came back to haunt him and undermine his carefully constructed policy nearly thirty years later (Nixon, 1980).

SUMMARY

- *Détente* and the Nixon Doctrine were part of a grand strategy to maintain American primacy in an era of considerable change.
- The grand design unravelled when faced with powerful domestic opposition and its failure to deliver on its promises.

7 CARTER AND THE LIBERAL ALTERNATIVE: 1976–1980

When Jimmy Carter won the election in 1976, his primary job was not to solve an international crisis like Vietnam, or to work out a new relationship with the USSR. Rather it was to restore the faith of the American people: in themselves, in their government and in their country's foreign policy. Damaged by Vietnam, bruised by Watergate and disturbed by revelations about US wrongdoing abroad, Americans were ready for a change; and in Carter's view were ready in particular for a more ethical approach to world politics. According to Carter, the Nixon Administration had done great damage to the nation; not because of its efforts to build new bridges to the USSR and China, but because of its shabby behaviour at home and appeasement of right-wing dictators around the world. Americans deserved better.

Carter's desire to restore the people's faith in the idea of the United States lent everything he did a heavy moral tone. In the area of foreign policy this expressed itself most forcefully in the strong emphasis he placed on human rights. US relations with other countries, he argued, had to reflect the nation's fundamental traditions and had to correspond to, rather than contradict its core democratic values. But to what end? This was not entirely clear. According to his supporters, Carter genuinely wanted to go beyond the narrow confines of power politics and so place the United States on the side of popular forces rather than unpopular states. His less generous opponents saw a more dubious motive at work. While human rights may have been a good thing in theory, in practice the primary objective of his campaign, they felt, was to put pressure on the USSR. Thus instead of moving beyond the Cold War, as he claimed he was doing, Carter was merely reaffirming its importance.

That Carter was prepared to use human rights as a way of forcing the Soviets onto the defensive is self-evident. At heart, however, he was not a Cold War president. Indeed, a strong case could be made that he was the first non-Cold War leader to have been elected to the White House since 1945. As he made clear when he took office, his administration, unlike previous ones, would not allow East-West issues to dominate and distort the foreign policy agenda. Instead, it would concentrate on solving what Carter intellectuals sometimes liked to call 'world order' problems. The USSR was one of these, but it was no more important than, say, building better relations with its economic allies, fostering closer links with progressive forces in the Third World, and getting Americans to adjust themselves to the fact that they now lived in a complex, interdependent world which they could no longer dominate or control. For too long, according to Carter, the United States had been overly preoccupied with international communism. Now it was time for a change of focus.

Carter's attempt to relegate the superpower relationship to the back-burner clearly set him apart from other post-war American leaders. The question is, why did he seek to do this? One reason, certainly, has to do with the USA's changing economic status in the world. In effect, by the mid-seventies, many policy makers were becoming increasingly preoccupied with issues such as competitiveness. As a result, there was a tendency to be less concerned with the classic national security problem of what to do about the USSR. But this was not all. A second answer is that many members of the Carter Administration (including his adviser on Soviet affairs, Marshall Shulman) were not that impressed by Soviet power. The USSR, they pointed out, remained militarily less capable than the United States. Its economy was confronted by major problems and clearly did not compete on world markets. Its East European empire had turned into a burden. And hardly anybody outside of the USSR was attracted to the Soviet economic model. The Soviet Union, in short, was an incomplete, one-dimensional superpower that repressed its own people and those of Eastern Europe, but hardly constituted a serious menace to the United States.

A third and final reason why many in the Carter team may have been inclined to play down Cold War themes was because of their relatively confident assessment of the superpower conflict in the Third World. Here, they believed that although the USSR was still making some headway, this was only in the most backward of countries. Moreover, these advances often turned out to be rather impermanent. In this regard, the Carter Administration was particularly struck by what had happened in Egypt; a country that had fallen into the Soviet sphere of influence in the fifties and sixties, only to fall out again in the mid-seventies. The question was why? The answer, they felt, was obvious. The USSR could supply the Egyptians with guns, but could not provide them with what they needed most in the form of economic aid, advanced technology and access to western markets for their goods. This was a vitally important lesson. What had happened in Egypt could easily happen elsewhere. There was no need therefore to resist Soviet influence everywhere. In the end those countries so influenced would be impelled to return to the international fold. Having momentarily dropped out in a fit of youthful radical anger, they would, in time, be forced to drop back in again when they discovered the Soviet Union had nothing to offer.

7.1 FAREWELL TO CARTERISM

Carter's more relaxed approach to the Soviet Union soon came under attack from his political enemies. Slowly but surely they wore his resistance down, and in the end he was forced to take a tougher line. Let us first examine the arguments used against him; and then explain the broader reasons why he felt obliged to change course.

The most important argument in the intellectual armoury of Carter's critics focused, naturally enough, on his original approach to the USSR. Kissinger and Nixon, it was noted, had the wrong strategy. But at least they took Soviet power seriously and attempted to do something about it. Carter, it appeared, had no understanding of the Russian threat at all. It was all very well talking about Soviet weakness, but the fact remained that the USSR still constituted a force in world politics. Moreover, during the seventies, it had made major gains at the West's expense: first in South-East Asia following the fall of South Vietnam in 1975; then in Africa between 1976 and 1978; and finally in Central America when the Sandinistas took power in Nicaragua in 1979. Thus far from Moscow being in retreat as Carter seemed to imply, it was, in reality, on the offensive.

This led Carter's opponents to a second conclusion by way of a question. Why, exactly, was the USSR taking the offensive? Here again his enemies came to much less sanguine conclusions than he about the international situation. Following the Vietnam War the USSR, it was argued, had opted for a policy of 'cautious expansionism'. In pursuit of this it had exploited both American weakness and a wave of revolutions that had engulfed the Third World. It had also exploited something else as well: its own increased military capability. Producing tables of statistics and detailed charts, Carter's critics not only managed to convince Americans that the USA was rapidly falling behind the USSR, but that as a result, Moscow was making enormous headway in the world. And unless the military imbalance was quickly rectified, this disastrous trend would continue.

For a time Carter tried to resist these arguments; and did so at first with skill and intelligence. But within two years of having been elected he began to buckle, and slowly, but surely, started to take an increasingly tough stance towards the Soviet Union. The first indication of this was when Washington tilted decisively towards China in 1978. The following year it then agreed to the deployment of cruise and Pershing II missiles in Western Europe. At the same time it adopted what many thought was a more aggressive nuclear strategy. Finally, in 1980 Carter announced a significant increase in the US military budget.

How do we explain this volte-face? One reason, though not a decisive one, was that the Carter team itself was never united in its approach to international affairs. Zbigniew Brzezinski, for one, rarely lost sight of the main strategic question; and that for Carter's chief adviser on National Security issues remained the Soviet Union. Always keen to find ways of forcing the USSR onto the defensive, Brzezinski, significantly, became more influential during the latter part of Carter's four year term. His harder line however may not have carried the day but for a second factor: Soviet actions themselves. Moscow, it seemed, wanted better relations with the United States but was unwilling to pay the price. Its continued repression of Soviet dissidents, the tough measures it forced upon its allies in Poland to control Solidarity, and most important of all, the invasion of Afghanistan in December 1979, made it almost impossible for more moderate voices in the Carter Administration like Cyrus Vance (Carter's Secretary of State until his resignation) to resist those advocating revitalized containment.

But in the last analysis Carter's attempt to redefine US foreign policy was undermined by something even more important than Soviet actions abroad: a drift to the right in American public opinion linked, and in some respects caused by, a general sense of malaise within the United States about the state of the nation. Clearly by 1980 a large number of Americans were convinced that the USA as a world power was in almost terminal decline —

something that was driven home in stark terms by the loss of Iran and the subsequent hostage crisis in Teheran. To add domestic insult to international injury, the country appeared to be both divided and rudderless. A new agenda was needed therefore. This had not been, and could never be supplied by the hapless Carter. He would thus have to stand aside and make way for someone who could provide what the USA and Americans so desperately required: firm leadership and a clear idea of where the country should now be heading. It fell to neo-conservative Ronald Reagan to provide it (Garthoff, 1985).

SUMMARY

- The Carter Administration sought to de-emphasize the Cold War struggle as the primary determinant of US foreign policy.
- The collapse of the Carter alternative was brought about by powerful domestic opponents and a series of international developments, the most important being the Soviet invasion of Afghanistan in December 1979.

8 REAGAN AND THE REVITALIZATION OF CONTAINMENT: 1980–1988

The Reagan Presidency will be remembered for many things: its deep hostility to all things liberal; its optimism; its ability to construct a broad conservative coalition that united philosophical libertarians and the authoritarian religious right; its suspicion of the role of government in the management of the capitalist economy; an almost child-like faith in the wonders of the free market; its pandering to the economic 'winners' in society; an apparent indifference to the plight of the 'losers'; and a deep and abiding faith in the American dream, interpreted by Reagan and the neo-conservatives at least as one in which the good guys (invariably rich and white) always won out over the bad guys.

8.1 REAGAN AND THE 'EVIL EMPIRE'

When the definitive history of the eighties is finally written however perhaps one thing more than any other will stand out about the incoming Reagan Administration: its profound suspicion of, its uncompromising attitude towards, and its determination to do something about the Soviet Union. The USSR, it claimed, was the source of all global problems; from terrorism in the Middle East to revolution in Africa and Central America. Its influence moreover was on the rise, while its goal still remained that of world domination. And unless it could be tamed, the international system would continue to be a highly unstable place. Indeed, reading through

Reagan's early speeches on the Soviet Union, one is forcefully reminded of themes developed thirty years earlier in NSC-68. There was the same highly emotional language about a deteriorating world situation. A similar level of exaggeration about the Soviet Union's intentions and capabilities. And the same clarion call to mobilize American power and to revitalize containment before it was too late.

Faced with such uncompromising rhetoric many have argued that Reagan, or at least those more intelligent people who advised him, could not really have believed what they were saying. Thus the only way of understanding or decoding his statements about the Soviet threat was in essentially functional terms; as if they served other purposes than the ostensible one of simply describing Soviet behaviour abroad. And what were these purposes according to the sceptics? They were firstly, an urge to intervene more effectively against a Third World that had of late become more assertive; secondly, an equally strong desire to re-impose discipline over an increasingly disobedient Western Europe; and finally a need to create a mood within the USA itself that would be supportive of a more muscular approach to international affairs. Talk of a growing Russian menace in 1980 hence told us less about Soviet actions and more about an underlying American determination to reassert its influence after a decade of decline (Chomsky, 1982).

There is a great deal to this argument. But it would be misleading, absurd even, to conclude that the Reagan administration was not concerned about the USSR; that somehow or another its alarmist rhetoric was but a mere cover, a thin veneer to disguise its true purpose. The fact of the matter was that the USSR had become militarily more powerful in the seventies. Moreover, it had been able to use this power to increase its political influence in the wider international system — especially in the Third World. These gains had been nowhere near as important as the new team in the White House suggested. But the fact that there had been any gains seriously undermined US credibility. This was the crucial issue. It was not a question of how much the Russians had acquired (or at what cost to themselves) but the fact that they had acquired anything at all. This is what alarmed the United States (see Map 2).

Indeed, so alarmed were the genuine neo-conservatives in the Reagan administration, that they saw no long-term possibility of international peace until the Soviet system itself had changed, or been changed. In this sense, the genuine ideologues amongst the Republicans did not aim just to revitalize containment, but to roll Soviet influence back in the hope that this would bring about a transformation (or even a break-up) of the Soviet empire itself. The name of the game therefore was no longer the defence of the free world, but the elimination of totalitarianism by all means short of war.

The success of Reagan's offensive strategy depended upon two things however. The first, which few in the White House doubted, was that the United States could place sufficient pressure on the USSR. The second, around which there was a good deal more debate, concerned the state of the

Map 2   US perception of Soviet global power projection (1987)

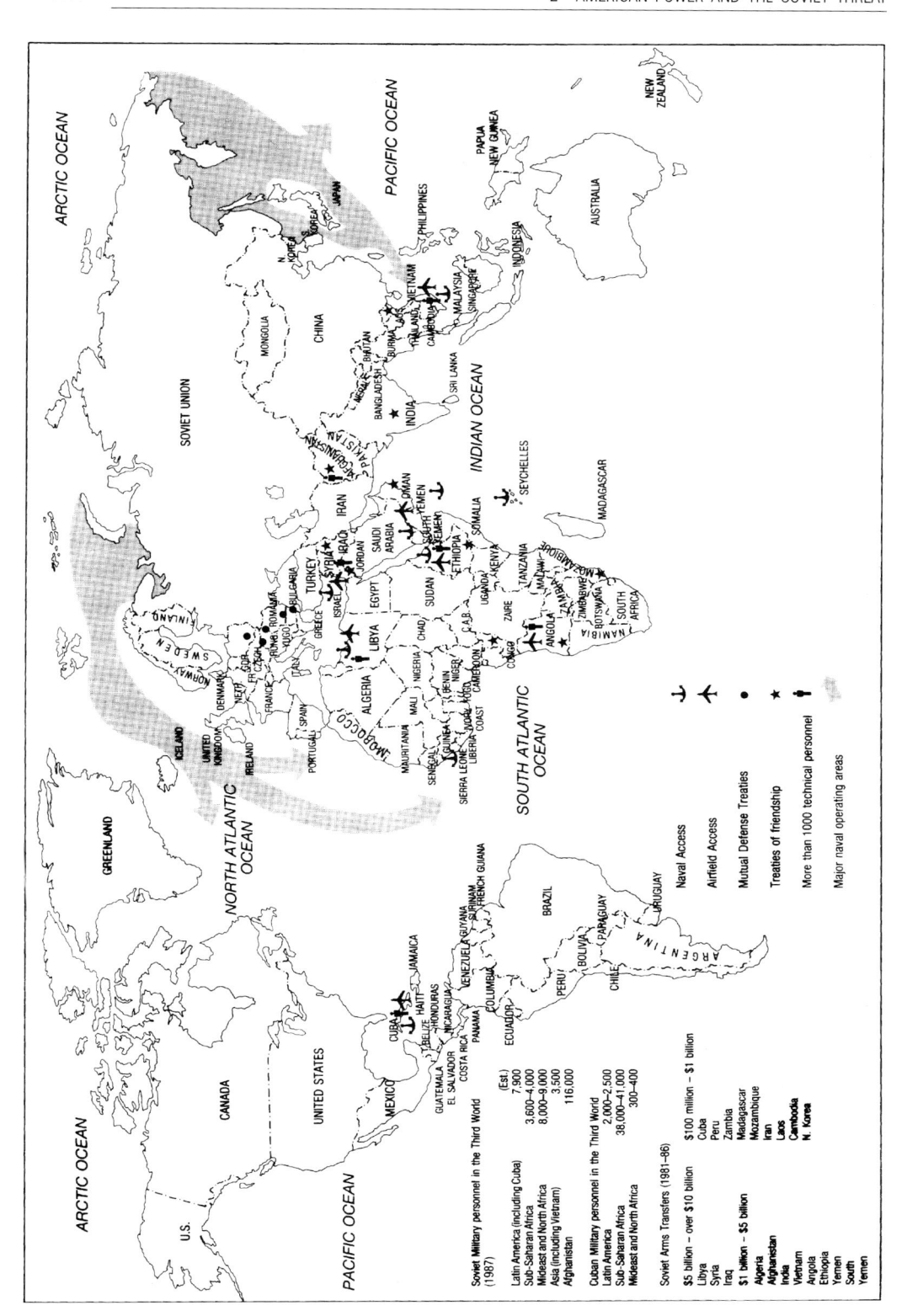

2   AMERICAN POWER AND THE SOVIET THREAT

61

Soviet system. Here the new administration almost seemed to be operating on two different levels. In its public announcements it spoke as if the USSR was more dangerous than at any time in its history. But privately (and sometimes not so privately) it accepted that the USSR faced the most horrendous internal problems. Indeed, Reagan frequently spoke of a 'crisis of totalitarianism' in which the economic forces of production were coming into increasing conflict with Soviet political relations. Richard Pipes, his adviser on Soviet affairs until 1983, talked in much the same way. According to Pipes in fact, the USSR faced problems it simply could not solve. This created a great opportunity, and if the United States had the courage to seize the moment, the rewards could be enormous (Pipes, 1984).

Thus in search of the holy grail called world order, the Reagan team set about rebuilding American power and contesting the USSR more effectively (see Map 3). This expressed itself in a number of ways, including a large scale military build-up, the arming and training of 'freedom fighters' in several Third World countries, the unleashing of the CIA, and a renewed emphasis in public fora on the Soviet Union's denial of human rights. In the process most of the core assumptions that had guided American foreign policy for a decade were jettisoned — the most significant one being arms control. Conceived of by Kissinger and Nixon as a reasonable way of managing the Soviet Union, and by Carter as a serious means of controlling the arms race itself, arms control was to all intents and purposes abandoned by Reagan. The aim now, it seemed, was not to control the arms race, but essentially to use it as a method of placing pressure on the USSR. In the short term, this might induce more reasonable behaviour by Moscow. In time, it could even bring about a change in the Soviet system itself. Only time would tell (Cox, 1990b).

8.2 REAGAN AND GORBACHEV: 1985–1988

Until 1984 or 1985 at least there was little sign that the Reagan strategy was bearing fruit. The most visible results of his project in fact were burgeoning budget deficits at home as military spending rose, the emergence of an increasingly influential peace movement in Western Europe, and deep strains within the NATO alliance as the West Europeans sought to moderate what they regarded as Reagan's unnecessary and premature abandonment of *détente*. Furthermore, by raising the nuclear stakes and questioning the legitimacy of the Soviet Union, his administration may, momentarily, have bolstered rather than undermined the integrity of the Soviet system. Confronted with such an uncompromising and apparently dangerous adversary as Reagan, many ordinary Russians rallied to the defence of the motherland; not out of ideological devotion to Marxism but for patriotic reasons.

Into this less than promising environment entered Mikhail Gorbachev, elected General Secretary of the Communist Party of the Soviet Union in March 1985. Between his elevation to power and the end of Reagan's second term, superpower relations underwent a revolution in the true sense of the word. To what extent that had been Gorbachev's original intention remains

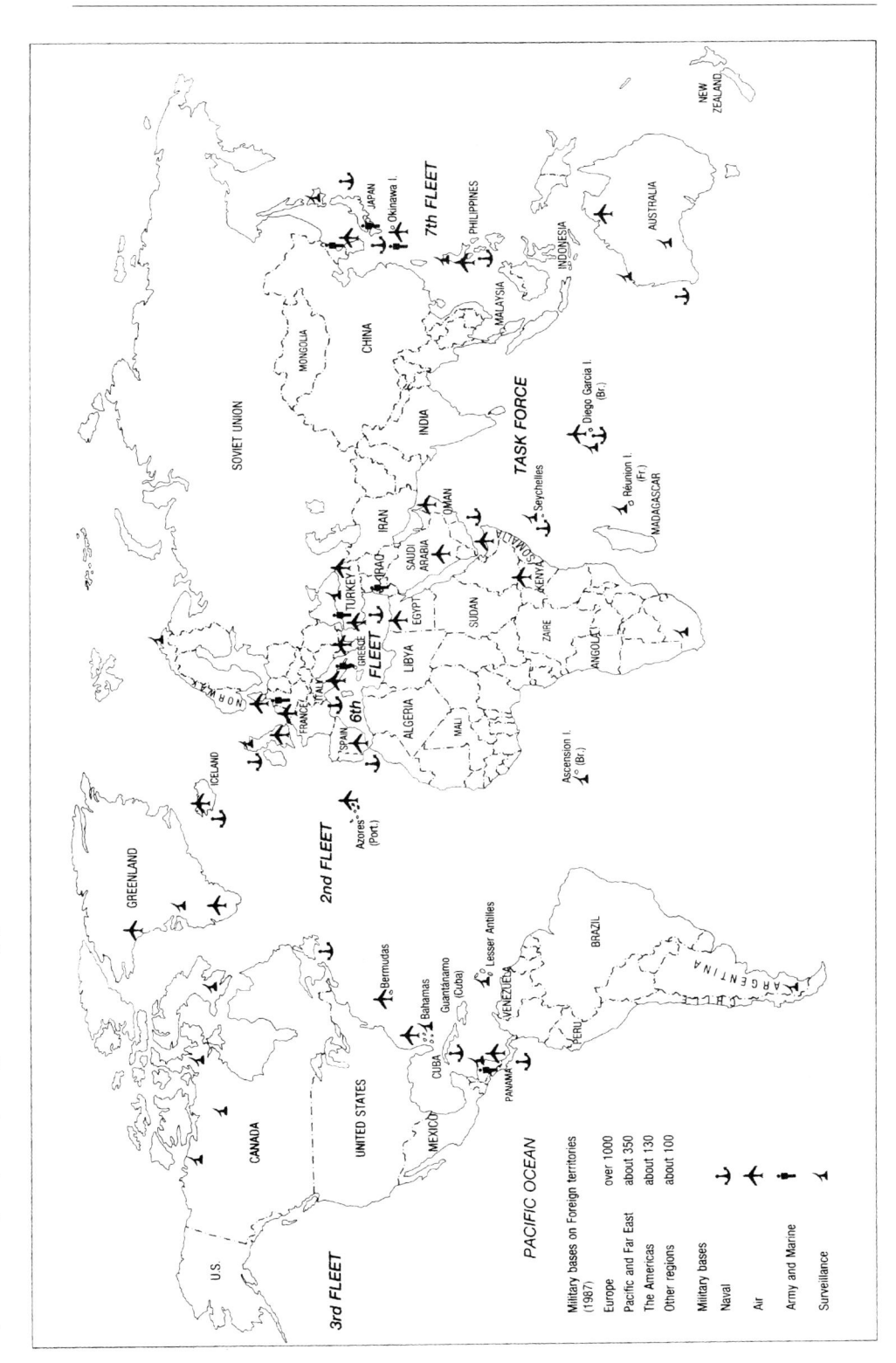

2 AMERICAN POWER AND THE SOVIET THREAT

Map 3 Soviet perception of US global military power (1987)

unclear. What is not in doubt however is that by the time Reagan left the White House, the world was a very different place to the one he had encountered when he entered it.

The initial American response to Gorbachev however was far from enthusiastic. Indeed, until 1989 at least, there were many within and without the Reagan administration who not only had their doubts about the new man in the Kremlin, but viewed him with greater suspicion than his less dynamic predecessors.

First, it was far from clear what Gorbachev actually wanted. If his aim was to reform the Soviet system, then all well and good. But it looked to many on the conservative right in particular that his primary purpose was not so much to reform the USSR, but to turn it into a more efficient and effective socialist superpower. If this was the case there was every reason to treat him, and his talk of *perestroika*, with great care. Moreover, although there was much that might be said in favour of his less aggressive foreign policy how could one really know that Gorbachev was telling the truth; that his honeyed words about peace were not some sort of deceit whose purpose was to undermine the western alliance by creating the impression that the USSR was no longer a threat? This scepticism ran particularly deep in the Reagan Administration, many of whose members assumed that Gorbachev's fine phrases were but a clever ruse aimed to slow down the American military build-up.

Finally, even if one could trust Gorbachev, there was no guaranteeing that he would remain in power. In fact, the general consensus in the second half of the eighties was that given his reformist inclinations, he was bound to be overthrown by those sections of the Soviet elite most opposed to him. And when he fell (as he almost certainly would) he would be replaced, inevitably, by a Soviet leader more overtly hostile to western interests. Thus the West in general — and the USA in particular — had best keep its powder dry and not go around making premature concessions to a man (however charming) whose days were numbered.

At first, Reagan shared many if not most of these concerns. But in the end even he was forced to concede that Gorbachev represented something completely new. More concretely, he was prepared (with all the enthusiasm of the convert) to enter into direct negotiations with Gorbachev in an attempt to settle outstanding issues. The process began slowly, starting with the first superpower summit in Geneva in 1985. Things then moved along reasonably briskly and concluded with a fourth summit in Washington in the middle of 1988. Progress was not always even, and at times it looked as if those opposed to negotiation in principle had the upper hand. But at the end of the day an extraordinary transformation had taken place in US-Soviet relations. How and why had this happened?

Part of the answer has to do with Reagan himself. A strong neo-conservative, nonetheless he was nowhere near as ideologically committed to pursuing the Cold War as some of his more intransigent advisers on the neo-conservative right. As more than one observer of the Reagan phenome-

President Ronald Reagan and Soviet Leader Mikhail Gorbachev leaving the talks in Reykjavik after the Summit in 1986

non has noted, his instincts were essentially co-operative rather than confrontational. Reagan moreover had sound domestic reasons for negotiating with Gorbachev. In 1984 he was politically on top of the world. Two years later he was in deep trouble as a result of the Iran-Contra scandal. However, by playing the role of the great and indispensable statesman on the world stage, he was able to divert attention away from his woes on the home front.

There was also the Gorbachev factor itself. Suspicious though many foreign policy professionals may have been of his intentions, millions of people in the West strongly welcomed his overtures of peace. Five years of superpower tension, the strong inclination to make some gesture towards him, and the desire to see some reduction in military spending (not to mention the attractive image of Gorbachev and his wife, Raisa) all played a part in winning over western public opinion. Reagan, as a democratically-elected politician with nervous allies across the Atlantic had to respond positively. Indeed, if he had not done so, there would have been a price to pay: both at home from those increasingly large numbers of Americans who liked what Gorbachev had to say, as well as in Western Europe where the Soviet 'peace offensive' seemed to be carrying all before it.

In the end, however, the single most important factor undermining the logic of confrontation was the sheer scale of concessions made by the Soviet leader. Recall what he did. He implemented far-reaching change at home. At the United Nations in December 1988 he effectively promised to eliminate the Warsaw Pact's offensive capability. In February of the following year, he took Soviet troops out of Afghanistan. In the Third World he placed pressure on his allies to surrender to the United States. And all this in the context of a thoroughgoing revision of Soviet ideology. Under such circumstances, it would have been strategically naive and politically foolish not to have engaged in serious discussion with Moscow. And Reagan, for all his faults, was neither naive nor foolish. Perhaps that is why he left the White House a more popular man than when he had entered it (Shultz, 1993).

> ## SUMMARY
>
> - Reaganism concerned the re-assertion of American global hegemony and a more confrontational approach to the Soviet Union.
> - The transformation of Soviet foreign policy under Gorbachev combined with domestic political problems forced the abandonment of confrontation and its replacement with negotiation.

9 BUSH AND THE END OF THE COLD WAR: 1989–1992

Unlike Ronald Reagan, George Bush was no ideologue, but nor was he a particularly bold politician either. By training and background, an instinctively cautious person he appointed those who shared his inclinations: Robert Gates at the CIA, Brent Scowcroft his National Security adviser, and Dick Cheney at the Department of Defense. For them, as well as for Bush, the exciting events of the previous four years posed rather special problems. They could hardly ignore what had taken place, and in their own low key fashion sought to encourage further reform on the Soviet side, with the promise that if it continued, the USSR would be re-admitted, or reintegrated back into the world community. On the other hand, they clearly did not wish to go too far. It may have been time to 'move beyond containment' as Bush argued in May 1989, but there were still good reasons to be careful. The Soviet Union, after all, remained a well-armed superpower. The situation in the USSR was extraordinarily volatile. And there was no guaranteeing that Gorbachev would not be overthrown tomorrow. The wisest course of action therefore was to do nothing and just await events in Russia (Cox, 1990c).

Bush's originally cautious approach to the USSR was soon rendered irrelevant by a torrent of events that threatened to overwhelm him, and those like him who had grown used to the Cold War.

The first and most significant of these events of course was the withdrawal of Soviet support for the existing regimes in Eastern Europe in 1989: the least expected and most extraordinary development in European history since the end of the Second World War. At a stroke this move changed everything, in particular the balance of military power on the continent. It also had serious economic consequences, for with the collapse of planning in the East the whole area was opened up to western economic penetration. And with the fall of planning in Eastern Europe, the case for it elsewhere in the world was thoroughly discredited. Finally, and perhaps most significantly, the events of 1989 appeared to confirm what many had been saying for decades: that Marxism was all very well in theory, but in practice was bound to lead to economies that did not work and political systems that were repressive. Little wonder that in the wake of 1989 western conservatives experienced a wave of euphoria. They had much to be euphoric about.

But hardly had the dust cleared on the continent, when the world was overtaken by another unexpected event: the Iraqi invasion of Kuwait in August 1990. According to Bush, this was one of the great defining moments of the post-war period. If Saddam Hussein were successful, this would be a major blow to the West. But if he could be thwarted (by whatever means) this would give an enormous boost to what Bush now termed the 'new world order', a world striving to be born in the post-Cold War era. It all depended on the USSR. Once again Gorbachev defied the sceptics and reversing the Soviet Union's traditional line, fell in behind the United Nations — first supporting sanctions and then, after some hesitation, the allied war effort against Saddam. The implications were clear. The USSR had given final notice that it had, at last, abandoned the anti-imperialist cause and thrown in its lot with the West.

But this was not all the USSR decided to abandon. Long before the Gulf War, many in the Soviet leadership had already concluded that although the Soviet economic system may have had a heroic past, it had a very dismal future. Planning, in effect, had outlived its usefulness and had to be replaced by something else; and that was the market. In effect, the long contest between social systems that had begun back in the thirties when Stalin proclaimed the USSR would catch up and overtake the West, had been fought to a conclusion. Unfortunately, from the point of view of the Soviet Union, the wrong side had won. The Stalinist pretence was over.

The final act in this great historic drama occurred in 1991 with the disintegration of the USSR following the abortive coup in August. This was something that the Bush Administration had neither looked forward to nor expected. Indeed, it had advanced sound arguments up to the bitter end for maintaining the territorial integrity of the Soviet Union. So long as the USSR remained intact, it reasoned, the region was likely to remain relatively stable. With Moscow in charge there was also a single point of authority with which to negotiate. Furthermore, if the USSR held together, there would be tight control over its nuclear arsenal. But this was not to be and the Soviet empire — which had been welded into a single unit by a combination of force and mutual economic need — simply fell apart. And with it collapsed the only other superpower in the world. The United States now stood alone.

Four great changes had thus occurred in just under three years: changes that brought about the end of the Soviet Union as a European power and a united state, witnessed the destruction of official communism as an ideological alternative and opened up the possibility at least of the former Soviet

Union (or parts of it) being pulled back into the international system. The Cold War had come to an end: more or less peacefully and almost (but not) completely without warning. And by sheer luck, it fell to George Bush to be present at the passing of one order and the coming into being of another. Not that this made much difference to the American people, who in the first post-Cold War election in 1992 dismissed the man who had overseen one of the most important transitions of the twentieth century. Such are the ironies of history (Cox, 1991b).

> ## *SUMMARY*
>
> - The collapse of Soviet communism and the events of 1989 made containment redundant and created new opportunities for American foreign policy.
> - The New World Order initially provided greater freedom of manoeuvre for American foreign policy makers, but this was to prove short lived in the wake of events in the Gulf.

10   CONCLUSION: THE UNITED STATES, THE COLD WAR AND BEYOND

Our story began with the origins of the Cold War in the immediate aftermath of the Second World War. It ends, rather neatly, with its final passing away in the last decade of the century. It would of course be comforting for conservatives to think that their great hero, Ronald Reagan, made it all possible and that he, more than anybody else, bears the greatest responsibility for having vanquished Russian communism. There is no doubt some truth in this assertion. Simply by raising the stakes at a crucial moment in Soviet history, it is reasonable to conclude that he forced the USSR into a corner from which it was difficult to escape. But the real cause of the end of the Cold War was not so much personal as structural. The inability of the Soviet Union to compete with capitalism lies at the heart of the great crash of the eighties; not the actions of Reagan. Yet Americans might still take heart for they can claim — with some justice — that if it had not been for the United States, then capitalism would not have been the great success story it was after 1947, and the Soviet alternative might have triumphed instead of the market. But as American policy makers contemplate the new world disorder that has followed the end of the Cold War they might be wondering what it is they have won exactly; and whether or not it was worth the winning. Some of the more subversive amongst them might also be asking another question as well. Why, if we have won, do so many of us feel so uncertain about the future? At least in the good old days of the Cold War the United States had a purpose and a vocation. Today it appears to have neither.

REFERENCES

Acheson, D. (1969) *Present At The Creation: My Years In The State Department*, New York, W.W. Norton.

Burnham, J. (1947) *The Struggle For The World*, London, Jonathan Cape.

Burnham, J. (1950) *The Coming Defeat Of Communism*, London, Jonathan Cape.

Chomsky, N. (1982) *Towards A New Cold War*, New York, Pantheon Books.

Clayton, J. L. (1970) *The Economic Impact Of The Cold War*, New York, Harcourt, Brace and World Inc.

Cox, M. (1985) 'From *détente* to the "New Cold War": the crisis of the Cold War system', *Millennium*, vol.13, no.3, pp.265–91.

Cox, M. (1986) 'The Cold War as a system', *Critique*, no. 17, pp.17–82.

Cox, M. (1990a) 'From the Truman doctrine to the second superpower *détente*: the rise and fall of the Cold War', *Journal of Peace Research*, vol.27, no.1, pp.25–41.

Cox, M. (1990b) 'Whatever happened to the "Second" Cold War? Soviet–American relations 1980–1988', *Review of International Studies*, vol.16, pp.155–72.

Cox, M. (1990c) 'From superpower *détente* to *entente cordiale*? Soviet–US Relations: 1989–90' in George, B. (ed.) *Jane's Nato Handbook, 1990-91*, Surrey, Jane's Information Group, pp. 277–86.

Cox, M. (1991a) 'Requiem for a Cold War critic: the rise and fall of George F. Kennan, 1946–1950', *Irish Slavonic Studies*, no. 11, pp.1–36.

Cox, M. (1991b) 'East–West relations in a year of uncertainty: 1990–1991' in George, B. (ed.) *Jane's Nato Handbook, 1991–92*, Surrey, Jane's Information Group, pp. 329–35.

Deporte, A. (1978) *Europe Between The Superpowers*, New Haven, Yale University Press.

Foreign Relations of the United States, 1950, Volume I: National Security Affairs; Foreign Economic Policy (1977) Washington, United States Government Printing Office.

Garthoff, R. L. (1985) *Détente And Confrontation: American–Soviet Relations From Nixon To Reagan*, Washington, The Brookings Institution.

Kissinger, H. (1981) *For The Record*, Boston, Little, Brown.

Lynch, A. (1992) *The Cold War Is Over – Again*, Boulder, Westview Press.

Mayall, J. and Navari, C. (1980) *The End Of The Post-War Era: Documents On Great Power Relations, 1968–75*, Cambridge, Cambridge University Press.

McCormick, T. J. (1989) *America's Half-Century: United States Foreign Policy in the Cold War*, Baltimore, The John Hopkins University Press.

Melanson R. A. (1991) *Reconstructing Consensus: American Foreign Policy Since The Vietnam War*, New York, St Martin's Press.

Nixon, R. (1980) *The Real War*, London, Sidgwick and Jackson.

Pipes, R. (1984) *Survival Is Not Enough: Soviet Realities And America's Future*, New York, Simon and Schuster.

Schlesinger J.R. (1977) *Defending America: Toward A New Role In The Post-Détente World*, New York, Basic Books.

Shultz, G. (1993) *Turmoil And Triumph: My Years As Secretary Of State*, New York, Charles Scribner's Sons

FURTHER READING

Ambrose, S. (1986) *Rise To Globalism: American Foreign Policy Since 1938*, Harmondsworth, Penguin Books, 4th rev. ed.

Bowker, M. and Brown, R. (eds.) (1993) *From Cold War To Collapse: Theory And World Politics In The 1980s*, Cambridge, Cambridge University Press.

Cox, M. (ed.) (1990) *Beyond the Cold War: Superpowers at the Crossroads?*, Lanham, University Press of America.

Gaddis, J. L. (1982) *Strategies Of Containment: A Critical Appraisal Of Post-war American National Security Policy*, New York, Oxford University Press.

Gaddis, J. L. (1987) *The Long Peace: Inquiries Into The History Of The Cold War*, New York, Oxford University Press.

Halliday, F. (1983) *The Making Of The Second Cold War*, London, Verso Books.

Hogan, M. J. (ed.) (1992) *The End Of The Cold War: Its Meaning And Implications*, Cambridge, Cambridge University Press.

LaFeber, W. (1993) *America, Russia And The Cold War: 1945–1992*, New York, McGraw Hill, 7th ed.

Leffler, M. P. (1992) *A Preponderance Of Power: National Security, The Truman Administration, And The Cold War*, Stanford CA, Stanford University Press.

3

PAX AMERICANA: MULTILATERALISM AND THE GLOBAL ECONOMIC ORDER

Stephen Gill ★

1 INTRODUCTION

The *Pax Americana* was not an entirely new world order: in theory at least, it was based upon the reconstruction of an international political system of sovereign states (reflected in the United Nations Charter), and, in the non-communist world, the restoration of the integrity of the world capitalist economy which had been torn apart in the turbulence of the 1930s. What was novel was the scope and intensity of American influence in the construction of the peace, and in the subsequent institutionalization and policing of this order.

This chapter explores the role of the United States in the creation, maintenance and transformation of the global economic order. More specifically it discusses:

- the relationship between American power and the emergence in the post-war era of a multilateral economic order;
- the role and functions of the USA in maintaining this order; and
- the global financial revolution of the 1980s and its implications for the US role in the governance of the global economy.

2 THE CONSTRUCTION OF THE *PAX AMERICANA* AND THE 'GRAND AREA' STRATEGY

American post-war strategic goals were based upon assessments of the causes of the Second World War. American leaders, such as President Roosevelt's Secretary of State Cordell Hull (and Treasury Secretary Henry Morgenthau), believed that the pre-conditions for war rested in the form of the inter-war international order. In particular, Hull associated the war with the disintegration of the inter-war international order. This led to the solidification of antagonistic and protectionist blocs and spheres-of-influence. At the same time, the Wall Street Crash triggered the Great Depression of the 1930s, and this was the cause of the subsequent collapse of the world trade and payments systems.

In the terms used by Kindleberger (1973) the world economy had no willing or effective leadership to avert the crisis. Thus, during the war, these New Deal leaders began to shift towards the idea that the USA should lead post-war reconstruction to eliminate tendencies towards rival imperialisms. Nevertheless, isolationist interests (as was discussed in Chapter 2) remained very strong. They argued for a return to a foreign policy which would give priority to hemispheric interests. Their viewpoint was founded upon the high degree of economic self-sufficiency and the virtual territorial impregnability of the USA. These relatively inward-looking, 'isolationist' forces were opposed by 'globalists' who wished to see the USA extend its power and influence world wide.

A 'multinational bloc' of interests (associated with leading industrial and financial sectors) came to countervail the isolationists. It was loosely organized in a nexus which included (parts of) the State Department, the Treasury, the Department of Defense, blue chip corporations, media and union leaders. It was brought together on occasion in influential private councils such as the New York Council on Foreign Relations (CFR). Many of the nation's top strategic thinkers were drawn into these efforts. Secretary of State Cordell Hull's economic liberalism — he associated peace with the growth of economic interdependence, that is the creation of collective interests in peace through a web of commerce — was synthesized with the philosophical and political realism of the strategist George Kennan and philosopher-columnist Walter Lippman. These 'internationalists' — drawn from both the public and private sectors — began, from as early as 1942, to advance a three-fold conception of a desirable post-1945 world order, which was called the 'Grand Area' idea (Gill, 1990).

The Grand Area was defined as the 'maximum living space' for the US economy. This meant, first, opening up closed territories for American investors and traders — the 'Open Door' idea which had long been associated with US economic imperialism in the Americas. The Grand Area thus required the break up of the economic empires not only of the Axis powers (for example, the Japanese Co-Prosperity Sphere in Asia), but also those of its allies (for example, the UK's Sterling Preference Area and Empire).

Second, and partly with this in mind, US leaders advanced the ideas of self-determination and national sovereignty, concepts enshrined subsequently in the United Nations Charter (the United Nations' headquarters were located in New York City, the International Monetary Fund (IMF) and World Bank in Washington, DC).

Third, the political and economic systems of the defeated Axis powers, as well as those of key allies, were to be reconstructed in the context of multilateral surveillance mechanisms supervised, ultimately, by the USA. This implied bolstering liberal democracy, the market economy, and the political centre *vis-à-vis* both communism and fascism: from the US viewpoint such policies were crucial to prevent old-style economic imperialism and the rival economic blocs of the inter-war years. US goals were to be achieved partly through developing new alliance structures (such as NATO) and in multilateral economic arrangements.

The Grand Area concept was premised upon the outward expansion of the material, institutional and ideological power of the United States. After it became clear that the USSR would not allow communist states to become incorporated into this order, the scope of its application shrank into a Cold War framework, especially after 1947, and after the Chinese Revolution ended in 1949 with the triumph of the communists led by Mao Tse Tung.

Especially with regard to its key allies and former Axis enemies, the construction of the *Pax Americana* was a complex, interactive process which required the USA not only to use its economic and military leverage, but also to make compromises and concessions, so as to politically embed its vision in a politics of consent. To a degree, this process was manifest in the creation of the 1944 Bretton Woods framework for post-war economic multilateralism, embodied in the International Monetary Fund and World Bank, as well as in a different way, in the General Agreement on Tariffs and Trade (GATT), founded in 1947. The plan for a World Trade Organization was defeated in the US Congress, and thus a less formal and centralized institutional framework for world trade emerged.

US strategy became clearer in the post-war Occupation administrations and the Marshall Plan. The broad aim was to establish new constitutional structures and market-oriented economic reforms. Especially in Germany and Japan, the post-war Occupation resembled an interim dictatorship pending the emergence and solidification of liberal democracy in these former Fascist and militarist powers.

The military settlements at the end of the war, and the subsequent forms of post-war reconstruction (both political and economic) provided the foundations for the so-called *Pax Americana*.

Atlanticism — or transatlantic political, military and economic co-operation — was at the centre of this post-war system of American hegemony. US leadership was perceived widely as legitimate by the strongest political forces in the transatlantic heartland, and, to a degree, in Japan. In this sense, 'American hegemony' was more intense and socially constructed in its centre than in its hinterlands: the Third World. Even here, despite interventions in the Americas, and support for several odious dictatorships, and despite wars in Korea and later in Vietnam, there was some support for the USA since Washington initially promoted decolonization and national self-determination. Moreover, Third World producers derived benefits from trading with the USA. Nevertheless, many Third World governments sought to distance themselves politically not only from the Cold War superpowers, but also from the former colonial powers. So developed the Non-Aligned Movement.

2.1 JAPANESE POST-WAR RECONSTRUCTION

Returning to the former great powers, the case of Japan is revealing since it indicates the contradictions associated with the US policies of economic liberalism and Cold War internationalism: the twin pillars of American post-war globalism. It also illustrates the coercive and consensual aspects of

American hegemony, or 'hegemony protected by the armour of coercion' (Gramsci, 1971). The US Occupation followed Japan's surrender after atomic bombs were dropped first on Hiroshima (a uranium device which instantly killed 118,661 persons) on 6 August 1945, and then on Nagasaki (a plutonium bomb where 73,884 died instantly) on 9 August 1945. The use of these genocidal weapons — especially the second bomb dropped on Nagasaki when to many it was clear that the Japanese surrender was imminent — demonstrated not only to the Japanese government, but also to the rest of the world, that the United States was willing and able to use its colossal destructive power to reshape world order.

Although US conventional bombing had been largely responsible for the devastation of many Japanese cities (greater casualties occurred in Tokyo than in Hiroshima because of fire-bomb attacks), many in Japan subsequently welcomed the superimposition of liberal democracy and a move towards market economics. For many Japanese this was partly because of the fear of the resurgence of militarism, given the atrocities committed by Japanese forces during the Pacific War, especially in Korea and China. On the one hand, the USA was feared (or hated, as in Okinawa, where fighting between the USA and the Okinawans was particularly fierce and involved enormous casualties). On the other, this fear was also mixed with feelings of admiration for the power and achievements of American society. Japan later became the launching pad and supplier of *matériel* for the US forces in the region, especially during the Korean and Vietnam Wars. This helped to boost the Japanese economy in its reconstruction efforts.

In Japan post-war reconstruction took the form of a new liberal democratic constitutional order. Occupation authorities attempted to dismantle the Emperor system (at least denying the Emperor's status as a god-king, and removing him from the inner circles of political power). The USA also attempted to dismantle the pre-war *zaibatsu* (massive industrial and trading conglomerates such as Mitsubishi which provided the material power to arm Japan) and to introduce an American-style market society. The rise of the Cold War in the late 1940s, and especially after the Chinese Revolution of 1949 meant, however, that key aspects of restructuring were largely abandoned. The USA sought to make Japan its Asian bulwark against both Chinese and Soviet communism. The *zaibatsu* were reconstituted as *keiretsu* (looser business groupings). The Japanese economic system remained highly protected from foreign penetration and Japan subsequently rose to the status of economic superpower, but as a close ally of the United States.

2.2 THE GRAND STRATEGY

The *Pax Americana*, then, involved a conscious political strategy of vast scope and ambition, intended to extend the global reach of American power. The strategy fused consensual and coercive dimensions of power to reconstruct world order at three levels:

1. at the level of the 'domestic' institutions and arrangements of the core states in the world capitalist economy (Japan, German etc.) by promoting liberal democracy and the development of a strong civil society; whilst at the same time opening them up to the emerging world economy;

2   at the level of production, involving the spread of the Americanist system of mass production and mass consumption with its utilitarian values and the primacy of market forces;

3   at the international level, through, for example, the institutionalization of East-West conflict and of American leadership in international organizations and in formal military alliances.

The strategy to achieve these objectives was three-fold: the creation of a strong military apparatus, the rebuilding of powerful allies and reorienting their economic activities towards US growth patterns, and the institutionalization of American power in a relatively consensual process of multilateralism. These policies were, from a US vantage point, largely successful in the 1950s and 1960s, as both Western Europe and Japan were rebuilt economically and politically, and the process of decolonization was linked to the new US-centred alliances and to the process of economic multilateralism. The international economy (a series of national economies interacting principally through trade and investment flows) gradually gave way to a more integrated global system of production, consumption, finance and exchange, at least among the richest countries of the world.

The post-war planning process culminated with the decision by the US leadership not to impose a Carthaginian peace in either Germany, Japan or Italy. At one point, for example, the US government seriously contemplated the so-called Morgenthau Plan, which argued for the prevention of the possibility of a resurgence of German militarism by turning post-war Germany into an agrarian economy. Unlike the peace exacted at Versailles after the First World War, Germany was not required to pay massive reparations (despite French and Soviet pressure for this). Rather the emphasis was upon a constructive peace. In the sections which follow we shall explore more systematically each of the three levels of *Pax Americana* in more detail: the domestic; the productive; and the international.

SUMMARY

- In planning for the peace the USA sought to avoid the disasters of the Versailles treaty and the autarchy of the inter-war international economy;

- *Pax Americana* involved the reconstruction of Germany and Japan reflecting American priorities, interests and values;

- *Pax Americana* embraced a multilateral economic order, policed through the IMF, World Bank and GATT, and based upon the principle of economic liberalism;

- *Pax Americana* was a conscious political strategy to establish a constructive peace which legitimated an American designed world order.

3 WELFARE-NATIONALISM AND POST-WAR RECONSTRUCTION

This decision to engage in a constructive peace was ultimately reflected in the Marshall Plan of 1947–1948. This plan allowed for the creation or reconstitution of welfare states in the transatlantic regions, coupled with a liberalizing orientation towards the world economy (Cox, 1987). Many of the European governments which came under US influence during the Marshall Plan era were Christian Democrat in nature, with Konrad Adenauer of Germany an exemplar in this regard.

The Marshall Plan was accompanied at the international level by a system of public multilateralism which linked the key bureaucratic, military and political, as well as class forces across a range of countries. Within most of the transatlantic nations the mediation of class conflict was frequently expressed in a form of 'corporatist' sharing of power that is, involving co-operation between government, organized labour and employers. This often meant conservative parties, although in a number of cases Social Democratic (but not Communist) parties came to power (a Socialist government took power in Japan in the early 1950s, albeit briefly). In Britain, this 'corporatism' took the form of 'Butskellism', named after the Conservative R.A. Butler and the Labour Leader Hugh Gaitskell. The term was meant to reflect a broad political consensus on the purposes and nature of post-war politics between the two major parties.

'Butskellism', then, was a particular form of welfare-nationalism: a combination of policies and institutions to ensure social peace and national determination of economic outcomes. The form of state which these policies implied assumed the continuation of the war-time co-operation and class compromise between labour and capital. It implied that state planning of the economy, and Keynesian macroeconomic demand management was to be continued. Radical tendencies (especially communists) were to be incorporated or marginalized politically. Worker interests were included in the policy-making framework of corporatism (where government, employers and unions shared in strategic decisions in the mixed economy).

The 'social' dimension of 'Butskellism' involved the shielding of workers from the effects of the marketplace in a number of key areas (for example, unemployment insurance in the labour markets) and the creation of universal provision of what were now deemed to be essential public services. By 'essential' we mean necessary for the broad reproduction of society. Thus worker and broader public interests were included politically in accord with the growing importance of organized labour. Such interests were reflected – with variations between nations – in the creation of the welfare state and a widened adult suffrage, including votes for women. The new provisions and entitlements included universal education and healthcare, retirement pensions and child benefits.

The economic function of welfare payments (and unemployment benefits) was to sustain aggregate demand when the business cycle was in slump. Thus spending power was injected into the economy when economic activity declined, and taxes were increased to cool the economy if it were to overheat. These policies presupposed some state control over economic activity within the boundaries of a particular nation-state. Indeed, some form of protection against foreign competition was widely held to be necessary to rebuild shattered industries. However, such support was viewed — by the US leadership — as temporary, with the goal of a more liberal movement of goods, services and capital when conditions allowed. This was the 'nationalist' dimension of the new post-war 'mercantilism'.

The 'nationalist' mix of policies associated with this stance included various types of economic protection against foreign competition, through the use of subsidies, nationalization of industry and prohibitions on foreign investment and control of firms in 'strategic industries' such as munitions, telecommunications, energy supply and the media. In Europe these 'nationalist' types of mercantilism were not pursued in as exclusionary a manner (with regard to foreign participation in the economy) as in Japan, at least with regard to foreign direct investment (FDI) and foreign control over strategic industries.

Mercantilism can be contrasted with economic liberalism in a number of ways. Whereas Liberals advocate virtually free movement of 'factors of production' (land, labour and money), mercantilists advocate and justify state intervention for purposes of national security and survival. Thus controls over emigration (to either encourage it or block it) and capital movements are very important for mercantilists. There is no historical example of a country pursuing pure liberal policies, at least for any significant length of time, although Britain in the period between the passing of the Corn Laws in 1842 and the start of the Great Depression of 1873–1886 approximated liberal international economic policies. The USA at the time was highly protectionist in trade, and in true mercantilist fashion, promoted rapid immigration as a means of state-building. Thus only when the USA had become a preponderant international economic power did its policies begin to become more 'liberal' (Gill and Law, 1988, pp.25–53).

Economically, then, the post-war reconstruction at the domestic level, was intended to create or to restore the conditions for the emergence of more integrated circuits for trade and capital across the Atlantic and the Pacific, and, in time, a fully Open Door to US foreign direct investment (FDI). Most of the post-war United States' FDI — in manufacturing — was focused in Western Europe and in parts of the Third World which contained strategic raw materials and energy supplies, especially oil, in the period when the USA pressed strongly for a liberal international economic order. (The USA had pressed aggressively during and after the war to enter British controlled territories in the Middle East, to secure control over international oil supplies.) Politically, reconstruction came to be associated with the policies of containment or roll-back of communism.

However, the liberal international economic goals of the USA were not fully achieved, in large part because of the onset of the Cold War. In particular, because of the Cold War, Japan was able to gain more room for manoeuvre in determining its own post-war reconstruction pattern, and, as a result, was able to use classic mercantilist policies to protect its infant industries and to rise up the economic ladder in a hierarchical international division of labour.

> ## *SUMMARY*
>
> - The USA assisted in the creation and maintenance of national welfare states in Europe and Japan;
> - such domestic political and economic arrangements were buttressed by a US managed liberal international economic order;
> - the USA sought to establish an increasingly free trade liberal global economic order as conditions allowed.

4   HEGEMONY, CIVIL SOCIETY AND FORDISM IN THE POST-WAR ORDER

In this section I shall relate the emergence of welfare-nationalist forms of state to the process of international organization. This presupposes some discussion of changes in the nature of production and consumption in the post-war era, and the way that US domestic production structures became more internationalized.

4.1   PRIVATE (TRANSNATIONAL) DIPLOMACY

The institutionalization of conflict and the promotion of trans-class consensus in political decision making were reflected in US-led forms of multilateralism. As already noted, this included the formal domain of international politics: inter-state alliances, treaties, etc. The public face of US globalism, however, had as its counterpart an emerging global civil society, in which private interests and agencies were active. This dimension involved the creation of transnational networks of business, trade unions, academia, the media etc., and private international relations councils such as the secret Bilderberg meetings and other Atlanticist forums (Gill, 1990, pp.122–41).

Indeed Bilderberg shows the way that 'public' and 'private' aspects of international diplomacy were fused. Created in the early 1950s, Bilderberg was a forum involving political, military, intelligence, business, academic, media and union leaders from the Atlantic region (and some from the Pacific, such as Australia). It sought to reconcile divergences of interest between the rising power of the USA and the relative subordination of the former imperial powers of Western Europe. Japan was not considered to be sufficiently powerful for inclusion at this particular high table of world politics. This situation was rectified in 1973 when the Trilateral Commission was created by US banking and industrial magnate David Rockefeller. (Later, Japan's new status was publicly consecrated when it was included in the seven power 'economic' summits in 1975–1976, now known as the Group of Seven [G7, involving Canada, France, Germany, Italy, Japan, the UK and the USA and the President of the European Commission].)

The existence of private international relations councils like Bilderberg shows that the consolidation of the American post-war order had not only a political, economic and security, but also a cultural and ideological dimension. The post-1945 capitalist restoration was linked, ideologically, to the rehabilitation of the nineteenth century idea which equated progress with the spread of the material civilization of capitalism. By the early 1950s it came to be associated with the old rivalry between capitalism and socialism, personified by Woodrow Wilson and V.I. Lenin following the Russian Revolution of 1917. Western propagandists juxtaposed the 'free world' with 'totalitarian' communism. The Cold War emerged as a central aspect of the 'new' world order.

This juxtaposition involved the universalization of the world view and social principles associated with American civilization. The political influence and popular appeal of these principles were related to the attachment of growing numbers of people to the idea of the realization of self through the process of consumption and the concepts of liberty and freedom associated with possessive individualism: aspects of what may be referred to as a process of 'Americanization'.

Another aspect of 'Americanization' was the spread of US production forms and the particular methods and processes associated with the manufacture and distribution of goods and services for mass consumption (see Chapters 2 and 3, Book 2). Many of the leading US industries had been organized since the 1930s to produce for a gigantic domestic market, a market which grew tremendously during the war. This mass-production and mass-consumption system was known as Fordism after the innovations of Ford Motor Company.

4.2 THE SPREAD OF FORDISM AND US CORPORATE CAPITAL

Fordism presupposed the technical rationalization of production and strict control over the workforce as well as an efficient system of storage and distribution. It also presupposed a system of economic management allowing producers to develop a longer-term outlook and to plan effectively, and to raise large amounts of credit for investment, so as to exploit economies of scale. Fordism involved workers giving up on efforts to control the labour process and to subordinating themselves to the rhythm of the assembly line. The acceptance of a high level of discipline in the factories was paralleled by rising real wages (especially during the 1950s and 1960s). Workers' families — and not just US workers — were thus able to acquire the artifacts of the American Dream such as the automobile, the television set, the washing machine and the refrigerator — the consumerist elements of 'Americanization'.

Moreover, the dominant US manufacturing firms tended to operate in oligopolistic markets — limited competition — and key industries were linked to the post-war military-industrial complex: electronics and appliances, capital goods industries, automobiles, energy, and finance. Oligopolistic structures were formed by the competition and occasional collusion between large corporations — such as the so-called 'Seven Sisters', international oil companies which dominated the international oil industry until the late 1960s. The growth of these key industries was co-ordinated by some elements of state planning, such as in the Pentagon's procurement and research and development policies (which produced, for example, the first mainframe computers) and through the state's application of Keynesian economic policies to influence the level of aggregate economic activity in order to promote smooth economic growth (Melman, 1970).

Kees van der Pijl (1984) has called this a system of 'corporate liberalism': it went with the mediation of conflict through corporatist forms of political (and industrial) management such as Butskellism, and was supportive of the liberalization of the world economy, allowing such companies maximum freedom of manoeuvre internationally. These firms tended to employ the most privileged workers, with the highest real wages, and thus, tended to drive a wedge within the ranks of working class unionism. Union representatives associated with corporate liberalism tended to be linked to anti-communism.

Fordism was imitated in Western Europe, and, subsequently, in Japan. Fordist production methods were used in both the public and private sectors — state industries and private corporations were equally Fordist in this respect. The Marshall Plan administration was in some respects the midwife of this process. Its Technical Assistance and Productivity Program involved 'the complete inventory of Taylorism and Fordism, like merit rating, job classification, shift labour in continuous process [with a] key component of Marshall Plan hardware deliveries ... the technology of continuous wide-strip mills for the steel industry ... capable of producing cheap steelsheet for automobiles and household appliances' (Van der Pijl, 1984, p.149). For example:

> Twenty years after their introduction in the United States, the wide-strip mills with American aid broke the cartel barriers which hitherto had prevented their installation in Europe. In 1939 Europe only possessed two such mills, with important restrictions on their output imposed by their cartelized competitors; by 1953, in contrast, France, Germany and Britain each had three wide-strip mills, with others in Austria, Luxembourg, the Netherlands and Belgium (two).
>
> (Van der Pijl, 1984, p.149).

These innovations — and others — underwrote the social dominance of interests associated with Fordist mass production, rather than finance, in the key capitalist countries in the 1950s and 1960s. This was in contrast to the situation in the 1920s when the dominance of international finance prevailed. In Britain, of course, the power of the financial interests of the City was never fully subordinated to those of industry. Nor were those associated with Wall Street in the USA.

US corporations too, like the Ford Motor Company, expanded rapidly in Western Europe after 1945. This meant, because of the strategic importance of the automotive industry, connections with heads of state and labour leaders in a range of European countries. Other US firms had long standing economic links with Germany. Prior to the war Henry Ford had been decorated by Hitler's representatives, as was Thomas Watson of IBM (he received the Order of the German Eagle from Hjalmar Schacht, the Nazi Minister of Economic Affairs in 1937). Rockefeller's Chase Bank had links with German banks as did a significant number of other US companies. The US Marshall Plan administrator was Paul Hoffman, the former president of Studebaker, the automobile company. When Hoffman spoke to US Senators about the initial plan — the Schuman plan — for a European Coal and Steel Community in a closed session in 1950, Hoffman said he backed the plan because:

> Heretofore, the price has been too high and wages too low for people to buy the products of the steel industry to the extent that they buy the products of the steel industry [in the USA]. We take a ton of steel and put it in an automobile and you know there are very few people who can afford to buy an automobile in Europe. So, if you start this process, raising wages and lowering prices, you get that great expanding market in Europe, and that will take care of this increased production. Henry Ford introduced us to that new principle, and, when he did so, he started a revolution that we are still benefitting by, and I think that the Schuman Plan may have that result in Europe.
>
> (Van der Pijl, 1984, pp.159–60)

An individual who symbolized the unity of this corporate-liberal, Fordist system was Robert S. Macnamara. He left a senior executive position at Ford Motor Company to become Secretary of Defense during the Vietnam War, and thus the *de facto* leader of the NATO alliance (the President, as commander-in-chief of the US armed forces is in effect the *de jure* leader of NATO). After stepping down at the Pentagon he became the President of the World Bank, and devoted himself to promoting Third World development. In the 1980s he became a key establishment voice advocating massive reductions in nuclear weapons.

The case of Macnamara also shows other dimensions of the way that the ruling elements of the major capitalist countries were linked through their shared outlook, material and political interests, and this was formalized at both the public and private level. Like Hoffman, Macnamara was both a business and a political leader, and a member of the Bilderberg group (and later, the Trilateral Commission). Bilderberg was constructed as an attempt to synthesize some form of transatlantic compromise on questions of international politics and economics. Bilderberg, like corporatism, brought together not only elements of the government and the representatives of capital, but also those of labour, in the political process. Often, the representatives of organized labour were the most militant anti-communists — international bankers like David Rockefeller were happy to make loans to communist countries and, later, to open a branch in Red Square (Chase Manhattan did this in 1975).

> ## SUMMARY
>
> - Private, transnational diplomacy was an important dimension of the creation and maintenance of the post-war international economic order since it generated transnational social networks through which the process of Americanization was diffused;
>
> - Americanization involved the spread of consumerism, Fordism, and US corporate capital;
>
> - Americanization was assisted and promoted by policies of economic reconstruction such as the Marshall Plan.

5 MULTILATERALISM AND THE INTERNATIONAL ECONOMIC ORDER

Any discussion of multilateralism needs to be placed initially in the context of the construction of a massive worldwide military-security apparatus anchored in United States alliance systems. The most important of these alliances was NATO (see Chapter 2). The US strategic posture rested on a global network of military bases and intelligence facilities. These not only encircled US Cold War enemies, but also were based within the territory of allies and clients. The military-intelligence installations (with their electronic eavesdropping capacities) thus directly and indirectly policed the range of political and economic alternatives open to the non-communist world.

5.1 MULTILATERALISM

Multilateralism in its simplest sense refers to a broad process of co-operation between three or more states in the making of economic policy and the conduct of international economic regulation. It usually refers to the system of international money, trade and payments which emerged under the aegis of the *Pax Americana*. It is associated with movement towards the full convertibility of currencies and the resumption of international capital flows which declined as the inter-war system fragmented into antagonistic economic blocs.

As has been noted in the previous section, the process of economic liberalization rested upon the reconstruction of the other great powers' economies, and the emerging welfare-nationalism, which allowed for some forms of temporary protectionism. Thus the American inspired international economic liberalism was socially embedded in the domestic institutions and politics of states in the capitalist heartland of the emerging world order. In the terminology used by John Ruggie (1982) it was a system of 'embedded liberalism'.

But the process was not, and is not solely confined to governments. As noted, it was also associated with private actors (see the discussion of Bilderberg and Fordism), whose international economic activity is regulated by the formal processes of public multilateralism. Large trading houses, international energy and raw materials companies, international investment banks and other providers of goods, services and capital across national boundaries form a key constituency in favour of economic multilateralism. This constituency has grown in size and power since 1945, along with the general internationalization of production and the globalization of finance. In other words, economic multilateralism means the development of arrangements which would facilitate the expansion of capital on a world scale — and not just US capital.

In the post-war period, this process has been associated with the so-called Bretton Woods institutions, but has never been confined to those institutions. At Bretton Woods in 1944, US leaders met with representatives from other nations to construct a blue-print for the post-war economic order. The blue-print can be understood as a type of 'economic constitution' for the emerging world order. As with any kind of constitution, its nature changes with practice. This was also true of Bretton Woods.

5.2   THE BRETTON WOODS SYSTEM

The discussions at Bretton Woods in 1944 were influenced by the ideas of Lord Keynes, the British negotiator, and those of Harry Dexter White, the leader of the US team. The US side was dominated by the New Deal thinking of the US Treasury. Both sides agreed on the need for state intervention to steer the 'mixed economy', deal with market failures and ensure smooth macroeconomic management. Each agreed that control over speculative flows of capital ('hot money') was necessary. In particular, they felt that finance should be the 'servant' rather than the 'master' of production: finance should lubricate trade flows and promote the development of the 'real' economy — and not be used to make speculative gains (as occurred in the 1920s and early 1930s) (De Cecco, 1979).

Each attempted to devise a multilateral and publicly regulated system of international money and finance, with control exercised 'at both ends' (Helleiner, 1991). Obligations were to be attached to countries which both sent and received capital to co-operate in the mutual adjustment of balance of payments, with the IMF projected to be a crucial link in this process. However, the New York financial community, and its counterparts in

Western Europe succeeded in diluting the public surveillance aspect and the proposals concerning capital controls. Thus countries with a balance of payments deficit were forced to bear the burdens of adjustment — with the exception of the USA which was able, in time, to run large balance of payments deficits. Adjustment here usually meant cutting back on domestic consumption through higher taxes to pay the overseas bills.

At Bretton Woods the USA insisted on the goal of an integrated liberal monetary system, with fixed exchange rates and free convertibility of currencies, with the US dollar the centrepiece of the system. All currencies were fixed in value relative to the dollar — the fixed exchange rate system — and the dollar tied to gold — in contrast to Keynes' suggestion that an international currency called 'bancor' be created and overseen by the IMF. The USA pressed for the impossible in terms of convertibility, since the European economies were devastated and could not hope to sustain their exchange rates against the dollar without the kinds of exchange controls for which Keynes had argued. Nevertheless, the USA pressured Britain in 1946 to restore the convertibility of sterling. After intense speculation against the pound, partly encouraged by the US government (holders of pounds sold them to buy dollars) the UK ran out of foreign exchange reserves and quickly returned to the use of exchange controls — controls which remained in place until 1979. Other European countries retained controls and general convertibility was not restored in Europe until 1958.

Thereafter, the workings of the international monetary system were almost totally dominated by the USA between 1947 and 1960. In 1947, the USA forced a structural change in the European economic landscape, when it

International Monetary Fund building in Washington, DC

encouraged investors to get out of European currencies (notably sterling) to force a massive devaluation. The USA also threatened to stop Marshall Aid to the UK if Britain did not acquiesce to US demands and fully dismantle the Sterling Preference Area — a legacy of imperial rule. This all had the result of turning the European economies into export economies (De Cecco, 1979, p.60). In addition, the Japanese yen was pegged at 360 to the dollar, a situation which also encouraged Japan to embark on the path of export-led growth. In both the European and Japanese cases, a large proportion of exports were destined for the giant US market, a situation which the USA was prepared to encourage because of its importance for post-war reconstruction.

The IMF was originally seen by its Bretton Woods founding fathers as an institution which would help to guarantee global financial stability and monitor and help to sustain the system of exchange rates based on the US dollar fixed in price in relation to gold. Its sister UN institution, the World Bank was intended to focus its efforts on development aid and technical assistance. The IMF mandate was inspired by the desire to avoid the kind of competitive devaluations of currencies and beggar-thy-neighbour policies, associated with the 1930s. However, the resources of the IMF and World Bank were modest and could not be expected to match the scale of the problems. The economic crisis of 1947 forced the hand of the USA, and the Marshall Plan was the result — a means of overcoming the dollar shortage which plagued the majority of European countries, and recycling the huge trade surpluses which the USA was running at the time (US aid included outright grants to sixteen west European countries of $17 billion between 1948–1952).

Between 1947 and the late 1950s the linchpin of US global economic diplomacy was confidence in the US dollar. This was based on the primacy of the US economy, its vast gold reserves and its commitment to convert dollars into gold. By 1958, however, due to large balance of payments deficits occasioned by a combination of overseas military expenditures, Marshall Plan aid in the form of the European Recovery Programme, and the investments overseas of US corporations, US overseas liquid assets began to exceed its monetary reserves (Calleo, 1982, pp.17–18). After 1958 the deficits got worse.

This led to what French President General de Gaulle later described as the 'exorbitant privilege' of the USA, since as the dollar was the primary international currency the USA could finance its deficits in its own currency, and so could pay for its debts by debasing the 'greenback'. In time, then, the massive outflow of dollars which accompanied American globalism undermined that confidence. This situation proved to be unsustainable, but it was not until 1971 that President Nixon formally severed the link between the dollar and gold, and ended the Bretton Woods fixed exchange rate system.

During the 1950s and 1960s the IMF played a relatively minimal role, with most of the elements of monetary politics dominated by the USA and a group of other key countries. For example, officials and ministers of these countries met regularly in Basle at the Bank for International Settlements (BIS), the secretive central bankers' bank, founded in the early 1930s (the USA joined in 1960). A second forum was known as the Group of Ten (G10), formed in 1961 to create the General Agreements to Borrow, a set of arrangements confined to its members: Belgium, France, Germany, Italy, the Netherlands, Sweden, Canada, Japan, the UK and the USA. The G10 was supplemented by Working Party III (WP3) of the Organization for Economic Co-operation and Development (OECD), a forum for finance and economics ministers to co-ordinate policies. All of these forums continue, with the high-profile Group of Seven summits the subject of an annual media circus.

After five years' negotiation in the G10 Special Drawing Rights (SDRs) were created by the IMF, the first truly international reserve assets and units of currency which could be used by central banks in international payments. This new form of liquidity was similar to Keynes' 'bancor': it was not managed by the USA alone, or even by the USA in tandem with an inner circle of countries. It was managed by an international institution (albeit one where the USA had preponderant influence). Nevertheless, what Joan Spero (1990) calls this 'high point' of post-war economic multilateralism occurred just as the world economy was ending its 'long boom' and entering a long period of economic crisis.

5.3 THE INTERNATIONAL TRADING ORDER

The forms of multilateral monetary management by a privileged and powerful inner circle dominated by the USA, can be contrasted with the more 'global' forms of co-operation and conflict management in the field of trade. In the politics of trade the term 'multilateralism' was, of course, associated with economic liberalization — but only up to a point, as a selective review of the GATT indicates.

An example of this is the 'most-favoured-nation' principle of inter-state commerce and the principle of non-discrimination (enshrined in the General Agreement on Tariffs and Trade, GATT, founded in 1947). What the latter meant was that all of the contracting parties (that is, governments) agreed to adhere to the principle whereby 'any advantage, favour, privilege or immunity granted by any contracting party to any product originating in or destined for any other country shall be accorded immediately and unconditionally to the like product originating in or destined for the territories of all other contracting parties' (Gardner, 1980). Exceptions to the principle of equal treatment for all were existing preferential arrangements and future customs unions (including the very important ones, such as the EEC) and free-trade associations (like the European Free Trade Association). Moreover, the 'national treatment' provisions in the GATT were designed to ensure that governments must treat imports the same way as domestically produced goods and services with regard to matters of taxation, regulation, and distribution. Codes were also established to deal with disputes over subsidies and dumping (selling goods in foreign markets at below-cost price to offset losses). A crucial rule was the prohibition of quotas (that is, fixing

Finalizing the agreement for the World Trade Organization — the successor to GATT, 1994

the numbers of a good which can be imported, for example, a certain number of cars or video cassette recorders) and quantitative restriction of trade. Separate provisions were made for agricultural trade, allowing for the welfare-nationalist forms of protection to continue and indeed to intensify after the GATT was signed. Indeed, the US agricultural sector had been fundamentally re-shaped and reorganized during the New Deal period by a system of production controls, price supports, subsidies and import protection.

Certain other aspects of trade were also omitted, such as commodity agreements and trade in services. The GATT included mechanisms for redressing grievances ('dispute settlement') but these were often accompanied by delays, or non-compliance by members. The GATT's pronouncements were not legally binding. The GATT advanced through a series of negotiating 'rounds' according to the principle of reciprocity: reductions of tariffs and barriers would occur if agreed by contracting parties. The GATT, like the IMF and World Bank, became a part of a wider multilateral process. This process even related to the management of industrial relations and the political orientation of trades unions, in the form of the International Labour Organization, which was, like the GATT also headquartered in Geneva.

As is clear from the development of these institutions in the immediate postwar period, the USA was prepared on the one hand, to take virtually complete control of certain aspects of economic multilateralism (for example, in the field of money) and in others to make a significant number of concessions over the speed of the implementation of liberalization (although not its direction), as in the GATT. This was partly because of the imperatives of

Cold War politics. It was also because a deepening of the post-war economic crisis in Europe might have had ominous economic repercussions for the USA. Apart from short-term crisis management, US leaders also sought to create the most hospitable long-term investment climate for the expansion of US capital. This meant that some interests of subordinate powers had to be given weight in the new institutional order.

> ## SUMMARY
>
> - Multilateralism was a dominant form of international economic governance promoted by the USA in the post-war period;
> - multilateralism involved the creation of international organizations such as the GATT, the IMF and the World Bank to police the international financial and trading systems;
> - multilateralism was a means by which the USA retained primary influence over the rules and operation of the global economic order;
> - multilateralism was essential to the expansion and vitality of the post-war international capitalist system.

6 GLOBAL FINANCE AND THE PROBLEMS OF ECONOMIC MULTILATERALISM

The 1970s and 1980s represented a major change in the development of the post-1945 global political economy, especially with the emergence of global finance as a major driving force for change. Many of the forces associated with the rise of international finance in the 1970s and 1980s had a contradictory, destabilizing, and polarizing character. This was also true in earlier periods of this century, with the inter-war years as the classic example of the way that financial movements, crises and collapse can have substantial effects on the 'real' economy, and the balance of class forces and state forms.

6.1 THE FORCES FOR TRANSFORMATION

Developments in the 1950s and 1960s coincided with the birth and expansion of the Euromarkets which became a key means through which the City of London could sustain its position as an international financial centre, as well as a means for US banks to develop their international business and avoid many of the capital controls imposed in the USA in the 1960s. The Euromarkets were the first relatively free international capital and money markets to be created after the Second World War, and their emergence is crucial to the internationalization of money capital which has been a feature of recent economic history. As Jeff Frieden (1987) has shown, the creation and growth of this Euromarket was a product of government policy, that is of the USA and UK governments. The offshore markets now constitute a gigantic pool of mobile capital, which has served to erode the 'international and domestic, economic and political underpinnings of the postwar world order' (Frieden, 1987, p.80).

Part of the political support for the offshore markets in the 1960s stemmed from their growing importance in the short- and long- term financing of the operations of American transnational firms, many of whom had influence in the Democratic administrations of the 1960s. Also, because of the openness of the City of London the markets grew quickly, creating a coincidence of interests between the City and New York finance similar to that of the 1920s.

The Euro-dollar market became attractive in the 1970s to the oil exporting states, who deposited their massively increased earnings in the London offshore markets. The value of these markets has now more than doubled from an estimated figure of over $1 trillion ($1,000 billion) in 1984: 'Its appeal for the oil states was that it was apparently beyond the reach of the US government; it was movable, it was secret; and it paid a handsome and floating rate of interest' (Strange, 1988, p.105).

The rise in capital mobility associated with the growth of the Euromarkets and the internationalization of production (transnational companies drew on the markets to help finance their investments) was a crucial influence in undermining the viability of fixed exchange rates, as was the spillover effect of US domestic economic expansion which contributed to the inflationary surge of the late 1960s and early 1970s. The Nixon shocks of August 1971, ending gold convertibility of the dollar, followed from the logic of the policies of the Johnson era, as US domestic expansion led to a rise in external trade deficits. The Nixon response reflected the US acceptance that the international monetary system was becoming more unstable and that the convertibility of the dollar into gold was not economically sustainable. US monetary reserves were dwindling and its external deficits were ballooning. These developments set the scene for the 'collapse' of the Bretton Woods system of fixed exchange rates. Nevertheless, the USA was still able to take advantage of the new more market-based system of flexible exchange rates — exchange rates would float against the dollar. This system would, albeit temporarily, be configured around the now super-exorbitant privileges of the USA in the international monetary system.

Attempts were made initially to co-operate among the USA and other countries, who agreed to reduce placements of funds in the Euromarkets in 1971 to stem their growth, a strategy which was undone as the markets were soon flooded with petro-dollars after the oil price rise in 1973–1974. The major OECD governments turned to the offshore markets for balance of payments financing, as did many Third World governments.

Eric Helleiner (1991) emphasizes, along with Susan Strange (1986) that at the time of the oil shock the authorities of the major OECD countries had a choice: they could have strengthened co-operation, for example, via the IMF and used international organizations to recycle the funds. That they did not do this reflected three things: (1) US veto power over any significant change in the international monetary and financial structures; and (2) a reduction in the policy autonomy of the transnational supervisory and regulatory structure characteristic of post-war central bank co-operation, for example, in the BIS; (3) a reduction of the collective power of the major capitalist states *vis-à-vis* the global financial markets.

The USA wanted to implement a more fully liberal financial system, whereas other major states favoured public multilateral collective action. The USA sought to devalue its foreign debts via a dollar depreciation and force other countries to expand to absorb increases in US exports (this tactic was repeated in 1985). Other countries were forced to accept the implications of the new US unilateralism (Gill, 1986; 1990). This was because of US centrality in the international financial system, reinforced by the role of the dollar and by the depth and liquidity of the US financial markets. Indeed, the offshore markets were largely Eurodollar markets.

Thus with more aggressive, unilateral means, the USA was able to sustain its ability to pursue a relatively autonomous macroeconomic policy, with foreigners underwriting US deficits by holding dollars. This also served to internationalize the costs of US adjustment to the oil shock. Indeed Helleiner (1991) cites a CIA report of the time arguing that the USA would receive the majority of OPEC overseas investment funds, and that therefore OPEC moves would in effect support US policy autonomy.

The social basis for this alteration in US policies away from the New Deal social compromise was partly based upon the transnational expansion of US capital. American corporations had been restricted in their overseas expansion by US capital export controls: they sought access to more 'liberal' international financial markets. In an alliance with neo-liberal and neo-conservative academics and financial interests, these firms often supported liberalization and deregulation of global finance (Hawley, 1987). As Robert Gilpin (1975) noted in the mid 1970s, no longer was there any simple correspondence between the domestic interests of the US population (that is, those of the bulk of US workers) and the needs of international business. This development was crucial to the fragmentation of the New Deal coalition, accelerated during the recessions of the 1970s and 1980s, as smokestack industries went to the wall, weakening organized labour, one of the bedrocks of Democratic Party support.

Indeed, the restructuring of the US economy has been disastrous in terms of the living standards of the average American. From 1973 to 1992 real per capita income rose 27 per cent (that is, adjusted for inflation). At the same time real average wages for the bottom 60 per cent of workers fell by 20 per cent, and fell most rapidly for young men and women aged between eighteen and twenty-four (Thurow, 1993). For much of the 1980s, many union members looked forward to their leaders negotiating pay cuts in the annual collective bargaining round.

US deregulatory policies let the genie out of the bottle. The rest of the 1970s and 1980s saw the rapid growth of offshore markets and a more liberal financial system, and the intensification of competitive pressures leading to the era of so-called flexible labour markets. It was also associated, then, with 'factor price equalization', namely the tendency for the cost of factors (notably labour) to fall towards Third World levels. Increased illegal immigration into the USA has accelerated this trend within the USA, in what has become an essential two-tier economy as a result (Thurow, 1993).

At the same time, global finance, whilst accentuating competitive pressures in the so-called real economy, created a new force field of constraints on the policy autonomy of all states, even those with large economies. Amongst the major economies, the constraints of the new financial order were first felt by the UK in 1976, in the form of a balance of payments crisis, followed by a political crisis over the terms of an IMF loan, which mandated substantial cutbacks in welfare state provision. A split emerged in the Labour government as its leaders opted for monetarist deflation, rather than the Keynesian autarky of the Alternative Economic Strategy. The same constraints were felt by the Socialist Mitterand government in France in the early 1980s when it tried a policy of Keynesianism-in-one-country, that is to reflate the economy by boosting government expenditures, leading to a growing fiscal deficit, and putting pressure on the franc.

Even the USA's room for manoeuvre was restricted during the 1978–1979, dollar crisis. The rise in US inflation which went with Keynesian expansion in the 1970s threatened the prospect, in David Calleo's (1982) words, of a 'catastrophic liquidation' in the international value of the dollar. In 1979 this prompted European discussions on the creation of the European Monetary System and eventually a single currency to countervail US dollar hegemony. These developments prompted a draconian response, with the US Federal Reserve tightening monetary policy and raising interest rates to increase the dollar exchange rate. This exerted a savage deflation on the USA and world economy. Real oil prices and world interest rates rose following the fall of the Shah of Iran. This squeeze was only reversed in 1982, when the threat of domestic and international financial collapse became manifest, for example, when the Mexican government threatened to default on the huge loans provided by the large US banks in the 1970s.

SUMMARY

- The globalization of finance, particularly the growth of the Eurodollar markets, contributed to the collapse of the Bretton Wood system;
- since the 1980s the dominance of global finance has imposed increasing constraints on the kinds of economic policies states can pursue, including the USA.

7 THE RENEWED CENTRALITY OF THE USA, ITS LIMITS AND CONTRADICTIONS

The 1970s and 1980s were characterized by recessions and restructuring, and a crisis of the post-war Fordist-Keynesian, welfare-nationalist states. Recessions contributed to the increasing liberalization of the global political economy. The 'new mercantilism' of the 1980s and 1990s is designed to increase the attractiveness of national economies to foreign capital, rather than to shut such capital out. This also involves competition to attract or retain skilled labour (or human capital), with competitive direct tax cuts (on both wages and capital gains). Such direct taxes were replaced by more regressive indirect or value added taxes (regressive taxes hit the poor more than the rich). Recessions promoted a restructuring of capital, and of capital-labour relations. For example, during 1979-1982 there were record bankruptcies, and the decline of older, less-competitive industries was accelerated, and 'flexible' work practices and real pay cuts for workers became more common. Labour became much more defensive than in the 1960s and early 1970s.

7.1 US DECLINE OR RENEWED PRIMACY?

In many ways the recession of the early 1980s can be seen as facilitating the renovation of American supremacy. This might appear paradoxical since recession was more severe in the USA than it was for its main economic competitors and military rival. However, in 1982–1983 the Reagan 'boom' took off. Reagan used a combination of fiscal stimulus (vastly increased military expenditures and some tax cuts, and thus a spiralling budget deficit) and supply-side measures to stimulate investment and improve the productivity and competitiveness of key sectors of the US economy.

At the same time, the US Federal Reserve kept real interest rates very high in part to quell inflation and support the dollar, and in part to finance the burgeoning public debt. Indebted countries, which had borrowed on the Euromarkets in the mid-1970s when interest rates were low, were now faced with very high debt service charges, and as such, many Third World countries were plunged into a debt crisis. As recession hit, their export earnings fell, and debt servicing costs spiralled.

The USA's capacity to expand out of recession in part by drawing in supplies of foreign capital contrasted with the position in other countries. Each had to exercise strict controls on the growth of public spending. Reaganomics provided a welcoming climate for foreign direct and portfolio investment (especially from Japan), as well as flight capital (for example, from Latin America), as a consequence of America's high real interest rates and the rising dollar between 1982–1985. Transnationalization in the 1980s was focused, therefore, on a growing American centrality (for example, as a destination for foreign investment) within the wider global political economy. This situation contrasts with the 1950s and 1960s when US foreign investments predominated, and went principally to Western Europe. The new investment flows into the USA have helped to make US policy ever more crucial to the interests of a wider circle of states and foreign capital.

On the other hand, the constraints on US policy autonomy in money and finance have increased during recent years. This is partly because of the size of US budget and balance of payments deficits; the USA is the world's largest international debtor and will have to service its debts; the US dollar appears to be declining as a reserve currency; US economic interdependence with the rest of the world is growing (and US self-sufficiency is eroded). The USA has increasingly come to rely on European and Japanese financing and is likely to continue to need further substantial funds from these sources throughout the 1990s, at the very moment when global economic growth and public confidence in established forms of political leadership has begun to falter:

> Ironically, while it might be said that US policy since the Nixon years has been driven by the desire to maximize US autonomy *vis-à-vis* the rest of the world, the result may have been to increase the constraints upon US freedom of manoeuvre both relative to its major allies and to international financial markets.
>
> (Walter, 1991, p.224)

At the same time as the Reagan 'revolution' was occurring, and accompanying the rise in international competitive and financial pressures, the global political economy shifted to higher levels of knowledge intensive information-based activity. This, the 'third revolution' in production and finance is premised upon new information technologies, but is occurring in the midst of economic depression in many parts of the world and a decay in the legitimacy of existing political structures on a world wide basis. This process has meant that state policies have become ever more 'internationalized', in the sense that they have become attuned to the cycles and rhythms of global economic forces. At the same time, the 1980s and early 1990s witnessed a period of fiscal and debt crisis, a weakening of the power of organized labour, and a growth in the structural power of capital on a world wide basis.

Given the deflationary bias in contemporary neo-liberal (market driven) economic policies an economic contradiction emerges: if all countries deflate, global recession is the necessary outcome. This points to what Keynesians call a massive drop in global aggregate demand, and what Marxists call a realization problem for the further accumulation of capital. For many parts of the world, the 1980s and 1990s have brought the second great depression of the twentieth century.

In this context, there is a growth in political disenchantment and alienation with the political formulas produced by mainstream parties and governments. In some ways the situation is similar to that which emerged in the 1930s. What the 1990s and 1930s may have in common, it would appear, is a dissatisfaction with, and increasingly a rejection of, 'politics as normal'.

US trade negotiator Mickey Kantor (centre) and his EC counterparts Leon Brittan and Rene Steichen prepare for final negotiations on the Uruguay GATT treaty

Moreover, the international financial system, both as cause and effect of globalization, is fragile and is only as strong as its weakest link. In 1992 Mr Hata, the Japanese Minister of Finance, revealed publicly that the Japanese banking system was near to collapse. The US system's fragility was exposed in the late 1980s with the Savings and Loan debacle, and it came near to failure over the Mexican debt rescue in 1982. The Wall Street Crash of October 1987 also raised the spectre of global economic collapse. Of course, there is greater internationalization of policy and corresponding support networks between central banks than was the case at the time of the Wall Street Crash of 1929 which precipitated the Great Depression.

Nevertheless, the spectre of a world-wide slump began to materialize during the 1990s, a decade that began with an investor boom associated with stock markets in the so-called 'emerging markets'. However, the boom proved to be unsustainable. By 1997 the world economy was in turmoil following the financial collapse of a number of countries. The collapse started in Thailand and spread throughout East Asia to finally engulf the Suharto dictatorship in Indonesia. In 1998 the Russian government defaulted on its debts and its economy went into a tailspin. This collapse was triggered, like the other financial crises of the late 1990s, by a combination of a crisis in investor confidence and the contagious effects of currency devaluation in a more integrated world economy. These crises helped to produce a second Great Depression across much of the world. In East Asia the situation was compounded by a worsening of the parlous state of the Japanese economy and the weakening financial system highlighted by Mr Hata in 1992. The Japanese economy was in absolute decline, with falling output, growing unemployment and a paralysis of its political establishment.

Some of what happened resembled the economic patterns of the 1930s — especially the competitive depreciation of currencies. However, in other respects the global economic order was moving into uncharted territory, partly owing to the proliferation of complex and exotic financial instruments (called 'derivatives') and other financial innovations that accentuated the hypermobility of short-term movements of capital. Much of the new hypermobile capital flows were the speculative 'vicious flows of capital' that the designers of the Bretton Woods system had sought to control. Indeed, much of this hypermobility was due to efforts by the international financial institutions to liberalize exchange and capital markets.

Thus a global financial collapse in the 1990s was by no means an impossibility, and one would need to be a Candide to be optimistic about the global economic outlook for the next decade. Following Polanyi's analysis of the 1930s, global liberalization and recession/depression were the immediate conjuncture for the remobilization of state and society against the logic of the self-regulating market — or what today we would call the 'process of globalization'. The repercussions in this period, it will be remembered, involved not only attempts to deal with the crisis through Keynesian policies (as in the New Deal), but also the imposition of neo-orthodoxies of sound money as well as Fascism and Nazism. Today nationalism and a backlash against globalization are beginning to resurface in a substantial manner in many parts of the world. For example, the problem would seem to be especially acute in east and central Europe and in those parts of the former Soviet Union that are in economic chaos. By late 1998 millions of Russian workers had received no wages for many months, and both the communists and the neo-nationalists were gaining in political strength.

Here it is worth remembering that the dramatic changes of the 1930s occurred in part in response to the failure of the market and the balance of power systems. The failure of the market was symbolized by the Great Depression, the collapse of the international gold standard, the Five-year Plans in Russia, the New Deal in the USA. Germany's decision to leave the League of Nations and the rise of Nazism were the harbingers of the collapse of the balance of power and the end of the international *status quo*. To put things in more Marxian terms, the superstructure of international economic and political order no longer corresponded to the more fundamental political and material forces operating at the more politicized and differentiated base of world society.

However, there has been no return to the autarchic blocs of the 1930s. Indeed, what has actually occurred is both a process of economic globalization and regionalization. This has been shaped and driven by the transnationalization of production, finance and exchange. It has been informed by an extension of market forces and market values associated with economic liberalization. These values are in some senses consistent with Americanization as I have defined it in this chapter.

> **SUMMARY**
>
> - Parallels exist between the emerging global economic order of the late 1990s and that of the 1930s;
> - contemporary developments confirm the centrality of the USA and processes of Americanization to the liberal international economic order;
> - the current world economic order contains contradictions and may not be sustainable, economically or politically.

8 CONCLUSION

This chapter provides considerable evidence from which we can draw some conclusions in respect of the following questions:

1. What is meant by American hegemony and how do we conceptualize it?
2. What sort of global economic order are we discussing?
3. What are its major characteristics and dominant forces?
4. Who benefits from such an order?
5. What form of stability is being pursued and how is it sustained?
6. What is the nature and role of international organization and multilateralism in this order?

First, I have conceptualized hegemony in Gramscian terms (see Gramsci, 1971). Changes in the post-1945 world order can be associated with the establishment of American preponderance in a transnational process of international conflict resolution and the legitimation of American leadership. This has involved the creation of a global civil society (including the process of international organization and the participation of private interests in the system of international politics) and the international extension of a mode of production (Fordism). These developments have been congruent with the outward emanation of American power and influence. For a period (that is, 1950–1970) this world order was relatively inclusive and universal in appeal, especially in its transatlantic heartland.

Second, the order in question is a predominantly and increasingly a capitalist one, but the form of capitalist development has shifted from traditional Fordism, to a disciplinary liberal form, with its flexible forms of production, distribution and changing patterns of consumption. It has changed, at least in its heartland from a politically inclusive and consensual, to a more disciplinary and neo-liberal order, albeit one still under US international leadership. One key feature of this change has been the political marginalization of traditional forms of organized labour. New forms of social discipline are increasingly market based. After the demise of the former Soviet Union, the security structures are dominated by the USA, which has become the chief protector of this neo-liberal order. After 1989, the communist states collapsed partly because their governments were unable to adapt to these new economic and political conditions. The historical defeat of Soviet-style communism is of course of crucial importance to world order prospects: now the USA is the world's only military superpower, and the communist alternative to capitalism is becoming a historical memory.

Third, the United States, understood in terms of both its state and civil society, has been at the heart of the creation of multilateral economic institutions and the post-war development of the process of international organization. The central forces in these developments have involved the globalization of production and finance and the growing militarization of the planet. Fourth, then, this order has tended to work more systematically in favour of some interests, rather than others, for example the interests of transnational capital, and especially financial interests have benefitted most from globalization. This situation is in contrast to the early post-war years when the fruits of American productivity and power were more equitably distributed within US society, and indeed elsewhere. Globally, social inequality has increased, especially since the late 1970s and the gap between the 'haves' and the 'have nots' of the world has grown to massive proportions.

Fifth, in comparison with the 1950s and 1960s, the global economy has become less stable and more prone to recessions, in ways that call into question the sustainability of the shift towards a more neo-liberal, disciplinary order, an order which is based, as it were, on a neo-Darwinist concept of the survival of the fittest. Much of this instability is related to the operation and character of global finance, which tends to promote a short-term outlook, one that is often inimical to long-term planning in production, education and so on.

Moreover, while many thought that the threat of nuclear annihilation would diminish with the end of the Cold War, it may be intensifying in other ways. The nuclear tests by India and Pakistan in 1998 were, in some senses, a nationalist backlash against the imposition of a globalized world economic order under American leadership. Indeed, the turmoil in Russia may also involve a backlash against neo-liberal globalization with unpredictable consequences, particularly given the enormous stockpiles of nuclear weapons possessed by the post-Soviet states.

More generally, however, we should analyse changes in the global economic order from the perspective of everyday life as well as from the viewpoint of high politics. For example, in the world of work and in the everyday lives of people a key social trend of the 1980s and 1990s has been towards ever-greater levels of personal and social insecurity. The forms of welfarism and social protection associated with the 1950s, 1960s and 1970s have been diluted by the competitive and harsh economic conditions of the 1980s and 1990s. Thus the paradox of the question of stability in the post-Cold War world order may relate to more than weapons of mass destruction. Security in this sense seems to be increasingly a commodity that only the affluent can afford, rather than a public good to be publicly provided and enjoyed by all citizens.

Finally, the process of economic multilateralism has changed in ways that reinforce this pattern of insecurity because of its relentless emphasis on defeating inflation (austerity) and the freeing of market forces via policies of liberalization. This is reflected in the changing role of the IMF, which — in concert with the Group of Seven and the World Bank — now effectively supervises the process of neo-liberal restructuring in many parts of the Developing World and in the former communist states. Earlier in its existence, the IMF was intended to oversee the rules of the international monetary system of fixed exchange rates, balance of payments adjustment, and the projected commitment to full currency convertibility among the major economies. The IMF was able to use its credits, based on member quotas, to oversee adjustments in a transitional manner. Nevertheless, these resources were modest, and in practice the US effectively controlled and managed the international monetary system, with *ad hoc* crisis management supplemented by the BIS and the G10 in more general financial matters. Now the IMF, in concert with the World Bank, places policy conditionality on its loans — forcing the process of liberalization and structural adjustment on loan recipients, and effectively supervising a wide range of economic and social policies to make countries conform to the dictates of the world market order. At the same time, this order has become more unstable. It has been associated with widening social polarization, greater inequality and a general rise in insecurity for the majority of the world's population.

In many respects, it is still the USA that sets the agenda for the international financial institutions, although in many parts of the world — for example, East Asia and the former Soviet Union — there is growing resentment at their policies, as well as concern that ultimately these organizations and the G7 are impotent to prevent financial crises and the world economic depression from spiralling into a slump. Of course, under these conditions the United States' centrality is reinforced, as is its supremacy in world politics, but in a more coercive and less consensual way than was the case in the Marshall Plan era. Thus while the United States presses for liberalization, the political appeal of US power is far from hegemonic, given that many millions in the emerging middle classes of the developing world are being economically wiped out by the brutal disciplines of the liberalized world capital and currency markets, disciplines promoted by American leaders and international financial institutions.

In summary, therefore, it is legitimate to ask whether the new forms of economic multilateralism — centred around the G7, as a new global economic directorate — will be not only legitimate but also effective in sustaining international economic growth, despite successes in reducing inflation, often at the cost of high levels of unemployment. The new phase of economic multilateralism — as has been the case for the entire post-war period — would appear to depend on the willingness of the US government to co-operate. Given the prospect of world-wide economic depression, a key political issue is whether the US is willing to share economic leadership, particularly with Japan and the European Union. It remains to be seen whether the inward-looking nature of the US political system and the often parochial outlook of its leaders will allow American leadership to become more multilateralized, in the sense of sharing power with other governments for constructive economic purposes.

REFERENCES

Arrighi, G. (1982) 'A crisis of hegemony' in Amin, S., Arrighi, G., Frank, A.G. and Wallerstein, I. (eds.) *Dynamics of Global Crisis*, New York, Monthly Review.

Block, F. (1977) *The Origins of International Economic Disorder*, Berkeley, University of California Press.

Calleo, D. (1982) *The Imperious Economy*, Cambridge, Ma, Harvard University Press.

Cox, R.W. (1981) 'Social forces, states and world orders: beyond international relations theory', *Millennium*, (10), pp. 127–55.

Cox, R.W. (1986) 'Social forces, states and world orders', revised version, in Keohane, R.O. (ed.) *Neorealism and its Critics*, New York, Columbia University Press.

Cox, R.W. (1987) *Production, Power and World Order: Social Forces in the Making of History*, New York, Columbia University Press.

De Cecco, M. (1979) 'The origins of the post-war payments system', *Cambridge Journal of Economics*, 3, pp. 49–61.

Frieden, J. (1987) *Banking on the World*, New York, Harper Row.

Gardner, R.N. (1980) *Sterling-Dollar Diplomacy in Current Perspective*, New York, Columbia University Press.

Gill, S. (1986) 'American hegemony: its limits and prospects in the Reagan era', *Millennium*, (15), pp. 311–39.

Gill, S. (1990) *American Hegemony and the Trilateral Commission*, Cambridge, Cambridge University Press.

Gill, S. (1992) 'Economic globalization and the internationalization of authority: limits and contradictions', *Geoforum*, (23), pp. 269–83.

Gill, S. and Law, D. (1988) *The Global Political Economy: Perspectives, Problems and Politics*, Brighton, Wheatsheaf; Baltimore, John Hopkins University Press.

Gilpin, R. (1975) *US Power and the Multinational Corporation: The Political Economy of Foreign Direct Investment*, New York, Basic Books.

Gilpin, R. (1987) *The Political Economy of International Relations*, Princeton, NJ, Princeton University Press.

Gramsci, A. (1971) *Selections from the Prison Notebooks of Antonio Gramsci*, translated by Q. Hoare and G. Nowell Smith, New York, International Publishers; London, Lawrence and Wishart.

Hawley, J. (1987) *Dollars and Borders*, New York, M.E. Sharpe.

Helleiner, E. (1991) 'American hegemony and global economic structure', PhD Thesis, London School of Economics.

Kennedy, P. (1987) *The Rise and Fall of the Great Powers: Economic Change and Military Conflict from 1500 to 2000,* New York, Random House.

Keohane, R. (1984) *After Hegemony: Cooperation and Discord in the World Political Economy,* Princeton NJ, Princeton University Press.

Kindleberger, C.P. (1973) *The World In Depression, 1929–39,* Berkeley, California, University of California Press.

Kolko, G. (1971) *The Politics of War,* New York, Harper and Row.

Melman, S. (1970) *Pentagon Capitalism,* New York, McGraw Hill.

Polanyi, K. (1957) *The Great Transformation: The Political and Economic Origins of our Time,* Second edition, Boston, Beacon.

Ruggie, J.G. (1982) 'International regimes, transactions and change — embedded liberalism in the post-war economic order', *International Organization,* vol.36, pp. 379–415.

Spero, J. (1990) *The Politics of International Economic Relations,* New York, St. Martin's Press.

Strange, S. (1986) *Casino Capitalism,* Oxford, Basil Blackwell.

Strange, S. (1988) *States and Markets,* London, Frances Pinter.

Thurow, L (1993) 'An American common market', *Guardian Weekly,* November 21, 1993.

Van der Pijl, K. (1984) *The Making of an Atlantic Ruling Class,* London, Verso.

Wallerstein, I. (1984) *The Politics of the World Economy,* Cambridge, Cambridge University Press.

Walter, A. (1991) *World Power and World Money,* New York, St. Martin's Press.

FURTHER READING

Calleo, D. (1982) *The Imperious Economy,* Cambridge, MA, Harvard University Press.

Gill, S. (1990) *American Hegemony and the Trilateral Commission,* Cambridge, Cambridge University Press.

Gilpin, R. (1987) *The Political Economy of International Relations,* Princeton, NJ, Princeton University Press.

Walter, A. (1993) *World Power and World Money* (2nd edition), New York, St Martin's Press.

4 THE UNITED STATES AND WESTERN EUROPE: EMPIRE, ALLIANCE AND INTERDEPENDENCE

Michael Smith ★

1 INTRODUCTION

President Clinton fought his first election campaign, the 1992 campaign, with the reminder that 'It's the economy, stupid!'. This was intended to imply that whatever else might catch the President's eye as the issue of the day, the one unavoidable problem was that of nurturing the domestic prosperity of Americans. The ending of the Cold War had produced not only great pressures for the declaration of a 'peace dividend' but also a feeling that US politics began — and for some, ended — at home. One implication of this stance was that relations with America's allies in Western Europe should be given a low priority, except when they were linked to domestic needs. During the remainder of the 1990s the President and ordinary Americans were reminded again and again that an easy retreat from their entanglement with Western Europe was impossible. Within six months of his inauguration, the President had been forced to recognize that his set of priorities was unachievable: the Americans were deeply enmeshed with their European partners in the conflict in the former Yugoslavia, the stabilization of the former Soviet Union, the reform of the North Atlantic Treaty Organization (NATO), the control of nuclear weapons, global trade negotiations and the management of world currencies. For the rest of the decade, this reality of entanglement and mutual concern continued, despite the pull of American domestic priorities. This chapter aims to identify the primary factors that have made this entanglement inescapable, and to assess the ways in which it has evolved throughout the post-1945 era.

Since the founding of the Republic, relations with Western Europe have been a central focus of US foreign policy and its changing role in the world arena. They have played a major role in the evolution of the American polity and in the 'domestic' aspects of the American economy and society. The USA itself was essentially a product of West European colonialism and the reactions to it, and developments in the nineteenth and early twentieth century gradually shifted the balance between the two sub-continents. Since the Second World War, and the confirmation of the USA's status as a superpower, there has been what some would describe as an essentially imperial relationship between the Americans and their erstwhile 'superiors'.

Partly because of this long historical adjustment, and also because of the political and economic evolution both of the Old World and of the New, the relationship between the USA and Western Europe has been central to the development of world politics and the global political economy more generally. Although it could be argued that in the nineteenth and early twentieth centuries there was a considerable 'distance' between the politics and economics of the two regions, their increasingly close connection in the period after the First World War, and their formal alliance in the post-1945 era, meant that the transatlantic 'partnership' came to dominate the world arena in a number of interrelated dimensions. To be precise:

- the transatlantic relationship came to be seen as the epitome of 'Western liberal democracy' and as the core of the 'free world' in the Cold War years, defining the 'West' as a bloc facing the rest of the world and led by the USA;

- the security relationship between the USA and Western Europe, institutionalized in NATO, was at the centre of the confrontation between the USA and the Soviet bloc, and underwrote the most remarkable integration of allied military strategies, force deployment and weapons development;

- the United States and its West European partners, especially those which were members of the European Community (EC), were at the centre of the industrial world, and thus dominant in trade, finance and technology on a global scale.

Such was the dominance of these concerns that at times in the period after the Second World War it appeared that the Atlantic Alliance held the key to the future of world politics as a whole — a perception which has persisted into the post-Cold War era. At the same time, it could be seen as holding the key to US foreign policy, and as a vital prop for American domestic tranquility and prosperity. But two processes of change have become central to the relationship, and to the ways in which it invites the attention of American political and economic elites.

- First, the growth of interdependence between the USA and the countries of Western Europe has made it increasingly difficult to define the boundaries to the relationship. On the one hand, there is no longer a clear guide as to what in the relationship is 'domestic' and what is 'international', and as a result there are difficulties of policy making and implementation. On the other hand, there is no clear separation between political, economic and security concerns, and this causes problems of priority, interest and co-operation. This is particularly the case given the changing nature of the USA, and the consequent debates about its role in the world; transatlantic relations thus have a great deal to offer in answer to the question: 'What kind of USA?'

- Second, the world has changed around the transatlantic partnership, in ways which underline but sometimes also throw into question its continued centrality and relevance as a guide to policy-making. For a long time, it appeared that such changes as took place could be contained within a remarkably long-lived and vigorous alliance, but from the mid-1980s onwards, there has been change of such scale and scope that it is appropriate to talk about a transformation both of Europe and of the broader world political economy. For the United States, these changes have great significance in terms of its world role and assumptions about world order.

The purpose of this chapter is to explore three central questions about US policies towards Western Europe.

- Why is the Atlantic partnership so central to US foreign policy interests, and how have American leaders formulated those interests in a changing context?
- How have US policy makers managed this vital relationship, and with what degree of success in adapting their policies to change?
- Does the evidence suggest that this has indeed been an imperial relationship, rather than one based on an alliance of interests or on the political and economic interdependence of its members?

This chapter will touch upon — although it cannot hope to explore in detail — several of the issues and questions raised in earlier chapters, and will illustrate how they have influenced a specific set of relations and policies.

2 THE FOUNDATIONS OF THE TRANSATLANTIC SYSTEM: 1946–1949

As Alfred Grosser (1980) has asserted, there is no 'year zero' in the relationship between the USA and Western Europe: the destinies of the two regions have been intertwined since the creation of the USA itself, and each has played a crucial role at turning points in the other's history. Even at the height of isolationist sentiment in the USA during the 1930s, the economic and political links between the two sides of the Atlantic were a vital focus of world politics. It was in the years after the Second World War, though, that it became possible to talk of an 'Atlantic system', with its characteristic institutions, forms of behaviour and patterns of relations. During the war itself, it could be argued, the foundations of the future system were laid in the shape of the Atlantic Charter of 1941, concluded by Roosevelt and Churchill in the course of US engagement in the global conflict. Although the charter was couched in global terms, it also had a particular resonance in setting out an agenda for the post-war world based around the Western democracies.

Global conflict had a pivotal role in the shaping of US attitudes towards the post-war world. As has been noted in earlier chapters, the focus on the United Nations, human rights and the open world economy were central both to US thinking and to the construction of the 'grand alliance', initially around the USA and the UK. But it is important to note that the building of the Atlantic or Euro-American system reflected much more direct and tangible forces. Chief among these was the growing awareness of a threat from the Communist world, led by the USSR — a threat which was initially masked by the wartime alliance and discounted by some Americans including Roosevelt himself. Chapter 2 has dealt with the evolution of the Soviet-American relationship, and that relationship was of crucial significance in defining the US approach to Western Europe during the late 1940s.

It could be argued on this basis that the Americans had no choice but to become or remain involved in Europe after 1945; the logic of the structure and the emergence of bipolar rivalry meant that only the details had to be settled. Events, however, were much less tidy or conclusive. In 1945 the Americans still assumed that they could withdraw their forces from Europe with considerable speed, and the forces of isolationism at home meant that there were considerable incentives to be seen to be disengaging. Although there were significant gains to be made from continuing economic involvement in the European market (not least because of the global economic dominance of the USA and the Europeans' desperate need for both American goods and supplies of dollars), these could be ensured through the exercise of arms' length influence within the context of an open world economy. The foundations for that economy had been laid in the Bretton Woods agreements of 1944 (see Chapter 3) and once European recovery had taken place, the USA would benefit from access to European markets. In the meantime, the need was for bridging finance in the shape of loans and for supplies of the goods and materials which would enable the Europeans to help themselves (Milward, 1984).

Between 1946 and 1949, these initial American assumptions were progressively challenged and eroded to the point at which a semi-permanent system of relations and institutions had been established between the Americans and Western Europe. The image of an undivided Europe fitting comfortably within an open world economy had been replaced by the reality of a divided Europe with the need for substantial and direct US support to its Western half through the Marshall Plan. The initial assumption of US abstention from the political and security concerns of Europe had been replaced by the reality of continuous and intense engagement, institutionalized within the North Atlantic Treaty of 1949 and further supported by the growth of intelligence and security networks involving governments in relations of almost wartime intimacy (Grosser, 1980; Ireland, 1981; Hogan 1987).

2.1 THE EMERGING TRANSATLANTIC SYSTEM

This 'revolution' can be interpreted in a number of ways. As has already been noted, the structure of the emerging Cold War system formed a compelling influence on the ways in which American leaders defined their approach to Europe. Not only this, but the threat of the Soviets was more than simply a military one; it could be defined as a challenge to the economic system, the political institutions and the values of European societies. European leaders themselves, led by the British, were keen to point out to Washington the dangers of any American withdrawal, and this was reinforced by the views of those in the State Department and elsewhere that the loss of Europe would fatally wound US interests. As Anton DePorte (1986) has noted, the redefinition of US interests and roles was not always knowing or calculated, but it had the effect of consolidating a two-bloc structure centred on Europe.

Structure thus pushed the Americans and the West Europeans together, and the convergence was reinforced by the distribution of power in the emerging Cold War system. Although West European armed forces were substantial in some cases, this concealed the extreme sacrifice into which their governments had been led by the war. The war effort had exhausted the economies of all involved, not merely the losers; and it must not be forgotten that apart from the British and the isolated Spaniards, all significant European states had been defeated at some stage in the conflict. Military power, economic potential and political institutions rested on a knife-edge in post-war Western Europe. In particular, the vacuum around Germany created the potential for incursion, subversion or chaos. The USA in this situation was in a unique position of power: militarily dominant, economically unscathed and with political institutions and values which were seen by many as the model for a new democratic order.

Its own raw power combined with the emerging division between East and West made the USA predominant in the developing Atlantic system. Did the arrival of a bipolar world make it inevitable that the Atlantic system would emerge with the Americans at its centre? In fact, there was considerable division of opinion in the USA about the wisdom of semi-permanent engagement anywhere, let alone Europe, and the efforts of European leaders such as Prime Minister Churchill and Foreign Secretary Bevin had to be bent towards encouraging the Truman administration to become committed. In this, they were helped by the USSR, and by the extension of Soviet domination to Eastern and Central Europe. The Communist seizure of power in Czechoslovakia in February 1948, and the imposition of the Berlin Blockade in the Summer of 1948, provided a catalyst not only for change in the views of American leaders but also for popular conviction that there was a cause to defend in the centre of Europe (Ireland, 1981; DePorte, 1986; Heller and Gillingham, 1992).

Importantly, the process of US entanglement in Europe was not simply a matter of traditional diplomacy and bilateral commitments. By the end of 1949, the building blocks of an institutional revolution had been laid; during the early 1950s, the American commitment was consolidated in a form which would have astonished the isolationists of the 1930s, and which assumed an all-but permanent form. At the centre of the process was the security relationship, expressed in the North Atlantic Treaty signed in April 1949. This set out the bones of a political and security guarantee which was in principle multilateral, but which was to all intents and purposes unilateral, with the Americans committed to aiding West European governments in the event of aggression from unspecified but obvious quarters. Although for some this guarantee provided the cover for continuing US withdrawal, it rapidly became clear that an American military presence in Western Europe was required: the evidence that the USSR had a nuclear capability, the example of the North Korean invasion of South Korea in June 1950, and the continuing military and economic weakness of the West Europeans provided the cementing forces. By 1951, the transatlantic security

Dean Acheson, US Secretary of State, signing the North Atlantic Treaty

architecture had become an elaborate and quasi-permanent framework for military planning and for US participation in the affairs of Western Europe. As will be seen later, this did not preclude conflicts and tensions, but it did settle much of the framework within which those would take place and the rules by which they were played out (Heller and Gillingham, 1992; Riste, 1985).

Alongside the institutionalization of the security relationship there went an indispensable economic dimension. Indeed, it has been argued that the key events and driving forces in US engagement in Europe after 1945 were economic more than political or military (Kolko and Kolko, 1972; Hogan, 1987; Block, 1977; Calleo and Rowland, 1973). To put it crudely, the Americans recognized at an early stage that they had a vital interest in the economic stability and prosperity of post-war Europe, and this underpinned their growing commitment in the political and military arenas. Both the federal government in Washington and US corporate business interests had a lot at stake in the economic revival and openness of Europe, and the chaos of the 1930s, when economic nationalism had gone alongside the development of Fascism and the onset of war, was vivid in peoples' minds. US economic support for European recovery started almost before the war ended, but it was initially based on rather traditional mechanisms such as loans, often on conditions which could not be met by enfeebled European economies. The winter of 1947–1948 was particularly harsh, raising the spectre not only of economic disaster but also of political unrest. The link between these conditions and the communist threat was relatively easy to make, and the emergence of a US policy for the post-war European economy was not long delayed.

On 5 June 1947, General George C. Marshall, the US Secretary of State, set out in a speech at Harvard University the essentials of what was to become the Marshall Plan. In the speech, he explicitly linked the economic fate of Europe with the political and security problems, and also with the vital interests of the USA. Aid would be given in novel forms, through grants and gifts rather than on commercial terms; eventually, nearly $20 billion was given between 1948 and 1952. Not only this, but the aid was given with the implicit assumption that it would be used to bolster market economies and to underpin democratic institutions. It could be argued that it was this condition which truly divided post-war Europe, given that the USSR and its satellite states could not accept the Marshall prescription. Another condition of the aid was that the Europeans should collaborate to distribute it and adopt collective mechanisms for its use. Through such collaboration and collective action, it was hoped by many Americans that progress could take place towards a 'united states of Europe', and it is clear that this played a major role in the encouragement of European integration. Initially, this was nurtured in the Organization for European Economic Co-operation (OEEC), an intergovernmental body, but there were early moves to introduce more sweeping and supranational elements (Hoffman and Maier, 1984; Grosser 1980; Hogan, 1987).

Through the creation of both a security and an economic framework for European-American relations, the events of the late 1940s effectively laid the foundations for continuing US involvement and intervention in the political structures of the continent. The Marshall Plan had implications for the role of governments in the economy and for organizations such as trade unions which were bound to affect 'domestic' politics in Western European countries. The North Atlantic Treaty by itself was a 'traditional' international treaty, but the growth of the North Atlantic Treaty Organization and the permanent stationing of US forces in many European countries meant a major intervention in European affairs. Not only this, but the anti-communist concerns of successive US administrations led them to intervene more or less directly in domestic electoral or party political processes, particularly in Italy and to some extent in France (both countries with strong indigenous communist parties) (Grosser, 1980; Serfaty, 1979).

Was the emerging pattern of US engagement a reflection of clear-cut decisions about the ways in which transatlantic relations should be conducted, and what kind of role did it imply for the USA? It would be tempting to conclude that US dominance was complete, and that any significant developments in Western Europe required US permission if not support. After all, it was only the USA that had the military and economic muscle to underpin the recovery and security of Europe, and it was only the USA that possessed political ideas and institutions of such a vigour and appeal as to form the basis for a new European order, or to justify active intervention against the communist threat. Such a conclusion, though, would miss some important points. As has been noted, the American assumption of a leadership role was not unhesitating or unqualified; there were many in the USA who argued that engagement in Western Europe should be reduced as the Europeans recovered and were able to bear more of the burden. At the same time, European leaderships were not simply putty in the Americans' hands: the recovery of economic vitality and political awareness was rapid, and the friction between this and American structural dominance was to prove an enduring theme in European-American relations (Calleo, 1987; Milward, 1984). By 1950, the framework for transatlantic relations was largely in place, but much development and consolidation was needed before it could be said to constitute a well-defined or uncontested system.

SUMMARY

Three points emerge from this initial survey.

- First, the nature and direction of US policies. Were Americans inclined or able to design a Western Europe that would fall in with their interests or preferences? As has been noted, at least part of the process was a response to events or situations in which there was a need for rapid commitment, and there was often little in the way of detailed planning or design. Nonetheless, US actions were bound to be influential, whatever their rationale, because of the dominance of the USA in the global security and economic systems.

- Second, the nature of the emerging 'Euro-American System'. How far was a systematic European-American relationship established by the early 1950s? Although a number of important principles were established through the Bretton Woods institutions, the Marshall Plan and the North Atlantic Treaty, it was far from clear how those principles would play out as Western Europe recovered its confidence and asserted its interests. It was also unclear to many of those involved in policy making how long the arrangements would last, given uncertainty about the future world order.

- Third, the nature of 'Europe'. How far were the Americans able to promote a 'united states of Europe'? Although Americans were at times inclined to talk in such terms, it was far from clear that there was actually or potentially such a thing. After all, the countries concerned had been in many cases long-established and in others strongly nationalistic in character. Although the USA was a vital part of the context, could US policy makers call the tune on detailed developments in the 'new Europe'?

These specific questions give rise to a more general set of issues. Did the Americans, either through their material strength or through the power of their institutions and ideas, have the capacity to get the Europe they wanted? Did they actually know what kind of Europe they wanted? As the transatlantic system developed in the 1950s and 1960s, the answers to these questions began to appear.

3 CONSOLIDATION AND CONFLICT: 1950–1960

For US policy makers, the dominating feature of the period which effectively began with the onset of the Korean War in 1950 was the consolidation of the commitments and institutions surrounding the transatlantic relationship, stimulated by Cold War security concerns and by the reconstruction of the capitalist world economy around the Bretton Woods system. At the same time, however, it became apparent that the fault lines in the European-American system, and the ambiguities of the American position, could not be forgotten. As a result, the 1950s saw not only consolidation of the system but also undertones of tension which threatened to emerge into open conflict across the Atlantic.

3.1 WESTERN SECURITY AND COLD WAR RIVALRY

Although the Korean War was distant and non-European, it presented a powerful analogy for what might happen if the Western allies relaxed their vigilance. In particular, for the USA it gave new force to the need to define the boundaries of the 'free world'. Whereas the Soviet threat in Europe had hitherto remained limited, it did not take a great leap of political imagination to envisage a situation in which the Red Army rolled across northern Germany, and in which the insidious influence of European communist parties would undermine the capacity of governments to resist. The forces of bipolar confrontation thus operated to keep security firmly at the head of the American agenda for transatlantic relations, and to increase the US commitment in NATO, which in the early and mid-1950s moved towards an 'integrated military coalition' (Hilsman, 1959).

At the same time, though, the forces working for increased transatlantic integration exposed a number of lines of cleavage, worrying to American leaders. In particular, these concerned the willingness and ability of the European allies to contribute to their own defence. Dwight Eisenhower, the first Supreme Allied Commander Europe (SACEUR) and later President of the USA, proclaimed that if NATO still existed in 1960, it would have failed, since in his view the alliance's purpose was to enable the Europeans to rebuild and defend themselves. The problem from an American point of view was that the Europeans seemed unwilling or unable to provide for themselves. The imperatives of domestic economic and social reconstruction, and the availability of overwhelming US power, combined to make the European allies 'civilian' in all but a few cases. To be sure, goals for force levels in NATO were agreed in 1952, but these remained largely unmet; it seemed that the preoccupations of the new Europe lay elsewhere as long as the Americans could be relied upon to provide the (increasingly nuclear) firepower (Mandelbaum, 1981; Riste, 1985; Gordon, 1956).

This is not to say that there were no efforts to create a more specifically European role in the Alliance. From an American perspective, a crucial element of all such moves was the rearmament of Germany. The most ambitious plans were those of the early 1950s for a European Defence Community (EDC), which were first proposed by the French in 1950. Under this scheme, the Europeans (particularly the members of the emerging European Community) would have created an integrated military force under multinational command, which would operate as the 'second pillar' of NATO. The plan was conceived for a number of reasons: to divert US pressure for the rearmament of West Germany, to contain West German military power within a multinational framework, to further the process of European integration more generally. But it can be seen that these reasons were not guaranteed to play well with American audiences, unless the EDC could be shown to make a material contribution to Western defence. In the early stages, US leaders and particularly Secretary of State John Foster Dulles were hard to convince of the plan's merits; by the time they were won over, the scheme was close to failure for a variety of domestic political reasons centring particularly on France. When the EDC failed to obtain the support of the French National Assembly in late 1954, it appeared that US hopes for a robust German and European presence in the alliance were doomed. Significantly, the British, who had been profoundly ambivalent about the EDC concept, stepped in to propose a means whereby the West Germans could be accommodated in the Western European Union, and thus become members of NATO by indirect means (Fursdon, 1980; Riste, 1985; Kaplan, 1988).

For Americans, the lessons of the early 1950s in Atlantic security relations were mixed, to say the least. The failure of the EDC threw profound doubts over the ability of Europeans to get their military act together; but the rearmament of West Germany within the WEU and NATO gave the USA almost all of what it had wanted, and without the disadvantages of dealing with a united European presence. As the 1950s progressed, this structural advantage of the USA was further cemented by the nuclearization of NATO. The alliance came increasingly to substitute nuclear strategy and hardware for conventional forces — a rational tendency given the difficulties of raising or justifying large conventional forces on both sides of the Atlantic (Mandelbaum, 1981; Kaplan, 1988; Freedman, 1981).

3.2 ECONOMIC IMPERATIVES

The world economy provided additional force to the consolidation of the Atlantic system. By the early 1950s, the USA dominated the capitalist world economy, both through its economic weight and through its influence in the multilateral framework set up under Bretton Woods. The Marshall Plan itself, which came formally to an end in 1952, expressed the division in the world economy between those who were part of the European-American sphere and those who were not. Within Western Europe, the plan had led to domestic restructuring and to an increasing American presence both through investment and through the adoption of mass production methods. Perhaps the most crucial development, though, was the creation of the European Coal and Steel Community (ECSC) in 1951, and the further establishment of the European Economic Community (EEC) in 1958. In a very tangible way, these developments completed the economic structure of the transatlantic system, and they were constructed within the overarching framework of US hegemony (Milward, 1984; Hogan, 1987).

US support for the ECSC and the EEC was not by any means unalloyed. In a broad sense, the Americans supported the initiation and growth of European integration for impeccably Cold War reasons: the stability and prosperity of the West European economies would be an invaluable support to the security system and in the struggle against communism everywhere. Thus, the State Department in the USA was the most enthusiastic convert to the integration process, whilst government agencies with a more purely economic brief, and above all some parts of private industry, were far from convinced of its merits. As Alan Milward (1984) has argued, this blend of motives in the US case was sufficient to ensure consistent political support for European integration, but also to make it likely that tensions and conflicts would arise in specific sectors. The very foundation of the ECSC gave rise to disputes about steel trade, and the far broader aims of the EEC made it inevitable that disputes would arise over a broad front (Smith, 1984; 1992a).

Despite the nuances and often open tensions accompanying US support for European integration, there is much to be said for the argument that in the 1950s it led to the 'completion' of the Western alliance. In the military sphere, NATO provided the structural focus for Cold War confrontation, whilst in the economic sphere the EEC could be seen as an economic alliance serving political ends, both internationally and politically. Although it clearly implied costs to the USA through loss of some markets, and it required exemptions for the EEC from some of the Bretton Woods trade rules, these penalties were seen by successive US administrations as well worth paying. Not only this, but some US commercial interests, particularly those of the multinational corporations, could see very positive effects from the creation of a larger European market to which they would have access. For these and other reasons, US support for British entry into the new Europe was strong and growing; it would add a final piece to the jigsaw and give more credibility to the political and economic balance across the Atlantic.

Much of what I have said so far implies that the impact of both NATO and the EEC in the 1950s was linked closely to US and European domestic politics (see also Peterson, 1996). For the Americans, the issue of domestic consensus was especially important. During the 1950s, the conservative internationalism which underpinned both NATO and the EEC was overwhelmingly dominant among US political elites and in governmental institutions. Whilst the Europeans could be and were castigated for their military failings and for their lack of economic openness, this dominant view held that stability and prosperity in Europe were in the vital interests of the USA, and that it was worth paying some costs to ensure that the newly established order was preserved or enhanced.

> ## SUMMARY
>
> During the 1950s, the transatlantic system effectively became and remained embedded in the institutions of the USA and in the broader international framework spawned by the Cold War. Amongst its key features were these:
>
> - US attention and resources became focused on the NATO alliance, there was no alternative if the Cold War was to be fought.
>
> - In addition US power and primacy in both the world security order and the world economy meant that the Western alliance could be paid for and the shortcomings of the allies could be accommodated, however reluctantly.
>
> - In return, certain rules of precedence and conduct came to be inseparable from the US role in the transatlantic system. For security purposes, the debates that mattered, about nuclear policy and about the operation of NATO, took place in Washington (and sometimes between Washington and London). Economically, the rule-book for the operation of the Bretton Woods system was safely lodged in Washington, and many of the institutions themselves were housed there; although the EEC was in some ways a deviation from the multilateral system, it was within the rules as interpreted by officials in Washington, and that was what counted. Politically and diplomatically, the Americans held the initiative: through their dealings with the Soviets they could shape the context for European-American relations, whilst they had the weight to ensure conformity even in cases of open deviation such as the Anglo-French intervention in the Suez Canal Zone (1956).
>
> In many ways, the 1950s saw the working out of the implications of decisions taken in the late 1940s, and although these did not add up to a blue-print for a transatlantic system, they gave formidable leverage to the Americans in pursuing their perceived interests.

4 PARTNERSHIP AND RIVALRY: 1960–1971

During the 1960s, a major change in atmosphere and conduct occurred in US policies towards Western Europe. As well as changes at the national level in both the USA and Europe, this reflected changes in the structure of the global security and economic orders, which affected the inclination and the capacity of both Europeans and Americans to nurture their mutual relationships.

4.1 FORCES FOR CHANGE

The growth of Soviet military capacity, particularly in the nuclear field, pushed Americans into a focus not only on the nuclear aspects of NATO but also on the threat to the USA itself. Whereas during the early and mid-1950s the central threat was that of a Soviet ground attack in Europe, the arrival of intercontinental ballistic missiles fundamentally changed the calculus of US nuclear strategy. At the level of doctrine, this was reflected in the switch from 'massive retaliation' to 'flexible response' based on the graduated use of first conventional and then nuclear forces — a notion whose formulation and implementation occupied much of the 1960s and 1970s. Another force challenging the primacy of NATO and the European-American security complex was the occurrence of conflicts outside the North Atlantic area, in the Middle East and South-east Asia (particularly Vietnam), which provided a powerful distraction for American Administrations and the potential for transatlantic tensions as perceptions of their significance diverged. By the end of the 1960s, the onset of *détente* between the USA and the USSR, expressing powerful forces for managing the Cold War contest, promised to reshape the links between the USA and its West European allies in ways which were not always comforting (Calleo and Rowland, 1973; Kaplan, 1988).

Alongside changes in the security order, US policies were strongly affected by global economic developments. The early 1960s saw two major trends: first, a loss of momentum in the US economy which, whilst still dominant, was subject to slow growth and loss of competitiveness; second, the continued recovery of West European economies, particularly those of the EEC, and most particularly of all the West Germans. Moreover, the emergence of the Third World and its need for economic and technical assistance constituted another major modifying force in the world economy. Whilst it was still clear that the Atlantic region formed the dominant core of the world arena, it could no longer function as a sealed system, if indeed it ever had done so. American policies were thus shaped strongly by the onset of global economic change (Calleo, 1982).

The forces of change in the security and economic contexts were reinforced by elements in the political environment, both at the transatlantic and at the national level. It has already been noted that the US concentration on Europe and the Atlantic Alliance was less exclusive during the 1960s than it had been in the 1950s, and this was brought sharply into focus by the Cuban Missile crisis of October 1962. For Americans, the significance of the crisis was a domestic as well as an international one, with the reinforcement of fears about the new vulnerability of the homeland. Later in the 1960s, there were further distractions for US policy, particularly those arising from the perception of communist threats both in Latin America and in South-east Asia. In simple terms, the security debate in the USA became less about Europe and more about the Third World, despite the crises in Czechoslovakia (1968) and elsewhere. At the same time, the increasing concern of Americans for their domestic prosperity, and the perception of competition from the EEC in particular, played an important role in changing the terms of debate and the focus of action. Ironically, just as many of the Bretton Woods institutions seemed to be functioning properly, the commitment of Americans to their maintenance was under challenge from perceived inequities and the need for national recovery (Calleo, 1982; Grosser, 1979).

4.2 THE GROWTH OF FRICTIONS

Political and economic change in Europe itself posed an additional challenge to US policy makers and public perceptions. Most dramatically, the rise of Gaullism in France brought to power a president who placed great emphasis on national independence and who saw the threat emanating as much from US dominance and 'protection' as from Soviet hostility. The tensions between General de Gaulle and successive American leaderships during the 1960s were at times sensational. Just as the US role in the world and in the Atlantic alliance was an issue at home, so it was in Western Europe, among the USA's closest allies. The intersection of the two forces set up tensions which could be contained, but which had debilitating effects for transatlantic security and economic co-ordination. Thus, the attempts in NATO to implement the ideas of 'flexible response' could be seen by the Gaullists — and not by them alone — as an attempt to reinforce US strategic dominance, and even to make Europe into a battleground on which the USA's confrontation with the USSR could be fought out. The trade negotiations between the USA and the EEC which became known as the 'Kennedy Round' (1963–1966) were bedevilled by the divergent priorities of both sides, and also by tensions in the international monetary system set up by the weakness of the dollar (Block, 1977; Calleo, 1982; Smith, 1984).

The result of these processes of change and divergence was a series of pressures on US leadership in the transatlantic system, leading to a growing uncertainty about the Americans' role and the proper conduct of relations. Whilst US leadership in NATO could survive the Gaullist challenge (despite the French decision in 1966 to withdraw from the NATO military structure), it was clear that implementation of US policies through the Alliance was subject to qualifications and that Europeans would not necessarily or automatically submit to US wishes. Even in the nuclear field, the development of the British and French nuclear forces set up new dynamics at the same time as the USA and the USSR were beginning to talk about arms limitations. Economically, the ambivalent relationship between the United States and the EEC, partnership alongside rivalry, meant that the Bretton Woods institutions and particularly the GATT became arenas for conflict rather than instruments of co-ordination. The growth of interdependence, ironically, meant both the increase of co-ordination and the growth of frictions; in fact, as Robert Keohane (1984) has pointed out, the two are inseparable and inevitable in an interdependent world, but this did not lessen the challenge and the need for mutual adjustment in European-American relations.

Despite — or perhaps because of — these tensions, it was during the 1960s that the Americans made their first explicit efforts to redesign Atlantic relations, and to carve out a formal division of responsibilities and effort between themselves and their allies. On 4 July 1962, President Kennedy made a speech in Freedom Hall, Philadelphia, which attempted to set a new agenda for transatlantic relations. Often known as the 'Declaration of Interdependence', the speech itself is short, but its consequences for Atlantic relations were extensive and echoed throughout the 1960s. At the rhetorical level, the speech declared the existence of an Atlantic Community, based on shared values, institutions and practices, and the need to establish this Community at the heart of the world order. More practically, the speech called for a new division of labour between the United States and a United Europe, within NATO, the Bretton Woods system and the wider world. But what kind of division of labour was this? In military strategy, it was based firmly on 'flexible response', with the Americans controlling nuclear forces and the allies contributing conventionally in larger measure than they had before. There was little evidence of provision for real involvement of the Europeans in nuclear planning or operational control. Economically, the speech could be read as an attempt to contain the EEC, by calling for new trade negotiations with the aim of establishing new rules about crucial areas of trade. Politically, the speech could be and was read as an attempt by the USA to re-establish its primacy in a world where the emergence of new institutions and issues placed it under threat (Calleo and Rowland, 1973; Kissinger, 1965; Pfaltzgraff, 1969). In the context of the 1960s, as it has been described above, it is possible to understand why the rhetoric of the speech was felt necessary, but also to understand why the translation of its sentiments into policy was fraught with difficulties. It appeared that American leaders had woken up to the need for prescription about the Europe they wanted just at the time when such a Europe was slipping out of their grasp; by the end of the 1960s, it was far from clear where the processes of change could or would lead.

SUMMARY

During the 1960s, a number of major trends converged to create uncertainty about US policies towards Western Europe. Among these were:

- Changes in superpower relations and US security policy which cast into doubt the centrality of Western Europe and the functions of NATO as a 'nuclear alliance', allied to the increasing salience of conflicts outside Europe.

- The emergence of Western Europe as an economic rival for the USA, rather than a junior partner in the running of the capitalist world economy, and the economic stagnation of the USA itself.

- The debate within the USA about the kind of transatlantic system policy makers wished to nurture.

The attempt to redesign US–European relations represented by President Kennedy's 'Declaration of Interdependence' of July 1962 in many ways acted not as the basis for a new 'Atlantic Charter', but rather as a catalyst for tensions and a focus for uncertainty.

5 EUROPEAN–AMERICAN RELATIONS IN A CHANGING WORLD: 1971–1981

The forces for change described in the preceding section meant that by the end of the 1960s, every dimension of the European-American system was up for debate and potential reform. But it must also be noted that there had been throughout the history of transatlantic relations a tension between the impact of change and the need for explicit reformulation of the institutions and policies around which the Western Alliance had centred. In particular, from the point of view of this chapter, United States perceptions of and policies towards Western Europe had been subject to a series of pressures and adjustments. Often, these had taken effect indirectly or implicitly, as the result of other adjustments in the domestic context or the broader international arena. During the early 1970s, these types of pressures and adjustments were to play a key role in the development of transatlantic relations, with a key period being that of 1973 — a year of crises and upheaval, but also the focus of renewed US attempts to redesign the relationship.

5.1 A DECADE OF CRISES

Perhaps the most dramatic forces for change in US policies emerged from the domestic context. The turbulence of the Nixon era, culminating in the Watergate episode and the resignation of the president, can be seen as an inherently domestic affair, but it had important resonances in European-American relations. In particular, it distracted American leaders from alliance affairs and threw into question the credentials of successive US leaderships, not only that of Nixon himself. Alongside this force went that of the Vietnam War — an international episode which had searing effects on domestic institutions and policies and which raised further questions about the appropriateness and credibility of US leadership. The legacy of Vietnam remained a factor in American policies well into the 1990s; during the 1970s, it created uncertainties about the commitment and will of all US leaderships, which were bound to make alliance management more taxing (Calleo, 1982; Destler, Gelb and Lake, 1984).

Both Watergate and the Vietnam War were more than simply political events. By placing strains on the political economy of the USA, and by shaping US international economic behaviour, they fed directly into the world economy and the tangled web of transatlantic economic relations. The Nixon leadership in its later years placed increasing emphasis on unilateral economic measures to preserve or enhance the USA's position in the world economy. As already noted, this was fragile during the 1960s, and the pressures came to a head in the early 1970s. The combination of domestic budget constraints — partly emanating from the Vietnam involvement — and a growing balance of payments deficit led in 1971 to the so-called 'Nixon Shock', in which the American administration effectively devalued the dollar and declared unilateral trade measures aimed largely against the EEC. Given the pivotal position of the dollar at the centre of the international monetary system, and the multilateral trade rules encapsulated in the GATT, the significance of these US measures cannot be overestimated: the country which had effectively written the rules and underwritten the system had defected. Whilst it is tempting to focus on Watergate, Vietnam or US-Soviet relations as formative influences for the 1970s, it could be argued that this economic transformation was if anything more fundamental. Certainly, the growing EEC and the Japanese spent the rest of the decade attempting to come to terms with the collapse of the Bretton Woods system. To this was added in 1973 the effects of the Middle East crisis and the fourfold rise in oil prices, which had profound effects both on the USA and on the EEC, but which were arguably more taxing for the Europeans given their dependence on imported oil and other natural resources (Chace and Ravenal, 1976; Kaiser and Schwartze, 1977; Serfaty, 1979).

Another major influence on US policies towards Western Europe during the 1970s was that of US–Soviet relations. As has been seen, this relationship was crucial both to the foundation of the Atlantic system and to its evolution; a central feature has been the linkage between fluctuations in the US-Soviet arena and US policies towards Western Europe. When Americans and Soviets were at daggers drawn, Europeans worried, but no less did they worry when Americans and Soviets entered into dialogue and *détente*. In the early 1970s, this happened on a grand scale, with the Nixon-Kissinger initiatives and the conclusion of agreements both in the arms control and in the political domains (see Chapter 2). For Europeans, the process smacked of US decoupling from the alliance, and of a process of consultation more honoured in the breach than in the observance. In the early 1970s, US policies raised dangers of a US-Soviet condominium, in which the big two made decisions fundamental to the future of Europe without European involvement. It also led during the 1970s to debate about the appropriate institutional focus for US policies.

5.2 INSTITUTIONAL ADAPTATION

Institutionally, the Atlantic and European security orders had been tied together essentially through NATO. The onset of *détente* during the early 1970s raised fundamental questions about the adequacy of the Alliance for what Americans called the 'era of negotiations'. In the late 1960s, the so-called Harmel Report had raised the issue of NATO as an instrument of *détente* rather than defence, and the tension between political and military priorities this reflected has been central to the Atlantic relationship ever since. From a US point of view, it was far from clear that NATO provided a good vehicle for their relationship with the USSR, in arms control and other domains, although it could clearly be used as a sounding board and a channel for consultation. Nor was it clear, in the era of global balance, that US interests *vis-à-vis* China or Japan, for example, were a proper concern of the North Atlantic alliance. Nixon and Kissinger were wont to refer to a 'pentapolar world' in which Europe was only one pole, and in which it had no necessary priority for Washington over the others (Hoffman, 1978; Kaiser and Schwartze, 1977; Serfaty, 1979).

As a result of these and other changes in institutional priorities, there arose in the early 1970s a tension between the global interests of the American leadership and the more regional interests of those concerned with the changing shape of Europe. As noted above, one symptom of this tension was the feeling in Europe that the Americans and the Soviets could shape their continent without more than a passing reference to their interests. At the same time, however, the early 1970s saw the first stirrings of institutional change focused on the redefinition of Europe and of the superpowers' roles in it. The process by which the Conference on Security and Co-operation in Europe came to meet in Helsinki during 1975, and the ways in which its deliberations reflected the changing shape of Europe, cannot be detailed here, but it is important to note that this was a process no longer under the control or patronage of the superpowers alone. By relating the political, the military and the economic aspects of security, it also began to build networks of negotiation and interaction which could not be contained solely within an East-West divide. At times, US policymakers seemed willing to let the Europeans (often centred around the EEC) get on with it; at others, they were decidedly uneasy about the growth of concern with humanitarian and other 'new' issues (Hoffman, 1978; Allen, Rummel and Wessels, 1982).

The later 1970s brought a number of these tensions to a head, both because of the changing nature of US policies and because of the changing structure of world politics. Whilst the Carter Administration placed great emphasis on human rights and related issues, it was not clear that this represented an attempt to transcend the Cold War, rather than fighting it in a new way. The Europeans, both in the CSCE and through their national or EC policies, had a stake in *détente* and new versions of security which was not the same as that felt in Washington, and as US-Soviet tensions grew in the late 1970s, the divergence was felt in a number of institutional contexts. The strength of the 'umbilical cord' linking US military and political weight to Western Europe was no longer unquestioned, and the breakdown of US-Soviet relations at the end of the decade exposed its fragility.

No less were there institutional strains in the economic sphere. Indeed, one of the features of the 1970s was growing awareness of the ways in which security policy entailed a linkage between military, political and economic elements. One of the problems facing US policy makers was that West Europeans had profited precisely from the disconnection of these elements; the EEC remained stubbornly a 'civilian power', and national governments in Western Europe, with some variations, saw little reason to jeopardize prosperity for ideological causes. As a result, the problem as seen from Washington became that of getting the Europeans to face up to their obligations and to balance their economy with broader security interests. It was far from easy to convince recalcitrant European leaderships that they should play a far greater role in sharing the security burden whilst allowing the Americans to defend their vital interests in dialogue with the Soviets.

Alongside this tension in the institutional framework of security went a number of more exclusively economic concerns. The 'Nixon shock' and the

1973 oil crisis placed great strain on the institutional framework of the transatlantic economy, not least because they seemed in the first case unilaterally to reject the established rules and in the second to exacerbate the differences in vulnerability between the USA and Europe. The proclamation by the Nixon Administration that the USA was now an 'ordinary country' flew in the face of the facts; to Europeans, it appeared that the Americans were intent on preserving their privileges, not least that of acting without regard for the international consequences of their domestic policies. From an American perspective, of course, the picture was different. The EEC was seen as an increasingly potent rival, but a rival which itself claimed privileges, such as abstention from the expensive areas of security policy or from the application of international trade rules to such areas as agriculture. Given the fragility of the US economy during the 1970s, it is not surprising that Washington spent a great deal of time attempting to contain or to reorient the troublesome economic policies of both the EEC and Japan, which were increasingly seen as a greater threat even than the Community. The problem was that Washington itself had undermined some of the central pillars of the world economic order, through its actions on monetary and energy policy, and that the instability of the dollar combined with very high levels of US imports in key commodity areas was perhaps the central structural issue for the world economy (Calleo, 1982; 1987).

In these circumstances, the institutional framework for transatlantic economic relations was at constant risk of being made hostage to unilateral interests and policy reversals. The politics of blame were characteristic of much transatlantic economic dialogue, and the dangers of economic nationalism were severe. Yet there was a certain degree of institutional rebuilding, in which the Americans were not always the dominant partner. Increasingly, the operation of the Western Economic Summits after 1975, and the development of mechanisms for handling floating exchange rates, were reflective of a triangular relationship. The Americans could no longer expect to dominate the EEC, and both had to cope with the rise of Japan and later the new industrial economies of Asia. The Carter Administration placed considerable emphasis on multilateral co-ordination of economic policies, although there were suspicions in some instances that co-ordination masked US attempts to shift the costs of interdependence onto their rivals (Keohane, 1979). During the late 1970s, therefore, the industrial nations through the GATT, the Western Summits and through central bank co-ordination made some progress towards reshaping the institutional framework. But such rebuilding was far from complete and far from reflecting any US blueprint.

It might be expected in this context that Americans would be cautious about proclaiming grand designs for the future of US-European relations. Nevertheless, in March 1973, Henry Kissinger ventured another such design, by proclaiming the 'Year of Europe' and calling for the conclusion of a 'new Atlantic Charter' to express the new reality of relations between the old and the new worlds. Reading his speech alongside that of Kennedy in 1962, it is intriguing to reflect on what had changed and what remained largely the same. Like Kennedy, Kissinger called for a greater effort on the part of the Europeans in burden-sharing within NATO; like Kennedy also, he excluded from this the privileged domain of nuclear weapons. He also excluded a new privileged domain: that of negotiations with the Soviets and the conduct of *détente*. Whilst the Europeans had legitimate interests in this field, their interests were essentially regional, whilst those of the USA were global. This may have reflected reality as seen from Washington, but it was guaranteed to arouse the strongest emotions in Europe. Feelings were further aroused by Kissinger's economic message, which was aimed both at the EEC and at Japan (an important new dimension). The call for fair trade and a kind of economic burden-sharing came ill from a source considered by many Europeans and Japanese to be inherently tainted after the 'Nixon Shock'. It was also, in true Kissinger fashion, linked to the broader security question, and appeared to many observers to constitute a threat of disengagement if economic demands were not met (Kaiser, 1974; Serfaty, 1979).

Kissinger's 'Year of Europe' initiative thus posed substantial questions about the USA's role in transatlantic relations. It seemed to constitute another attempt by the Americans to redefine Europe into an image of their choosing, and to remind Europeans of their dependence on the USA. Not only

Henry Kissinger

this, but it appeared to be primarily for domestic consumption in the context of an increasingly embattled presidency and growing demands for unilateral US military and economic initiatives. The EEC reacted, as many Americans might have predicted, by rejecting the American message but failing to come up with a substantial policy of their own. At a time when the EEC was absorbing three new members and still adjusting to the 'Nixon Shock', this might have been anticipated; and the situation was made worse by the impact of the Arab-Israeli October War and the oil crisis at the end of 1973. The war demonstrated a divide between American demands for assistance in their supply of Israel and European reluctance to comply, whilst the oil crisis exacerbated the economic divergence which meant that for Europeans oil was worth almost any economic or political sacrifice. By December 1973, Kissinger was accusing Europeans of acting as if NATO did not exist, and US-sponsored attempts to co-ordinate Western policies on oil supplies in the face of an embargo by OPEC were largely in disarray. Although these tensions were muted for much of the rest of the decade, the Carter administration's response to the Soviet incursion into Afghanistan during 1980 was to reveal that they had not disappeared.

SUMMARY

In many ways, the failure of the 'Year of Europe' can serve as a metaphor for the 1970s as a whole in US-European relations:

- It was an initiative conceived for ill-defined reasons against a background of domestic uncertainties in the USA itself. Launched unilaterally, it was derailed not only by the deficiencies of the transatlantic partners but also by the turbulence of the global arena. Such factors bedevilled transatlantic relations throughout the 1970s.

- Its fate appeared to demonstrate the fragility of the existing military, political and economic orders, and also to underline the increasingly ambivalent role played by the Americans in the system. Not only this, but the growing linkages between economics, security and political leadership were central to Kissinger's strategy; they were also central to its failure, and to the problems which beset US policy throughout the 1970s.

- The speech signalled a key phase in the redefinition of transatlantic relations, but not quite in the ways envisaged by Kissinger.

On each side of the Atlantic, by the end of the 1970s the other appeared to be a major problem rather than a support or a partner in the construction of world and regional order. Could the structure survive in the face of challenges both from within and from outside, from changing American and European positions as well as from the global arena?

6 THE REAGAN CHALLENGE

The challenge of change in US policies and the world arena was posed in a stark form by the first Reagan Administration. Almost from its inception in January 1981, it threatened a direct confrontation with the West Europeans on a number of fronts. In doing so, it reflected not only the particular characteristics of the president and his policies but also the effects of structural changes which had begun in the 1970s and which were to become more pronounced during the later 1980s. One of the most important from the point of view of this chapter was to be found within the USA itself. The loss of any established consensus within the US political system, institutional fragmentation, economic stagnation, foreign policy uncertainty and apparent loss of direction; all of these lay behind the ascendancy of the New Right and the calls for a reassertion of US values and muscle. The question, central to US-European relations, 'What kind of USA?', had become increasingly difficult to answer in the 1970s. Reaganism promised to banish the confusion, but not in a way which would reassure the West Europeans. The new emphasis on US strength, on confrontation with the USSR, on economic unilateralism and on diplomatic abrasiveness with both adversaries and allies was bound to create divisions within the Atlantic alliance and within Western Europe itself (Joffe, 1987; Treverton, 1985).

The domestic politics of Reaganism were complemented by international changes which further injected uncertainty into transatlantic relations. The New Cold War (see Chapter 2) can be seen in some ways as a creation of US domestic tensions embodied in the rise of the New Right, but it also rested upon the diffusion of conflict in the global arena, and on the increasing tendency of the superpowers to be drawn into local conflicts. When coupled with continued economic turbulence and global pressures for protectionism, the context for transatlantic reconstruction was as challenging in the early 1980s as it had ever been.

As a result, US assertiveness and US power set the tone of transatlantic relations in the early 1980s. The Reaganite agenda was for a national revival and for an accumulation of muscle whether that was through a strong military or a strong economy (and an intimate link between the two was often seen). Most dramatically, the US-Soviet confrontation over arms control threatened a deterioration of the security order and thus increased tension in Europe as well as in the Third World. Once again, US policies seemed to assume that vital interests could be defined for Europeans in Washington, and protected through US-Soviet dialogue or confrontation. This was coupled with the American demand that Europeans fulfil their commitments to the stationing of intermediate-range nuclear missiles (cruise and Pershing-II) in NATO countries. In a partial parallel with the European Defence Community dispute of the 1950s, this issue became deeply intertwined with the domestic politics of NATO countries, particularly Britain, West Germany and the Netherlands (Eichenberg, 1989).

Accompanying the focus on US power in the NATO and arms control context was a broader concern with the pursuit of the New Cold War and confrontation with the 'evil empire'. The Reaganite view that 'who is not with us is against us', and the Washington tendency to look for any instrument which could be used against the forces of darkness, was not easy for many Europeans to accept. In particular, the Reagan Administration's demands that Europeans fall in with economic sanctions against Eastern bloc governments and that they should not trade with the enemy in sensitive areas caused a good deal of acrimony. Thus, in 1981 and 1982, the US imposition of sanctions against the USSR and Poland in the wake of martial law meant that pressure came on West European governments to control not only European companies but also the activities of US subsidiaries operating from their territory. This use of extra-territorial power by the USA was resented and often defied, challenging as it did the ability of European governments to control their own economies or legal systems (Allen and Smith, 1990; Woolcock, 1982).

The practice of 'Reaganomics' in the USA caused further disruption to transatlantic relations. By espousing supply-side economics and reducing taxes at the same time as spending on welfare entitlements and defence were increasing, the US economy was thrown into a vicious circle of high interest rates and later government deficits which profoundly affected European economies. It has been noted already that the late 1970s saw a partial rebuilding of the transatlantic economic order; Reaganism threatened to overturn it again, through a unilateral focus on the problems of the US economy and the needs of national revival. In vain might Reaganites argue that in the long run this 'domesticism' would regenerate the world economy as a whole. Helmut Schmidt, the West German Chancellor, accused the President in 1982 of visiting on Europeans the highest interest rates since the birth of Christ. Whether or not this was historically accurate, the transatlantic economic tensions of the early 1980s seemed likely to hold back growth, to destabilize the remaining institutions of economic co-ordination and to add fuel to the flames of a possible European-American 'war' (Nau, 1984; Bergsten, 1981; Tsoukalis, 1986; Calleo, 1982).

Yet the 'war' was contained. By the end of 1984, when Ronald Reagan was re-elected as president, the European commitment to deploy cruise and Pershing-II had largely been implemented, representing in some views a triumph for NATO and allied co-ordination. There were still disputes about strategic trade issues and economic sanctions, but the line had largely been held or fudged. Reaganomics was still a cause for concern, but the beginnings of the late-1980s boom were beginning to make themselves felt despite continuing instability of currencies. The mechanisms of co-ordination had not collapsed, although in many areas they had come under enormous pressure. The question is: To what extent did this reflect any US plan, or the purposeful use of residual US power? There is no doubt that power had made itself felt, but that was often as much by accident or indirection as by conscious design. Inasmuch as there was a design, it was not one for Atlantic relations; rather, it was a design for a new America which had consequences for the West Europeans in a number of areas. There is considerable evidence that the shifting centre of political gravity in the USA during the early 1980s — away from the East Coast, towards the South and the West — and the preoccupation of many Americans with the Pacific Rim, whether as challenge or as opportunity, meant a decline in the attention paid to all matters European. In March 1984, Assistant Secretary of State Lawrence Eagleburger made a well-reported speech in which he effectively warned West Europeans that they could not count on the continued attention and support of the USA. The evidence surveyed above might suggest that such a distancing from Western Europe was inherent in the structure and role of the USA during the early 1980s. What it did not foreshadow was the transformation of the late 1980s and the 1990s.

> *SUMMARY*
>
> During the first Reagan administration, US policies towards Western Europe were shaped by a number of dominant forces:
>
> - The new emphasis on the regeneration of America, and so on a unilateral style of leadership, placed major strains on the transatlantic relationship. There was a new tendency in Europe to define interests in distinction to those of the USA, and in the USA to marginalize the needs of allies. Such views were not unprecedented, but they were sharpened by Reaganism.
>
> - The practice of 'Reaganomics' placed a severe burden on the mechanisms of economic policy co-ordination developed during the 1970s, and they threatened to lead to all out confrontation. Such conflict was contained, though there were some very sharp skirmishes and attacks on existing institutional structures.
>
> - Developments in US-Soviet relations were of major importance for the transatlantic relationship. It appeared that the rivalry of the New Cold War marginalized European interests, whilst placing strong US demands for conformity to Reaganite policies on all European governments.

7 FROM CHANGE TO TRANSFORMATION

When Ronald Reagan was re-elected president in November 1984, there was some speculation about the ways in which 'Reagan II' would differ from his predecessor; amongst the most frequent observations was the feeling that in his second term the president would seek to be more of a world statesman, seeking agreement where there had previously been only confrontation and aiming to leave a legacy of diplomatic achievement. In addition, it was argued that the president would come up against the constraints of his own legacy: the burgeoning deficits both in the federal finances and in the balance of payments, and the weight of an inflated military establishment looking for a mission. Certainly, one of the key structural factors in the evolution of the European-American relationship during the second Reagan Administration was the changing nature of the US leadership at home, which had important spillover effects in the international domain. But this factor was implanted in a global arena which by the end of his second term in 1988 increasingly seemed to be on the edge of transformation and upheaval. Both factors acted in important ways to condition the US-European relationship (Allen and Smith, 1989; Oye et al., 1987).

7.1 'REAGAN II' AND THE EUROPEANS

There is a good deal of evidence that by the second term, Ronald Reagan and his administration had learned the limitations of their leverage on world politics, and had also become aware of the increasing linkages between what was done at home and what happened to US interests abroad. Although Reaganism in its early form had rejected the 'politics of limits' exemplified by the Carter years, it was apparent that US policy was increasingly circumscribed and occasionally outflanked as it attempted to reassert US power. At home, the key expression of this set of limits was the 'double deficit', which increasingly drew boundaries around what the president could achieve through budgetary means, and gave Congress a new voice in the making of policy. But there was also increasing concern about the vulnerability of the USA to economic competition and penetration from both Europe and (more sharply) Japan. Whereas the president's 'military Keynesianism' had delivered a powerful boost to the economy through defence spending in the early 1980s, by the middle of the decade it was clear that the downside included a distorted pattern of economic growth and a loss of competitiveness in vital industrial sectors. Domestic debate about the security implications of technological dependence on the Japanese in particular led to a series of attempts both under Reagan and his successor to redress the balance. But the financial limitations prevented major rebalancing and new initiatives. It was apparent early in the new administration that some awkward questions about finances would need to be confronted, and Europeans could observe that when this had happened in previous episodes the fallout had affected them very directly (Tsoukalis, 1986; Smith, 1988a).

As it happened, the denouement in October 1987, with the stock market crash and the effects of Black Monday, was more dramatic than anyone had expected. Although there was an apparent recovery in the following months, both Europeans and Americans were made acutely aware of the imbalances in the world economy at the centre of which were the American deficits. It was also clear that the structural interpenetration of the US and European economies had made it increasingly difficult to disentangle one from the other; economic shocks could no longer be contained within national or continental boundaries, and the US economy as much as any other was dependent on international conditions. Since the Americans were in the process of becoming the world's largest ever debtors in absolute terms, this was perhaps not surprising, but after 1987 it could no longer be shrugged aside. One of the results of Black Monday had been an increase in the attempts to manage exchange rates, initiated by the US Secretary of the Treasury James Baker; as a result of his and others' efforts, first the Plaza Agreement of 1985 and then the Louvre Accord of 1987 had seen the industrial countries setting targets for exchange rates and attempting to contain fluctuations in them. But the size of the structural imbalances, and the speed with which financial speculation could be transmitted through the system, made any such efforts difficult to maintain (Thurow, 1992; Bergsten, 1990).

At the same time as currencies and government finances were in turmoil, there were new attempts to manage US-European trade relations. Since the inception of the EEC, there had been a series of trade disputes between the Europeans and the Americans, in which US administrations had generally seen themselves as the injured parties. In particular, agricultural trade had been the source of almost continuous conflict, with the EC's Common Agricultural Policy attracting the venom of both US farmers and the federal government. The entry of Spain and Portugal into the Community in 1986 led to US sanctions against the Community, with the aim of compensating for an estimated $400 million of lost trade. There were other disputes over citrus and pasta products, steel and the European Airbus, each of them fuelled by the activities in the USA of lobbyists and the Congress. But at the same time as these disputes were taking place, there had begun a new effort to negotiate reforms in the GATT, through the so-called Uruguay Round. From 1986, there was thus a formal effort to deal with a very wide range of trade issues, including some of the most contentious such as agriculture. Such negotiations were necessary to deal with the changing structure of world trade itself, for example the growth of trade in services and problems of intellectual property rights, but they were bound to bring the USA and the EC into confrontation (Woolcock, 1991).

US concerns with the EC in relation to trade were conditioned by another structural force: the increasing creation of regional blocs in trade and other areas of economic activity, of which the Community's Single Market Programme (SMP) was the most ambitious example. The creation of a truly integrated market in Western Europe had been an aim of the EEC from the outset, and one which was welcomed by some US producers and investors. Others, though, saw it as a threat, and the spectre of 'fortress Europe' loomed. This issue intersected neatly with another already mentioned: American perceptions of their own economic and technological vulnerability faced with the dynamic economies of Europe and the Pacific Rim. As a result, there was a series of US attempts to exert leverage over the SMP through governmental means, some at least of them not appreciated by US corporations going about their business in Europe (Hufbauer, 1990; Smith, 1992b; Hocking and Smith, 1997).

Economic restructuring and perceptions of vulnerability in the USA thus had major implications for US-European relations. There were also major challenges to be faced in the security arena, many of them arising from the policies espoused by the first Reagan Administration. For West European governments, the course of US foreign policy in the late 1970s had been a cause of unease, demanding new clarifications and commitments on both sides. Thus, ironically, the commitment to deploy cruise and Pershing missiles to meet the threat of new Soviet 'Eurostrategic' forces was the result of pressures initially from the Europeans and particularly from the West German government led by Helmut Schmidt. From December 1979, the programme to enhance the intermediate range nuclear forces available to NATO was under way, accompanied by the commitment to negotiate with the Soviets even before the missiles were deployed in 1983. To this situation, the Reagan Administration brought its own mixture of hard-nosed confrontation both with the Soviets and with its own allies. As George Bush, then Vice-President, put it in September 1983, 'the United States is the leader of the free world, and under this President we are beginning to act like it' (Allen and Smith, 1989; Treverton, 1985).

What were Europeans thus to make of the changes that came over US policies in the second Reagan Administration? From the situation in which the Americans refused point-blank to negotiate in areas crucial to its allies, and in which the USSR continued its nuclear build up, a transformation occurred during 1985 and 1986. Suddenly, it appeared as if everything was negotiable; most notably, the Reagan-Gorbachev meeting in September 1986 in the Icelandic capital, Reykjavik, promised (or threatened) a Soviet-American agreement to eliminate all intermediate range nuclear forces in Europe, and to aim at the elimination of all nuclear forces by the end of the century. Alarm among European leaders was widespread, not only because of the implied 'decoupling' between the USA and Western Europe, but also because it appeared that the president was increasingly prone to being outflanked by the newly-sophisticated Soviet diplomacy.

For European-American security relations, the second Reagan Presidency awakened visions — and sometimes nightmares — that had been present but suppressed in the transatlantic relationship almost since its beginning. As in previous episodes, it appeared that US-Soviet agreement, and the strategic unpredictability of Washington, could undermine the stability of Europe. Arms control or reduction was not the only area of concern. In 1983, the president had announced the Strategic Defence Initiative (or 'Star Wars'), which seemed to imply that the USA might build an 'astrodome' of high-technology defences over its territory. If the USA could defend itself against the Soviets in this way, what need was there for NATO or her allies? Not only this, but the president had asserted that when the US defences were perfected the technologies would be offered to the USSR. The vision of two heavily defended superpowers surrounding Europe and agreeing on its future status appealed to some diplomats in Washington, but was decidedly less attractive in European capitals, in both the East and the West (Kanter, 1985).

During the mid-1980s, therefore, both the economic and the security dimensions of American-European relations were in flux, reflecting political changes in the USA and also in the USSR. The linkage between superpower diplomacy, US policy and European interests was once again central, but in a new form. When this was allied to doubts about the integrity and predictability of US leadership under 'Reagan II', it was to be expected that

American policies would encounter resistance and often open defiance. In this context, the 'Irangate' affair of 1986–1987 played a crucial role, rather as Watergate had done in the early 1970s. If the president was embattled at home, from the White House perspective there was much to be said for dramatic foreign initiatives, but these were precisely the kind of policy changes which cast doubt into the minds of allies. During the later years of the Reagan era, it was not clear where US policies were being made, what were their motivations and what might be the outcomes from the European perspective.

The shifting foundations of policy in the USA, and of US-Soviet relations in particular, thus contributed significantly to a decline of confidence in transatlantic processes during the second Reagan Administration.

7.2 FROM BUSH TO CLINTON

Within this uneasy context of structural change, uncertainty about US power and debate about the proper role of transatlantic institutions, the Bush Administration came to power at a crucial juncture. Perhaps not surprisingly, the new administration spent its first months in office attempting to review and revise its foreign policy priorities, to the extent that many West European leaders wondered where and when the policies might emerge. It is clear, though, that the administration did recognize the need for some fundamental debate given the coincidence of radical changes at both the global and the transatlantic level. What they could not fully foresee was the extent to which the radical transformation of global politics would be centred on Europe itself, leaving the USA in some respects an influential and concerned observer (Smith and Woolcock, 1993).

It is not the purpose of this chapter to give an exhaustive account of the ways in which radical change took place in Europe from the late 1980s on. Rather, the focus is on the extent to which the changes could be and were influenced by the USA, either through the exertion of power or through the use of institutional mechanisms, and on the ways in which US leaders attempted to preserve leverage over the process. It is necessary briefly to outline the nature and extent of the transformation, so that relatively informed judgements can be made. Three central dimensions can be discerned, each of them pregnant with implications for US policies (Smith and Woolcock, 1993).

The first area of transformation was the emergence of a new global and European security context, which had at its core the unification of Germany and the collapse of the Soviet Union. Between 1989 and 1992, the seemingly permanent division of Europe, which was one of the foundations of the transatlantic relationship, disappeared. It was replaced not by a stable European order based on recognized and legitimate states, but by a mosaic of often fragile politics and security arrangements, and by an eruption of seemingly new (but often very old) conflicts within the shell of existing states.

Alongside this, there were global echoes arising from the end of the Cold War system and the power vacuums created in a number of potentially volatile regions such as the Middle East. From an American point of view, this set of changes could be and was often presented as a triumph: the disappearance of one superpower left only one pretender to global responsibility, and this was illustrated most dramatically in the Gulf War. But in the European context, it was not clear where US power fitted any more. To be sure, the collapse of the USSR created a new arena for the exercise of US ideas not only about security, but also about markets and democratic institutions. But the relative cosiness and predictability of the Cold War had gone. Not only this, but the continuing uncertainty in the USA itself about its power, status and role provided an uncertain foundation for a new security order. The new security issues demanded close engagement, economic assistance and military adaptability — three elements which the USA after the Reagan years was not always ready or able to provide. There was thus in some respects a strong desire in Washington for the West Europeans to take up the burden. In Yugoslavia, in the former Soviet Union and elsewhere, the White House and the State Department were partially persuaded that the hour of Europe had arrived, but the European Community proved in many respects unready to take up the burden (Smith, 1992a).

Alongside the transformation in the European security context went the contribution of major structural changes in the world economy. In many ways

President George Bush signs the Charter of Paris at the end of the Conference on Security and Co-operation in Europe in 1990

the late 1980s and early 1990s saw a rebalancing of the world economy, in which the changed positions of the USA and the EC were key features. The perception both in Washington and in the European capitals that the respective weights of the USA and the EC had changed was bound to have important policy effects. These were magnified by the growing self-confidence of Community policy makers and by the self-doubt of US governmental and industrial elites; a rash of books and articles could be found in Washington assessing the state of play in the 'new world power game', which was centred on the USA, the EC and Japan. Although the early fears of a 'fortress Europe' were progressively diluted, continuing difficulties with the Community in the GATT Uruguay Round which came to a peak in 1991 and 1992 were seen as evidence of a new structural conflict (Thurow, 1992; Bergner, 1991; Silva and Sjogren, 1990).

A third element of radical structural change affecting American-European relations was the growing interpenetration between national political and economic systems, and the consequent difficulty for US policy makers in determining national policy priorities. There were two particular ways in which this problem made itself felt. First, there was an increasing tendency to see linkages between economic policy and national security, and to base political argument on this interconnection. In Washington, there was a rash of concern about competitiveness and about technological elements of national security, and whilst much of this was targeted at Japan, the Community came in for its share of blame. By the nature of the issue, though, it was very difficult to see how US policy makers alone could change the structure: global methods of production, and the existence of increasingly global business elites, provided a potent modifying force. If measures were taken against the EC in a specific area, among those harmed would be US corporations. This highlighted another dimension of linkage — between 'domestic' and 'international' problems. The world economy of the 1990s — and nowhere more so than in the transatlantic system — is characterized by high and growing levels of market interpenetration and interdependence. In these conditions, it is unclear that 'domesticism' of the kind preached by Reaganites of the early 1980s could work. Even the USA cannot cut itself off from the world, and indeed the world is firmly implanted in the USA through the activities of overseas investors, chief among them the countries of the European Community (see Chapter 5) (Reich, 1991).

For the Bush Administration, the coming together of these radical structural changes with continuing debate and uncertainty about the USA's role in the world presented a fundamental policy challenge. The 'notes for guidance' for policy making in the transatlantic arena had held good for policy makers since the early 1950s, with some significant but not fundamental modifications. Now, they were shredded. The policy challenge affected the central elements of the European-American system: the policy agenda, the institutional framework, the often implicit but always powerful 'rules of the game' shaping ideas of leadership and legitimacy. Tests for the Bush Administration were severe and inescapable, beginning with the initial 'Europhoria' as the Berlin Wall fell, moving into increasing concern about the stability of the

USSR and then into the near-anarchy of events in the former Yugoslavia and Central Asia. In the economic sphere, the vast demands of reconstruction in the former Soviet Union, the relaunching of the European Community with the aim of economic and monetary union, and the continuing tensions in the Uruguay Round formed an equally taxing agenda. In both the security and the economic domain, the Bush Administration faced the challenge of a semi-formed 'new Europe' in which there was a plethora of institutions — NATO, the EC, the CSCE, the United Nations, regional and sub-regional bodies — all of them searching for a new role and meaning. No longer did the Americans hold the master key to these institutional structures, and despite the awesome display of US power in the Gulf War it was not clear how far this could be applied to any foreseeable situation in the European arena (Smith and Woolcock, 1993; Williams *et al.*, 1993).

The Bush Administration thus could not escape the need to define or redefine the US position in Europe. But at the same time, it lacked the position of dominance and privilege which had been available to its predecessors in the late 1940s and the 1950s, and which had given them structural power even when it appeared that they could not get their own way in specific areas of dispute. Not surprisingly, there were voices in the USA which called for disengagement from the affairs of the old continent, for the construction of a regional fortress in the Americas — perhaps based around the embryonic North American Free Trade Agreement (NAFTA) — and the transfer of responsibility for European order to the Europeans themselves. In the context of a global economy and linked regional security systems, these calls were quixotic, but none the less appealing. They did not reflect the views of the Bush White House, led as it was by one of the last of the Second World War generation and a president who had spent the 1980s shuttling across the Atlantic to serve the needs of the Reagan Administration. The Bush Administration's position was thus one of engagement, but often without the leverage which could have shaped events into an American mould.

These intersecting dilemmas reflected a fundamental change in the transatlantic relationship which posed problems for all US policy makers. Internally, the links between the USA and Western Europe had been affected by a major rebalancing, most notable in the economic domain but increasingly in the security arena. Externally, the relationship itself was no longer automatically to be seen as the centrepiece of the Cold War, of the world economy or the democratic world. There was still a lot of life in it, but the challenges it faced were substantial and far-reaching. For American policy makers, most notably for George Bush's successor, Bill Clinton, the challenge of Europe was in some respects akin to that which had faced the Truman Administration between 1945 and 1950, but in a vastly changed Atlantic and global context.

In the attempt both to justify continuing engagement in Europe and to exert leverage over its evolution, the Bush Administration produced during 1989 and 1990 another in the series of designs for the transatlantic system. The most notable expression of this design came in a series of speeches by James

Baker, the Secretary of State, in which he envisioned a 'New Atlantic Architecture' based on a negotiated division of labour between the USA and a widening European Community. The first was made in Berlin in December 1989, not in the USA; it envisaged a treaty-based relationship between the EC and the USA, covering a wide range of political and economic issues; and it provided for the establishment of detailed mechanisms for consultation and co-ordination in those fields. It was not the only attempt to redefine relationships across the Atlantic in those years; indeed, in late 1990 there was a rash of pronouncements and declarations in the context of NATO, the CSCE and other institutions which began to redraw the institutional map of transatlantic relations. The US-EC negotiations themselves led in November 1990 to the Transatlantic Declaration, which established much of the network of working groups and co-ordinating bodies referred to by Baker.

Did this amount to an effective renegotiation of the 'transatlantic bargain' on which American-European relations had been based for the previous forty years? It was very difficult to arrive at a conclusion on this question given the degeneration of the European security order during the early 1990s and the emergence of new political and economic challenges.

7.3 THE LATE 1990s: TOWARDS A NEW TRANSATLANTIC BARGAIN

As was noted at the beginning of this chapter, President Clinton came into office in January 1993 with the avowed aim of concentrating first on the domestic needs of the US economy and on the broader regeneration of American society. Within a month he was deeply embroiled in the affairs of Europe, contemplating intervention in Bosnia, staking considerable US prestige on support for Boris Yeltsin in Russia, and negotiating hard about trade and monetary co-operation in the context of the GATT and the Group of Seven industrial nations (the G7). No clearer indication of the importance of Europe to the USA could be imagined; not only this, but the Americans found themselves dealing with a situation in which a number of key Euro-Atlantic institutions were given new life and new orientations.

The first and most dramatic impact of the radical changes in the 'new Europe' was felt in the area of security. When the Berlin Wall came down, it called into question many of the established institutions and assumptions of the Euro-American system, including the central 'pillars' of NATO and nuclear weapons. As I have already noted, the Bush administration responded uncertainly but with considerable adaptability to this new context. For the Clinton administration, the task was more difficult in many ways, since it entailed a reassessment in the longer term of some fundamental assumptions and expectations. Thus by the mid-1990s American policies towards NATO had been essentially re-shaped. Although the US position in the alliance was still regarded as a key element in American political and security leverage, the alliance in many respects had been 're-invented': first, by placing a greater emphasis on joint actions between Europeans and Americans through devices such as Combined Joint Task Forces to deal with conflicts in the new Europe if not beyond; and second, by moving towards the enlargement of NATO itself through the admission of new members from the central and east European 'candidates'. Thus there was a far greater emphasis on the political management of a new form of partnership, based on collective action by a variety of European countries and the Americans (Peterson, 1996; Smith and Woolcock, 1993).

This did not mean that US security dominance was necessarily diluted. Indeed, for Europe, and more specifically for the European Community, the mid-1990s saw some dramatic demonstrations of its continuing limitations. In the conflict in the former Yugoslavia, the EC was forced to retreat from an initial enthusiasm for its role in establishing order to a recognition that only the United States had the hardware and the leadership to create a settlement. There was a great irony here, for in December 1991 the Treaty on European Union (TEU) had proclaimed the establishment of a Common Foreign and Security Policy for the European Union (as it was to become after 1993). What the CFSP did not do was create the means to pursue policies in the realm of 'hard security' and defence. When the 1995 'end-game' in Bosnia led to large-scale bombing of the Bosnian Serbs and then to the Dayton Accords, which established a temporary stability, three features were notable: first, the Americans were central to the military action; second, the accords themselves were framed by US power and signed in the deepest Middle-West; and third, the Implementation Force set up to administer the accords was under the aegis of NATO. Combined with the institutional adaptation of the alliance and its impending enlargement, this seemed to many to confirm the centrality of the transatlantic dimension and of US power within it (Zucconi, 1996); a centrality reaffirmed during the 1999 Kosovo crisis.

This picture was not, however, replicated in the area of economic leadership. The European Union, as noted previously, had established itself as a partner and rival to the USA during the 1970s and 1980s, and was firmly cemented into institutions of global economic management such as the GATT. During the 1990s this status was if anything enhanced. The conflicts between the EC and the US during the later stages of the Uruguay Round negotiations centred on what might be described as the 'old' and 'new' agendas in Atlantic trade relations. One the one hand agriculture nearly caused the collapse of the Round as a whole, while on the other hand French resistance to US demands on audio-visual trade indicated that pressures for global subjection to American popular culture would be resisted by at least some Europeans. Indeed, for many members of the EU in the late 1990s the issue of resistance to 'globalization' was closely allied to the need for defence against US economic dominance. In many ways, the EU was well placed to carve out a leading role in this effort. As the GATT turned into the World Trade Organization (from 1995), the EU could take a leading position in building coalitions to pursue new trade issues, such as those associated with financial services, telecommunications and information technology. The Americans often appeared rather defensive as they responded to the interests of domestic producers in these areas (Smith, 1998b). Although the EU economies were markedly less dynamic than the US economy in the mid to late 1990s they showed signs of recovering from the economic shock of the end of the Cold War and German unification. Perhaps the most symbolic issue was that of Economic and Monetary Union (EMU), which had been decided in principle in the TEU and came to fruition for most EU member states with the inauguration of the single currency, the Euro, in January 1999. For some American commentators, and for an increasing number of policy-makers, this act was the most tangible symbol yet of Europe's new status. Some could even see the imminent emergence of a 'bipolar' international monetary system, with the Dollar and the Euro in — hopefully friendly — competition (Bergsten, 1997). Such a perception was strengthened immeasurably by the onset of financial crisis in the Asia-Pacific during 1997, and by the feeling that only the USA and the EU could be seen as havens of financial stability.

These developments in security and economic relations across the Atlantic had important effects on the perceptions and expectations of US policy-makers. These effects were often paradoxical, with evidence of continued US predominance accompanied by the feeling that the Europeans were both more influential and less than willing to take up the political burden (Newhouse, 1997). US leaders were compelled to respond to the need for new institutional arrangements in the post-Cold War context, but for a variety of reasons they could not act without being seen to do so as part of the broader Euro–American partnership (Gompert and Larrabee, 1997). Action came in two institutional forms. First, as noted above, there was the move to 're-invent' NATO through a search for new roles and new members, and to underline its place within a new 'Atlantic Community'. The US Secretary of State, Warren Christopher, used a speech in Stuttgart, Germany, in September 1996 to lay out the American understanding of this new relationship — fittingly, on the anniversary of a major speech made in 1946 by his predecessor, James Byrnes. The 'enlarged NATO' element of this new community was given tangible expression at the Madrid NATO Council of 1997, at which the entry of Poland, Hungary and the Czech Republic was agreed. Second, and at the same time, there was a move to institutionalize the EU–US relationship, which in December 1995 took the form of the so-called New Transatlantic Agenda (NTA). This not only set out a range of broad principles and procedures, but was accompanied by an Action Plan of around 150 'joint actions' at the transatlantic and the global levels. Significantly, this new EU–US agenda was accompanied by the rapid growth of a Transatlantic Business Dialogue bringing together representatives of the top 100 EU and US corporations (Smith, 1999). By September 1997 the US Under-Secretary of State, Stuart Eizenstat, in a speech to the American Chamber of Commerce in Brussels, was able to present the NTA in general as the foundation of a new 'habit of co-operation' between the EU and the United States.

The picture of US relations with Western Europe that emerged from these processes during the late 1990s was thus one of both continuity and radical change. At one level, US leadership was still seen as essential, particularly in areas of 'hard security', but was also seen as conditional. On the other hand, there was the progressive institutionalization of processes of economic, social and political dialogue, and a move towards joint actions in many global forums. These processes can be seen as responses to the post-Cold War transformation of Europe, but they can equally be seen as the outcome of up to 40 years of transatlantic interactions, which have continually affected US policy-makers and policy-making.

SUMMARY

US administrations from the late 1980s to the late 1990s have faced a number of radical changes in the global and the European context, and their responses to these changes have been vital to the redefinition of US–European relations. In particular:

- US policies had to come to terms with a major paradox relating to American power and influence. While the collapse of the USSR appeared to vindicate the Reaganite focus on unilateral power, the changing nature of the world economy and the shifting focus of conflict meant that US leverage in any given set of circumstances could not be predicted. This paradox intersected with continuing uncertainty in the USA itself about the appropriate role for the country in the new world of the 1990s.

- The growing interpenetration of domestic and international processes and the intensification of linkages between economics and security meant that the transatlantic relationship had to be managed in a new context, in which there were no clear divisions between 'them' and 'us' and in which the renewed vitality of the European Union posed a challenge for policy-makers (both because of its new assertiveness and because of the limitations still all too evident in some areas).

- The focus of policy was increasingly on multilateral mechanisms of management and consultation rather than on unilateral action, and this demanded an adjustment of US policies based on the achievement and exercise of leadership. In many cases neither the USA nor the EU was capable of dominating events, and in some cases neither was inclined to do so. Processes of consultation and collaboration were increasingly institutionalized at the transatlantic level or within global institutions such as the WTO.

8 REASSESSMENT AND CONCLUSIONS

At the beginning of this chapter, a number of issues were set out as the basis for investigation of US-European relations since 1945. The starting point was the observation that transatlantic relations have been central to the evolution of policies in both the USA and Western Europe, and central to the development of world politics more generally. As the chapter has proceeded, this centrality has become apparent in many ways, which need not be recapitulated here. More important are the twin focuses which emerge from the general observation, on processes of change and on the ways in which these relate to the underlying issue of 'empire'. This reassessment and conclusion thus takes as its cue the following two questions.

- First, the question of change. Is it fair to conclude that since the mid-1980s there has been a far-reaching transformation of the European-American system? How has the development of US policy towards Western Europe reflected the operation of structures, institutions, roles and designs generated both within and outside the transatlantic relationship? How has US policy responded to such changes?

- Second, the question of empire. Does the evidence suggest that US policies towards Western Europe can be evaluated through an imperial model? What other models are available and perhaps more relevant? In particular, what can an 'alliance' or an 'interdependence' model tell us about the nature and development of US policies?

8.1 THE QUESTION OF CHANGE AND TRANSFORMATION

Whilst the significance of the transatlantic relationship both to its prime movers and to the outside world has been one of the most enduring features of the post-1945 world arena, it is clear that things have changed. Along with this process of change have come new challenges for US policy makers and a variety of groups in American society, for example corporate interests. It is thus of great importance to try to identify the key phases of change, and to isolate the key features of successive historical periods.

This chapter has argued that the process of change in US policies towards Western Europe has moved through four major phases, the last of them as yet unfinished and even undefined in important respects. In the period 1945–1950, the foundations of a long-running mutual involvement were laid, often in response to urgent pressures and with little idea of their long-term implications. As a result, and inevitably, a number of fault lines and areas of tension were built into the transatlantic system. The consolidation of the system in the 1950s and 1960s brought to the surface a number of these tensions, often in the form of open recriminations and conflicts, but the period also saw a great intensification of the relationship and a process of institutionalization which increased its resilience. During the 1970s, changes not only in the USA and Western Europe but also in the broader world arena placed increasing pressures on the conduct of US policies, to such an extent that at important junctures policy makers were tempted to ignore the rules and misuse the institutional channels. The 1980s and 1990s saw an accelerating process not of change within the system but of transformation, in which the central policy assumptions and institutions were questioned at a fundamental level; although there is increasing evidence of institutionalization, it is unlikely that there will be a definitive new transatlantic 'settlement' for the foreseeable future, and US policies will have to accommodate this fact.

What has this process of change meant for US policy makers? At every stage of the relationship, they have been forced to examine their assumptions about its foundations and its future evolution, and about the role to be played by the USA. The entanglement with Western Europe has been inescapable yet problematic, not least because of the intensity of the mutual involvement it has generated. It has also been an 'open marriage', in the sense that developments in the domestic or the world arena have had direct and immediate reverberations within Atlantic relations. For American administrations this has been a central policy preoccupation, since it has been impossible to seal off the transatlantic domain from their other areas of concern.

It is thus not at all surprising that American approaches to transatlantic relations have demonstrated a persistent ambivalence. The relationship is central, yet challenged; it is a relationship of affinity, but one in which diversity and pluralism has to be accommodated; it is one of shared material and ideological interests, but also one in which there can be sharp clashes and differences of world view. As the post-1945 era has lengthened into the post-Cold War era there is substantial evidence, as noted in this chapter, not only that the transatlantic relationship has changed extensively since 1945, but also that certain themes and issues retain their primacy in its evolution and conduct. What now remains is to evaluate the relationship in terms of its 'deep structure'.

8.2 EMPIRE, ALLIANCE AND INTERDEPENDENCE

How far can the US-European relationship since 1945 be described in terms of 'empire'? It was noted at the beginning of the chapter that a number of analysts have presented the transatlantic system as one of dominance by the USA and dependence on the part of the Europeans (Van der Pijl, 1984; Calleo, 1987 and others). It is not only Marxist thinkers who have seen in the European-American system a structure which privileges the superpower and makes the others more or less subordinate or even client states. Nor is it clear that the relative decline of the USA in the 1970s and 1980s rules out explanation from an imperial viewpoint; in fact, the rise of troubles at the periphery of empires and the influence of 'imperial overstretch' can be accommodated within such a perspective (Kennedy, 1988; Tucker and Hendrickson, 1992). The question here is not whether a view centred on 'empire' is wholly right or wrong, but rather the extent to which such a view captures the complexity of the transatlantic system as it has been described in this chapter.

One way of approaching this is through the themes outlined in the previous section and throughout the chapter. From an imperial perspective, it is possible to see US policies towards Western Europe as manifesting a number of general characteristics. Perhaps the central feature was a structure which — until the early 1990s at least — privileged the USA and US–Soviet relations, and which subordinated the regional needs of Europeans to the global needs of superpower competition. Alongside this assumption went the promotion of what some would call the 'infrastructure' of a US imperial presence in

Western Europe: the network of investment, production, elite solidarity and cultural domination which could be seen as providing a foundation far beyond that established through NATO and other bodies. Institutions such as NATO, the GATT and even the European Community were there as mechanisms for the exertion of US power: they embodied assumptions about security and the economic order which were congenial to Washington, and they acted to reinforce the system. The combination of structural and institutional constraints meant that patterns of behaviour and the informal 'rules of the game' were weighted in favour of the USA, and that Western Europe had to accept a position of subordination to US leadership, not only at the practical level but also at the ideological level. Finally, the USA had the capacity to design and shape the transatlantic system because of its power over the agenda and its capacity to communicate to what was more often than not a divided Western Europe. Even where the message aroused strong resentment, it shaped the transatlantic debate and thus could redesign the system whether or not it was accepted directly.

There is no question that this image of the transatlantic system has some validity as a historical analysis, and that US assumptions and policies have at many points been imperial in nature, if not actively imperialist. The overwhelming dominance in the late 1940s and early 1950s of US military and economic power, and the potent forces exercised by the Cold War confrontation, provided considerable evidence of such a situation, recognized both by US policy-makers themselves and by European leaders. To be sure, there were European leaders who resented and reacted against the situation, but in many ways this served only to underline the potency of US domination. Even General de Gaulle could not remove France from the system, either politically or ideologically. The institutions of the Atlantic system in many cases operated to privilege the US position, and in doing so reflected material power as well as structural dominance. Even when the USA itself shook the system and broke its own rules, as in 1971, there was a rebuilding process which took on board many of the USA's aims. Although the Americans' attempts to design the Europe and the Atlantic system they want have aroused opposition and been opposed, they have profoundly shaped the actions and reactions of the Europeans themselves.

Does this mean that we should view the 'imperial' model simply as a historical curiosity, relevant as far as the end of the Cold War and no further? During the 1990s two new variants of the model have been apparent, one of them based on 'hard security' and US power and the other based on the evolution of the global economy. In the first case, the disappearance of the Soviet Union has meant that the USA is now the only superpower, with the capacity at least in theory to shape the world security order unilaterally. In fact, as we have seen, this is not the only aspect of such a situation: American policy-makers have often felt themselves to be the 'lonely superpower', looking for support and building coalitions. This does not entirely do away with lingering European resentments that the US — and only the US — can deal with some of their most pressing security challenges (for example, in the former Yugoslavia). In addition, the emergence of powerful processes of 'globalization' has led some European commentators and political leaders to discern a new threat of US imperialism, taking advantage of the 'infrastructure' laid down in the 1960s and 1970s and based on the globalization of US business, US popular culture or other aspects of US society. There is considerable power in such interpretations, as we have seen, since they emphasize the continuing power of the US in the 'new agendas' of global security and the global political economy and the relatively limited capacities of the Europeans to defend themselves or retaliate.

But such a judgement does not capture all of the complexities which are subsumed in the label 'transatlantic relations'. Two alternative models — those of **alliance** and **interdependence** — can be used to criticize the imperial view, and to add different dimensions to the picture. In the first place, there is the model which sees the European-American system not as imperial but as an alliance between independent sovereign states, led by the USA. According to this view, the key to understanding the system and US policies is the force exerted by a dominant external threat, and the ability of the various Atlantic countries to meet the threat. There is a strong element of voluntarism here: alliance is a choice, made by both the Europeans and the Americans, and there is thus the possibility that it will be rejected or cease to be necessary as conditions change. Institutions such as NATO are reflective of the interplay of their member-states, and may cease to be effective or relevant as conditions change. The USA can exercise considerable influence on the rules of the game and on behaviour, but there always remains the possibility of defection by countries whose interests demand it and are willing to accept the costs. Thus General de Gaulle represented not a quixotic and doomed attempt to buck a dominant system, but rather a genuine and far from unique assertion of national identity. In the same way, Richard Nixon could assert US interests against the perceived costs of the system even for a dominant power, and Ronald Reagan could adopt an apparently perverse emphasis on insular interests of the most powerful country in the system. The examples of the 'Nixon Shock' and Reaganism raise important questions: whilst states are seen as having legitimate and differing interests, it is assumed that they will pursue these in a responsible and responsive way so as not to bring about consequences damaging for all. The responsibility, by implication, is greatest for the most powerful, and both Nixon and Reagan can be accused of flouting this principle. The post-Cold War uncertainties of US leadership demonstrated another facet of alliance politics, in that the Americans have found it difficult to come to terms with the disappearance of the Soviet threat at the same time as the Europeans have become unsure of their capacity for collective action.

The alliance view can be criticized, as can the imperial perspective, for missing out or downgrading some vital elements in US policies. Most particularly, the focus on alliance and on security needs tends to beg questions about economic interdependence and transnational relations. From the outset, the relationship has been one not only of military and political alliance, but also one in which economic networks have grown up around trade, investment and production. An imperial perspective, as noted above, does include this component, and this is one of its strengths: the USA in Western Europe can be seen as an example of 'imperialism without colonies' or, as one recent study put it, of 'empire by integration' (Lundestad, 1998), in which territorial occupation and even formal governmental power are less important that the sinews of economic domination. But this misses a central point which has recurred at many points in this chapter. The economic relationship between the USA and Western Europe has not been a one-way phenomenon; indeed, from the mid-1950s onwards there has been an increasing element of competition, accompanied by ever-increasing interpenetration of the US and the EC economies. At many points, this has intersected with the military security of Europe, and has caused frictions, but it has less and less been a relationship of dominance and dependence. As time has gone on, it has become a vital part of an increasingly global economy, and the efforts of American policy makers to defend themselves on a national or regional basis against its effects have often proved self-defeating as well as ineffective. US policies at home and abroad have undergone painful adjustments in this process, and as has been seen, the adjustments continue today. The realities of intense market and political interdependence have not always been matched in Washington by a recognition of the resulting policy interdependence, and from this has stemmed some chronic problems. Perhaps most significantly, the 1980s and 1990s have brought home to US policy makers the growing linkages not only between domestic and international concerns but also between military security and economic well being, linkages which are extremely difficult to recognize and to manage in a turbulent world.

The development of transatlantic relations has seen a fluctuating blend of all three models — empire, alliance and interdependence — which in itself has raised problems for US policy. Alongside elements of imperial domination have gone the pressure of national interests and the constraints of alliance, with the Soviet threat or its absence playing a vital role both in the Cold War period and after. At the same time, the growth of interdependence and interpenetration between the USA and its European partners has created a situation in which it is difficult to identify purely national interests or to pursue effective policies on a national basis alone. As successive American administrations have had to recognize, they are doomed to exist in a process of 'competitive co-operation' with Western Europe. The radical transformations of the 1980s and 1990s have certainly changed the symptoms of this problem, but they have not removed the problem itself. For American policy-makers, the fundamental question as they contemplate the new millennium is not whether the USA is going to be involved in Western Europe, or in the 'new Europe' as a whole, but how.

REFERENCES

Allen, D., Rummel, R. and Wessels, W. (eds.) (1982) *European Political Co-operation: Towards a Foreign Policy for Western Europe*, London, Butterworth.

Allen, D. and Smith, M. (1989) 'Western Europe in the Atlantic System of the 1980s: towards a new identity?' in Gill, S. (ed.) *Atlantic Relations in the Reagan Era*, Brighton, Wheatsheaf, pp.88–110.

Bergner, J. (1991) *The New Superpowers: Germany, Japan, the US, and the New World Order*, New York, St. Martin's Press.

Bergsten, C.F. (1997) 'The Dollar and the Euro', *Foreign Affairs*, vol.76, pp.83–95.

Bergsten, F.W. (1981) 'The costs of Reaganomics', *Foreign Policy*, no.44, pp.24–36.

Bergsten, F.W. (1990) 'The world economy after the Cold War', *Foreign Affairs*, vol.69, pp.96–112.

Block F.L. (1977) *The Origins of International Monetary Disorder: A Study of United States International Monetary Policy From 1945 to the Present*, Berkeley and Los Angeles, University of California Press.

Calleo, D.P. (1982) *The Imperious Economy*, Cambridge, MA, and London, Harvard University Press.

Calleo, D.P. (1987) *Beyond American Hegemony: The Future of the Western Alliance*, New York, Basic Books.

Calleo, D.P. and Rowland, B.C. (1973) *America and the World Political Economy: Atlantic Dreams and National Realities*, Bloomington and London, Indiana State University Press.

Chace, J. and Ravenal, E. (eds.) (1976) *Atlantis Lost: The United States and Europe After the Cold War*, New York, New York University Press.

DePorte, A.W. (1986) *Europe Between the Superpowers: The Enduring Balance*, 2nd edition, New Haven, Yale University Press.

Destler, I.M., Gelb, L.H. and Lake, A. (1984) *Our Own Worst Enemy: the Unmaking of American Foreign Policy*, New York, Simon and Schuster.

Eichenberg, R.C. (1989) *Public Opinion and National Security in Western Europe: Consensus Lost?* London, Macmillan.

Freedman, L. (1981) *The Evolution of Nuclear Strategy*, London, Macmillan.

Fursdon, E. (1980) *The European Defence Community: A History*, London, Macmillan.

Gompert, D. and Larrabee, S. (1997) *America and Europe: a Partnership for a New Era*, Cambridge, Cambridge University Press.

Gordon, L.W. (1956) 'Economic aspects of coalition diplomacy: the NATO experience', *International Organization*, vol.10, pp.1–11.

Grosser, A. (1980) *The Western Alliance: The United States and Western Europe Since 1945*, London, Macmillan.

Heller, F.H. and Gillingham, J.R. (1992) *NATO: The Founding of the Atlantic Alliance and the Integration of Europe*, New York, St. Martin's Press.

Hilsman, R. (1959) 'NATO: the developing strategic context' in Knorr, K. (ed.) *NATO and American Security*, Princeton, NJ, Princeton University Press, pp.11–36.

Hocking, B. and Smith, M. (1997) *Beyond Foreign Economic Policy: the United States, the Single European Market and the Changing World Economy*, London, Cassell/Pinter.

Hoffmann, S. (1978) *Primacy or World Order: American Foreign Policy Since the Cold War*, New York, McGraw-Hill.

Hoffman, S. and Maier, C. (eds.) (1984) *The Marshall Plan: A Retrospective*, Boulder, Co., Westview.

Hogan, M.J. (1987) *The Marshall Plan: America, Britain, and the Reconstruction of Western Europe, 1947–1952*, Cambridge, Cambridge University Press.

Hufbauer, G.C. (ed.) (1990) *Europe 1992, An American Perspective*, Washington, DC, Brookings.

Ireland, T. (1981) *Creating the Entangling Alliance: The Origins of the North Atlantic Treaty Organization*, Westport, Conn., Greenwood Press.

Joffe, J. (1987) *The Limited Partnership: Europe, the United States and the Burdens of Alliance*, Cambridge, MA, Ballinger.

Kaiser, K. (1974) 'Europe and America: a critical phase', *Foreign Affairs*, vol.52, pp.85–110.

Kaiser, K. and Schwartze, H.P. (eds.) (1977) *America and Western Europe: Problems and Prospects*, Lexington, MA, D.C. Heath.

Kanter, A. (1985) 'Thinking about the strategic defense initiative: an alliance perspective', *International Affairs*, vol.61, pp.449–64.

Kaplan, L. (1988) *NATO and the United States: The Enduring Alliance*, Boston, MA, Twayne.

Kennedy, P. (1988) *The Rise and Fall of the Great Powers: Economic Change and Military Conflict from 1500 to 2000*, London, Unwin Hyman.

Keohane, R.O. (1979) 'US foreign economic policy toward other advanced capitalist states: the struggle to make others adjust' in Oye, K.W., Lieber, R. and Rothchild, R. (eds.) *Eagle Entangled: US Foreign Policy in a Complex World*, London, Longman, pp.91–122.

Keohane, R.O. (1984) *After Hegemony: Co-operation and Discord in the World Political Economy*, Princeton, Princeton University Press.

Kissinger, H. (1965) *The Troubled Partnership: A Reappraisal of the Atlantic Alliance*, New York, McGraw-Hill.

Kolko, J. and Kolko, G. (1972) *The Limits of Power: The World and US Foreign Policy 1945–1954*, New York, Harper and Row.

Lundestad, G. (1998) *Empire by Integration: the United States and European Integration 1945–1997*, Oxford, Oxford University Press.

Mandelbaum, M. (1981) *The Nuclear Revolution: International Politics Before and After Hiroshima*, Cambridge, Cambridge University Press.

Milward, A. (1984) *The Reconstruction of Western Europe, 1945–1951*, London, Methuen.

Nau, H. (1984–85) 'Where Reagonomics works', *Foreign Policy*, No. 57, pp.14–38.

Newhouse, J. (1997) *Europe Adrift*, New York, Pantheon Books/Council on Foreign Relations.

Oye, K.W., Lieber, R. and Rothchild, R. (eds.) (1987) *Eagle Resurgent? The Reagan Era in American Foreign Policy*, Boston, Little Brown.

Peterson, J. (1996) *Europe and America in the 1990s: Prospects for Partnership*, London, Routledge (2nd edn).

Pfaltzgraff, R. (1969) *The Atlantic Community: A Complex Imbalance*, New York, Van Nostrand-Reinhold.

Reich, R.W. (1991) *The Work of Nations: Preparing Ourselves for 21st Century Capitalism*, New York, Knopf.

Riste, O.W. (ed.) (1985) *Western Security: The Formative Years*, Oslo, Universitatsforlaget.

Serfaty, S. (1979) *Fading Partnership: America and Europe After Thirty Years*, New York, Praeger.

Silva, M. and Sjogren, B. (1990) *Europe 1992 and the New World Power Game*, New York, Wiley.

Smith, M. (1984) *Western Europe and the United States: The Uncertain Alliance*, London, Allen and Unwin.

Smith, M. (1988a) 'The Reagan Administration's foreign policy, 1981–85: learning to live with uncertainty?', *Political Studies*, vol.36, pp.52–73.

Smith, M. (1998b) 'Competitive co-operation and EU–US relations: can the EU be a strategic partner for the US in the world political economy?', *Journal of European Public Policy*, vol.5, pp.561–77.

Smith, M. (1992a) '"The devil you know": the United States and a changing European Community', *International Affairs*, vol. 68, pp.103–20.

Smith, M. (1992b) 'The United States and 1992: responding to a changing European Community' in Redmond, J. (ed.) *The External Relations of the European Community: The International Response to 1992*, London, Macmillan, pp.31–54.

Smith, M. (1999) 'The United States, the European Union and the new transatlantic marketplace: public strategy and private interests' in Philippart, E. and Winand, P. (eds) *Decision-Making in United States–European Union Relations*, Manchester, Manchester University Press.

Smith, M. and Woolcock, S. (1993) *The United States and the European Community in a Transformed World*, London, Pinter.

Thurow, L. (1992) *Head to Head: The Coming Economic Battle Among Japan, Europe, and America*, New York, Morrow.

Treverton, G.F. (1985) *Making the Alliance Work: The United States and Western Europe*, London, Macmillan.

Tsoukalis, L. (ed.) (1986) *Europe, America and the World Economy*, Oxford, Blackwell.

Tucker, R.W. and Hendrickson, D.C. (1992) *The Imperial Temptation: The New World Order and America's Purpose*, New York, Council on Foreign Relations.

Van der Pijl, K. (1984) *The Making of an Atlantic Ruling Class*, London, Verso.

Williams, P., Hammond, P. and Brenner, M. (1993) 'Atlantis lost, paradise regained? The US and Western Europe after the Cold War', *International Affairs*, vol.69, pp.1–18.

Woolcock, S. (1982) *Western Policies on East-West Trade*, London, Routledge.

Woolcock, S. (1991) *Market Access Issues in US/EC Relations: Trading Partners or Trading Blows?*, London, Pinter.

Zucconi, M. (1996) 'The European Union in the former Yugoslavia' in Chayes, A. and Chayes, A.H. (eds) *Preventing Conflict in the Post-Communist World*, Washington, DC, Brookings Institution, pp.237–78.

FURTHER READING

Calleo, D.P. (1987) *Beyond American Hegemony: The Future of the Western Alliance*, New York, Basic Books.

DePorte, A.W. (1986) *Europe Between the Superpowers*, 2nd ed., New Haven, Yale University Press.

Grosser, A. (1980) *The Western Alliance: The United States and Western Europe since 1945*, London, Macmillan.

Peterson, J. (1996) *Europe and America in the 1990s: Prospects for Partnership*, London, Routledge (2nd edn).

Smith, M. and Woolcock, S. (1993) *The United States and the European Community in a Transformed World*, London, Pinter.

5 GLOBALIZATION AND THE FOREIGN–DOMESTIC POLICY NEXUS

Brian Hocking

1 INTRODUCTION

> To renew America we must meet challenges abroad as well as at home. There is no clear division today between what is foreign and what is domestic — the world economy, the world environment, the world Aids crisis, the world arms race affect us all
>
> (President Clinton's inaugural address, 21 January 1993).

One of the dominant preoccupations of successive generations of US policy makers — as reflected in George Washington's farewell address to Congress in 1796, Ronald Reagan's attachment to the Strategic Defence Initiative during the 1980s and President Clinton's response to the bombings of the US embassies in Kenya and Tanzania in 1998 — has been the conquest of potential vulnerability through maximum self-reliance and minimum dependence on others. Indeed, it is this search for absolute security that has been a major determinant of the patterns of behaviour associated with the United States as an imperial power. But invulnerability is increasingly elusive, as challenges come not only from external events, such as the 1998 embassy bombings, but also from a growing sense of internal vulnerability, clearly demonstrated in the reactions to the bombing of the New York World Trade Center in 1993.

Of course, a more closely integrated global community embracing complex networks of linkages together with pressing global issues, not least those presented by growing environmental challenges, confronts all national communities to a greater or lesser extent. But the central position of the US within the international system together with the scope of its global interests, and the openness of its social and political systems, ensures that it remains, to an exceptional degree, the object of external pressures related to a broad range of policy issues. Thus whereas in the post-Cold War environment, the relative power of the USA appears to be underscored by its status as the sole claimant to superpower status, so the degree to which American society and the political processes are open to external influences is equally apparent.

This carries with it implications that extend far beyond traditional concerns with foreign policy. Indeed, whilst much of the discussion in this book is directed towards foreign relations and the degree to which US hegemony has shaped the contemporary international system, this chapter adopts a reverse perspective. In what ways, and to what extent, has the dominant role discharged by the USA in world affairs impacted on its domestic structures and processes? In attempting to answer this question, the chapter focuses on the growing interactions between international and domestic economic, political and social forces that pose problems for time-honoured distinctions between domestic and foreign policy as separate realms of political activity.

The discussion begins with an examination of the factors underpinning the growing nexus between the foreign and domestic spheres, paying particular attention to economic and social factors; it then proceeds to examine their impact on policy processes, focusing on the changing roles of Congress and the states in the management of external relations. Not surprisingly, given the global significance of the US economic and political arenas, foreign interests have recognized the need to operate within a more diversified policy milieu and to influence its outcomes. The consequent growth of foreign interest lobbying has prompted what are probably the clearest manifestations of a heightened sense of vulnerability in a United States beset by images of economic threat and decline.

The chapter concludes with an evaluation of the impact of international forces for a policy agenda marked by enhanced patterns of interaction between the external and domestic policy arenas. What are the implications for the United States as it seeks to establish a role in a world very different from that of the Cold War era?

2 THE CHANGING NATURE OF FOREIGN POLICY

As is the case in other national communities, the USA is confronted by a changing foreign policy environment which has considerable implications for those who live within its borders, but also — given the dominant role that it has come to play in post-1945 international politics — for the international community as a whole. The character of this changing environment can be examined in terms of three dimensions:

- the content of foreign policy;
- the participants in foreign policy;
- the patterns of interaction generated by foreign policy.

2.1 CONTENT

There is a strong, perhaps instinctive, inclination to think of foreign policy as something removed from other areas of public policy. Its association with the defence of national territories from external threat and with the very symbols of statehood and national sovereignty help to set it apart from more mundane issues which confront policy makers and publics. In particular, and because of its identification with the preservation of national interests in a hostile international environment, foreign policy has traditionally been equated with military security. Of course, in the case of the USA, given its superpower status in the context of the Cold War, this image of foreign policy has had much to sustain it.

However, long before the world could contemplate the problems of a post-Cold War order, it was clear that foreign policy had become far more complex as a range of issues — economic, social and environmental — crowded onto the agendas of national governments. Indeed, as the linkages binding national communities have grown, there are few areas of what have hitherto been viewed as 'domestic' policy which do not find their place at the international level.

2.2 PARTICIPANTS

Inevitably, this has affected the second dimension of foreign policy transformation, namely, the expansion of those agencies, groups and individuals involved in its formulation and implementation. The traditional image of foreign policy stresses the primary role of a policy elite centred on the foreign ministry — the State Department in the case of the USA — which acts as the point of interface between the national community and its international environment. Even prior to the collapse of the Soviet Union, however, the influences on US foreign policy were becoming more diverse. As we shall see later in this chapter, the Nixon-Kissinger era witnessed a resurgence of congressional involvement in the conduct of foreign relations which reflected both a concern with their content, especially in the context of US involvement in South East Asia, and a more general sense of unease of the use, or misuse of presidential power, greatly reinforced by the Watergate scandal in the early 1970s.

Alongside the growth of congressional interest in international affairs, the increasing diversity of foreign policy has brought into the process an ever-expanding cast of 'domestic' players, breaking down the barriers once perceived to exist between the two sectors of public policy. Not only is this evident at an official level as 'bureaucratic politics' impinges on the conduct of foreign relations, partly the product of tensions created by the international interests of departments — such as transport and agriculture — assumed to be domestic in character, but also at the non-governmental level as a wide range of non-governmental organizations seek to influence a policy agenda which no longer recognizes national boundaries. The diversity of actors involved in the conduct of foreign policy can be seen at its clearest where domestic and international priorities intersect, as in the case of environmental issues.

Here, the juxtaposition of domestic interests, both governmental and non-governmental, has been demonstrated by the interaction of domestic and international diplomacy in climate change negotiations, as the US position on reducing greenhouse gases emerged prior to the Kyoto (1997) and Buenos Aires (1998) conferences. The phenomenon was especially visible during the development of the US position on the control of chlorofluorocarbons (CFCs) during the negotiations which resulted in the 1987 Montreal Protocol on Substances That Deplete the Ozone Layer. By late 1986, through an intensive round of internal diplomacy involving a number of government agencies and led by the State Department and the Environmental Protection Agency, a formula for the US international negotiating position — incorporating ambitious targets for the phasing-out of CFCs — had been established. However, the considerable opposition to environmental regulation within the Reagan Administration began to assert itself even as the international diplomatic campaign to win over other countries to the US position got under way. In addition to some voices from within Congress, a coalition of opponents embracing officials in the Departments of the Interior, Commerce and Agriculture together with members of the White House staff, attempted to undermine the negotiations by questioning the scientific and economic bases of the US position. Ultimately, the disarray created by this bureaucratic and political dissensus required the active intervention of Secretary of State George Schultz and the endorsement of the negotiating stance by the President himself (Benedick, 1991, pp.57–65).

2.3 PATTERNS

Thirdly, the transformation of foreign policy is reflected in the patterns of interaction between national communities. International politics can no longer be viewed simply as a matter of relationships between governments. Certainly, despite the arguments of those who suggest that national governments are being rapidly eclipsed by powerful 'non-state actors' such as the multinational corporation, they remain dominant players on the world stage. Nevertheless, they are constrained to operate in a far more complex milieu wherein their room for manoeuvre is determined by a variety of cross-cutting webs of interaction. On the one hand, governments themselves are by no means monolithic entities: they are, in fact, complex organizations and, as suggested above, different elements of these structures can build relationships with departments and agencies in other countries. This creates 'transgovernmental' webs of officials which can greatly affect the way foreign policy is conducted.

Similarly, factors such as the emergence of a global economy and the revolution in communications and information technology have opened up national societies, creating patterns of 'transnational' relationships between a variety of groupings and organizations such as trade unions and religious groups.

SUMMARY

Summarizing the points made in this section, it has been suggested that the nature of foreign policy as an activity is changing in important respects:

- the issues subsumed under the term 'foreign policy' have expanded dramatically;

> - partly as a consequence, a far greater range of actors are involved in the foreign policy processes;
> - the patterns of interactions between national communities is more complex, both at the governmental and non-governmental levels.

3 MANAGING FOREIGN AND DOMESTIC POLICY

One of the major consequences of these developments has been to erode the distinction between foreign and domestic policy in two senses. At one level, it is now far harder to distinguish the precise content of an 'international' and a 'domestic' issue. Taking the long-running trade negotiations within the framework of the General Agreement on Tariffs and Trade (GATT) launched in 1986, the Uruguay Round, as an example, the disputes between the USA and the European Union (EU) over agricultural subsidies are, clearly, an international issue affecting the patterns of relationships between Washington and member states of the EU. Yet the character of the dispute is an intensely domestic one, touching as it does on key sectoral interests in the countries involved. This fact ensures that governments are going to treat it at least as much as a matter of domestic politics as one of foreign relations.

At a second level, the foreign-domestic distinction is weakened by the political interactions which such an issue generates. Whilst, clearly, the USA-EU dispute over, for example, oilseeds, engaged the attention of the respective governments on both sides of Atlantic, so did it generate patterns of pressure group activity more traditionally associated with domestic politics. Thus when in 1992 French farmers marched in Paris and Brussels in protest at the USA-EU oilseeds deal, American farmers joined their ranks. Furthermore, to promote their cause, representatives of French farmers' groups such as the *France Confederation Paysanne* and the *Federation des Producteurs de Lait* visited Washington in December 1992 to alert members of Congress, US farmers and the general public to their objections to the GATT deal.

Instances such as this illustrate the complex patterns which the growing interaction between domestic and foreign policy produces. They reflect the fact that national communities, such as the United States, are subject to apparently paradoxical trends.

On one hand, we are witnessing a growing 'globalization' of public policy as national governments respond to an expanding range of international linkages, economic interdependence and the demands of policy issues which can no longer be managed within the framework of individual political systems. On the other, a growing 'localization' of what have hitherto been seen as policy issues belonging to the sphere of foreign relations as subnational interests, both governmental and non-governmental, are alerted to these pressures through their effects on an expanding range of domestic constituencies and those who represent them at the local level.

There is a tendency to regard the relationship between these processes of globalization and localization of the foreign policy milieu in 'zero-sum' terms, suggesting that they are fundamentally incompatible rather than complementary to each other. Hence Evan Luard argues that the 'globalization' of politics has created a situation in which national political arenas have become redundant. In the context of the environmental agenda for example, he stresses the importance of the international over the national:

> ... effective political activity relating to the environment today can only take place at the global level. Because it is there, not in the relatively insignificant decisions of national states, that the important steps for safeguarding the world's threatened natural heritage must be taken, it is there too that in the future the significant political struggles will occur.
>
> (Luard, 1990, p.12)

Whereas there is, at first glance, an apparent logic to such an argument, it fails to recognize the complexities that the growing integration of foreign and domestic policy referred to above are creating. Globalization and localization of the policy arenas are, in fact, complementary processes whereby policy issues touch several levels of political activity, often simultaneously from the subnational, to the national and international. Achieving policy objectives, therefore, as in the case of the negotiations leading to the Montreal Protocol on ozone depletion discussed above, require policy officials to operate in several political arenas, often simultaneously.

SUMMARY

Summarizing the argument so far, it has been suggested that:

- Fundamental changes have occurred in the character of foreign policy both in terms of the issues which it encompasses and the processes through which it is formulated and implemented.

- These have, in turn, contributed to the crumbling of the walls separating foreign from domestic policy.

- Consequently, alongside the globalization of the policy agenda, pressures from the external environment are impinging on domestic interests which project localized concerns into the international arena.

4 GLOBALIZATION AND LOCALIZATION

In this sense, globalization and localization go hand-in-hand. As has been noted, such developments as these can be found to a greater or lesser extent in many national communities. What makes them of particular significance in the US context, is, on the one hand, the myriad external linkages which the USA has developed and, on the other, the fundamental character of US society and its political institutions. Not only is the USA an open society in terms of the plurality of the interests within it and the opportunity afforded them to voice their concerns, but the structures of government, with their territorial power divisions between federal and state levels, together with the separation of powers between Congress and the executive, offer multiple points of access. Moreover, as will be shown later in the chapter, this openness can be exploited by foreign interests anxious to influence the shaping of US domestic and external policies, thereby reinforcing the growing linkages between the global, the national and the local. Bearing this in mind, let us now turn more specifically to the United States in order to see how the twin processes of localization and globalization have developed and with what consequences.

4.1 THE USA AND THE CHANGING GLOBAL ECONOMY

Earlier chapters in this book have traced the emergence of the United States as a global superpower in the vastly changed international order which was the product of the Second World War. Just as in the military sphere, Washington was prepared to assume a leadership role, and was urged to do so by its allies (whose aim in the late 1940s was to secure American involvement in the rehabilitation and defence of Western Europe), so did it become the dominant force in the shaping and operating of the emerging post-war economic order. In world trade, the USA was competitive in all major industrial sectors; in Spero's words: 'the United States acted as the world's central banker, provided the major initiatives in international trade negotiations and dominated international production' (Spero, 1990, p.25).

By the 1970s, however, fundamental changes in the political and economic character of the international system were challenging US dominance of the international economy. On the one hand, US pre-eminence and leadership were less and less accepted within the group of states constituting the advanced industrialized economies. With the growing economic strength of Western Europe and Japan, US leadership and the advantages that went with it, were less readily conceded. Moreover, from Washington's viewpoint, the advantages of leadership became decreasingly apparent. On both sides of the Atlantic, of course, the gradual lessening of East-West tensions helped to weaken the security arguments for continued US leadership. At the same time, claims for a voice in the management of the international economy from the emerging Third World and the Soviet bloc were increasingly heard.

Underpinning these developments was the relative weakening of US economic dominance associated with the growing internationalization of the US economy. From 1960 to the early 1990s the contribution of foreign trade to GNP doubled from approximately 6 per cent to 12 per cent, and it is estimated that some 70 per cent of US economic growth is now attributable to international trade (Fry, 1998, p.7). But at the same time, the areas of production in which the USA enjoyed a dominant share fell, as did its overall share of world manufacturing production. In the mid-1950s this stood at more than 40 per cent; by 1980 it had declined to 30 per cent (Nye, 1990, p.76). Furthermore, the changing nature of global production combined with the appeal of the US market, in terms of its size and diversity, encouraged a rapid growth in foreign direct investment (FDI). Between 1975 and 1987, this grew by 845 per cent (Glickman and Woodward, 1989, p.32).

Developments during the 1980s encouraged these trends. On the trade front, the strong rise in the value of the dollar in the early part of the decade pushed it to a point 40 per cent above the level at which US firms were competitive in world markets (Destler, 1995, p.9). As a result, imports flooded in, swelling a growing trade deficit which, combined with an escalating budget deficit, was to turn the USA into the world's largest debtor nation. (According to some estimates, its foreign debt will have reached $1 trillion by the end of the 1990s.) In the late 1980s, the decline in the dollar's value encouraged a spurt in FDI as foreign investors took advantage of the situation to gain direct entry to the US market. Reflecting on the implications of these changes for the United States since 1945, the 1989 report from the National Governors' Association Task Force on Foreign Markets summarized the position in the following terms:

> As the global marketplace has emerged, the United States' role as an economic decision maker has changed. During the 1960s, when the US economy was partially insulated from global influence, it was possible to influence the economy by then-traditional fiscal and monetary policies. With the development of the Euro dollar market, foreign ownership of a large portion of the federal debt, and huge increases in foreign trade, the economic sovereignty once enjoyed by the United States has been reduced.
>
> (National Governors' Association, 1989, p.iv)

The impact of these events has been, firstly, to alert the public and political elites, not least Congress, to the impact of external economic forces. Foreign investors, especially the Japanese, are very visible presences in particular communities, such as Tennessee. The percentage of the US workforce employed by overseas firms, whilst small nevertheless grew by 147 per cent between 1977 and 1986 (Glickman and Woodward, 1989, p.32). By 2000, it is suggested, 20 million jobs will be related to international trade, investment and tourism (Fry, 1998, p.4). Such trends have helped to reinforce a growing sense of vulnerability, symbolized by the debate on American 'decline'. This had come to assume a significance which stands apart from the considerable debate on the merits and demerits of specific arguments, such as that advanced by Paul Kennedy in his influential book, *The Rise and Fall of the Great Powers*, published in the late 1980s (Kennedy, 1987). As Nye amongst others has argued, the indices relating to US economic power are often ambiguous and cited selectively by those anxious to portray the United States as being in a condition of terminal decline (Nye Jr, 1990, Chapter 3).

But however the statistics are interpreted and whatever conclusions are drawn from them regarding the status of the United States, the fact is that the globalization of the world economy is having a profound impact on American society and politics. As Destler observes, 'Between 1970 and 1990, trade doubled as a share of US gross national product. Hence more industries are exposed internationally, and more are hurt by import competition' (Destler, 1995, p.286). The fact that the USA is experiencing, along with other communities, the impact of changes in global production methods — the emergence of 'global webs' as Robert Reich has termed them — marked by the ease with which the factors of production — factories, capital, expertise, scientific knowledge and technology — slip across national boundaries, does little to help local communities come to terms with the anxieties that external economic pressures create (Reich, 1991, Chapter 10).

In this section, we have seen that the twin forces of globalization and localization are particularly marked in the USA, partly because of the openness of its political and social systems. These processes have been reinforced by the growing internationalization of the US economy which has greatly enhanced the sensitivity of domestic constituencies to international economic forces, creating thereby a sense of vulnerability. Equally, however, expanding international-domestic linkages have enabled groups, and even individuals, to operate in the international arena and this provides a further dimension to the overall picture.

4.2 SOCIAL ACTIVISM AND THE FOREIGN–DOMESTIC NEXUS

The internationalization of the traditional domestic policy agenda has also helped to condition the ways in which the proliferation of interest groups seek to achieve their objectives. To a considerable degree, groups — and even individuals — have a far greater access to the international system and mobility within it than in any previous era. Projecting influence outside national boundaries no longer presents the insuperable problems that once it did: 'acting internationally' is now within the grasp of determined local groups in pursuit of their objectives. One instance of this can be seen where the interests of US employees of foreign firms are involved, as in the case of the Illinois-based corn syrup producer, A.E. Staley, owned by Britain's Tate and Lyle. Objections by the workforce to changes in working practices at Staley led to the development of a strategy that was by no means confined to the United States. Hence in January 1993, a union delegation from the USA attended the annual meeting of Tate and Lyle in London with the intention of publicizing their cause.

Beyond situations such as this (one consequence of the globalization of the US economy discussed in the previous section) we find a large range of organizations increasingly active at both the domestic and international levels on issues such as those embraced by the broad human rights and environmental agendas. In some cases, this reflects a dissatisfaction with government policy, extending on occasions to defence policy.

Shuman, in his survey of 'local' foreign policies in the USA points to the disenchantment with the Reagan administration's attitudes towards arms control, Central America and South Africa as major factors in the development of what he terms 'citizen diplomacy' in the 1980s (Shuman, 1986). In the case of nuclear weapons the 'nuclear freeze' campaign which originated from the Massachusetts referendum proposing a moratorium on their acquisition was reflected in the decision of a number of local authorities to declare themselves as nuclear-free zones and had a substantial impact on US public opinion (Dumbrell, 1990, pp.174–5). However, it is in the sphere of foreign economic policy that activist groups have been most in evidence, often linking human rights matters to trade and foreign investment issues.

Acting on the principle 'think globally, act locally', pressure groups have become adept at using the locality as a route to participation in, and influence over, external policy, once again reinforcing the significance of the US political system in terms of the access it offers to groups seeking to influence the policy processes. In this instance, the economic powers and financial structures of subnational authorities offer an opportunity to exert influence both on Washington and selected targets in the international arena. This can be clearly seen in the attempts by a diverse range of groups and organizations to encourage institutions and organizations to adopt economic sanctions in pursuit of human rights objectives, as in the cases of South Africa, Northern Ireland and Burma.

Such sanctions have assumed several forms: pension fund disinvestment, bank deposit denial, procurement denial and (in the specific case of South Africa) regulation of the Krugerrand. Amongst these, pension fund divestiture appears to be the most potent. In the wake of the 1976 Soweto riots, a number of communities in the United States enacted measures to remove investments in companies operating in South Africa which did not adhere to a code of practice (known as the Sullivan principles), from the portfolios of pension funds (Love, 1985). Michigan was the first state to adopt sanctions legislation but with the 1984 disturbances in South Africa, it was joined by a growing number of state and local governments. In 1989, one author noted that 'some 23 states, 14 countries, 80 cities and the Virgin Islands have enacted various kinds of divestment or procurement legislation or ordinances directed at South Africa's apartheid policies' (Bilder, 1989 p.822).

As these sanctions policies became more popular, their scope extended to other countries, including the USSR and Iran, whose actions attracted the disapproval of various interests. In later years, the list has included Northern Ireland. Unemployment amongst the Catholic population of the province has become an issue on state and local political agendas, particularly in communities containing significant Irish American populations. Again, pension funds have been used as weapons, in this case to persuade US companies to implement the MacBride principles drafted by the New York City Comptroller's office in 1984. These principles are intended to protect the interests of religious minorities in the Northern Ireland workforce and to relieve the high levels of Catholic unemployment through such measures as increased representation of religious minorities and bans on religious and political emblems in factories. During 1989, the MacBride campaign gathered momentum with 10 states and 12 cities having passed legislation in support of it by February of that year.

More recently, in a development that threatened to become increasingly embarrassing to the Administration in 1997 and 1998, several state and local governments, led by the city and state of New York City, focused attention on the record of Swiss banks and companies before and during the Second World War and, in particular, on their reluctance to settle the claims of Holocaust victims. Faced with the threat of phased sanctions (for example, banning Swiss banks and investment firms from selling city and state debt), sanctions that would be extended to all Swiss companies if no agreement was reached, the banks agreed a settlement in September 1998. In the same month, a different sanctions dispute took a new twist as the European Union and Japan called for a World Trade Organization disputes panel over a highly controversial 1996 Massachusetts state law prohibiting procurement from companies trading with Burma.

Swiss banks expect sanctions this week

By John Authers in New York

Swiss banks expect to have sanctions imposed on them this week by US state and city officials over the "Nazi gold" affair, and they intend to respond with legal action.

Officials leading the negotiations on behalf of UBS and Credit Suisse, giving their first press interview on the issue, also made it clear they thought divisions among negotiators for Holocaust victims lay behind the failure to reach a settlement.

Last week lawyers acting on behalf of Holocaust survivors rejected a public offer of $600m (£360m) in addition to the amount proved by an independent audit to be left in dormant accounts, which the banks had made to settle the US legal actions against them. The lawyers called it a "shabby" offer.

Robert O'Brien, global head of credit and loan management for Credit Suisse First Boston, said: "We've reached a point now where we realise we are dealing with two agendas. One is the substance of the issue. The other is the political agenda." He added: "Some politicians basically see this as an opportunity. Notwithstanding the facts, they will pursue their own ends for their own purposes."

He also questioned whether some lawyers in the case, who have been criticised by Holocaust victims themselves for failing to keep the plaintiffs informed, were motivated primarily by the attempt to generate fees.

The interview marked a new departure for the banks, which have so far taken a low profile. Obviously angered by the failure to reach a settlement, and by continued negative publicity in the US press, they said they were prepared to fight the legal actions in court.

On Wednesday, a group of elected finance officials led by Alan Hevesi, the New York city comptroller, will meet in New York to hear representations from the parties to the talks over a global settlement. Mr Hevesi has said they may impose sanctions on the banks.

But Mr O'Brien said: "Sanctions at this point in time would be counter-productive. Sanctions are probably illegal because they are unconstitutional. It's the US government which carries out the foreign policy of the US, and not New York City."

Richard Capone, managing director of UBS in the Americas, said they were prepared to take legal action even though this might put them in the uncomfortable position, for Wall Street institutions, of suing the city of New York.

They have been criticised for moving too slowly. The audit of their dormant accounts, carried out under the direction of Paul Volcker, former Federal Reserve chief, has already lasted two years, involving 500 accountants at a cost to the banks of $200m.

But Mr Capone said of the $70m, subsequently raised to $200m, which the banks made available for a humanitarian fund two years ago, to ensure speedy recompense for ageing Holocaust survivors, only $11m has thus been paid out.

Swiss banks are challenged by New York City
Source: Financial Times, *29 June 1998*

WTO drawn into row over anti-Burma law

By Neil Buckley in Brussels

The European Union and Japan will this month call for a World Trade Organisation disputes panel over a controversial Massachusetts state law barring procurement from companies trading with Burma.

The call for a WTO panel is expected to be made on September 22, and follows three sets of inconclusive talks with the US.

It comes as the National Foreign Trade Council (NFTC), representing 580 companies, including many of the biggest US multinationals, seeks to overturn the 1996 Massachusetts law at a federal court in Boston. The law effectively bars companies doing business with Burma from bidding for public contracts in Massachusetts, worth $2bn a year.

Papers filed in the federal court this summer by the NFTC suggested 346 companies were affected, and Apple, the computer group, has cited the law as one reason for withdrawing from Burma. The NFTC argues that the law violates the US constitution, which says making foreign policy and regulating foreign trade are federal rights.

The European Commission, the EU's Brussels-based executive arm, first complained to the WTO about the law in June 1997, with Japan joining a month later.

They argue that the law breaches the WTO's government procurement agreement, which is designed to prevent procurement decisions being based on political factors.

"The US had promised there would be amendments, but these simply haven't happened," said one Brussels official yesterday.

The call for a panel also reflects growing concern in Europe over the increasing tendency of the US to impose sanctions, often with extraterritorial effects.

The EU and US narrowly avoided a damaging clash this year over the Helms-Burton anti-Cuba law and the Iran-Libya Sanctions Act.

Massachusetts insists the law is not unconstitutional, and has called the NFTC action an attack on state sovereignty by wealthy companies motivated by greed. It points to the success of sanctions in forcing political change in countries such as South Africa.

● The UK has called on its EU partners to take further steps to support Burma's opposition leader, Aung San Suu Kyi, including fresh discouragement on trade, investment and tourism and new visa restrictions for Burmese citizens, **adds Peter Montagnon, Asia Editor, in London.**

Derek Fatchett, UK Foreign Office minister, condemned the latest detentions of opposition figures. He said he had raised with other EU countries the possibility of a top-level mission to see Ms Suu Kyi and other opposition figures and to establish dialogue with the regime.

The EU and Japan fight Massachusetts in the WTO

Source: Financial Times, *10 September 1998*

These campaigns have also helped to focus attention on the role of ethnic groups as influences on both domestic and foreign policy. In particular, there has been considerable speculation as to the impact of the United States' changing demographic profile on the character of its external relations. Figures from the US Census Bureau suggest that by 2050, the non-Hispanic white population will have declined from 75 per cent to 53 per cent of the population whilst Hispanic groups will have increased from 9 per cent to 21 per cent and Asian and Pacific groups will have increased from 3 per cent to 11 per cent. Interpretations of the consequences of such changes vary. Coker, for example, has suggested that they present significant challenges to America's place in the world:

> It is not that American society is disintegrating but that it is being transformed into something quite different, with all the attendant violence and loss of orientation which the transmutation of any society brings in its wake. Transform itself America will have to, if it is to play a significant role in the twenty-first century.
>
> (Coker, 1992, p.420)

Others point to the inherent diversity of the Hispanic and Asian-Pacific communities, their lack of political influence (even in California where the latter make up some 10 per cent of the population) and question whether ethnic origin is any guide to international orientations. Nevertheless, whatever the future holds, it is the case that US society has witnessed a growing interaction between the ethnic groups which constitute it and the agenda of world politics that offers such groups anxious to use them increasing opportunities to achieve their goals at all levels of political activity (Dumbrell, 1990, pp.176–81). Alongside this, other demographic changes have had a significant impact on US foreign policy. Population movements from the north-east to the Sunbelt have, it is suggested, enhanced the Asian-Pacific dimension of US foreign policy, and by the mid-1990s the experiences of Vietnam were replacing those of the Second World War as the dominant events affecting the international perceptions of significant elements of the population (Haass, 1997, p.15).

SUMMARY

Summarizing the points made in this section, we have seen that the processes linking globalization of the policy agenda on the one hand and localization on the other have been underpinned by the following major developments:

- the globalization of the US economy and the responses to this at both national and local levels;

- a creeping sense of economic 'decline' as the impact of international economic challenges are felt by various domestic constituencies;

- the opportunity offered to a range of groups and individuals to pursue their concerns at both the local and the international levels, thereby linking domestic and foreign policy issues.

What consequences have these factors, together with trends discussed earlier in the chapter, had on the conduct of public policy?

5 THE FOREIGN-DOMESTIC NEXUS AND THE POLICY PROCESS

The twin processes of globalization and localization outlined above have contributed towards the profound changes which have occurred in the foreign policy process. More accurately, they have helped to meld together the spheres of domestic and foreign policy and in so doing, have altered the role of institutions and agencies in both areas. In this section, the main focus is on Congress and the patterns of relationships between the federal government and the states as the latters' international interests have developed.

The background to what might be regarded as the growing localization of foreign policy or the globalization of domestic policy has to be seen in the context of the broader relationship between domestic politics and foreign policy. In the immediate post-war years, the existence of a dominant security threat in the shape, firstly, of the Soviet Union and then a perceived global communist challenge provided a focus, coherence and legitimacy to US foreign policy expressed in the evolving concept of 'containment'.

To a considerable degree, this masked a growing list of domestic problems embracing education, health care, civil rights, urban decay, to be joined later by the challenges posed by drug addiction and law and order, in urgent need of attention. However, as the external threat became more ambiguous in its character with the decrease in tensions marked by various phases of *détente*, so the domestic agenda became more prominent. The Reagan years (1981–1989) disguised the growing pressures confronting Washington by resurrecting the Cold War and focusing attention on reinforcing American military power. Not only did this fail to address these compelling domestic issues, it succeeded in enhancing them by adding the burdens of budget and trade deficits and associated indebtedness. As the 'New Cold War' of the first Reagan Administration was replaced by a renewed relaxation of tensions with the USSR during the second, so the domestic agenda with its attendant demands on the administration stood in stark relief. During the Bush Administration (1989–1993), the collapse of the USSR simply served to weaken further the conceptual framework underpinning post-war US foreign policy, ensuring that President George Bush, despite the uncertain triumphs in the Gulf War, would be judged on his domestic record and found wanting. Significantly, Bill Clinton's 1992 campaign focused on economic and social issues rather than foreign policy, a pattern largely repeated in 1996.

A decreasing security threat, a more hostile economic environment and growing domestic pressures on the White House have brought about fundamental changes in the relationships between political institutions and, thereby, the processes of which they are part. At the most general level, this has resulted in an increasing pluralism in foreign policy making. The 'national security state' established during Truman's presidency weakened under the twin pressures of diminished external threat and internal dissatisfaction and disillusion with the institutional frameworks which that threat had created. This pluralism was no more clearly manifested than in the reassertion of a congressional role in foreign relations.

5.1 CONGRESS

During the period of US ascendancy in the international system — indeed, since its entry into the Second World War — Congress played a largely subservient role to the executive in the conduct of foreign policy. This was not the case by the 1970s and 1980s, two decades in which Capitol Hill came to assert its influence over, and took a direct hand in, the conduct of foreign policy. In part, this reflected the growing plurality of influences on foreign relations generated by the more relaxed atmosphere in superpower relations produced by the Nixon-Kissinger era of *détente*. At the same time it was stimulated by a growing unease at the growth of presidential power in the conduct of foreign policy, particularly in the context of the war in Vietnam. Of course, this was greatly enhanced by the erosion of presidential authority resulting from the Watergate scandal, but it was the Ford (1974–1977) rather than the Nixon Administration (1969–1974) which reaped the harvest of congressional interventionism. As the following comment from Henry Kissinger's memoirs indicates, he viewed this development in highly negative terms:

> The Congress progressively weakened the constraints on Soviet conduct without providing us with the tools to see it through in the form of increased defence ... It was a part of a larger pattern — the product of the Vietnam trauma and the corrosion of Watergate — that stripped away both the incentives and penalties needed to conduct an effective policy toward Moscow.
>
> (Kissinger, 1982, p.255)

Bearing in mind the experience of the 1974 Jackson-Vanik amendment which sought to use congressional influence over trade policy to pressure Moscow to allow Jewish emigration from the USSR, one can appreciate his irritation. This was a relatively minor excursion into the realms of foreign policy, however, when compared with the 1973 War Powers Resolution, followed in 1974 by the War Powers Act. This attempted to put into place clear procedures which the president would need to follow in order to deploy US troops in a fighting war. It is not our purpose here to examine the application of the Act in the various circumstances that have arisen since its passage, but the experience of the Reagan Administration in committing troops to Grenada and the Lebanon in 1983 demonstrated the weaknesses inherent in the Act. Nevertheless, events since the Ford and Carter Administrations have shown how the domestic political consensus which underpinned US foreign policy in the years of its international ascendancy began to evaporate as its role looked increasingly uncertain in a more challenging environment.

Congressional assertiveness was, moreover, to be reinforced by the globalization of the US economy described earlier in this chapter. To understand the connection here, it is necessary to recall the experience of the inter-war years and the protectionist policies implemented by Congress, symbolized by the 1930 Smoot Hawley Act. The common perception that it was such legislation which had plunged the international community into a downward spiral of tit-for-tat protectionist measures, helps to explain why, from the Roosevelt Administration onwards, Capitol Hill sought, in co-operation with the White House, to divert the domestic political pressures bearing down on it from economic interests that tariff-setting naturally produces. In the post-war environment, the consensus in favour of free trade combined with practices which insulated Congress from domestic trade policy pressures and the obvious dominance which the US economy enjoyed, created a situation in which trade was not a major source of political conflict.

This consensus began to erode during the 1970s as the economic power of the United States weakened. Not surprisingly, the emergence of a trade deficit in 1971, even though this was balanced by returns from large overseas investments, alarmed Congress because it affected economic interests selectively. Those firms and workers most vulnerable to foreign imports not unnaturally pressured their congressional representatives to act on their behalf. Not only did the belief grow on Capitol Hill that the Commerce Department was consistently undervaluing the challenge to the economy that the trade deficit posed, but the conviction that this was the result of unfair competition on the part of America's trading partners also gained acceptance. In particular, during the 1980s, the accusatory finger pointed to the Japanese, seen as the arch-perpetrators of 'mercantilist' policies designed to penetrate foreign markets in an aggressive fashion whilst denying others access to their domestic market.

Two factors underscored the growing sensitivity of Congress to international trade issues. Firstly, there was the fluctuating value of the dollar. During the period 1980–1985, the dollar rose dramatically in value, making US goods more expensive overseas and foreign imports cheaper at home. Second, the success of the GATT as a framework within which trade liberalization could be negotiated lessened as new power centres outside the Euro-Atlantic theatre emerged. A more diverse set of players made trade rules harder to devise.

Moreover, the agenda of trade negotiations began to shift during the 1970s from reducing tariffs to the far more difficult — and in domestic terms more politically sensitive — problem, of non-tariff barriers to trade (NTBs). Here, the issues were complex, touching on such practices as government procurement, product standards and government subsides to specific industries. In part, this reflected a clash of political cultures and political philosophy. Non-interventionist, free market America confronted countries whose governments operated within a more regulatory, interventionist culture. Thus, for example, practices regarded by Canada (one of the United States' largest trading partners) as being socially desirable for purposes such as regional development, might well be viewed by Congress as unacceptable subsidies disadvantaging American firms.

To these factors were added the transformation of Congress as a political arena. The era of US international dominance was marked by the power wielded within Congress and its committee system by such figures as Senator Arthur Vandenberg, chairman of the Senate Foreign Relations Committee in the early post-war years. During the 1970s, there was a 'revolution' on Capitol Hill whereby power became increasingly decentralized and the role of such figures as Vandenberg was undermined by a new generation of legislators far more attuned to localized politics. Decentralization within both the Senate and the House Foreign Affairs Committees to a proliferation of sub-committees helped to weaken the overall authority of these bodies.

As the political agenda moved increasingly towards domestic issues in the 1980s, membership of the committees appeared to become electoral liabilities rather than sources of power. As Destler has argued, these developments were particularly crucial in their effects on the politics of foreign economic policy. Effectively, the insulation of Congress from the domestic pressures of trade politics was destroyed as legislators responded to the growing protectionist sentiments that were emerging. During 1985 alone, '634 trade bills were introduced of which 99 were directly and seriously protectionist' (Destler, 1986 p.84).

The consequences of these developments and the growing importance of Congress in foreign policy, particularly foreign economic policy, can be seen in its impact on a variety of trade negotiations. It was an influential actor in the negotiation of the Free Trade Agreement between the USA and Canada which came into force in 1989. At one stage it seemed likely that a congressional committee would stall the international negotiations aimed at creating a free trade area embracing Mexico, Canada and the USA (the North American Free Trade Agreement). NAFTA met considerable opposition in Congress. Here the concerns related not only to fears that the deal would result in the loss of jobs in the USA through competition from cheaper labour in Mexico, but also to what many in Congress regarded as lax environmental standards. The NAFTA treaty was finally approved by Congress in November 1993 but only following an extensive lobbying campaign by President Clinton.

A growing concern with the domestic impact of globalization was reinforced by the 1994 congressional elections, which produced a Republican-dominated Congress. The 'Contract with America' made scant reference to foreign policy, and a growing disenchantment with international trade negotiations was reflected in the 1997 refusal to renew the President's authority to conduct such negotiations within the 'fast-track' system designed to smooth their path on Capitol Hill. At the same time, international and domestic issues were becoming increasingly entangled. Thus legislation introduced in 1998 to provide the International Monetary Fund with an additional $18 billion to deal with the consequences of the Asian financial crisis was held up in the House of Representatives, in part because of the growing links between social policy issues — such as abortion — and foreign policy. Alongside this, there was a strengthening of the congressional impulse to employ economic sanctions as a foreign policy tool (for example, the 1996 Helms-Burton Act directed at Cuba and its trading partners), to the increasing concern of both US and foreign businesses (Haass, 1998).

In short, the changing international context in which United States' foreign relations were conducted interacted with major shifts in the domestic political scene. Congress's growing assertiveness in the foreign policy sphere reflected, on the one hand, the disappearance of the intense bipolarity of the early Cold War years. Under any circumstances, the logical consequence of this was likely to be a policy process more open to domestic influences. But when to this was added the twin forces of unease at the fundamental character of foreign policy and the way in which it was conducted together with domestic pressures generated by a more competitive international economy, then the linkages between foreign and domestic policy were, inevitably, strengthened. It was not only at the centre that such pressures occurred, however, but also in the regional communities comprising the United States and their institutional voices at state and local levels.

5.2 STATES AND LOCALITIES

The constitutional position of the states in the conduct of US foreign relations is clearly defined: 'No state shall, without the consent of Congress ... enter into any agreement or compact with another state, or with a foreign power ...'. However, as we have seen, given the fundamental transformation that has occurred in the nature of foreign policy, particularly the erosion of the divide between the spheres of foreign and domestic policy, constitutional prescriptions of this kind decreasingly accord with reality. One consequence of this process has been to project issues under state control into the sphere of foreign relations, as in the case of environmental diplomacy. Thus the Center for Clean Air policy, established by a group of US State governors in 1985, has pointed to the challenge that global warming poses for all levels of government. Noting the key role of the federal government, the Center's policy statement goes on to argue that it is at the state level that much of the effort to combat global warming must be directed since the states regulate the charges that their utilities levy on their customers, may control the policies of power utilities, and can adopt a variety of measures (for example, through building code standards) to promote energy-saving and conservation of resources (Driver and Nixon, 1989, p.3).

Furthermore, the globalization of the marketplace together with its growing regionalization through the North American Free Trade Agreement, the EU Single Market Programme and other initiatives, has focused attention on the very structure of federalism and the allocation of powers amongst the governments which make up the United States. Here again we are confronted by the consequences of the transformation of foreign policy. When the federal constitution was drafted, the images conjured up by the term 'foreign policy' were far more closely identified with those matters, defence and military security, for which the central government was responsible. As foreign policy came to embrace a broader set of issues, many closely related to the powers and functions of the state governments, the claims of the centre to an exclusive role in the management of foreign relations became more difficult to sustain.

Additionally, during the 1970s against a background of economic uncertainty reinforced by the energy crisis, the US populace appeared to look increasingly to their localities as a source of economic security where Washington often appeared incapable of action. With the moves towards regional trading blocs such as the EU, however, the fragmentation of the US marketplace itself was highlighted. The plethora of state regulations in the health and safety areas, for example, stand in contrast to the goals of a Single European Market. When the Secretary of the Treasury introduced a bill in 1991 to reform the dual banking system incorporating state and federal regulations, he noted the apparent absurdity whereby a bank in California could open a branch in Birmingham, England, but not in Birmingham, Alabama. Increasingly, then, globalization is having an impact on the fundamental structures of US government with its traditional assumptions as to 'who does what' in the processes of policy making.

As the barriers between domestic and foreign policy have been breached and state and local governments have come to acquire an 'international voice', considerable attention has been paid within the United States to what is sometimes referred to as 'local foreign policy'. This usage is not usually intended to suggest that subnational governments are usurping Washington's prerogatives in the conduct of foreign policy (although there are some observers who tend towards this position). Rather, the reality is that state and local governments are finding their interests determined as much by events in the international as the national environment and that, consequently, they seek either to influence national policy on external issues bearing on those interests or, in some circumstances, to become international actors themselves. We have just examined a fundamental factor underlying this development, namely the internationalization of what were once regarded as intrinsically domestic issues. But there are other considerations which need to be taken into account.

One of these is the growth in local activism discussed earlier in the chapter. On a range of issues, from nuclear weapons, South Africa and Northern Ireland to the campaigns directed towards the Swiss banks and Burma, local and state governments have been encouraged to adopt policy stances by vocal groups who see local politics as one means by which foreign policy issues can be addressed. This can have the effect of creating internal centres of opposition to national policy which, whilst in no sense constituting rival foreign policies, can have the effect of reducing the capacity of the federal government to pursue its objectives, and greatly complicate the conduct of external relations.

However, it is in the areas of foreign trade and investment that state and local governments have assumed a growing role. Just as a more competitive international economic environment has stimulated congressional interest in trade policy, so at the local level the impact of global economic forces has encouraged governments to devise methods of ameliorating their impact on the local economy. In this context it should be remembered that the developments outlined above had varying effects on regions within the United States. Thus in high technology industries, the trade surplus grew during the 1970s whilst regions dominated by more traditional industries, the so-called 'rustbelt' states such as Michigan — saw their industrial base decline and unemployment escalate.

The response of the states has been vigorous as they have attempted to counter the effects of economic decline. The chairman of the National Governors' Association described the changing role of the states in the following terms: 'Twenty years ago, states were bystanders as international events changed the economic landscape. That, too, has changed. Our boundaries are no longer the borders of our states, but every corner of the globe. As Governors, we are challenged to confront this new reality' (National Governors' Association, 1989, iv).

The main manifestations of state activism lie in trade promotion and investment attraction. Figures from the National Association of State Development Agencies indicate that during the fiscal year 1987–1988 state expenditure on trade development increased by 195 per cent and that the average state budget devoted to such activities rose by 141 per cent between 1984 and 1988. Part of the states' strategy has been to open overseas offices: between 1986 and 1994 these increased from 66 to 162 (National Association of State Development Agencies, 1995, pp.5–6). The state governors have become active advocates of regional economic interests. Governors from 27 states made 81 overseas visits related to economic development in 1993 (Fry, 1998, p.69).

A similar, frenetic level of activity has marked the quest for scarce foreign investment. Whereas trade promotion has encouraged co-operative ventures amongst groups of states, attempts to persuade foreign firms to locate in a particular state have generated battles as states seek to outbid each other in offering incentives. Robert Reich provides one example of the results that this can produce: Hyster, the US forklift truck manufacturer, having announced to the five states and four countries in which it operated that some plants would be closed, succeeded in acquiring $72.5 million in aid from the various jurisdictions involved (Reich, 1991, pp. 295–6). Similarly, another study of foreign investment found that Kentucky had, effectively, paid an incentive cost to Toyota of $108,000 per job created to move to the state (Glickman and Woodward, 1989, pp.241–4).

State foreign economic interests have inevitably extended from trade promotion and foreign investment to trade policy making. One manifestation of this trend is the development of local foreign trade policies. These, we have already seen, reflect a growing willingness of state and local governments to exploit the economic linkages created by globalization, as in the case of Massachusetts's Burma sanctions legislation and the campaign

Georgia.
Europe's New U.S. Headquarters.

Over 500 companies from nearly twenty European countries are located in Georgia. A primary reason is that our state is in the center of the Southeast, the fastest growing region in all of the United States.

Atlanta's Hartsfield International Airport, the world's busiest, means you can get here in a matter of hours on a direct flight from most European business centers. And our airport also means your products and services are just two hours away from 80% of the U.S. population. To complete a highly efficient transportation system, we've developed two advanced deep water ports, as well as excellent rail and highway systems that provide quick access to the free world's largest market.

Georgia's government does everything possible to make European firms feel at home, too. Our corporate tax rate hasn't increased since 1969. The costs of land, construction and labor in Georgia are among the nation's lowest. Yet the productivity growth rate of our work force is 36% higher than the U.S. average.

To learn all the other reasons why Georgia is the successful U.S. location for hundreds of European businesses, contact Bill Hulbert, Managing Director, European Office, Georgia Department of Industry and Trade, 380 Avenue Louise, 1050 Brussels, Belgium; phone 32-2-647-7825.

GEORGIA
The International State

State activism in action

directed against the Swiss banks. More commonly, however, they are the expression at the local level of the protectionist sentiments which have become so visible in Congress. Some states have operated 'buy-American' laws for decades (despite questions as to their legality) and these began to proliferate during the 1970s. The State Department, a vehement opponent of the practice, estimated that by 1981, thirty-two states had adopted such legislation. Not surprisingly, as the trade agenda has shifted from tariff reduction to non-tariff barriers, the galaxy of NTBs operated by state governments, such as government procurement, have commanded increasing attention, both from the federal government and from America's trading partners such as the European Union. Despite unilateral and multilateral agreements to limit 'buy-American' legislation at state and local levels, some states (for example, New Jersey) continue to maintain such legislation in specific areas.

Beyond local action, however, the states have developed a keen interest in the shaping of national foreign trade policy. A briefing document for state governors issued by the National Governors' Association is indicative of the trend:

> A governor's role in the making of US trade policy is that of a participant in the national debate on the issues. Governors participate through direct lobbying of Congress and the White House regarding their state's needs, through membership on various intergovernmental trade policy advisory committees, through co-operation with other Governors at the national level (NGA), and through their work with federal agencies.
>
> (National Governors' Association, 1986, p.4)

The role of states in the trade policy area depends on several factors, not least the resources available to exercise influence. Not surprisingly, California, a major actor in the world economy, is an influential player in US trade policy. Alone amongst the states it maintains a full-time trade policy adviser in Washington, and the guides to international trade issues produced by the California World Trade Commission are impressive documents. (Its guide to the Uruguay Round was used by the US GATT negotiating team in Geneva as a key study of the potential impact of the negotiations on American industry.)

The policy and research section of the California World Trade Commission also works with industry to promote changes in trade policy as in the case of the electronics industry's campaign to have US export controls on 'dual-use' products such as personal computers relaxed. In this instance, the CWTC helped to establish, in conjunction with electronics industry leaders, a set of priorities for reforming US export controls, including an enhanced level of involvement of the Commerce Department in the licensing process and the transference of munitions control administration from the Department of State to Commerce.

In recent years, however, there has been a greater emphasis on the role of the states in enhancing US competitiveness in the global marketplace, as is made clear by the following statement by a former governor of Virginia, Gerald Baliles, in the context of growing US awareness of the potential significance of the European Single Market Programme (SMP):

> EC '92 is a clarion call for the states. It signifies the growing interdependence of the world economy or, in essence, the unity of the international economy. State governments, with their unique degree of flexibility, creativity and accountability, are best poised to answer this call and serve the needs of our public now and into the future.
>
> (quoted in Hocking and Smith, 1997, p.97)

In the late 1980s and early 1990s state development agencies played a significant role in alerting local business communities to the significance of the SMP. As in a number of other states, the Division of International Trade of the New Jersey Department of Commerce and Economic Development, in co-operation with KPMG Peat Marwick, produced a guide to the SMP for New Jersey Business. In Tennessee, the Tennessee–European Economic Alliance, a public–private sector joint venture, sought to build public awareness of the significance of the SMP and the possibilities for business in the state.

Inevitably, there are some misgivings amongst federal officials at the growing trade activism on the part of the states. These misgivings were most obvious in the context of state and local involvement in the campaign against the Swiss banks. But it has to be recalled that it is, at least in part, a reflection of the policies pursued by successive administrations. The Carter Administration actively encouraged the participation of the states in trade promotion. The 'New Federalism' of the Reagan era reinforced the trend and enhanced it by reducing federal expenditure in the area. During the 1980s, the initiative for economic development appeared to pass to the states (Fosler, 1988). Certainly, the United States and Foreign Commercial Service recognizes the need for partnership between the federal and state governments.

The picture is more uncertain in the trade policy area but even here, the impact of the growing foreign-domestic nexus on the conduct of all levels of public policy means that the need to involve domestic interests in foreign economic policy is an increasingly compelling reality if the outcome of international negotiations are to be accepted by those they affect at home. Indeed, the problem for federal trade negotiators may frequently be not so much limiting state and local involvement in trade policy issues but encouraging an intelligent interest in them so that international deals — as in the case of the North American Free Trade Agreement linking the USA, Canada and Mexico — will not unravel in the face of opposition from regional economic constituencies.

5.3 THE GROWTH OF FOREIGN INTEREST LOBBYING

The fact that the conduct of US foreign relations is now open to a greater plurality of influences demands that actors on the international stage operate within this more diffuse framework. Increasingly, governments, international business and the vast proliferation of non-governmental bodies have recognized that the route to political influence lies not through the White House but, in many contexts, Congress and even the states. Consequently, foreign interest lobbying has become big business: in 1988 it was estimated that 152 Japanese companies and government agencies employed 113 lobbying firms to represent them in Washington, paying more than $100 million dollars for their services. The use of professional lobbyists is most often dictated by the need to gain information and to devise strategies whereby objectives can be attained in an increasingly complex political milieu; in short, to guide those who are unfamiliar with them through the mysteries of a foreign political terrain.

In one sense, the desire to exercise influence in these domestic political arenas reflects the continuing importance of the United States, yet it is often interpreted as one manifestation of weakness and decline. Not only is the US economy being threatened by external forces, these same forces are subverting the political system itself. So runs the argument. Much attention here has focused on the activities of former government employees, such as Robert Strauss, previously United States Trade Representative, who have subsequently established themselves as lobbyists. The fear has been voiced that foreign interests — especially the Japanese — monopolize the lobbying networks in the United States, have more influence over senior government officials than do subordinate officials within departments and, even, are determining key trade policy appointments.

These fears rest, ultimately, on the belief that such foreign interest lobbying is distinct from domestic political lobbying and that it threatens, in some sense, 'national security'. Clearly there are problems here; the activities of former public servants turned political lobbyists may well pose ethical dilemmas. However, the realities underlying many instances of foreign interest lobbying simply reflect the fact that globalization has created far more disparate patterns of relationships in which it is often hard to differentiate domestic from foreign interests.

One example is provided by the dispute over unitary taxation which focused on the attempt by some state governments to tax the profits of subsidiaries of foreign owned corporations on the basis of their global earnings, rather than those generated within the state. Needless to say, this was highly unpopular within the international business community and prompted the launching of a highly sophisticated transnational lobbying campaign in which British interests played a leading role. What is interesting from the viewpoint of the present discussion is the interpenetration of foreign and US interests. Generally, during the 1980s, the US federal authorities, particularly the Treasury, shared a

Mexico 'spending $30m' to boost Nafta in US

By Nancy Dunne and Lisa Bransten in Washington

MEXICO is to spend as much as $30m (£19.4m) on lobbying efforts by the end of this year, to try to ensure the passage of the North American Free Trade Agreement, according to the Centre for Public Integrity in Washington.

"Mexico has employed a veritable phalanx of Washington law firms, lobbyists, public relations companies and consultants," said Mr Charles Lewis, executive director of the Centre, which draws about 10 per cent of its support from labour unions.

Basing its conclusions on an eight-month analysis of Justice Department records, researchers found that 33 former US officials had been hired by Mexico to try to ensure the implementing legislation for Nafta gets congressional approval. Among those working for Mexico are former US trade representative Bill Brock and former analyst for the International Trade Commission Ruth Kurtz.

The report is the latest snag in the Clinton administration's efforts to sell Nafta to Congress.

Negotiations among the three governments on labour and environmental supplemental agreements are now stalled over a US proposal to allow trade sanctions against companies which demonstrate a pattern of failure to enforce environmental laws. However, Mr Mickey Kantor, the US trade representative, said this week he still expected to complete negotiations this summer.

The most serious threat to Nafta may come from Mr Ross Perot, the former presidential candidate, whose "infomercial" against the accord is due to run nationwide on television on Sunday night. Mr Perot's folksy presentations have done much to arouse fear that Nafta will draw jobs from the US to Mexico.

While many Democrats are in open rebellion against Nafta, Republican senators and some business groups are threatening to oppose it if the president succeeds in negotiating strong side agreements.

Union leaders, meanwhile, have given no sign that they will be satisfied by the proposed tripartite commission on labour standards, which the side pact would establish.

Congress, lobbyists and US trade policy
Source: Financial Times, *28 May 1993*

common concern with overseas business interests in seeing this policy ended. Even at the state level, politicians and government agencies were divided, some fearing that unitary taxation would deter foreign investors. In brief, this was an issue on which foreign and American interests coalesced in ways which made it as much an exercise in conflicting domestic political priorities as an insidious exercise of foreign influence.

A second example is to be found in the case of Congress's attempts to penalize the Japanese company Toshiba for selling American-designed milling machines — used in the production of submarine propellers — to the USSR. The Senate proceeded to cut off Toshiba's US markets, estimated to be in the order of $2.5 million per annum. It soon became apparent to members of Congress, however, that they were dealing with a global industry, not an individual company. Thus Capitol Hill rang to the complaints of representatives of US industry — firms such as Tektronix and Hewlett-Packard — dependent on Toshiba products, particularly semiconductors, or which sold Toshiba goods under their own brand labels.

In the face of this pressure it was not surprising that by April 1988 congressional 'punishment' of Toshiba had been reduced to an annual ceiling of $200 million on its sales in America. The pattern of events clearly surprised most of those involved, including Toshiba, who had not appreciated how closely its interests were linked to those of American companies. They also demonstrated in dramatic fashion the extent to which lobbying on behalf of domestic and foreign interests can become part of a political campaign in which the interests of each are inseparable.

> *SUMMARY*
>
> Given the concerns within the United States at growing foreign economic influence, especially from Japan, it is not surprising that the exercise of influence by foreign interests within the various arenas of US politics should reinforce the sense of external threat and vulnerability so clearly expressed in much contemporary commentary. But rather than viewing this phenomenon as a natural outgrowth of the continuing significance of the USA both in political and economic terms, it has been widely regarded as yet another symbol of 'decline'. In fact, it is possible to view the desire of foreign governments and other actors to influence US policy as symptomatic of the developments with which this section of the chapter have been concerned. These can be summarized as:
>
> - the growing plurality of actors involved in the shaping and conduct of US foreign policy as the challenges posed by the threat of global communism became more ambiguous;
> - as a result, the reassertion of a congressional role in foreign policy stimulated by an unease at the conduct of foreign policy, especially in Indo-China, underscored by the loss of confidence in the presidency generated by the Watergate scandal;
> - the emergence of an international voice on the part of state and local government particularly, although not exclusively, in the sphere of foreign economic policy.
>
> In other words, foreign interest lobbying is one logical consequence of the general theme with which the chapter is concerned; namely, the growing interaction between foreign policy and domestic politics in a political system marked by its openness and the diversity of points of access available to those desiring to influence the shaping of public policy.

6 CONCLUSION

The dominant position of the United States in the immediate post-war international system was underscored by the immediacy of the external threat presented by the onset of the Cold War, its economic ascendancy and the relative insulation of external policy from domestic pressures that these factors helped to create. Consequently, Washington's leadership role in the emerging bipolar order was reinforced by both an international consensus amongst its alliance partners and bipartisanship at the domestic level.

As this hegemonial position began to erode, so the picture altered dramatically. As we have seen, this has been due in part to a general transformation in the character of foreign policy, the result of growing global interdependence, which has weakened the traditional distinction between foreign and domestic policy. Accompanying this, however, there were factors peculiar to the United States.

Firstly, the diminishing external threat accompanying the phases of *détente* combined with a growing sense of unease regarding US foreign policy produced by the conflict in Indo-China. Second, American economic supremacy of the early post-war period gradually disappeared. In retrospect, it was hardly likely that it could be sustained at those levels indefinitely. But the emergence of rival centres of economic power in the shape of the EC, Japan and the 'newly industrializing countries' of the Asia-Pacific region, provided not only economic competition but a growing sense that the USA might be entering a period of decline. In turn, this was strengthened by concern with the political process. The presidency was weakened by the experience of Watergate and the belief that, in general terms, the constructive tensions marking executive-legislative relations had deteriorated into 'gridlock' whereby the pressing domestic issues, for long subordinated to the imperatives of foreign relations, could not be addressed. Attempts by the Reagan Administration to alleviate this problem by re-inventing the Cold War in the early 1980s collapsed under the weight, firstly, of its economic consequences as trade and budget deficits soared and then, ironically, the virtual disappearance of the threat itself.

Against this background, domestic politics and foreign policy came together and re-awakened a traditional American concern with vulnerability; but a vulnerability which now embraced not simply the traditional issues of military security but also economic security. As domestic constituencies were alerted to the pressures bearing down on them from the international environment, so the interactions between domestic politics and foreign relations were strengthened. Not only did foreign policy become a more diffused activity at the centre, it also became 'localized' as regional interests and their local representatives responded to the challenges and opportunities that these developments presented.

At the century's end, this growing nexus between foreign policy and domestic politics presents the United States with a considerable challenge. This is partly constituted by the fact that relative economic decline has not made the USA the 'ordinary country' that commentators of the 1970s suggested. On the contrary, part of its problem derives from the fact that, in the post-Cold War environment, in many senses it remains an extraordinary country, possessing considerable power resources and the object of intense international pressures. Yet, at the same time, it is a society beset by tremendous social problems which encourage self-examination and introspection. The preoccupation with 'decline' which became such a feature of this condition in the late 1980s is symbolic of the problem. In this sense debates about whether the statistical evidence of economic decline supports the case or not are almost irrelevant. It is what the public perceives to be true that becomes significant.

Looking at the situation in a positive vein, it is, of course, possible to argue that enhanced linkages between foreign and domestic policy are a positive feature. Indeed, at a time when the fundamental character of US foreign policy stands in need of conceptual re-evaluation, it may be that a closer dialogue between the broad community of interests that make up American society and those who shape that policy is a step towards the emergence of a new consensus akin to that which underpinned the policy of containment in the late 1940s. The problem is that the domestic debate may well, in misunderstanding the root causes of the changed American place in the world, perceive the future in terms of choices which do not exist. Decline is not to be reversed by neo-isolationism; the United States is too enmeshed in the webs spun by the global economy for that to be an option. Rather, the challenge is to determine an appropriate American role in a changing interdependent world. Ultimately, this turns on the resources of the political system to produce innovatary policies as the authors of one study of the dilemmas confronting Washington suggest:

> The alternative of selective engagement and co-operative introversion requires a skill, creativity and imagination that are hindered by a fragmented, acrimonious political system which places a premium on short-term results, not long-term visions. In these circumstances, the balance between international obligations and domestic needs seems more likely to swing toward parochial competitiveness than towards the maintenance of the altruistic self-interest which has characterized US policies towards Western Europe since the late 1940s.
>
> (Williams *et al.*, 1993, p.17)

At its most fundamental level, the problem lies in the traditional interaction between the character of American society, its political culture and the relationships it maintains with the world around it. As often noted, US foreign policy has swung between the belief that its values could best be protected by insulating itself against the external forces bearing down on it and, alternatively, the conviction that this goal could be achieved by re-shaping the world in its own image. The first strategy is no longer a viable one: the second demands a certainty regarding what is to be secured and a domestic environment capable of securing it in a world where power is diffused and hegemony the property of no one country.

REFERENCES

Benedick, R.E. (1991) *Ozone Diplomacy: New Directions in Safeguarding the Planet*, Cambridge Massachusetts, Harvard University Press.

Bilder, R.B. (1989) 'The role of states and cities in foreign relations', *American Journal of International Law*, 83.

Clinton, B.J. (1993) 'Inaugural address', 20 January 1993, *The Times*, 21 January.

Coker, C. (1992) 'Britain and the new world order: the special relationship in the 1990s', *International Affairs*, 68 (3).

Cuomo, M. (1993) Press conference reported in *The Sunday Times*, 28 February.

Destler, I.M. (1986) *American Trade Politics: System Under Stress*, Washington, DC, Institute for International Economics, NY, Twentieth Century Fund.

Destler, I.M. (1995) *American Trade Politics*, Washington, DC, Institute for International Economics, and New York, NY, Twentieth Century Fund (3rd edn).

Driver, B. and Nixon, E. (1989) *Healing the Environment: State Options for Addressing Global Warming*, Washington, Center for Clean Air Policy.

Dumbrell, J. with Barrett, D. (1990) *The Making of US Foreign Policy*, Manchester, Manchester University Press.

Fosler, R.S. (1988) *The New Economic Role of American States: Strategies in a Competitive World Economy*, New York, Oxford University Press.

Fry, E.H. (1998) *The Expanding Role of State and Local Governments in US Foreign Affairs*, New York, NY, Council on Foreign Relations.

Glickman, N.J. and Woodward, D.P. (1989) *The New Competitors: How Foreign Investors are Changing the US Economy*, New York, Basic Books.

Haass, R.N. (1997) *The Reluctant Sheriff: the United States After the Cold War*, New York, NY, Council on Foreign Relations.

Haass, R.N. (ed.) (1998) *Economic Sanctions and American Diplomacy*, New York, NY, Council on Foreign Relations.

Hocking, B. and Smith, M. (1997) *Beyond Foreign Economic Policy: the United States, the Single European Market and the Changing World Economy*, London, Pinter.

Kennedy, P. (1987) *The Rise and Fall of the Great Power: Economic Change and Military Conflict from 1500 to 2000*, New York, Random House.

Kissinger, H. (1982) *Years of Upheaval*, London, Weidenfeld and Nicolson and Michael Joseph.

Liner, B. (1990) 'States and localities in the global market place', *Intergovernmental Perspective*, 16(2).

Love, J. (1985) *The U.S. Anti-Apartheid Movement: Local Activism in Global Politics*, New York, Praegar.

Luard, E. (1990) *The Globalization of Politics: the Changed Focus of Political Action in the Modern World*, London Macmillan.

National Association of State Development Agencies (1995) *State Export Program Database, 1994*, Washington, DC.

National Governors' Association (1986) *Program Brief: International Trade, Office of State Services*, Washington, DC., National Governors' Association.

National Governors' Association (1989) *America in Transition: the International Frontier; Report of the Task Force on Foreign Markets*, Washington, DC., National Governors' Association.

Nye Jr, J.S. (1990) *Bound to Lead: the Changing Nature of American Power*, New York, Basic Books.

Reich, R.B. (1991) *The Work of Nations: Preparing Ourselves for 21st-Century Capitalism*, New York, Knopf.

Shuman, M.H. (1986) 'Dateline Main Street: local foreign policies', *Foreign Policy*, 65.

Spero, J.E. (1990) *The Politics of International Economic Relations* (fourth edition), London, Unwin Hyman.

Williams, P., Hammond, P. and Brenner, M. (1993) 'Atlantis lost, paradise regained? The US and Western Europe after the Cold War', *International Affairs*, 69(1).

FURTHER READING

Cohen, S.D., Paul, J.R. and Blecker, R.A. (1996) *Fundamentals of US Foreign Trade Policy: Economics, Politics, Laws and Issues*, Boulder, Col., Westview.

Destler, I.M. (1995) *American Trade Politics*, Washington, DC, Institute for International Economics, and New York, NY, Twentieth Century Fund (3rd edn).

Dumbrell, J. and Barrett, D. (1990) *The Making of US Foreign Policy*, Manchester, Manchester University Press.

Fry, E.H. (1998) *The Expanding Role of State and Local Governments in US Foreign Affairs*, New York, NY, Council on Foreign Relations.

Glickman, N.J. and Woodward, D.P. (1988) *The New Competitors: How Foreign Investors are Changing the US Economy*, New York, Basic Books.

Haass, R.N. (1997) *The Reluctant Sheriff: the United States after the Cold War*, New York, NY, Council on Foreign Relations.

Haass, R.N. (1998) *Economic Sanctions and American Diplomacy*, New York, NY, Council on Foreign Relations.

Hocking, B. (1993) *Localizing Foreign Policy: Non-Central Governments and Multilayered Diplomacy*, London, Macmillan.

Hocking, B. and Smith, M. (1997) *Beyond Foreign Economic Policy: the United States, the Single European Market and the Changing World Economy*, London, Pinter.

Love, J. (1985) *The US Anti-Apartheid Movement: Local Activism in Global Politics*, New York, Praegar.

Luttwak, E.N. (1993) *The Endangered American Dream*, New York, Simon & Shuster.

Nye Jr, J.S. (1990) *Bound to Lead: the Changing Nature of American Power*, New York, Basic Books.

Snow, D.M. and Brown, E. (1994) *Puzzle Palaces and Foggy Bottom: US Foreign and Defense Policy-Making in the 1990s*, New York, NY, St Martin's Press.

Tolchin, M. and Tolchin, S. (1989) *Buying into America: How Foreign Money is Changing the Face of Our Nation*, New York, Berkley.

6

THE DEMOCRATIC IMPERATIVE

Michael Foley

1 INTRODUCTION

The United States has always had an ambiguous relationship with the rest of the world. This chapter seeks to examine the implications of America's unsettled, provisional and fluctuating position in what it regards as the outside community of other nations. Following this introduction Section 2 will make a number of observations on the traditionally imprecise connection between the United States and the rest of the world. It will acknowledge America's self-conscious exceptionalism both as a nation apart from other nations and as an exemplar of Western principles and enlightenment aspirations.

Section 3 will examine the United State's historic allegiance to those liberal democratic ideas which are widely assumed to be both the agent and the object of America's national identity. It will study the way in which the democratic culture of the United States is seen to be the natural outcome of indigenous social dynamics and political developments. It will also acknowledge the implicit potential of such values to provide an evaluative frame of reference for American behaviour abroad.

Sections 4 and 5 will assess in general terms the different relationships between the United States' domestic characteristics and the external realm of international relations. Section 4 will appraise the ways in which American values have been translated into the manner and conduct of foreign policy. Section 5, on the other hand, will describe the ways in which 'the world' outside has acted as an independent variable upon American perspectives and policies.

Section 6 will trace these historical tensions through to present day problems in contemporary foreign policy. It will illustrate and analyse a number of procedural and substantive points of friction that continue to characterize the United States' position within the international community.

The seventh and final section will examine America's traditions and perspectives in the context of the collapse of communism and the onset of the post-Cold War world.

2 THE USA AND THE EXTERNAL WORLD

America's outlook upon the world has always been coloured by its conviction that whilst it is self-evidently *in* the world, it remains equally convinced that it is not *of* the world. Its identity remains strongly dependent upon the conception that America is separate from, and different to, everywhere else. Americans take pride in the fact that their society was formed and developed by multitudes of settlers who sought emancipation from previous conditions of European destitution and oppression through the simple recourse of physical flight to the protean expanse of America's 'virgin lands'. 'New' rapidly became the leitmotif of everything American. The American was the 'new man who acts on new principles' (St John de Crevecoeur quoted in Lerner, 1958, p.61). America itself was a new world of disaggregated peoples from other nations reconstituted into an alternative nation by nothing other than their collective experience of America. As a consequence, 'the United States may properly claim the title of the first new nation. It was the first major colony successfully to break away from colonial rule through revolution' (Lipset, 1979, p.15). This was more than a simple act of political independence. It provided public evidence that the peculiar dynamics of both America's social organization and its geographical isolation were sufficient to defeat the British army and, thereby, to defy the authority of a major power. America's successful declaration of independence not only seemed to substantiate a pre-existing separatism in outlook and conditions, but served to fuse America's early consciousness of itself and its purposes with an act of violent rebellion against a European superpower. The implications of spatial distance were in effect turned into a form of political distance.

This forceful and unexpected emancipation would have profound implications for America and the rest of the world. America was now established as the 'new world' in several senses: 'America was new in nature, new in people, new in experience, new in history. Nothing had prepared the old world for what now confronted it fearfully, alluringly, and implacably' (Commager, 1978, p.64). America was no longer merely an asylum for European dissenters, it began to see itself as a prototype new world that could act as a model for the rest of humanity. 'We have it in our power to begin the world over again,' exhorted Tom Paine in 1776. 'A situation, similar to the present, hath not happened since the days of Noah until now. The birth-day of a new world is at hand' (Paine, 1976, p.120). Such sentiments became commonplace during America's subsequent development. They reflected the core conviction that American liberty, democracy and virtue could best be measured and appreciated by a disparaging construction of the old world — namely as a moribund collection of feudal entities wracked by ancient class divisions and dynastic strife, by religious oppression and ethnic hatred and by corrupt government and civil disorder. The propensity towards new world orders also underlined the American belief that in any contact between the United States and the 'old world', it was assumed that the latter would in the end always have to come to terms with the providential and progressive nature of the former. A new world order to an American was a revised international order in the shape of the new world.

These inflated suppositions were not to become relevant in a global sense until the United States itself expanded to a point where its size could match its presumptions. During its first one hundred years, the American republic was almost wholly preoccupied with assimilating the vast land mass of the continent's interior. By purchase, treaty, war and annexation, the United States was rapidly enlarged in size, resources and population. The enormous acquisitions exacerbated pre-existing tensions to the point of a cathartic civil war between the North and the South. The Union Army's victory conclusively established the indissoluble nature of the American federation. It also ensured that the American republic would evolve as an integrated continental entity and, with it, generate the potential to be a world economic and military power. That promise was largely fulfilled in the years of rapid industrialization and urbanization which followed the war. By the turn of the century, the number of businesses had grown to over 1,000,000 from under 250,000 in the 1850s and 1860s. Agricultural employment fell from two-thirds of the labour force in mid century to just one-third by 1900. At the beginning of the twentieth century, the United States had become the world's leading producer of coal, iron ore, pig iron, steel and gold. The enormous potential of its natural resources and its massive internal market, allowed the USA to become an economic giant within a generation. A *laissez faire* economy had produced an essentially *laissez faire* nation centred firmly on the spontaneity and dynamics of America's own purportedly inner directed social experiment and organization. As unprecedented numbers of immigrants poured into the country, the American interior began to swell with towns and cities. At the beginning of the nineteenth century, Thomas Jefferson believed that there would be enough new land to satisfy a thousand generations of settlers. But by 1890, the frontier was officially closed. Within a hundred years, the United States had tripled its land possessions, its population had grown from 5.3 million to 75.9 million and the number of states had increased from 16 to 45.

The United States gave the impression of a nation so absorbed with itself and its own economic and social development, that it inadvertently stumbled out into the world backwards. The outside world was always taken to be dangerous and corrupting, but it was also assumed to be distant and only accessible through choice. America had no consciousness of being a great nation in the sense of constituting one of the major powers. The nation had been formed *in vacuo*, as a nation apart from others. Its greatness, therefore, had come not from any aspirations to gain entry into Europe's power politics, but as a consequence of its internal consolidation and an abhorrence towards being entrapped in the responsibilities and restrictions of any international balances of power. The nation was vindicated by its own aggrandisement. It was conditioned to believe that America was so massive, it could always accommodate its own voracious economic developments without compromising its idiosyncratic status as not merely a new nation but a new kind of nation. In the twentieth century, however, America repeatedly had to come to terms with the ramifications of being an island race set on a subcontinent in a shrinking world.

America's ambivalence towards the old world was compounded by an increasing ambivalence towards itself. America had always felt threatened by the world outside, but as a result of a number of paradoxical developments, the country was also threatened by its own size and composition. For example, the United States had become a nation by being apart from other nations; it had developed as a country by developing away from Europe both culturally and literally by westward expansion. And yet its success in this respect had increasingly brought it back into the orbit of international affairs and the European powers. By cutting itself off so effectively, it had succeeded in generating the growth that undermined its own isolation and brought it into closer contact with outside interests and obligations. Another example of this type of self-generated ambivalence towards the world was provided by the enormous influx of immigrants. For example, in the first twenty years of the twentieth century, 14.5 million people emigrated to the United States. In 1920, over 15 per cent of the American population was classified as foreign born. This created anxieties over the extent to which such large numbers of newcomers could be assimilated within American culture. The fear was that the success in attracting large-scale immigration was also a sign of decay in that these new immigrants brought the old world to America, instead of leaving it behind. This suspicion led to spates of internal cultural conflict involving conspicuously homogenous American forces defending individual liberty from the 'Un-American activities' of those 'subversive elements' who wished to challenge the orthodoxy of American society in the name of their constitutional rights to diversity (Higham, 1963).

Many other examples exist of the contradictory tendencies and interpretations generated by America's changing place in the world. For example, it can be argued that America's marked attachment to, and development of, science and technology not only served to integrate the nation and the economy, but neutralized the spatial boundaries of America's oceanic distance from other continents. It can also be claimed that America's very success in acquiring land in the nineteenth century gave the country a sense of being so open-ended in nature that it massively reduced the number of reference points in the new world demarcating which were areas of legitimate expansion and which were not. When its economic empire spilled out into the Pacific and Latin America during the late nineteenth century, it drew political interests and even military engagements in its wake. Later, American forces were sent to Europe, thereby allowing the process of American expansion to transcend the society's original *raison d'être* and to project the United States into the very centre of old world power. America's entry into the First World War, to fight alongside the British Empire against German imperialism, marked the emergence of the United States as a world power. In doing so, it might be said to have signified that the United States had expanded into an ordinary nation as dedicated to imperial outreach as any great power. On the other hand, the American impulse to withdraw can be said to be even more consistent than its imperialist disposition to intervene. In spite of its considerable economic interests in Europe and the Far East, for example, the USA nevertheless engaged in an emphatic, and quite unrealistic, isolationist stance in the 1930s. Even as late as 1939, 'the dominant political mood was isolationism. America's physical security, the *sine qua non* of foreign policy, seemed assured, not because of American alliances or military strength but because of the distance between America and any potential enemy' (Ambrose, 1991, p. xi). These types of developments have generated a profusion of inconsistencies, and even contradictions, in the United States' approach to the rest of the world. The unresolved nature of the strains entailed in these historical and cultural processes continue to cause marked fluctuations in America's approach to international affairs. But there is one element in America's composition that has had a particularly profound effect in this area. It could even be claimed to be the central feature in the United States outlook upon the world and the medium through which most American anxieties and mixed reactions concerning its international position are expressed. The element in question is the United States' relationship to its adopted values of liberty and democracy. These have the effect of couching the condition and behaviour of America in an indigenous moral framework, thereby, deepening even further America's ambivalence toward what lies outside itself; what is at risk with worldly contact; and what America's responsibilities are to itself and to the rest of the world.

> *SUMMARY*
>
> Historically the USA has had an ambivalent relationship with the outside world.
>
> This ambivalence is a product of the nation's 'exceptionalism' combined with its geo-strategic isolation and its enormous resource base.

3 THE USA AND ITS INTERNAL DEMOCRACY

Central to America's self-image is the conviction that it is a wholly exceptional society not just because of its position in the new world, but because its unique social chemistry allowed it to become synonymous with the sort of advanced social principles which in most countries remain only aspirations. In the United States liberty, equality, and democracy are taken as merely traditional and self-evident features of America's indigenous experience. They are not regarded as a set of values to be striven for, so much as a set of pre-existing conditions to be protected and embellished. They are widely assumed to embody the essence of America — what makes America different, what makes it the new world.

3.1 EXCEPTIONALISM: UNIQUENESS AND UNIVERSALITY

These suppositions have a long and well established pedigree. As early as the 1830s, Alexis de Tocqueville was pointing out that the United States had produced a democratic society that was extraordinary in scale and spontaneous in origin. 'The great advantage of the Americans is that they have arrived at a state of democracy without having to endure a democratic revolution and that they are born equal, instead of becoming so' (De Tocqueville, 1946, p.370). This theme of democracy as an expression of American existence became such a dominant feature in the identity of the United States that the main questions raised by it have traditionally been those of causes rather than effects. For example, in his highly influential interpretation of American culture and ideas Louis Hartz asserts that the origins of America's overwhelming liberal tradition lay in the absence of a feudal past. Without an *ancien régime*, America 'lacks a genuine revolutionary tradition … and this being the case, it lacks also a tradition of reaction' (Hartz, 1955, p.5). As a consequence, America never developed the class divisions and political tensions that have traditionally afflicted European politics. Instead, it produced an intuitive social consensus centred upon liberal individualism, economic opportunity and widespread property acquisition — what Hartz terms 'democratic capitalism'.

Alexis de Tocqueville

> Amid the 'free air' of American life something new appeared: men began to be held together not by the knowledge that they were different parts of a corporate whole, but by the knowledge that they were similar participants in a uniform way of life.
>
> (Hartz, 1955, p.55)

This view of American life arising spontaneously from the very nature of American conditions — arguably from a state of nature — is a common theme underlying the conception of society in the USA. In Daniel Boorstin's opinion, for example,

> The United States is the *land* of the free ... No nation has been readier to identify its values with the peculiar conditions of its landscape: we believe in *American* equality, *American* liberty, *American* democracy ... American ideals are not in books or in the blood but in the air, [where] they are readily acquired; actually, it is almost impossible for an immigrant to avoid acquiring them. He is not required to learn a philosophy so much as to rid his lungs of the air of Europe.
>
> (Boorstin, 1958, pp.25, 28)

American democracy in this respect is not just a condition of democracy existing in the United States. It is a qualitatively exceptional form of democracy whose idiosyncratic nature is derived from the peculiarities of America itself. According to this perspective, American democracy is not comparable to other democracies. More precisely, America is not comparable to other countries because it is a democracy — the definitive democracy which other countries may seek to emulate but which never succeed in doing so because they lack the social chemistry of the new world. Democracy in this guise is the climactic end product of America's naturalistic experience and, therefore, the supreme expression of America's inherent nature. It serves to define American identity in relation to outsiders, to explain and vindicate America's unequalled economic and social expansion, and to provide a reassuring defence against the degenerate corruption of the old world. In short, American democracy conveys the idea that America is unique and that its democracy is not transferable.

This perspective is qualified by another, and equally traditional, interpretation of American democracy. In one sense, it can be used to support the proposition that American democracy is indeed exceptional. But this perspective carries quite different implications and can serve to inflate even further American pretensions to superlative uniqueness. It is the belief that American democracy is different in scope but not in kind, and that as a consequence it should be seen more as a model democracy capable of being copied elsewhere. The notion of America acting as a vanguard of social progress goes back to the late eighteenth century. In Peter Gay's words, 'the American Revolution converted America from an importer of ideas into an exporter. What it exported was, of course, mainly itself, but that was a formidable commodity — the program of enlightenment in practice' (Gay, 1970, p.21).

While the old world could only imagine and formulate sets of enlightened social proposals, it was the United States that enacted them. America, liberated from imperial rule and British orthodoxy, served to enhance an intellectual emancipation that in its turn led to a more secular and practical application of intelligence to human affairs. The belief in the systematic examination and appraisal of human nature and in the construction of political institutions on the basis of autonomous and collective experience was central to America's reputation for humane progress. America's professed contempt for history and established authority and its attachment to science and technology, practical utility, social progress and personal liberty stands not only as a general inspiration to the rest of the world but as a realisable objective for other countries. America's status as a democracy may have been special and unusual, but not unique. In the spirit of the Enlightenment, it can and has been seen as something universal — as an international example whose authenticity as a model of democracy is equated with its applicability to other nations and cultures.

It follows that the United States can conceive itself as either the embodiment of emancipation from the malaise of European traditions, or the exemplar of Western civilization and the living fulfilment of its social and democratic ideals. Both outlooks support the notion of American exceptionalism, but each possesses different implications for America's view of the world and its own society. What is clear is that liberal democratic values constitute both the agent and the object of America's national identity. The very conception of the world lying outside America is itself a product of the core conviction that the new world is separated from the old world by an ocean of democratic principles and ideas. It has often been observed that America is peculiarly dependent upon its sense of differentiation from anything else. To David Campbell, for example, no state relies more upon the posited distinction between the 'self' and the 'other' for its imagined community.

> Arguably more than any other state, the imprecise process of imagination is what constitutes American identity. In this context, the practices of 'foreign policy' come to have a special importance. If the identity of the 'true national' remains intrinsically elusive and 'inorganic', it can only be secured by the effective and continual ideological demarcation of those who are 'false' to the defining ideals.
>
> (Campbell, 1992, p.105)

This has led even within an avowedly open society to the characteristically American compulsion to equate outsiders with subversion, strangers with heresy and foreigners with the danger of un-American ideas. It is the alien world therefore that generates the deepest anxieties over the nation's identity and evokes the strongest reactions over the integrity and strength of its democracy. The beliefs in both the uniqueness and universality of American democracy serve to highlight the ambiguous nature of America's perspective of, and posture towards, the world — that is its mixed reactions, its fluctuating attitudes, and its inconsistencies over engagement and detachment. In fact, it is the unique and universal attributes of American democracy, together with the strong moral overtones invested in both constructions, that are central to the perennial question that afflicts America's international position — namely whether the world provided a service or a disservice to the United States.

> ## SUMMARY
>
> The ideological underpinnings of American foreign policy reflect two contradictory sets of beliefs: the uniqueness of its democratic experiment versus its universal appeal.
>
> These two opposing tendencies support very different kinds of foreign policy orientations namely isolationism versus interventionism or detachment versus engagement.

4 AMERICAN DEMOCRACY AND THE WORLD: CAUSE AND EFFECT

In one sense, the relationship between American democracy and the external world is seen as one of indigenous values and experiences being successfully applied to areas lying outside their immediate point of origin. According to this perspective, the world is a proving ground and a vindication of America's democratic integrity. Its democratic principles and obligations are not compromises so much as fulfilled by their outward movement. Indeed, the belief in the United State's exceptional status as the embodiment of democratic values is so strong that it has often led to the equally firm belief that such values cannot be confined to America but must inevitably find their expression on a world-wide basis. With this outlook, any encounter between the USA and the international arena can be interpreted as a relationship in which America is necessarily the independent variable.

4.1 MANIFEST DESTINY

Originally, this notion of America as an improving template for the rest of humanity took the form of a moral example and a model for republican emulation. America was 'a city upon a hill'; a social laboratory in which the feasibility of the republican ideal would be affirmed and acclaimed to a hopeful world. As the United States multiplied in size, its sense of passive example began to assume a more active dimension. The scale and speed of its acquisitions gave weight to the view that the USA possessed an inner virtue and a providential design. It also encouraged the view that America had a national mission to annex new lands, in order to maximize the spread of republican institutions of liberty to the furthest reaches of the continent.

American expansion in the nineteenth century bred a self-confidence both in its own social and political arrangements, and in the malleability of new lands and old societies to adapt to the American enlightenment. In one respect, physical expansion had always been central to American consciousness. The outreach of the original maritime colonies had been deepened, compounded and extended by the availability of vast tracts of western land. The founders of the American republic wove this natural resource into their conception of liberty and into the theoretical foundations of their systems of government. Republicanism became a geo-political construct in which expansion was directly related to the preservation of freedom. James Madison wrote,

> Extend the sphere and you take in a greater variety of parties and interests; you make it less probable that a majority of the whole will have a common motive to invade the rights of other citizens; or if such a common motive exists, it will be more difficult for all who feel it to discover their own strength and to act in unison with each other.
>
> (quoted in Hamilton, et al., 1961, p.83)

Even the libertarian, Thomas Jefferson, came round to the idea that where the American republic was concerned, it was a case of 'the bigger, the better'.

> I know that the acquisition of Louisiana has been disapproved by some, from a candid apprehension that the enlargement of our territory would endanger its union. But who can limit the extent to which the federative principle may operate effectively? The larger our association, the less will it be shaken by local passions; and in any view, is it not better that the opposite bank of the Mississippi should be settled by our own brethren and children, than by strangers of another family? With which shall we be most likely to live in harmony and friendly intercourse?
>
> (quoted in Peterson, 1977, pp.317–18)

What had begun as a largely benign and speculative statement of intent by an apprehensive and defensive young republic had changed by the 1840s into a solid belief that the United States possessed a special role in the world. Its universal presumption was 'to overspread and to possess the whole continent which providence has given us for the development of the great experiment of liberty and federated self-government' (John O'Sullivan quoted in Kohn, 1957, p.183). The end result was now no longer in doubt. American expansion could only be explained by reference to a 'manifest destiny' (Weinberg, 1963) to become a continental power, and in the process 'to establish a new order in human affairs ... to teach old nations a new civilisation ... (and) to unite the world in one social family' (William Gilpin quoted in Smith, 1950, p.40). Given the virtue of its strength and the strength of its virtue, the United States could not fail simply to prevail as the exemplar of the new world and, by implication, the proselytising model for the old world. To Ray Alan Billington, the American people in the middle of the nineteenth century:

> ... sincerely believed their democratic institutions were of such magnificent perfection that no boundaries could contain them. Surely a benevolent Creator did not intend such blessings for the few; expansion was a divinely ordered means of extending enlightenment to despot-ridden masses in near-by countries! This was not imperialism, but enforced salvation.
>
> (Billington, 1949, p.572)

Half a century later, America's position and its democratic presumption had simply been scaled up. It had become a world power but not one that was engaged in the process of international security management. It had entered the First World War but claimed to have done so not as an ordinary nation involved in a conflict with other ordinary countries, but as an extraordinary intervention through selfless moral choice and sacrifice 'to make the world safe for democracy' (Woodrow Wilson quoted in Heffner, 1976, p.249). Woodrow Wilson made it quite clear in the peace process that the United States had no interest in the moribund arrangements of the old powers. He condemned balances of power, spheres of influence and imperial protectorates, and pressed for national self-determination, free trade and open diplomacy. He wished to invest the process of collective security with American principles of democracy, liberty, natural rights and the rule of law.

The rejection of the League of Nations, and therefore, of American progress, began the United States' retreat into isolationism. The implacable and myopic nature of its political isolation in the 1930s was itself a testament to America's continuing belief in the uniqueness of its own position and status as a nation. Convinced that the European powers had failed to appreciate America's altruism or to respond to its visionary and progressive leadership, the USA engaged in one of its periodic reactions against what it believed to be the chronically regressive and illiberal nature of the old world. Even though the USA speculated on whether Europe was beyond redemption, it nevertheless continued to expand its economic empire and, with it, to become ever more closely implicated in international markets, commerce and trade. Eventually, the irresistible force of America's growing presence in the international economy opened the way to the United States' entry into the Second World War and, subsequently, to its pre-eminent position as a global superpower. Within ten years, the United States changed from being merely 'the arsenal of democracy' to the 'leader of the free world.'

4.2 A MORALISTIC SUPERPOWER

At the end of the Second World War, the United States was in the ascendency. It was the supreme military power and the only country with access to nuclear weapons. In the highly unstable international environment following the war, American forces were often the only means of providing protection and order, in areas threatened with civil strife subversion or invasion. The supremacy of the American military was matched by the American economy which, for similar reasons, had benefited by default from the devastation of its competitors. By 1950, the United States was responsible for over half of the world's foreign investment, half of the world's gross national product. As the dollar was the most dominant and reliable currency, it provided the foundation to the post-war system of international exchange. The United States used its economic power to become the chief guarantor to a series of measures designed to rebuild Europe's shattered economies and to restore stability to its currencies and its investment and banking systems.

The projection of American military and economic force was underpinned by the political conviction that the Soviet Union was a 'slave state' set upon the 'complete subversion and forcible destruction of the machinery of government and structure of society' (Nitze, 1978, p.387) in all free countries. In contrast to 1918, the end of the Second World War witnessed a power vacuum in Europe and the Far East. To the United States the devastation was analogous to the sort of *tabula rasa* on which the USA itself had been formed in the new world. America's belief in the spontaneity and universalism of the social dynamics supporting liberal democracy was affronted by the Soviet Union's rejection of the natural authenticity of the American way. To Americans, communism was a denial of America's own experience of nature and it, therefore, amounted to a perversion of nature itself. American freedom was simply taken to be genuine freedom.

As the political and ideological impasse between the United States and the USSR intensified, America's confidence in its own guiding principles became dependent upon its capacity to impart those principles to as many countries as possible in the international arena. The conflict was seen as 'momentous, involving the fulfillment or destruction not only of the Republic but of civilization itself' (Nitze, 1978, p.385). Given that the assault on free institutions was world-wide and that liberty was now conceived to be internationally indivisible, the confrontation with the Soviet Union 'impose(d) on us, in our own interests, the responsibility of world leadership' (Nitze, 1978, p.390). The Cold War drew the United States decisively onto the world stage and into a host of alliances that would ensure its active engagement in international politics on a permanent basis. It was no longer enough that American democratic values were transferable to other countries. It was now strategically and ideologically imperative that they were actually transferred and established in as many nations as possible. The validity of America's democratic principles, and the sense of national purpose activated by these principles, had been given an international dimension. As Paul Nitze made clear,

> The assault on free institutions is world-wide now, and in the context of the present polarization of power a defeat of free institutions anywhere is a defeat everywhere. We must lead in building a successfully functioning political and economic system in the free

world. It is only by practical affirmation, abroad as well as at home, of our essential values, that we can preserve our own integrity.

(Nitze, 1978, pp.389–90)

The Cold War succeeded in polarizing world politics and in creating an ideological dichotomy in which co-existence was interpreted as illegitimate and any victory for American liberal democracy was bought at the price of a more intense animus against the USA and its values in the 'communist bloc'. The scale and commitment of the Cold War conflict ensured the USA of an ideological security in the west, and especially so in America itself, where critical dissent was discouraged and tolerance was circumscribed for the greater good of America's war effort in the war of ideas. The United States has often been described as nothing other than the mobilization of liberal and democratic ideas. The Cold War provided a mobilization that was different in scale but not in nature. The American disposition to regard 'truths to be self-evident' (Thomas Jefferson quoted in Heffner, 1976, p.15) was extended to American behaviour abroad to defend such truths. Democracy was equated not only with American democracy but with whatever American leaders and forces ascertained to be necessary to the American defence of the free world. As a consequence, American foreign policy decisions and actions overseas came to be explained and defended according to a set of permanent first principles of Cold War intentions and objectives.

This compulsion towards deductive rationalization combined American history and contemporary purpose in a highly enclosed and unified system of premises and conclusions. The Cold War was a distinctly American responsibility and one characterized by American notions of virtue and vice. It was also an extrapolation of America's past development, and of the moral purpose and benign mission served by the nature of its unprecedented growth. The international confrontation with communism, therefore, was not merely a test of American democracy's universality; it was also a means by which America might revive itself through an enhanced self-awareness of its unique democratic credentials (Muravchik, 1986, pp.221–37). Even forty years after the Second World War, an American president found it was possible to sustain his public popularity for two terms of office by using the world outside to restore America's faith in its own democracy. Ronald Reagan exemplified the force of this Cold War outlook in substantiating American claims to indigenous virtue and ancient destiny (Chace, 1988). Reagan wished to recommemerate American democracy in the face of a renewed threat from a resurgent Soviet Union. To Reagan, the outside world made it clear that America was still a shining 'city upon a hill'. Even after two centuries, it was still a beacon, 'still a magnet for all who must have freedom, for all the pilgrims from all the lost places who are hurtling through the darkness towards home' (Reagan, 1989, p.97).

America's sense of its remedial qualities was enhanced still further by the decline of communism and the disintegration of the Soviet Union. To President Bush, the end of the Cold War era represented 'a victory for all humanity' and one which demonstrated that: 'America's leadership is indispensable. Americans know that leadership brings burdens and sacrifices. But we also [know] why the hopes of humanity turn to us. We are Americans. We have a unique responsibility to do the hard work of freedom' (Bush, 1992, p.6E). President Clinton, the first post-Cold War chief executive, has shown little sign of deviating from the hallowed norm. In Clinton's view, American democracy remains 'the envy of the world'. As such, '[c]learly America must continue to lead the world we did so much to make ... our mission is timeless' (Clinton, 1993).

According to this perspective, the old world may pose dangers to the United States, but it still provided the main contributory factor in America's democratic consciousness and the chief reason behind the society's self-assurance in seeking to enlighten and redeem the remainder of humanity without compromising its own principles.

> ## SUMMARY
>
> The notion of 'manifest destiny' involved a belief in the universalization of American ideals, a moralistic expansionism, and the commitment to a new kind of world order.
>
> For many post-war foreign policy makers the Cold War was conceived as a 'war of moral purpose' the aim of which was to promote the democratic spirit across the globe.

5 THE WORLD AND AMERICAN DEMOCRACY: CAUSE AND EFFECT

The alternative construction of the United States' relationship with the external world views the latter as the independent variable and the former as the dependent object. In this guise, the world reveals Americans to be just as worldly as everyone else — so much so in fact that it reduces the notion of one external world differentiated from the United States to something of a chimera. Whether America's contact with the international community is seen as having had a corruptive influence on the new world, or as simply demonstrating that the United States is not immune to original sin and human nature, the net effect has been to create a tension between America's professed ideals and the conduct and consequences of its foreign policy. Sometimes this tension is regarded as an inconsistency inherent in the United States' position as a vanguard of social and moral improvement at work in a degenerate world. But on many other occasions, the United States is condemned for using the external world as a separate dimension of values and conduct in which its domestic principles are deliberately suspended for the sake of America's national interests and security. In this respect, the USA is only different to the extent that it seeks to conceal its motives and objectives by an enriched rhetoric of selfless devotion to human rights and the welfare of humanity. The net effect of this deception is an implicit denial of its own democracy and of the rationale of its cultural distinctiveness.

5.1 AN IMPERIAL REPUBLIC

In contrast to the traditional conception of the United States having been reluctantly and even inadvertently 'driven onto the world stage by events' (Hartz, 1955, p.286), this more critical perspective of America's relationship with the international community places the emphasis on historical continuity and mundane social behaviour rather than of cultural exceptionalism. A different combination of uniqueness and universalism applies in this case. The United States may well have begun its development with a strong identity geared to spreading the democratic creed by force of example. Nevertheless, it can be claimed that this passive message of moral propagation was soon displaced by a pattern of presumption more reminiscent of imperialism than of an ideal republic. Mission was progressively superseded by the conviction that the United States possessed a manifest destiny to make the sub-continent American for the greater good of humanity.

The imprimatur of manifest destiny lent weight to the republic's increasingly aggressive foreign policy goals in the nineteenth century. It justified a *de facto* internal imperialism in which new lands were to be liberated by becoming American. This would be achieved either by coercion, or by the displacement of its people. The progressive and enlightened nature of America's indigenous democracy was now cast as the overriding rationale for the borders of the United States to be extended over and against the claims of either the moribund and corrupt powers of the old world (Spain, Britain), or the regressive and savage nature of inferior peoples like Mexicans and the American Indians. To Arthur Ekirch, manifest destiny represented a sea-change in America's national consciousness. Whereas the concept of mission gave emphasis to the peaceful propagation of American ideas, manifest destiny implied a belligerent form of expansion.

> It turned the defensive and idealistic notions of isolationism and mission toward the course of a unilateral, nationalist, political and territorial expansion. And, in so doing it also transposed broader, more universal values of genuine international importance — the natural rights philosophy, for example — into a narrower doctrine of the special rights of Americans over and against other people.
>
> (Ekirch, 1966, pp.43–4)

It can be argued that the sheer magnitude of American expansion concealed the extent to which it was becoming an imperial power comparable in nature to the European empires. Manifest destiny wrapped America's enlargement in a circular analysis of justification. Since the United States' growth was said to be motivated by virtue and progress, then the consequences of expansion necessarily increased the sum of virtue and progress on the continent and provided the justification for future growth. Democracy was a progression in both senses of the word. Virtue could be equated with a spatial dimension. Such expansion therefore was not imperial at all. It was the extended autonomy of free people — a self-made nation of self-made men and women whose values and motives know no bounds and who did not respect any artificial boundaries to enlightenment and emancipation. An empire by democratic means was by definition no empire at all.

The ethical myopia that accompanied America's internal imperialism began to break down towards the end of the nineteenth century. The comfortable licence of righteous and providential fulfillment became infused with more worldly ingredients — namely, America's own industrial and financial power, the Darwinian imperatives of competitive interaction between nations and the rise of a new imperialistic international order involving the global projection of force and the drive by each participant to co-opt as much available land as possible to prevent it from falling into the hands of others. As a consequence, American attitudes towards neighbouring and competing powers grew more belligerent.

Even by the beginning of the twentieth century, the United States was engaged in an Asian land war. As part of its effort to liberate Cuba from Spanish imperial control in the Spanish-American War of 1898, the United States had sent a naval force to destroy the Spanish fleet harboured at Manilla in the Philippine Islands on the other side of the Pacific Ocean. Here as in Cuba there was a local insurrectionist movement dedicated to relieving Spain of its colonial possessions. Led by Emilio Aguinaldo, it was initially supported and armed by the United States. When an American invasion force was sent to capture Manilla itself, it was assisted by Aguinaldo. But when President William McKinley forced the Spanish in the peace negotiations to cede control not just of Manilla but of the whole Philippine archipelago, and when he subsequently issued the order to American troops to occupy the country, Aguinaldo's forces resisted the United States. The principle of national self-determination could not be allowed to withstand America's prerogative rights of defining the terms of Filipino emancipation and freedom. The Senate passed a treaty of annexation in 1899 and for the next three years United States' forces were engaged in crushing the resistance to American liberation. Over 125,000 Americans fought in the war and 4,234 died as a result of it. Approximately 10,000 Filipinos died in battle; another 200,000 lost their lives in 'reconcentration camps'. An unknown number were killed in civilian massacres taken in reprisal for guerilla attacks. By 1902, the United States had prevailed but had in the process destroyed Asia's first genuine experiment in democracy (Bain, 1985).

It is true that this sort of overt and crude imperialism did not become established American practice. American intervention has been too intermittent and, at times, startlingly episodic to rank alongside any conventional imperial power. Nonetheless, when American force has been applied it can, and has been, brutal in nature and aggressively self-serving in its righteousness. To many, the United States' relationships with the rest of the world reveal it to be simply another country given to self-interest and power politics. Just as references to the Wilsonian axiom that America is the only idealistic nation in existence, are dismissed as delusions, so the idea that 'the American "empire" can be called empire by invitation' (Lundestad, 1990, p.55) is seen as pure casuistry. The world either acts as a lens through which America's *un*exceptionalism is demonstrably refracted, or it constitutes the actual agency of corruption which turns American innocence into a state of mortal affliction. On the one hand, it is possible to assert that America has always been an expansionary and imperialist power. Just as the pattern of its interior settlement was tantamount to a *de facto* internal imperialism, so its later pattern of influence over other countries (that is a *de facto* external empire) was merely an extension of the same pre-existing set of dynamics. To William Appleman Williams, for example, both patterns of United States history reveal the same controlling impulse towards empire which ranks as the defining characteristic of the American experience (Williams, 1972a; Williams, 1972b). In this light, America serves to affirm the existence of the universal motives and impulses to acquire interests, exploit resources and increase power to the fullest possible extent. On the other hand, the same evidence can support the contention that America may have begun as a unique national entity and undergone an exceptional form of development, but was then shown to be as corruptible as any other social order once the USA had become massively engaged in the international system. In fact, given the United States' avowed commitment to a public philosophy of democracy, freedom, equality and natural rights, it could even be said that America had shown itself to be exceptionally corruptible — that is uniquely more mundane than ordinary nations in its failure to live up to the high ideals which characterize its historical traditions and which continue to inform its contemporary political rhetoric.

Whichever contention is adopted, American democracy stands condemned through its contact with the rest of the world. The record of American foreign policy can be made to show that in the furtherance of American welfare and security, the United States has not only compromised the rights of self-determination in other nations, but has actively intervened abroad to ensure that the shape and policy of overseas governments conform to the overriding interests of the 'master democracy' (Kissinger, 1979, pp.657–9). Contrary to its own revolutionary origins and the implicitly revolutionary principles of its declared national ethos, the United States has been a potent force for counter-revolution in the twentieth century. To Michael H. Hunt, America's record is clear and consistent. Since its inception, a single ideology has informed and motivated foreign policy. This ideology, which has been conspicuously prominent since the Second World War, is composed of three elements — namely, a conception of national mission, the classification of other peoples according to a racial hierarchy and an overt hostility towards social revolutions (Hunt, 1987). This outlook had legitimated over forty military and covert interventions in the United States 'sister republics' in Latin America since 1900 (La Feber, 1993; Arnson, 1983; Pearce, 1981; Cingranelli, 1993, Chapters 6 and 7). Very often they have been made on behalf of palpably undemocratic governments and forces. But to a critic like Noam Chomsky, American behaviour in Latin America is only part of a much larger pattern of malignant American policy around the world.

> We invaded South Vietnam, overthrew the democratic capitalist government of Guatemala in 1954 and have maintained the rule of murderous gangsters ever since, ran by far the most extensive international terror operations in history against Cuba from the early 1960s and Nicaragua through the 1980s, sought to assassinate Lumumba and installed and maintained the brutal and corrupt Mobutu dictatorship, backed Trujillo, Somoza, Marcos, Duvalier, the generals of the southern cone, Suharto, the racist rulers of southern Africa, and a whole host of other major criminals and on, and on.
>
> (Chomsky, 1992, pp.13–14)

The embarrassment of American democracy by the world is not, however, limited to foreign lands. The United States itself is endangered by its own activities abroad, not just from the point of view of being morally compromised, but from the harmful effects that its foreign policy poses to its own democratic structures and processes. The huge military establishment and its central role in the American economy, the vast array of intelligence and security services, the enhancement of the executive's prerogative powers, and the use of secrecy as an instrument of government have all become permanent features of American society. The United States has found it difficult to reconcile these accoutrements of a national security state with the declared principles of its democratic government. The efforts to accommodate these devices within the US constitution have been far from straightforward and less than convincing in character.

In similar vein, the Cold War consensus for many years mobilized American society on a war footing for an international ideological confrontation. The consequent subordination of diversity and dissent in favour of a disciplined closure of ranks in the face of a common enemy fostered an atmosphere of domestic intolerance and the enactment of illiberal measures against minorities. Liberty at home was jeopardized by its defence abroad. Even more paradoxically, 'liberty might be undermined by its very exercise' (Hunt, 1987, p.26). Certainly Max Lerner believed that in spite of America's 'genius for equilibrium' it would be a hard task 'to balance the struggle for world power with the moral sensitivity it would need to save its democratic soul' (Lerner, 1958, p.371). NSC-68, America's Cold War catechism, made it clear that liberty was to a large extent the freedom to mobilize and demonstrate American democracy's 'unique degree of unity' (Nitze, 1978, p.402). According to NSC-68, the 'democratic way is harder than the authoritarian way' because it demands that the individual 'distinguish between the necessity of tolerance and the necessity for just suppression. A free society is vulnerable in that it is easy for people to lapse into excesses — the excess of a permanently open mind [and] the excess of tolerance degenerating into indulgence of conspiracy' (Nitze, 1978, p.403).

In this way, the pressures of the world, and of America's role within it, served to endanger the democratic order of the United States, and with it, the very substance of America's example to other nations.

> *SUMMARY*
>
> The USA has at various times pursued an imperial foreign policy motivated in part by democratic imperatives.
>
> Democracy at home, in its turn, has been compromised and endangered by such imperial adventures.

6 AMERICAN FOREIGN POLICY AND THE DEMOCRATIC CONSCIENCE

The position of the United States as a liberal, yet historically insular society that became a modern superpower, operating in the largely illiberal world of power politics, has led to a profusion of tensions surrounding American foreign policy. Nowhere are these instrumental and substantive strains more starkly revealed than in the response of America's political system to the varied requirements of international relations. According to de Tocqueville's classic dictum, democracies are 'decidedly inferior to governments carried upon different principles' where foreign relations are concerned (De Tocqueville, 1946, p.160). 'Foreign politics demand scarcely any of those qualities which a democracy possesses; they require, on the contrary, the perfect use of almost all those faculties in which it is deficient' (De Tocqueville, 1946, p.160). The qualities he had in mind were secrecy, perseverance, patience, unity and speed of action. His conclusions on the generic inadequacies of democracy in these respects were drawn from the governing arrangements of the United States in the 1830s. Fortunately for the young republic, its early democratic development coincided with a diminished need for a foreign policy. It was only later that De Tocqueville's observations would come to haunt the United States.

6.1 THE IMPERIAL PRESIDENCY

As America rose to become a great power, anxieties multiplied over the extent to which a cogent foreign policy could be squared with the maintenance of an informed public, making choices through a fully representative and accountable government. The fragmentation of America's political system and its corollary of checks and balances, together with the cultural tradition of open government and the transmission of public opinion, appeared to fly directly in the face of the structural and substantive needs of foreign policy making. So severe was the apparent disjunction between the disarray of American democracy and the order, reason and perseverance required of a foreign policy that it repeatedly led to a general anxiety 'about the difficulties the American system face[d] in fashioning a coherent and effective foreign policy' (Nathan and Oliver, 1987, p.1).

The main response to this conundrum came in the form of an expanded presidency. In the same way that the presidency came to symbolize the centralized provision of services in the positive state, so it came to rationalize the rise of a national security state. In both instances the presidency facilitated and signified the transformation of American government in response to recognized need. The presidency provided the focal point of political energy that made change not only possible but also legitimate. It was the very singularity of the presidential office which evoked the idea of the American nation being realized by central executive power. The conjunction of popular sovereignty, conveyed through a presidential election and the social solidarity and collective purpose suggested by an active president animating central government, fundamentally altered the relationship within government, and between the government and society. This was especially evident in the field of foreign relations.

The rise of the modern presidency coincided with the rise of the United States as a superpower. The two developments were not unconnected. The presidency was the main agent and the chief beneficiary of America's enhanced status in the international community. In many respects, the presidency became synonymous with the American nation. The state of the presidency came to be regarded as the state of the nation. A crisis in the presidency represented a crisis for the nation. This is not just because the president had become the 'democratic symbol of national unity' (Hirschfield, 1968, p.245). It was because of the widespread recognition that the presidency was the only agency in American government with the functional capacity to respond decisively to international events. It is also the only part of the political system with the capability of evoking that level of national trust that would permit the constitution to be circumvented for the sake of America's security. Where foreign relations were concerned, the presidency was the necessary instrument of adaptive change in an international environment that did not operate according to the principles of the American constitution. America's successful evolution in these dangerous and even anarchic conditions, therefore, was attributable to the comparable evolution of its political system towards progressive executive power in the service of a higher obligation to save American democracy. For the presidency to be cast into doubt in these conditions was tantamount to endangering America's continued evolution and, ultimately, its very survival.

The implications of these brutal but compulsive realities were recognized by the Supreme Court as early as 1936. In the landmark decision of *United States v. Curtiss-Wright Export Corporation*, the guardians of the USA's constitution all but excused the presidency from constitutional constraint in the area of international relations. The Court recognized that the presidency possessed not only powers implied in the constitution, but also powers inherent to the nature of the executive function. The president's position was not limited to constitutional provisions and Acts of Congress, but was drawn from historical precedent, forces of circumstance and the 'nature of foreign negotiations'. As a consequence, the president was afforded 'a degree of discretion and freedom from statutory restriction which would not be admissible were domestic affairs alone involved'. The Court's conclusion that the president possessed a 'very delicate, plenary and exclusive power ... as the sole organ of the federal government in the field of international relations' (*United States v. Curtiss-Wright Export Corporation*, 299 U.S. 320), was driven by a realistic appraisal of the state of international security in the 1930s. The threats posed by such severe instability transformed sweeping executive prerogative into a simple necessity. The explosion of American interests in, and anxiety about, the world outside brought with it a commensurate implosion of internal powers towards the executive centre. The Court inferred that such powers were not simply a legitimate extension of external sovereignty but were in fact derived from sources outside the constitution and were, therefore, not limited by it (Henkin, 1972, p.19–28; La Feber, 1987, pp.710–17; Koh, 1990, pp.93–100). As Harold Koh concluded, 'if the president actually possessed such extensive extra-constitutional powers, it is unclear why his actions in foreign affairs should ever be subjected to the consent of the governed' (Koh, 1990, p.5).

It was only later that the full significance of the decision became clear. Following the Second World War, when the United States no longer had the option of isolation to resolve its international problems, and when it became committed to the ambitious global policy of 'containment', it built up a very large military and national security establishment. The presidency's wartime position was not merely sustained in the ambiguous 'peacetime' of the 'Cold War'. It was enhanced by the progressive institutionalization of central executive power, by the statutory obligation to manage and co-ordinate the national security bureaucracy (see, for example, the National Security Act 1947) and by the ever-increasing need to centralize power further, in order to subject what was an ever-increasing military capability to full civilian control. 'The militarization of the American government during the Cold War' was justified as 'a creative response to a challenge' (May, 1992, p.227).

With the loss of America's nuclear monopoly (1949) and the subsequent heightening of tension between the 'communist bloc' and the 'free world', the need for presidential dominance became even more evident. Given the potential precariousness of the international system, as well as the continuing strides made in the accuracy, speed and destructive force of ever more advanced weapon systems, it was regarded as simply a matter of course that America should have the most sensitive, informed and effective decision-making apparatus that its political system was capable of providing. It was a testament to the proven track record of the presidency in crisis conditions that hardly anyone seriously contested the view that the ultimate life and death decisions concerning America's security (that is the most important choices for any democracy) should be made by the single occupant of the White House. He was to make them on behalf of the American people; in their absence; often without their knowledge or opinion; and probably even against their implicit wishes.

The problem of democracy and foreign policy making during the Cold War was as a consequence largely resolved by dividing politics and the requisites of democracy into two. The governing principles and processes in domestic policy making were simply regarded as separate from the governing principles and process in foreign policy making. The former conformed to the norms of traditional American democracy, while the latter were recognized as necessarily subject to different principles for the sake of the former, and for the wider national interest of the United States. This bifurcation was most clearly expressed in the popular 'two presidencies' thesis which suggests that while presidents were weakened at home by an array of competitors for power, they were conspicuously devoid of such rivals in foreign policy. 'Compared with domestic affairs, presidents engaged in world politics [were] immensely more concerned with meeting problems on their own terms' (Wildavsky, 1968, p.101). Foreign policy was conceived as a matter of stimulus and response — that is the best way of making the appropriate reaction to a set of forces external to indigenous control. Only the presidency was able to lay claim to the prerogative first of ascertaining what the response had to be, and then of providing it. While domestic policy making centred upon options, alternatives, choices and differing objectives, foreign policy making was generally assumed to be devoid of voluntarism and autonomy. In this realm, the normal processes were simply immaterial. As a consequence, Aaron Wildavsky writing in 1966 could conclude that in foreign policy that there had 'not been a single major issue' since the Second World War 'on which presidents, when they were serious and determined [had] failed' (Wildavsky, 1968, p.93).

The 'two presidencies' conception provided an acceptable device not only for explaining the differences in presidential power between the domestic sector and the international arena, but also for giving legitimacy to the centralized structure of foreign policy decision making. The 'two presidencies' gave expression to the idea of two different political systems co-existing with one another on the basis of shared functions and responsibilities to a common citizenry. It was in essence an extrapolation of America's traditional notion of a federal democracy. The power of the foreign policy presidency signified the corporate identity and collective purpose of the United States as a nation in the dimension of international relations. The comparative weakness of the presidency in domestic policy reflected the intrinsically plural nature of American society and politics. The central force of the foreign policy presidency attended to matters of national security, in order to make America safe for American democracy. The very fact that the presidency could not muster the equivalent political resources at home was in itself both an affirmation of the continued vitality of American democracy, and a confirmation of the need to protect foreign policy making from the conventional operations of such a democracy. Where 'the world' was concerned, the presidency was different from normal because the world was abnormally different from America.

6.2 DEMOCRATIC DILEMMAS

The rise of presidential government in this most important area of governmental responsibility raised a host of problems concerning the principles and practices of a functioning democracy. It prompted the creation of various 'democratic dilemmas'. For example, the president's position in foreign policy raised the question of the extent to which the office had neutralized the constitution's checks and balances in favour of a concentration of power in the executive branch. Presidential pre-eminence prompted concern over the existence of a foreign policy elite that could limit, and even preclude, broad democratic participation. It was possible to argue that open government and accountability were continually jeopardized by closed hierarchical decision making, by executive secrecy and by covert actions. Even the rule of law itself might be compromised by the chief executive's prerogative powers and by the general emphasis upon reaction and realism over process and form. It was difficult to discern whether the foreign policy apparatus amounted to a legitimate derivative of American democratic government, or to a suspension of normal governing arrangements. Was it a genuinely democratic response to undemocratic conditions? Or was it simply a necessarily *un*democratic reaction to the international system, but one which was leavened by democratic motivations and justified by public acquiescence. To Clinton Rossiter, it was simply a matter of democratic survival — 'in time of crisis, a democratic, constitutional government must be temporarily altered to whatever degree is necessary to overcome the peril' (Rossiter, 1948, p.5). If American democracy did not adapt, then it would cease to be anything — least of all a democracy. On the other hand if, as De Tocqueville believed, that democratic governments could not cope effectively with foreign policy, then it might be concluded that, to the extent that the United States had successfully adapted to the requirements of foreign policy making, it had ceased to be a democracy.

Some of the questions concerning the effects of foreign policy on American democracy and in particular the democratic status of the Cold War presidency, were answered in the late 1960s and early 1970s when a severe reaction set in against executive government. The presidency was held directly accountable for the mistakes and mismanagement of the Vietnam War and for the social dislocation and civil disorder generated by it. With the disarray in the economy and the perceived 'failures' of progressive and presidentially sponsored social programmes, the political consensus, which had supported presidential power for a generation, came under enormous strain. Now it was widely believed that the 'imperial presidency' had not only usurped powers from other parts of the political system, but had misused and even abused them. The problems of America were compulsively reduced to the problems of concentrated and, therefore, excessive power in the executive branch. Presidents were accused of breaking the rationale of the two presidencies by directly exploiting their executive prerogatives in the foreign policy area to enlarge their powers, and to defend their position, in the field of domestic politics. The extension of such prerogative privileges in order to harass political opponents, or to spy on American citizens, or to evade political responsibility, were seen as unwarranted and quite out of proportion to the asserted threats of internal subversion. To Arthur Schlesinger,

> The all purpose invocation of 'national security', the insistence on executive secrecy, the withholding of information from Congress ... the attempted intimidation of the press, the use of the White House itself as a base for espionage and sabotage directed against the political opposition — all signified the extension of the imperial Presidency from foreign to domestic affairs.
>
> (Schlesinger, 1974, pp.ix–x)

The outcry over the 'Caesarism' of the presidency led to a general reaction against the ethos and scale of executive power, and to a remarkable revival in the constitution's original principles of institutional dynamics and reciprocal controls. Running counter to the evolutionary direction of the presidency and against its purportedly irreversible development towards greater executive hegemony, critics and reformers set about containing the 'greased pig' (Ambrose Bierce quoted in Cunliffe, 1972, p.201) of American politics within the ancient fences of checks and balances. Animated by a resurgent constitutional fundamentalism and a restored conviction in the plurality and democratic benevolence of balanced government, the Congress passed a raft of legislation designed to monitor, supervise and control the president. The most significant aspect of the restoration of constitutional mechanics was Congress's incursion into foreign policy making. For over a generation, Congress had been unwilling to press its constitutional claims in this area. It was thought to be functionally ill-equipped and politically incapacitated to serve as a co-equal branch of government. But through much of the 1970s, Congress sprawled all over American foreign policy. Fired with the Cold War heresy that foreign policy could, and should, be susceptible to more democratic methods and objectives, Congress passed an array of measures designed to publicize and constrain decision making in such sensitive areas as arms sales, military intervention, human rights, weapons systems, nuclear strategy, arms limitation and war powers (Franck and Weisband, 1979; Hodgson, 1979; Lehman, 1976; Spanier and Nogee, 1981). Despite being previously regarded as congenitally unsuitable for the intrinsic authoritarian necessities of foreign policy, Congress proceeded on the assumption that foreign policy and national security decisions could be democratized by making them approximate more to the former mechanics of the constitution.

This faith in the interchangeability of the legislative and the executive, and, with the substitution of a closed hierarchical control with an open and more pluralistic form of management took Congress to the point of challenging the Central Intelligence Agency. Previously its supervision of the agency had been characterized by a deep reluctance even to acquire information about its activities (Marchetti and Marks, 1976, pp.371–9). It appeared to appreciate that there was something in the very essence of a secret service which rendered it, by definition, inconsistent with the normal standards and procedures of democratic supervision. To many both inside and outside the intelligence community, the CIA, by the nature of the function it was expected to perform, was simply not amenable to the customary norms of democratic control and direction. It might be said to have been 'born on principle, out of control (and) formed expressly to escape accountability' (Wills, 1976). Problems like these were further compounded by the fact that the CIA was formally under presidential direction and represented one of the fullest expressions of his obligation to preserve, protect, and defend both the security and the interests of the United States. The existence of such an organization seemed to bear witness to the critical threat facing America and its western allies, and the need to resort to extraordinary, and even extra-constitutional, means to meet it. Whether it was possible to impose democratic standards of control and accountability on the CIA, therefore, became bound up with whether it was consistent with the national good even to attempt to do so. 'Democracy depends upon secret intelligence for its survival, yet the relationship between the two has always been controversial, and, at times, mutually harmful' (Jeffreys-Jones, 1989, p.1). The feasibility of control became obscured by the Cold War consensus that resolved all such problems in favour of allowing the CIA to evade external constraints and for the American public to place their trust in the self-restraint of honourable men.

By the mid-1970s, however, perceptions had changed. 'The public's often easy tolerance of presidential abuse of intelligence evaporated into open dissent' (Jeffreys-Jones, 1989, p.250). From being a heroic adjunct of national destiny and American purpose, the CIA was derided as the 'action arm of the imperial presidency' (Wills, 1976) and as a 'Frankenstein's monster' (Wicker, 1975). It stood accused of large-scale surveillance of US citizens, unauthorized domestic intelligence gathering, drug experimentation, intelligence operations against political dissidents, wiretapping, break ins, mail opening, clandestine military engagements abroad, destabilizing foreign governments, and, most controversially of all, attempting to assassinate or being implicated in the assassination of foreign political leaders. In the 1950s such matters might well have been viewed fatalistically as examples of 'the ways of the world'. But such equanimity was absent in the 1970s. The CIA's activities were seen as being motivated more by considerations of executive power at home than by the power of the country's adversaries — more on behalf of the presidency's interests than the long-term interests of the United States. As a consequence, Congress immediately introduced a range of measures designed to monitor and control the CIA. The working assumption was that by taking action which suggested a balance between Congress and the presidency, it would be possible to acquire a balance between democracy and secrecy (Foley, 1990, pp.167–75).

Despite the fervent affirmations of a solution being secured through balanced government and restored democracy, it remains unclear whether either condition was ever achieved and whether they were even necessarily related to one another. Serious doubts remained over what a congressional check consisted of in an area like intelligence and covert operations; whether such a check was operationally feasible; and how the effectiveness of a legislative check might be determined one way or the other. Scepticism over the plausibility of public restraint upon a secretive body were further compounded by uncertainty over the point at which constraint might lead to impotence and ineffectiveness in an agency like the CIA. By democratizing the process of intelligence and undercover work, it was possible to strengthen the democratic credentials of national security policy making but at the price of undermining its effectiveness in the external world — thereby weakening the USA and jeopardizing America's internal democracy.

Where the CIA was concerned, it was widely believed at the end of the 1970s that Congress's checks had been too effective and that as a consequence the CIA had become so disabled that it had failed to predict the Soviet invasion of Afghanistan (1979) and the Islamic revolution in Iran (1979). Perception of American decline and of American foreign policy in disarray led to a re-evaluation of Congressional insurgency in international affairs. With the onset of the Reagan presidency and with the rise of public pressure for a more aggressive posture abroad, Congress adopted a more expansive approach to the statutory limitations on the CIA. This was symptomatic of a general relaxation in Congress's foreign policy incursions. It did not rescind any of its measures, but neither did it enact any substantial additions. Its original restraints had always included qualifying clauses to preserve the president's discretion to respond to the exigencies of changing international situations. Now these saving devices of executive prerogative were given free rein. Congress still assumed a position of co-partnership but was more prepared to give the presidency the general responsibility for foreign policy while reserving the right to monitor and to intervene on a selective basis (Foley, 1989). Control was now more a matter of deterrence than sustained constraint. In spite of the spectacular advances made by Congress in the 1970s, and in spite of the allusions at the time to a clear foreign policy 'revolution' (Franck and Weisband, 1979, p.3) and to a balance between democracy and foreign policy making, the net effect had been been to displace one form of ambiguity with another (Foley, 1990; Olson, 1991) — that is formal measures of control that were brittle in construction and unpredictable in effect were replaced by more informal, imprecise and discretionary forms of negotiated limitation.

While the measures of the 1970s show that democratic insurgency can penetrate into foreign policy making, the reactive *realpolitik* of the 1980s reaffirms the existence of the inherent cross-pressures of internal democracy and foreign policy making (Destler *et al.*, 1984; George, 1990). On no occasion was this more evident than during the Iran-contra affair. This complex scandal centred upon the Reagan Administration's efforts to continue to support the contra guerillas in Nicaragua, despite Congress's varied attempts to prevent American involvement in the insurgency campaign against the revolutionary Sandinista government. The administration regarded Nicaragua as a test case in its crusade against communist expansion in Latin America. It devoted prodigious amounts of political capital into persuading the American public that the Sandinista regime was a client state of the Soviet Union and, thereby, a strategic threat to the United States. To the administration,

Nicaragua provided an example of how the spread of communism could be halted and, thereupon, reversed so long as the United States adopted a sufficiently aggressive posture.

The American public was never convinced. It was left to Congress to reflect its misgivings. Through a series of measures (that is, the five Boland Amendments), Congress sought to impose a measure of democratic control and accountability upon foreign policy making in this area, while simultaneously reserving the president's discretion to monitor the Nicaragua situation and to prevent the collapse of the contra forces. Congress attempted to bring all contra aid to the surface; to regularize its transfer in the light of Congress's policy choices on Latin America; and to reduce and subsequently to eliminate military aid in favour of humanitarian assistance to the contras. Reagan was loathe to abandon those whom he regarded as 'freedom fighters'. His administration, therefore, went to extraordinary lengths to exploit both the rights of executive prerogative in foreign affairs, and the opportunities for inventive legal construction, in order to circumvent the Boland Amendments and to defy their objectives.

Some efforts to challenge and to evade legal restrictions were always to be expected in the traditional rules of engagement between the presidency and Congress. A president will always be convinced that he had to be in a position to react to changing conditions and to use his judgement and coercive executive powers to serve the national interest. By the same token there are dangers for Congress achieving too tight a control of foreign policy. If such restrictions are seen to be reducing the presidency to a state of impotence, the chances are that there would be a public backlash against Congress. Both sides have things to gain from the relationship but, more significantly, they also have a great deal to lose. If Congress exceeds the bounds of tolerance, then the president can publicly smear the legislature with culpability for policy defects and even failure. If the president breaks the spirit of what are normally tacit arrangements with the legislature, then the Congress can drag often sensitive policies into public debate and accuse the executive branch of an abuse of power, a failure of judgement, or a breach of the law. In the high profile-high stakes case of Nicaragua, it was generally:

> Understood that the administration would adhere to the letter of the Boland prohibitions but would unilaterally use its inherent foreign-policy powers to pursue its policy of helping the contras. President Reagan would do what he could for the contras outside of authorised appropriations, while Congressmen who opposed any aid could rest assured that they had done what they could to cut the contras off.
>
> (Crovitz, 1987, p.24)

The level of gamesmanship within the rules of the game was set and understood by both sides.

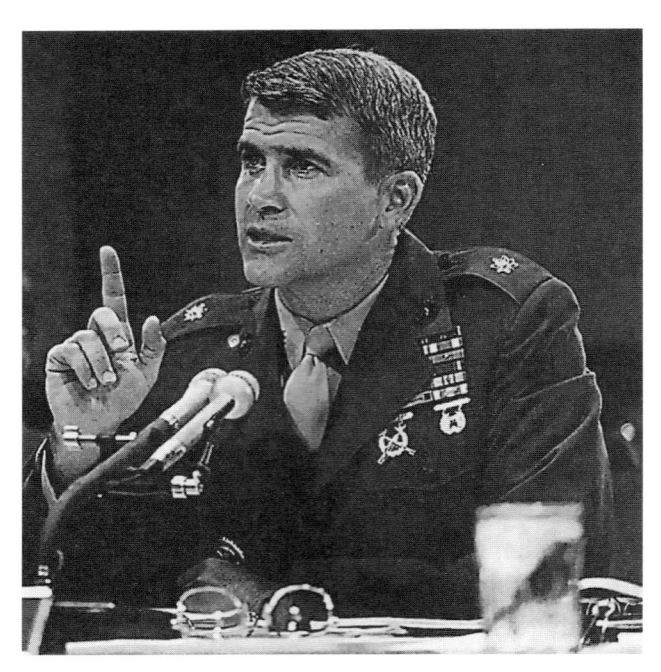

Lieutenant-Colonel Oliver North

The game rules were not breached by the administration's efforts to evade them, but by its conspiracy blatantly to defy them. In the White House, Lieutenant-Colonel Oliver North's 'Project Democracy' was designed to break the sanctions of the Boland Amendments by the use of private donations. North's team even went so far as to transfer to the contras monies which had been acquired from secret 'weapons for hostages' deals with Iran — deals which were themselves in contravention of the administration's own publically stated position against negotiations with terrorists or with states sponsoring terrorism. Through such means, 'Project Democracy' acquired warehouses, supplies, ships, aircraft, vehicles, maintenance facilities, communication equipment, munitions and a secret air strip in Costa Rica to assist the contras in their military attacks upon the Sandinista government.

> The facilities amounted to a semiprivate network in which government security managers subcontracted out security policy and financed it with private contributions and donations from foreign governments. The secret network was the most blatant attempt to protect administration doctrine from constitutional and democratic controls since those controls had been reinvigorated in the wake of Vietnam.
>
> (Sharpe, 1987, p.34)

The failure of 'Project Democracy' to recognize and accommodate Congress's role, its rights and its sensitivities brought discredit to all sides. Congress's response was immediate. It invoked explicitly constitutional sanctions. It refused to bail the executive out and transmuted what had been spongy legislative measures into rock-ribbed embodiments of the rule of law. Oliver North and his fellow conspirators were presented as law-breakers, holding Congressional instructions in contempt and ignoring legislative restraint at will.

As criminal proceedings followed top level resignations, the contras were effectively abandoned, the Reagan presidency collapsed in public esteem and American foreign policy was plunged into disarray. Attempts to exert internal democracy had prompted the executive into elaborate efforts at deep cover foreign policy which included a secretive White House unit designed explicitly to act independently from the conventional apparatus of foreign policy making.

The question posed by De Tocqueville concerning the compatibility of an operational democracy and a coherent foreign policy, therefore, not only remains unresolved but, in the light of America's recent experience, is confirmed as fundamentally insoluble. As Volkman and Baggett state,

> No one has yet been able to figure out a system where the Legislative and Executive branches can share responsibility for the conduct of foreign policy — and at the same time act with great speed in the event of a sudden crisis. It is one of democracy's central flaws. Still, democracy is a flawed process, and it may well be that this central question will remain a permanent source of tension, so long as there is a constitutional system.
>
> (Volkman and Baggett, 1989, p.228)

SUMMARY

The realm of foreign policy poses acute dilemmas for American democracy.

Foreign policy has been associated with the emergence of 'two presidencies' or two separate political systems.

Attempts in the 1970s and 1980s to reassert the principle of democratic accountability through Congressional oversight of foreign affairs have not been resoundingly successful.

The dilemma identified by De Tocqueville of the conflict between an effective foreign policy and democratic practices remains unresolved.

7 CONCLUSION: PRIMACY VERSUS DEMOCRACY

As the United States nears the end of the 'American century', the country remains deeply affected by the ambivalent relationship that exists between democracy and great power. The disjunctions between ideals and self-interest, principles and practice, intentions and consequences, and between the ethics of liberal morality and the morality of power and security all continue to play a part in America's consciousness of the world and of its role within it. It may be thought that the 'collapse of communism' would have clarified America's international position. According to Francis Fukuyama, America should have no reason any more for apprehension. With the Cold War won and the dominance of liberal democracy and the free market assured, the United States and its values can be regarded as marking an 'end to history' (Fukuyama, 1992). Despite its flaws, no other system of thought has survived the twentieth century. The United States, therefore, stands not only as the predominant single superpower but as the archetype of a society that can be represented as the culminating point of social and political evolution. The sentiments echoed by Fukuyama and others suggest that the United States might adopt a more consistent posture towards the rest of the world. In the words of Louis Hartz's classic maxim, Americans in the past seemed 'to oscillate between fleeing from the rest of the world and embracing it with too ardent a passion. An absolute national morality is inspired either to withdraw from "alien" things or to transform them: it cannot live in comfort constantly by their side' (Hartz, 1955, p.286).

It could be said that Fukuyama's view neutralizes Hartz's duality. With America's democratic supremacy and cultural hegemony assured, the world is now no longer qualitatively different to the United States. There is no reason for America to retreat into its own democracy because it would now only be withdrawing from its own mirror image. By the same token, it is arguably more likely that the United States will increasingly move out in the world, and feels less restraint in intervening to punish aggression and to facilitate the release of societies into the norm of liberal democracy.

American military action in the Persian Gulf and in the Horn of Africa would seem to have affirmed a radical shift of focus. In April 1991, *Time* magazine speculated on whether the United States was assuming the role of a 'Globo-Cop' on behalf of democracy and human rights (Walsh, 1991). According to the *Washington Post*, '[c]ountries that fail to care decently for their citizens dilute their claim to sovereignty and forfeit invulnerability to outside political military intervention' (quoted in Jenkins, 1992). Simon Jenkins in *The Times* deplored such views. To him, the fighting in Somalia or in the former Yugoslavia were scandals, but not world scandals requiring international intervention. Should the United States defer to the sentiments expressed in *The Washington Post* and a host of other media outlets, it would amount to a 'caring imperialism' going 'far beyond the Cold War doctrines of Dulles, Kennedy, Nixon and Kissinger, that foreign intervention was justified only if invited to save a nation from communism. If the *Post* is right, three-quarters of the globe is now at risk of attack from America or its UN proxies' (Jenkins, 1992).

On closer examination, however, the universalism of the United States remains more apparent than real. America objects to melting into the rest of the world as dangerous, unresponsive and costly. The United States commitment to the Gulf War, for example, was made strictly dependent on limited objectives and immediate disengagement. More important than the decision to leave for the Gulf War was the display of democratic autonomy in returning home on time. Despite President Bush's insistence that 'we've kicked the Vietnam syndrome once and for all' (quoted in Cloud, 1991), America's premature departure demonstrated the reverse. Fear of becoming sucked into a larger and longer commitment ensured an outcome of victorious retreat. Contrary to expectations, Saddam Hussein remained in power and the defeated Iraqi army was strong enough to crush the popular uprisings against the regime. During the deadlock negotiations between the United States and Iraq prior to the war, Fred Greenstein commented that: 'what we're dealing with here is a basic limitation on the capacity of leaders in a democracy to play a game of chicken' (quoted in Lichfield, 1990). At first, Bush appeared to have won the game by invading Kuwait and Southern Iraq. But by correctly gambling on the United States' reluctance to press on to Baghdad, it might be said that the authoritarianism of Saddam Hussein ultimately prevailed in the international game of chicken with American democracy.

The second reason for Americans to object to the concept of one world is that they fear the direction of the process. They are concerned that the USA is simply becoming like the rest of the world instead of the other way around: 'that Americans are in the same boat as the rest of humankind rather than being the owner-passengers on a separate and uniquely privileged ship of state' (Thorne, 1992, p.327). Whether it is the spectre of economic decline, the drugs problem, the breakdown of law and order, the alienation and destitution of the inner cities, or the multicultural fragmentations of American society, the fear is that harmful transnational trends are making parts of the United States into an equivalent of the Third World (Rieff, 1992). The presidential election of 1992 demonstrated the extent to which the American public wished to turn its back on a successful foreign policy president and on the rest of the world, in favour of giving markedly more attention to domestic problems. In a year which also witnessed the Los Angeles riots and the federal government in Washington deteriorating further into scandal, gridlock and stagnation, the emphasis turned to an agenda of American renewal through the exertion of democratic will to make the United States less like an altogether more deplorable outside world.

The third reason behind America's objection to being cast as an ordinary nation is its instinctive insistence that it is, and must remain, a wholly extraordinary country. Uniqueness remains an axiomatic element of American identity. It is integral to America's exceptionally demonstrative nationalism and its fervent patriotism. This American need to feel unique is satisfied more than anything else by the importance of democracy to America's culture and identity. The United States can only ever feel different through what it considers to be its exceptionally democratic society — that is its only serious historical claim to uniqueness. The circularity of this view is far less important than its effect, which is to satisfy America's need to be different from the world and to fulfil its *raison d'être* of having something to offer the world. In essence, America needs to be unique to be universal in an active, originating and controlled way.

As a consequence, the United States remains with essentially two dimensions of democracy. On the one hand, is a cultural democracy which finds expression in displays of national consensus and patriotic zeal. On the other hand, is its instrumental democracy of critical public opinion, pluralistic division, and embattled institutions. In many respects, the cultural democracy of the Cold War allowed the United States to withstand the fissiparous effects of its instrumental democracy. But with the grandeur of the East-West challenge having dissipated and with the decline of the social discipline and solidarity that it once elicited the United States has now become much less predictable in foreign policy than it once used to be. It has always had a reputation for relative inconsistency because of its geographical isolation and its democratic impulses. The growing interdependence of the world has reduced the former. At the same time, America's emancipation from the strictures of the Cold War has helped to compensate for this diminishment of American independence. There is now a greater perception of choice in foreign policy making than there used to be in the bi-polar conditions of East-West confrontation. The growing susceptibility of foreign policy issues to America's instrumental democracy means a much greater unpredictability as to what means and objectives will receive the assent of America's cultural democracy. The scale of the international mass media, for example, can now immediately and directly suck issues into American public opinion with the effect of derailing presidential agendas and prompting erratic American action. Harrowing television pictures of famine and lawlessness in Somalia, for example, led President Bush to extend America's ancient mission of democracy to the banditry and clan warfare of Mogadishu, Kismayu and Badera. In Bush's words, 'Operation Just Cause' was a humanitarian obligation. 'You are doing God's work,' he told his troops. 'We will not tolerate armed gangs ripping off their own people' (quoted in Walker, 1992). Just as important as the divine nature of the intervention, however, was the emphatic assurances given by the president that the operation would not stretch further than the public's tolerance and would, therefore, be of very limited duration. American public opinion that would be served by lurching into a country, would be equally served by lurching out of a country.

In the post-Cold War context, the possibilities of intervention or other forms of American action are huge. By the same token, the potential for inconsistency and unpredictability is also extensive. America's cultural democracy can still be harnessed to foreign commitments, but increasingly the causes to which the United States will subscribe are being determined on the basis of running battles for American public opinion (Isaacson, 1992). In the current climate, De Tocqueville has been turned on his head. The impoverishment of foreign policy making in the United States is now taken to be not a vice so much as a redeeming virtue — a sign of democratic choice and autonomy in a complex and interdependent world. America's 'instrumental democracy' is supporting instead of detracting from America's 'cultural democracy'. The possible disarray of American foreign policy is not seen especially as a problem to be overcome, but as proof of a functioning democracy that makes the United States satisfyingly different to other countries. With so much of the world actively engaged in attempts to court American public opinion, especially through television, it is understandable that the United States considers itself confirmed as being uniquely democratic in character and, thereby, universal in purpose.

> ## SUMMARY
>
> In the post-Cold War era the temptation for an American interventionist response to international problems may be tempered by the fear of entanglement, domestic constraints and its very uniqueness of character.
>
> Despite this the potential for inconsistency and unpredictability in the conduct of foreign affairs remains evident because the disarray in foreign policy is paradoxically a product of the triumph of the democratic spirit.

REFERENCES

Ambrose, S.E. (1991) *Rise to Globalism: American Foreign Policy Since 1938*, 6th edn, Harmondsworth, Penguin.

Arnson, C. (1983) *El Salvador: A Revolution Confronts the United States*, Washington D.C., Institute for Policy Studies.

Bain, D.H. (1985) *Sitting in Darkness: Americans in the Philippines*, Boston, Houghton Mifflin.

Billington, R.A. (1949) *Westward Expansion: A History of the American Frontier*, New York, Macmillan.

Boorstin, D.J. (1958) *The Genius of American Politics*, Chicago, Phoenix/University of Chicago Press.

Bush, G.H.W. (1992) 'State of the Union address,' January 29, 1991, Washington D.C., *Congressional Quarterly Almanac, 102nd Congress, 1st Session, 1991, Volume XLVII*, pp.6E–8E

Campbell, D. (1992) *Writing Security; United States Foreign Policy*, Manchester, Manchester University Press.

Chace, J. (1988) 'Dreams of perfectability: American exceptionalism and the search for a moral foreign policy' in Berlowitz, L., Donoghue, D. and Menand, L. (eds.), *America in Theory*, New York, Oxford University Press, pp.249–61.

Chomsky, N. (1992) *Deterring Democracy*, London, Vintage.

Cingranelli, D.L. (1993) *Ethics, American Foreign Policy and the Third World*, New York, St. Martin's.

Clinton, B.J. (1993) 'Inaugural address,' January 20, 1993, *The Times*, January 21, 1993.

Cloud, S.W. (1991) 'Exorcising an old demon,' *Time*, March 11, 1991.

Commager, H.S. (1978) *The Empire of Reason: How Europe Imagined and America Realized the Enlightenment*, London, Weidenfeld and Nicolson.

Crovitz, L.G. (1987) 'Crime, the constitution, and the Iran-Contra affair,' *Commentary*, October 1987, pp.23–30.

Cunliffe, M. (1972) *American Presidents and the Presidency*, London, Fontana/Collins.

Destler, I.M., Gelb, L.H. and Lake, A. (1984) *Our Own Worst Enemy: The Unmaking of American Foreign Policy*, New York, Simon and Schuster.

De Tocqueville, A. (1946) *Democracy in America*, London, Oxford University Press.

Ekirch, A.A. (1966) *Ideas, Ideals and American Diplomacy: A History of Their Growth and Interaction*, New York, Appleton-Century-Crofts.

Foley, M. (1989) 'Mumbling across the branches: the Iran-Contra scandal, the Boland Amendments, and the American foreign policy making process', University College of Wales, Aberystwyth, *International Politics Research Papers*, Number 6.

Foley, M. (1990) *Laws, Men and Machines: Modern American Government and the Appeal of Newtonian Mechanics*, London, Routledge.

Franck, T.M. and Weisband, E. (1979) *Foreign Policy by Congress*, New York, Oxford University Press.

Fukuyama, F. (1992) *The End of History and the Last Man*, Harmondsworth, Penguin Books.

Gay, P. (1970) *The Enlightenment: an Interpretation, Volume II, The Science of Freedom*, London, Weidenfeld and Nicolson.

George, L.N. (1990) 'Tocqueville's caveat: centralised executive foreign policy and American democracy', *Polity*, 23, no.3, pp.419–41.

Hamilton, A., Madison, J. and Jay, J. (1961) *The Federalist Papers*, New York, New American Library.

Hartz, L. (1955) *The Liberal Tradition in America: An Interpretation of American Political Thought Since the Revolution*, New York, Harcourt Brace Jovanovich.

Heffner, R.D. (1976) *A Documentary History of the United States*, New York, Mentor.

Henkin, L. (1975) *Foreign Affairs and the Constitution*, New York, Norton.

Higham, J. (1963) *Strangers in the Land: Patterns of American Nativism, 1860–1925*, New York, Atheneum.

Hirschfield, R.S. (1968) 'The power of the contemporary presidency' in Hirschfield, R.S., *The Power of the Presidency: Concepts and Controversy*, New York, Atherton, pp.238–54.

Hodgson, G. (1979) *Congress and American Foreign Policy*, London, Royal Institute of International Affairs.

Hunt, M.H. (1987) *Ideology and U.S. Foreign Policy*, New Haven, Yale University Press.

Isaacson, W. (1992) 'Sometimes, right makes right,' *Time*, 21 December 1992.

Jeffreys-Jones, R. (1989) *The CIA and American Democracy*, New Haven, Yale University Press.

Jenkins, S. (1992) 'This caring imperialism,' *The Times*, 5 December 1992.

Kissinger, H. (1979) *White House Years*, Boston, Little, Brown.

Koh, H.H. (1990) *The National Security Constitution: Sharing Power after the Iran-contra Affair*, New Haven, Yale University Press.

Kohn, H. (1957) *American Nationalism: An Interpretive essay*, New York, Macmillan.

LaFeber, W. (1987) 'The constitution and United States foreign policy: an interpretation', *Journal of American History*, 74, no.3, pp. 695–717.

Lehman, J. (1976) *The Executive, Congress and Foreign Policy Studies of the Nixon Administration*, New York, Praeger.

Lerner, M. (1958) *America as a Civilisation: Life and Thought in the United States Today*, London, Jonathan Cape.

Lichfield, J. (1990) 'Doves spoil Bush's game of chicken,' *The Independent*, 25 November 1990.

Lipset, S.M. (1979) *The First New Nation: The United States in Historical and Comparative Perspective*, New York, W.W. Norton.

Lundestad, G. (1990) *The American 'Empire' and Other Studies of U.S. Foreign Policy in Comparative Perspective*, Oxford, Oxford University Press.

Marchetti, V. and Marks, J.D. (1976) *The CIA and the Cult of Intelligence*, London, Coronet.

May, E.R. (1992) 'The U.S. Government, a legacy of the Cold War' in Hogan, M.J. (ed.), *The End of the Cold War: Its Meanings and Implications*, Cambridge, Cambridge University Press, pp.217–28.

Muravchik, J. (1986) *The Uncertain Crusade: Jimmy Carter and the Dilemmas of Human Rights Policy*, Lanham, Hamilton.

Nathan, J.A. and Oliver, J.K. (1987) *Foreign Policy Making and the American Political System*, 2nd edn, Boston, Little, Brown.

Nitze, P. (1978) 'NSC 68: United States objectives and programs for national security' in Etzold, T.H. and Gaddis, J.L. (eds.), *Containment: Documents on American Policy and Strategy, 1945–1950,* New York, Columbia University Press, pp.385–442.

Olson, W.C. (1991) 'The U.S. Congress: an independent force in world politics?', *International Affairs*, 67, no.3, pp.547–63.

Paine, T. (1976) *Common Sense*, Harmondsworth, Penguin Books.

Pearce, J. (1981) *Under the Eagle: U.S. Intervention in Central America and the Caribbean*, London, Latin America Bureau.

Peterson, M. (ed.) (1977) *The Portable Thomas Jefferson*, Harmondsworth, Penguin Books.

Rieff, D. (1992) *Los Angeles: Capital of the Third World*, London, Jonathan Cape.

Reagan, R. (1989) 'Farewell address,' January 11, 1989, *Congressional Quarterly Weekly Report*, January 14, 1989, pp.95–7.

Rossiter, C. (1948) *Constitutional Dictatorship: Crisis Government in Modern Democracies*, New York, Harcourt Brace.

Schlesinger, Jr., A.M. (1974) *The Imperial Presidency*, London, Andre Deutsch.

Sharpe, K.E. (1987) 'The real causes of Irangate,' *Foreign Policy*, 68 (Fall 1987), pp.19–41.

Smith, H.N. (1950) *Virgin Land: The American West as Symbol and Myth*, New York, Vintage.

Spanier, J. and Nogee, J. (eds.) (1981) *Congress, the Presidency and American Foreign Policy*, New York, Pergamon.

Thorne, C. (1992) 'American political culture and the end of the Cold War,' *Journal of American Studies*, 26, no.3, pp.303–30.

United States v. Curtiss-Wright Export Corporation (1936) 299 U.S. 304.

Volkman, E. and Baggett, B. (1989) *Secret Intelligence*, London, W.H. Allen.

Walker, M. (1992) 'U.S. troops in Somalia will do God's work, says Bush,' *The Guardian*, 5 December 1992.

Walsh, J. (1991) 'Global Beat,' *Time*, April 1, 1991.

Weinberg, A.K. (1963) *Manifest Destiny: A Study of Nationalist Expansion in American History*, Chicago, Quadrangle.

Wicker, T. (1975) 'Destroy the monster,' *New York Times*, 12 September 1975.

Wildavsky, A. (1968) 'The two presidencies' in Wildavsky, A. and Polsby, N.W. (eds.), *American Governmental Institutions: A Reader in the Political Process*, Chicago, Rand McNally, pp.93–102.

Williams, W.A. (1972a) *The Tragedy of American Diplomacy*, 2nd edn, New York, Dell.

Williams, W.A. (ed.) (1972b) *From Colony to Empire: Essays in the History of American Foreign Relations*, New York, Wiley.

Wills, G. (1976) 'The CIA from beginning to end,' *New York Review of Books*, 22 January 1976.

FURTHER READING

Campbell, D. (1992) *Writing Security: United States Foreign Policy*, Manchester, Manchester University Press.

Chomsky, N. (1992) *Deterring Democracy*, London, Vintage

Henkin, L. (1990) *Constitutionalism, Democracy and Foreign Affairs*, New York, Columbia University Press.

Hunt, M.H. (1987) *Ideology and US Foreign Policy*, New Haven, Yale University Press.

Spanier, J. and Uslaner, E. (1982) *Foreign Policy and Democratic Dilemmas*, Boston, Houghton Miflin.

7

A SECOND AMERICAN CENTURY? THE UNITED STATES AND THE NEW WORLD ORDER

Anthony McGrew

1 INTRODUCTION

On 19 November 1990 the Cold War officially became history. Somewhat overshadowed by the threat of war in the Persian Gulf, the presidents of both superpowers, George Bush and Mikhail Gorbachev, signed the Charter of Paris which affirmed that East and West were 'no longer adversaries' (CSCE Joint Declaration, 1990). With its resonances of the 1918 Versailles Peace conference this final act of the 'Great Contest' held out the welcome prospect of a new era in European and world history: an era of possibilities. For the United States, the 'Charter of Paris' was a historic document since it echoed, in many key respects, the basic principles of the post-war peace settlement which President Roosevelt had articulated almost five decades earlier in the Atlantic Charter and the Yalta Accords. To most Americans it also vindicated the strategy of global containment and delivered the final judgement on the many tragedies, both personal and national, which had been borne in the struggle to defend 'freedom and democracy' across the globe.

In his famous 'X' article (published in 1947 at the beginning of the Cold War) George Kennan, the father of containment, observed that the 'issue of Soviet–American relations is in essence a test of the overall worth of the United States as a nation among nations' (Kennan quoted in Gaddis, 1992, p.48). But 'victory' bequeathed to American foreign policy makers an uncertain legacy; with no clear rival, the nation's purpose and role in the global system is no longer self-evident. Its manifest destiny appears to have been realized. Accordingly the foreign policy establishment has been somewhat ambivalent in its celebration of 'victory' since it is confronted with a complex 'reality': on the one hand, the end of the Cold War appears to confirm American global preponderance and the opening of a further chapter in the 'American Century'; but, on the other hand, years of relative economic decline, combined with the unsustainable burdens of 'Empire', suggest that the end of the Cold War could be just as convincingly (some would argue more convincingly) interpreted as the closing chapter of the 'American Century'. As the new millenium beckons, the United States approaches another historic assignment in responding to the conflicting meanings of its Cold War 'triumph'.

Any attempt to prophesy about the future trajectory of American foreign policy is subject to innumerable pitfalls. John Gaddis, a respected historian of post-war American foreign policy, has drawn attention to the failure of academic accounts written during the Cold War to predict the end of the conflict (Gaddis, 1992). Consequently, this chapter aims primarily to identify the forces which are implicated in the restructuring of the nation's foreign and national security policies at the end of the twentieth century. It is concerned with how the USA is adapting its role and foreign policy posture to the changed circumstances of a now increasingly interconnected, but fragmented, global system. This chapter is concerned also with how far the architecture of this new world order is being defined by the exercise, or even the withholding, of American power. In attempting to understand the dynamic interface between American power and the new world order this chapter will explore:

- how the termination of superpower rivalry has transformed the global 'stage' upon which American foreign policy decision makers have to act;

- the contemporary strategic debates and intellectual controversies which inform the restructuring of foreign and national security policies;

- the complex interaction between domestic and international priorities in the reshaping of the nation's external relations;

- why issues of national identity, morality and ideology have become pivotal in the reconstruction of foreign policy at the 'century's end'; and finally,

- whether the end of the Cold War effectively represents the final stage of the 'American Century' or the renaissance of American power: a second American Century.

2   ENDINGS AND NEW BEGINNINGS

In his recollections of his time in office, Henry Kissinger observes that: 'Any statesman is in part the prisoner of necessity' (Kissinger, 1979, p.54). For almost fifty years the Cold War imposed a single logic on American foreign policy. But with the collapse of the Soviet Empire in Eastern Europe and the demise of the Soviet Union this bipolar world came to an abrupt end. The requirement to maintain 'eternal vigilance' against the perceived Soviet threat was eliminated almost overnight. The ever present risk of a nuclear Armageddon, amongst the most chilling and sobering reality of the Cold War, has diminished steadily. By early 1994 the United States and Russia had agreed not to target each other with their dwindling nuclear arsenals; a largely symbolic gesture but one which nevertheless consolidated the end of the 'great contest'. In this transformed political environment the USA has become freed from the political logic and necessities of a bipolar world; it now confronts a unique 'opportunity to reconstruct foreign policy free of the constraints of the Cold War' (Hyland, 1990).

2.1 THE UNEXPECTED ANSWER

It is instructive to compare the American response to allied victory in the Gulf War with its response to the ending of the Cold War. In the case of the former, a national celebration was inaugurated with a victory parade in New York which recalled scenes from Times Square in 1945. By comparison, the end of the Cold War received a considerably less euphoric and more subdued national reception. Admittedly, the Gulf War delivered dramatic television images whilst the end of the Cold War proved a somewhat more ambiguous and complex story for the media to convey. Yet ironically in the latter case the outcome was as close to the notion of 'total victory' as can possibly be conceived. What was the reason for this subdued reaction?

In part, the answer lies in the rapidity with which the Cold War system unraveled itself, and, in part, with the fantastic, almost inconceivable, scale of the transformation in the geo-political landscape which it precipitated. Throughout the critical period of 1989–1990 the American public were bombarded with news of developments in the Soviet bloc. They watched, from the comfort of their own homes, the scaling and destruction of the Berlin Wall, the street demonstrations, and the people's revolutions which brought about the collapse of communist regimes in East Germany, Hungary, Poland, and the other Eastern bloc states. In August 1991 they listened nervously to reports of the *coup d'état* in the Soviet Union and observed the subsequent break-up of the Union of Soviet Socialist Republics, whilst at the same time Germany was busily engaged in the process of national reunification. Moreover, as they contemplated the impact of the European revolutions, the United States was engrossed in assembling, and deploying to the Persian Gulf, the largest military force since the Second World War, in order to liberate Kuwait. For a public which normally demonstrated little interest in the world beyond its shores, this unrelenting cascade of historic world events tended to numb minds to the profound consequences of these combined developments for the United States.

Amongst the political classes and foreign policy establishment the events of 1989 'and all that' proved only somewhat less surprising than for the informed public. Domestically, the American 'victory' over Soviet communism was exploited to its maximum political effect to combat those opponents who regarded the Reagan–Bush era as the culmination of America's decline. Abroad, the Bush Administration adapted a more measured rhetoric. Indeed, there was a certain caution in its responses to developments in Eastern Europe and to German reunification in particular. This caution issued from a realization that politicians, of both the East and the West, had little direct control over events. Moreover, there was the ever present possibility of military repression and counter-revolution. In such circumstances misguided political interventions could prove entirely counterproductive whilst the traditional instruments of foreign policy, as the Soviet coup demonstrated, retained only a limited utility. The administration too was conscious of the need to encourage Soviet acquiescence in respect of Operation Desert Shield in the Gulf. Nevertheless, the USA and the West in general continued to support at every opportunity the progressive forces of change. But it was only following the Gulf War that the full impact of the on-going geo-political transformation registered fully on the American public and its leaders.

Despite great uncertainty there is much that Americans welcome about the post-Cold War world. The threat of a nuclear Armageddon and the need to maintain a constant state of preparation for war has been removed. By 1992 the nation's nuclear forces had been placed on a 'peacetime' status of alert. With the eradication of the Soviet threat came the prospect of a huge 'peace dividend' as military forces were scaled down to meet the very different requirements of the new geo-strategic environment. For instance, following the dissolution of the Warsaw Pact there was no longer a need to retain over 200,000 American troops and scores of military bases in Europe. Beyond Europe the demise of superpower rivalry enhanced the prospects for settling regional rivalries and conflicts which had become imbued with a Cold War logic. In South Africa, Central America, the Middle East and South-Central Asia a stable peace became a feasible objective. Moreover, the emergence of a new international order, in which there was the realistic possibility of creating effective collective security arrangements, whether globally in connection with the United Nations or at a regional level, invited the prospect of a more circumscribed global role for the USA. Yet whatever new security architecture was constructed, it was self-evident that global containment, the basis of post-war US national security policy, was effectively redundant. As a consequence, the policy agenda of the Bush Administration was hijacked by the urgent need to rethink the nation's strategic posture and its global role in the post-Cold War world.

Even before the fall of the Berlin Wall the Bush Administration had set in train a major review of foreign policy. Initially motivated by the need to respond to Gorbachev's 'new thinking', which championed an interdependent world freed from superpower confrontation, it also became a mechanism for addressing the fiscal pressures on the defence budget. Urgent action was required to curtail an escalating budget deficit, brought about in part by significant tax cuts in the early years of the administration, with the consequence that defence expenditure had to be cut back. In effect the review was an acknowledgement that, irrespective of events in Europe, the Reagan military build-up and the policy of reasserting American hegemony was unsustainable. In the Reagan era annual defence spending had more than doubled (from over $150 billion in 1979 to over $300 billion in 1989) and reached levels (in real terms) not witnessed since the height of the Vietnam War. Given limited economic growth and a burgeoning government deficit the defence burden was unmanageable and increasingly, within the domestic political arena, unsupportable. Events in Eastern Europe and the Soviet Union undermined the legitimacy of growing defence expenditures and the strategy of global containment. Even the Gulf War provided only temporary respite for the administration from those groups, both conservative and liberal, who sought to realize a significant 'peace dividend'. Indeed it is important to recall that whilst the Berlin Wall was being torn down the political debate in Washington was focused on the question of American decline. An industry of 'declinists' argued that Reagan's attempt to reassert global hegemony had accelerated the underlying process of imperial decline. The United States, as Paul Kennedy observed — in the only book which Ronald Reagan publicly claimed to have read — was experiencing the historical fate of all great powers as they came to terms with 'imperial overstretch' (Kennedy, 1988). This 'declinist' rhetoric infiltrated key Washington policy-making circles and became an influential discourse framing the early debates concerning the post-Cold War reconstruction of American foreign policy.

No longer the prisoner of circumstance the nation confronted a decisive moment in its history without the luxury of a strategic compass, a vibrant economy, or an agreed vision of its purpose or identity. Then came the Gulf Crisis in August 1990; very much, for the Bush Administration, the unexpected answer. The crisis delivered a genuine global threat in the form of regional instability and expansionism which in turn provided a new mission — a kind of Containment Part II. In one sense the unfolding crisis was a critical catalyst in reconstituting the national mission. It underlined the continuing importance of American military power and global primacy whilst also robustly demolishing, at least superficially, the claims of the 'declinists'. Accordingly, Operation Desert Shield and Desert Storm, became intimately connected with a distinctive global project: the construction and maintenance, in President Bush's words, of a 'new world order' backed by the unassailable primacy of American power.

President George Bush responding to press questions on the Gulf Crisis

2.2 'THE NEW WORLD ORDER'

President Bush explained the concept of the 'new world order' to the American people in an address to a special Joint Session of Congress on 11 September 1990. In this address, delivered in the month after Iraq's annexation of Kuwait, the president clarified his vision for the post-Cold War world:

> We stand today at a unique and extraordinary moment ... Out of these troubled times ... a new world order can emerge; ... Today, that new world order is struggling to be born, a world quite different from the one we have known, a world where the rule of law supplants the rule of the jungle, a world in which nations recognize the shared responsibility for freedom and justice, a world where the strong respect the weak.
>
> (Bush, 1990)

Although not articulated in as precise or legalistic language as Woodrow Wilson's Fourteen Points, the 'new world order' reflected a similar vision. This new world order, like President Wilson's, emphasized mechanisms of collective security and international solidarity in the face of threats to peace and stability. Collective action was to be achieved through the rehabilitation of the United Nations to its original role in world politics, as envisaged by its founders at the end of the Second World War. Respect for international law and the promotion of liberal democracy across the globe were considered the cornerstones of this new order, essential to the maintenance of global peace and prosperity. Explicitly rejecting the criticism that this vision expressed a new *Pax Americana*, President Bush emphasized the limits to American power and the necessity, in a more interdependent world, for collective, as opposed to unilateral, action.

In this context, the Gulf Crisis was represented by the Bush Administration almost entirely as a threat to the 'new world order'. This fuelled suspicions that the concept was merely convenient rhetoric devised both to cement the unity of the allied coalition against Iraq and to mobilize a domestic political consensus in the USA as war became inevitable. But this argument fails to recognize the genuine and serious attachment of the administration to the 'new world order' project as the distinctive foundation to which post-Cold War foreign and defence policy were to be anchored. The project had its genesis in the reviews of foreign policy undertaken from 1989 onwards and issued from a wide-ranging intellectual and policy debate concerning America's future global role. It expressed the national aspirations of the Reaganite New Right coalition which considered 'victory' in the Cold War as a vindication of a strategy of global primacy. New Right thinkers placed considerable emphasis on the role of the Reagan military build-up and the strategy of ideological confrontation as the two primary causes of the collapse of the Soviet empire. From this reading of events the conclusion was drawn that the USA had to maintain its primacy in order to ensure a world order that nurtured the forces of freedom and democracy against the forces of disorder and instability. As the Wilsonians firmly believed, a world of liberal-democratic states was considered an essential ingredient of stability since democracies, it was argued, were inherently pacific (Knock, 1993). Embedded in this 'new world order' project, was a set of principles which had their roots in the Wilsonian diplomatic tradition and the ideology of American exceptionalism. It therefore found support amongst a broad coalition of interests, both within and outside government, which was united by the fear of global disorder and instability and the threat these posed to the 'city on the hill'.

In the national debate on foreign policy, unease was expressed in some quarters about the 'new world order' idea. Far from conceiving it as solely empty rhetoric, or a pragmatic political cover for military intervention in the Gulf, critics of the concept viewed it with deep suspicion. Many conservatives considered the whole notion utopian and therefore an inherently dangerous foundation for the determination of future foreign and national security policy. In 1951 the distinguished academic Hans Morgenthau had authored a critical treatise on American foreign policy entitled *In Defense of the National Interest* (Morgenthau, 1951). This classic realist analysis of US foreign policy roundly condemned the 'intellectual errors' of utopianism and legalism evident in the world order schemes of Wilson, and even Roosevelt. For many conservatives this classic critique applied with equal force to the 'intellectual errors' of Bush's 'new world order'.

Dean Acheson, Secretary of State in the Truman administration, acknowledged that in the very early days of the Cold War his political rhetoric was designed as much to neutralize the isolationists at home as it was to intimidate the Soviets. In his memoirs, entitled *Present at the Creation*, he noted: 'If we made our points clearer than truth, we did not differ from most other educators and could hardly do otherwise' (Acheson, 1969, p.375). To some extent the rhetoric of the 'new world order', and the emphasis upon regional threats to global stability, was an important element in the Bush Administration's strategy to mobilize American public opinion behind a clear internationalist foreign policy posture in the context of a growing isolationist sentiment within American society. Although there was no serious clamour for a return to the isolationism of the inter-war period there was considerable public pressure to give priority to the domestic agenda over foreign affairs. With the collapse of the Soviet threat neo-isolationists saw the historic opportunity to initiate a process of disengagement, to reorientate American foreign policy towards a more circumscribed global role and an agenda which gave priority to national economic security. The neo-isolationists considered that with the demise of communism, the USA, in effect, had fulfilled its global purpose and could now concentrate its energies and resources upon a process of domestic renewal. Accordingly the Bush Administration's call for the nation to unite behind the construction of a 'new world order' received a hostile reception amongst this growing political constituency. Even victory in the Gulf War did not erode continued public sympathy and expanding support for the neo-isolationist cause.

Alongside the isolationist critique of the 'new world order' vision arose a more radical one. The harnessing of American power to the creation of a new world order was perceived in some quarters as a dangerous illusion which ignored the fact that the world had changed dramatically. It was considered a misguided project and a doomed attempt to maintain the status quo. It was conceived as misguided because it failed to confront the real lessons of the Cold War and the Gulf War triumphs: the decline of American power and the end of the superpower era. Whilst the USA had won the Cold War this had been achieved, it was argued, only at the cost of the nation's economic security and social solidarity; and despite its status as the only remaining superpower it was nevertheless Japan, Germany and Saudi Arabia who had borne the financial costs of the Gulf War. Critics therefore considered that it was both dangerous and feckless to define the nation's role primarily as the ultimate defender of the 'new world order': a kind of twenty-first century 'globocop'. Such a role was inherently dangerous since, as Tucker indicates, it would inevitably lead to an 'imperial temptation'; a desire to intervene and impose order wherever threats to international stability arose (Tucker and Hendrickson, 1992). However benignly conceived, this prospective role as 'globocop' was deeply unpopular with the majority of politicians and the public too. For, despite the success of Operation Desert Storm, the 'Vietnam syndrome' remains deeply embedded in the national psyche.

In his final months of office, President Bush continued to define the future role of the USA in terms of the construction of a 'new world order'. In December 1992, shortly before relinquishing the Presidential Office to Bill Clinton, he remarked in an address to a convocation at Texas A&M University:

> ... today we're summoned again. This time we are called not to wage a war, hot or cold, but to win the democratic peace, not for half a world as before, but for people the world over. The end of the Cold War ... has placed in our hands a unique opportunity to see the principles for which America has stood for two centuries — democracy, free enterprise, and the rule of law — spread more widely than ever before in human history ... For the first time, turning this vision into a new and better world is, indeed, a realistic possibility.
>
> (Bush, 1992)

Yet few Americans have responded enthusiastically to this new summons. Daily television news reports of tragic events in the former Yugoslavia, Eastern Europe, Russia, East Asia and Africa have generated confused and contradictory domestic responses. No robust domestic consensus has been forthcoming on the most urgent global problems of today. Rather than a 'new world order' the forces making for 'ethnic cleansing', economic dislocation, extremist nationalism, and inexplicable violence, appear to represent a return to a distant era; an era which, somewhat ironically, also began with an American inspired vision of a new world order.

> ## SUMMARY
>
> The end of the Cold War took American foreign policy makers and the public by surprise making containment completely redundant.
>
> The Gulf Crisis provided a temporary focus for a reassertion of American primacy around the concept of the 'new world order'.
>
> The 'new world order' project was received sceptically by American elites and public opinion.

3 THE RETURN OF HISTORY

As Schurmann observes 'the novelty of the present era is the discovery of the past' (Schurmann, 1993, p.214). The demise of the East-West confrontation — the bipolar world — has brought about a return to a multipolar international system — a system, as in the inter-war period, in which multiple centres of political and economic power coexist. Moreover, the growing resurgence of nationalism, the clamour for national self-determination, the dire problems associated with economic development and modernization have provoked the reinvention of old enmities and conflicts suggesting some historical parallels with the period following the end of the First World War. As James Schlesinger (Secretary of Defense in the Nixon Administration) observes: 'The world order of the future will revert to that which existed before 1939, and most notably after World War One: It will be marked by power politics, national rivalries, and ethnic tensions' (Schlesinger, 1991). For the architects of US foreign policy this is a world order to which Americans, on past experience, will find it difficult to adapt.

3.1 BACK TO THE FUTURE

Although historical analogies are significant in shaping the strategies and actions of policy makers, particularly in times of crisis or transition, of equal significance are the intellectual fashions which filter past events to produce guides to the present. Conventional accounts of the changing global order reflect a preoccupation with the structure of international power and the geo-political balance. As will become apparent, this kind of 'realist' analysis does not capture fully history's shifting tectonic plates, delivering only a partial view of the forces of global change. Nevertheless, for policy makers in Foggy Bottom (the local address of the State Department) and the Pentagon, the most pressing consideration in reconstructing foreign and national security policy has been the changing structure of global power relations.

Before the events of 1989 were even consolidated, an essay entitled 'Why we will all miss the Cold War' became popular reading in Washington policy-making circles (Meirsheimer, 1990). A somewhat pessimistic analysis of the US predicament, the Meirsheimer argument turned on the demise of bipolarity. Meirsheimer affirmed the conventional wisdom that bipolarity imposed its own logic on world politics: that in order to prevent direct confrontation in a nuclear world both superpowers learnt to act with mutual restraint and kept control over subordinate states so underwriting global stability and peace. In this bipolar system the rules of the game were transparent, global conflicts and tensions were actively managed, and the competition for power channelled into proxy conflicts, the arms race or ideological rivalry. Since the military threat was unambiguous and since the implications of superpower conflict were so potentially devastating, bipolarity tended to create the conditions for international stability — a freezing of the world into two armed camps — more so than in any previous historical epoch. Hence Gaddis refers to the post-war era as the 'long peace' (Gaddis, 1988). The demise of bipolarity therefore implies the arrival of a less predictable and less stable world order. This is necessarily so, in Meirsheimer's view, because the logic of restraint imposed both on the great powers and upon the behaviour of weaker states in the international system is no longer operative. Conflicts of interest which previously were subordinated to alliance solidarity or managed by superpower diplomacy (or even submerged within spheres of influence) may now go effectively unchecked. The consequence is greater insecurity and a greater probability of conflict.

For the United States the end of the bipolar era has had profound ramifications for national security. It poses in particular, three acute policy dilemmas: a security dilemma; a leadership dilemma; and an autonomy dilemma. In security terms the collapse of Soviet power has involved redefining threats to national security. Potential new threats, in particular regional threats (for example, Iraq or North Korea) to global stability, have acquired greater salience. But by devising military plans to deal with these potential threats, new 'enemies' may be created unintentionally. Indeed the identification of potential threats can provoke the 'target' states to build up their military capabilities as a prudent measure to guard against what may be perceived as a future threat of US intervention. In doing so perceptions of regional insecurity may be reinforced, confirming US fears and inviting further defensive action. A spiral of worsening regional and global security could thereby be initiated. Alternatively, to ignore a potential threat may signal an unwillingness to act and so create the conditions for future insecurity. This 'security dilemma' becomes all the more acute in times of historic change and turbulent international conditions.

During the 'long peace' the West had a clear identity and sense of 'mission'. The existence of a common threat subdued serious inter-capitalist rivalries and legitimized US dominance of the Western camp. With the demise of the Soviet threat significant differences of interests and foreign policy priorities are emerging between the USA, Europe and Japan. Indeed, the possibility of a return to the intense inter-capitalist rivalries of the late nineteenth century cannot be fully discounted (Halliday, 1990). This creates a leadership dilemma for the USA in terms of how to manage future alliance relations. If it attempts to reassert its primacy it confronts the risk of fuelling discord and the disintegration of the 'West' whilst if it abandons any pretence to leadership it entertains the equally dangerous risk of international instability through a return to the old style balance of power politics.

The reconstruction of American foreign policy involves a serious debate about the changing nature and forms of American power. There are those who argue that in the post-Cold War era the USA needs to adopt a more unilateral approach to international affairs, particularly in the economic domain, in order to protect the nation from an increasing vulnerability to global forces. In this view, global economic and military supremacy are the only foundations of true national security and national autonomy — security and autonomy being conceived in absolute terms. Alternatively, there are others who emphasize that such a strategy can only be counterproductive since power in the world is becoming more widely diffused, and effective power divorced from the possession of military capabilities. Greater complexity suggests that real national autonomy and the achievement of national security can only be attained through multilateral diplomacy and international co-operation; national security and autonomy are therefore conceived in relative terms. The choice for policy makers is therefore between a foreign policy strategy predicated upon unilateralism, involving absolute notions of security and autonomy, or a strategy emphasizing multilateralism, and thus relative autonomy and security. In the case of the former there is a greater risk of conflict, whilst in the latter case American power and vital national interests may be compromised in the search for international consensus. To complicate matters this autonomy dilemma is connected with the issue of the changing configuration of power in the contemporary global system.

During the Cold War the USA confronted an unambiguous threat to its security. Only the Soviet Union had the potential capability to inflict 'unacceptable damage' on the USA. In the post-Cold War era the USA is almost invulnerable to attack. Nevertheless, since the 1970s, when Nixon and Kissinger talked in terms of a pentagonal or multipolar world order, there has been a growing realization that emerging new powers would eventually challenge its political dominance. The end of the Cold War has accelerated that challenge. Japan, a united Germany, and China, increasingly exert global political and economic influence whilst Russia too remains a considerable regional power. In the 1990s the structure of power in the international system has come to resemble that of the inter-war, or even pre-First World War, era when five or more great powers dominated global politics. In a multipolar world foreign policy is a highly complicated activity since it involves an intricate balancing of power. Instability is ever-present and potentially greater, since the larger the number of powers the higher the probability of great power rivalry, misperceptions and conflict. Indeed the historical evidence is somewhat depressing in this regard, as the inter-war years and period leading up to 1914 confirm.

Within Washington the current fascination with the great power politics of the pre-First World War and inter-war era is very much connected to a desire to 'learn' the lessons of history, assuming there are any to be learned. There is in particular a distinct concentration on the 1920s period when the USA became aware of, but refused to accept, its global power status. However, there are significant differences between the position of the USA today and its position in the inter-war period. In the 1990s and beyond the USA is likely to remain the world's dominant military power and the largest single economy. It is therefore likely to be *'primus inter pares'*, rather than just another great power. As the world recombines into a patchwork of regional blocks its claim to global primacy is becoming devalued since it confronts extremely powerful regional actors. Within Washington think tanks and policy-making circles there is a developing recognition that the transformation in global power relations which is underway requires a continuing readjustment on behalf of the USA to the politics of a multipolar world. In this new environment the USA's role is being transmuted into that of the 'regional balancer': acting in other words as the primary stabilizer of the balance of power in the world's key regions, Europe and the Pacific basin. Whatever its specific role, the existence of a world of many powers means that the USA is having '… to learn a role it has never played before: namely, to coexist and interact with other great powers' (Waltz, 1993).

3.2   THE NEW SECURITY AGENDA: FRESH CHALLENGES AND STRATEGIC PRIORITIES

This shift towards a more multipolar world has been a conspicuous theme in official thinking about post-Cold War foreign policy. In August 1991 a reassessment of US national security strategy acknowledged that 'One of the most important and far reaching strategic developments of the new era … is the emergence of Japan and Germany as economic and political leaders' (The White House, 1991, p.6). That same document also went on to identify the new 'opportunities and concerns' which confront US decision makers in their attempts to construct a national security strategy for the twenty-first century. Among the key issues identified were: the changing geo-political environment; the emergence of new security threats; and the transformation of the national security agenda.

With the collapse of the Soviet threat one of the foremost challenges confronting the USA is how to maintain the integrity of the Western alliance in the absence of any 'clear or present' danger. NATO and the defence pact with Japan have been the foundations of post-war American security. But the political cement provided by the existence of a common enemy is already beginning to crack as interests diverge and the burden of alliance commitments is called into question, both at home and abroad. Growing political and economic competition jeopardizes the future cohesion of the 'Western' security system. Since the 'West' as a global political force was constructed in relation to the 'Eastern bloc', 'It is extremely doubtful whether it can now survive the disappearance of that enemy' (Harries, 1993, p.42). Although an overly pessimistic conclusion, one which overlooks the civilizational and ideological bonds of the 'West' as a political community, divergent responses to developments in the 'New Europe' and elsewhere suggest it is not without foundation.

Stability and security in the 'New Europe' continue to be threatened by the emergence of hyper-nationalism, territorial and ethnic conflicts, social turmoil resulting from economic restructuring, and the political problems associated with democratic reform. Moreover, the unification of Germany, combined with the dissolution of the Soviet Union, has stimulated the resurgence of old fears and insecurities. Despite the European Union's attempts to develop more autonomous security arrangements, the centrality of the USA to the emergence of a stable security architecture for the continent has not diminished. This is evident specifically in the expansion of NATO membership and the significant support given to the Conference on Security and Co-operation in Europe (CSCE) as a key forum for addressing continental security issues. But this continuing engagement poses distinctive challenges for the USA both in respect of the entangling nature of its commitment and the way in which the costs of the continued engagement are to be distributed between its allies and the American taxpayer. Accordingly the problems of the 'New Europe' continue '... to be the centre-piece of the broader challenge confronting the US, its policy and politics, after the Cold War' (Treverton, 1992).

Beyond Europe, the most pressing security issue for the USA relates to 'a process that has been underway for some time, namely the regionalization of regional conflicts' (Kemp, 1993, p.207). As the Cold War has receded regional rivalries have become more salient, but also more dangerous, since there is no longer the automatic discipline of superpower intervention. As a result, in East Asia, and the Indian subcontinent in particular, regional powers have accelerated their acquisition of formidable military capabilities. India, for instance, is now a nuclear power and has the world's third largest army and seventh largest navy (Kemp, 1993). As the Gulf War and subsequent military campaigns demonstrated, even the US military machine was stretched in its attempt to ensure the defeat of Iraq. In this new geo-political context the relationship between regional and global security has become much more complex. For the USA, the existence of significant regional power centres in those areas of the world — such as the Middle East and the Asia Pacific — which are considered vital to national security, poses a critical new security problem as well as a direct challenge to its global power projection. As a consequence US defence strategy, according to General Colin Powell (former Chairman of the Joint Chiefs of Staff), has replaced its 'focus on global war-fighting [with] a focus on regional contingencies' (Powell, 1993).

This process of regionalization is directly connected to a further security concern: the proliferation of weapons of mass destruction. For an increasing number of states industrialization, the diffusion of sophisticated civil and military technologies, combined with the existence of an illegal global market in sensitive military technologies and hardware, has opened up the possibility of acquiring weapons of mass destruction. Nuclear, chemical and biological weapons are no longer the preserve of a few advanced states. Iraq, for instance, embarked on its nuclear weapons programme in the 1980s; South Africa developed a nuclear capability in the 1970s; India and Pakistan acquired a nuclear capability in the 1990s; and North Korea is believed to be close to acquiring a nuclear capability. In addition, the spread of sophisticated delivery platforms, such as ballistic missiles and advanced combat aircraft, has compounded the dangers posed by weapons proliferation. As a consequence the prevention of weapons proliferation has become an urgent priority amongst the guardians of US national security.

Whilst proliferation poses a continuing danger, a convincing argument can be made that the more immediate and tangible threats to US national security arise from economic, rather than military, rivalries. It is, for instance, instructive that the Bush Administration's and the Clinton Administration's National Security Strategy documents devoted much space to the economic security agenda (The White House, 1991, 1996). There is a certain irony in this since the very success of the post-war liberal international economic order, constructed under US hegemony, is now deeply implicated in the economic insecurity felt by communities across the country. For, in the last five decades, the globalization of the American economy has intensified the nation's vulnerability to foreign economic competition, not just from Japan but also from the newly industrializing economies of the former 'Third World'. The North American Free Trade Agreement (NAFTA) too may further compound these problems of economic insecurity. Yet the traditional security agenda, dominated as it is by military conceptions of national security, fails to address this critical issue. The new security agenda therefore acknowledges both military and economic security as the twin foundations of a coherent national security strategy for the post-Cold War era.

In reconstructing foreign and national security policy to meet the challenges posed by the new political environment and the new security agenda, the question of priorities is ever present; policy makers cannot realistically attach equal priority to all of these challenges simultaneously. Three themes in particular seem to dominate the controversies about priorities: the political question of the relative balance between a Eurocentric and a Pacific-focused foreign policy; the relative emphasis to be given to economic versus military security; and the balance between national security and collective security. Clearly the choices posed are relative rather than absolute, that is, matters of degree or of emphasis.

Since the nineteenth century America has had important ties with and interests in the Asia-Pacific region. During the post-war period, however, foreign policy acquired a Eurocentric bias. But the economic dynamism of the Pacific region, combined with the rising status of China and Japan as great powers, has provoked serious consideration of the need to re-balance foreign policy in the sense of giving greater priority to Asia-Pacific affairs. Since the early 1980s American trade with the Asian-Pacific region has overtaken that with Europe (Linder, 1986, p.16). And if present trends continue the Pacific region is likely to remain a key centre of economic activity in the global economy of the twenty-first century. There are, accordingly, powerful reasons to believe that the post-war priority accorded to European affairs will be subject to continuing demotion as American diplomacy comes to terms with a shifting geo-economic balance of power towards the Pacific. This is because 'the US should be determined to play a central role in a region that may well have a greater impact on America than US-Soviet relations or the new European order' (Chace, 1992, p.82).

During the Cold War there were many occasions upon which the USA subordinated economic objectives to national security requirements, a prime example being the denial of lucrative high-technology trade with the East. But today the question is whether economic objectives should take priority over military security. This is most explicit in the on-going controversy concerning burden sharing. The USA considers it bears an unfair proportion of the costs of Western defence, resources which otherwise could be devoted to industrial investment and improving its global competitive position. Given the increased vulnerability of the American economy to its competitors, the priority accorded to economic security, as opposed to military security, has become a sensitive issue on the national political agenda. Reductions in defence spending, and by implication the contraction of overseas security commitments, are considered by some as a necessary step towards domestic economic renewal (Nordlinger, 1995). Others promote more aggressive (protectionist) foreign economic policies, or explicit trade-offs between security commitments and bilateral economic diplomacy, to help stem the nation's relative economic decline. What is at stake here is the relative priority to be attached to economic as opposed to military security. In the absence of any serious threat to the latter, the emphasis, in the past few years, has shifted markedly towards the former.

A corresponding debate is simmering in respect of the relationship between national security goals and the developing emphasis on mechanisms of collective security. The historical antipathy to 'entangling alliances', which has its origins in the early diplomacy of the Republic, is evident in the more strident critiques of contemporary diplomacy. Since the Senate's rejection of membership of the League of Nations, the American public has shown a distinct dislike of any arrangements involving an open-ended security commitment, which is the very essence of the collective security idea. Such a fear re-appeared in the domestic debate with respect to US intervention in the Gulf and was assuaged only by the USA assuming effective control, on behalf of the UN, of the entire military operation. More recently cautious domestic responses to requests for US or NATO intervention in Bosnia betrays the continuing legacy of a deep national suspicion of the collective security idea. The consequence is a profound ambiguity about how national security interests relate to the renewed emphasis upon collective security. That ambiguity is partly deliberate, and partly the consequence of a failure to finally resolve more fundamental questions concerning the USA's role in the post-Cold War world, namely: 'What should the USA do?', and of equal importance, 'What should the USA be?' (Chace, 1992, p.7).

> ## SUMMARY
>
> The end of the Cold War has transformed the global power structure from bipolarity to multipolarity, although the US, as the only superpower, remains *'primus inter pares'*.
>
> The USA now confronts a security dilemma, leadership dilemma and an autonomy dilemma.
>
> The new security agenda emphasizes regional threats, the integrity of the West, the proliferation of weapons of mass destruction and economic threats to national security.
>
> The growing significance of the Pacific region, economic diplomacy and collective defence are challenging the established priorities of post-war national security and foreign policy.

4 PLANNING FOR PEACE

The political response to these questions has elicited considerable rhetoric but little conclusive action. In Layne's view the rhetoric of change emanating from Foggy Bottom and the White House conceals an essential continuity in the American approach to foreign affairs; an approach which seeks to maintain global preponderance and thereby '...aims at preserving the Cold War status quo, even though the Cold War is over' (Layne, 1993). Others disagree and emphasize the apparent lack of any coherent or sustained strategy informing post-Cold War foreign policy (Wolfowitz, 1994; Naim, 1997). It is, in this respect, instructive to recall that the strategy of containment was never systematically articulated until 1950, almost five years after VE day. Indeed, a parallel could be drawn between today and the early post-war years. According to Leffler's acclaimed study of foreign policy making during the Truman Administration (1945–51), there was a similar mood of 'muddling through': 'Initially, US policy makers made little effort to define priorities concerning their national security objectives. Moreover, they had enormous difficulties mobilizing resources and designing tactics capable of achieving their goals ... In an administration that still lacked effective leadership and effective co-ordination machinery, American policy looked rudderless' (Leffler, 1992, p.55).

By the end of Truman's period of office the strategy of containment had been formulated and implemented, a strategy which defined the nation's national security and foreign policy posture until the collapse of communism in 1989. History teaches caution in coming to definitive judgements.

4.1 THE END OF EMPIRE?

In commenting upon the post-war British predicament Dean Acheson suggested that the country had 'lost an Empire and not yet discovered a role' for itself. Today a similar predicament confronts the USA, involving a parallel process of 'imperial' readjustment to a new post-Cold War environment. But there is evidence to suggest that this readjustment, as in the British case, is proceeding, if at all, with extreme caution. Irrespective of the prevailing political rhetoric it is the (in)actions of decision makers, according to many respected foreign policy analysts, which betrays a stubborn commitment to the status quo: to a strategy of preponderance or, as the great thinker Reinhold Niebuhr characterized it many years ago, to 'the empire which is so desperately anxious not to be an empire' (Niebuhr, 1959, p.28).

Amongst the severest critics of what is characterized as a failure to grasp the challenges of the post-Cold War world are Tucker, Layne, Harries and many former Cold War warriors including James Schlesinger, Henry Kissinger and Zbigniew Brzezinski (President Carter's national security adviser). Although they each propose distinctive remedies their analyses share certain common themes. Specifically there is concern at the slow pace of adjustment to the realities of the new era, in particular, much greater concern is expressed with regard to the continuing attachment to a Cold War strategy of US preponderance, or hegemony, in the global system. Whether disguised in the rhetoric of the 'new world order', the slogan of 'American leadership', or the language of 'collective security', the policies pursued as well as the underlying political motivations, it is argued, reflect a misplaced conviction in the necessity for continued American primacy.

Layne, in particular, identifies in current policy a powerful reaffirmation of the Cold War strategy of hegemony (Layne, 1993). He associates the desire of policy makers to forestall the emergence of a multipolar world order with a virulent attachment to the reassertion of American primacy. Underlying this belief in primacy, he argues, is an assumption that multipolar systems are inherently unstable and prone to the kinds of great power rivalries which, in previous eras, have culminated in war. Equally, there is a conscious recognition that, as noted earlier, the shift to a world of many great powers would involve considerable adjustment for the USA. A multipolar world would necessarily involve a more complex game of power balancing than existed during the Cold War. It would impose new constraints upon US freedom of action and engage other states, such as Japan and Germany, in framing the rules of the newly emerging global order. Without preponderant power, it is argued, American global interests and national security will become vulnerable to the ambitions and actions of other great powers. For a nation which fought and won the Cold War such a predicament might be considered, not simply an infringement of its 'historic mission', but tantamount to a fundamental affront to its national interests and national purpose. Without preponderant power, so the argument goes, democracy and freedom, both at home and abroad, will be compromised. This is a recurring theme — stretching back to Madison and Jefferson — in American diplomacy and nowhere better expressed than in the advice of the State Department's Policy Planning Staff to President Truman in 1949: 'To seek less than preponderant power would be to opt for defeat. Preponderant power must be the object of US policy' (PPS Staff, quoted in Leffler, 1992, p.446). What accounts for this apparent attachment to preponderance given the end of the Cold War?

One explanation is to be found in the inertia of power. Harries notes there is '...the weight of habits of involvement and leadership acquired over the last half century. Americans have got used to their country being a superpower and a leader, and they like it more than they care to admit (or possibly know)' (Harries, 1993, p.50). Another factor is the popular belief that, in the post-war period, American hegemony underwrote the creation of a global economic and political order which brought prosperity and the 'long peace' both for the nation and for the West. Whilst this assertion is superficially correct it radically oversimplifies the historical relationship between hegemonic power and international order. Nevertheless, it is an argument which is used to legitimate a continuing strategy of primacy. As Layne and Schwarz note: 'Underpinning US world order strategy is the belief that America must maintain what is in essence a military protectorate in economically critical regions to ensure America's international trade and financial relations will not be disrupted by political upheaval' (Layne and Schwarz, 1993).

There is also a curious sense in which the attachment to American primacy can be traced to the relative erosion of American power in the world. Without entering into the debate about the validity of the 'declinist' argument it is certainly the case that since the 1970s perceptions of relative decline have been influential in shaping the direction of national security policy. Kissinger's *détente* strategy, for instance, was widely regarded as an attempt to manage the erosion of American power whilst Reagan's attempt to reassert US global hegemony was a direct response to perceptions of American decline. Since the 'triumph' in the 'Great Contest' a distinctly simplified and (perhaps deliberately) misleading caricature of the strategic choices confronting the nation has tended to become fixed in the public imagination: a choice between preponderance or simply adjusting to relative decline. Given that the electorate closely associate the former with 'victory' in the Cold War and the latter (for those with long memories) both with the 'failed' policies of *détente* and the Carter years, there has been little incentive for politicians and the bureaucracy to engage in the kind of fundamental reassessment of the strategy of 'primacy' which the collapse of communism would appear to demand.

According to Tucker and Hendrickson this apparent failure to rethink America's global role is linked to a more deeply rooted 'imperial temptation' (Tucker and Hendrickson, 1992). In some political circles, the remarkable triumph over the Soviet Union, the Gulf War 'victory', the unassailable nature of American power, the worldwide 'democratic revolution', and the global reach of American capital, represent the foundations of a truly liberal world order and present the USA with a historic opportunity to 'make the world safe for democracy'. As Tucker and Hendrickson note:

> The US is today the dominant military power in the world. In the reach and effectiveness of its military forces, America compares favourably with some of the greatest Empires known to history ... Its historic adversaries are in retreat ... Under these conditions, an age old temptation — the imperial temptation — may prove compelling for the US. That this temptation is pursued under the banner of a new world order, an order that promises to universalize both peace and the institutions of freedom, does not relieve it of its dangers...
>
> (Tucker and Hendrickson, 1992, p.16)

Justifying the benign exercise of great power, in terms of the creation of a 'better world', finds echoes in other formative episodes in American diplomatic history. In explaining the doctrine of Manifest Destiny in his inaugural speech in 1845, President Polk asserted that '...foreign powers do not seem to appreciate the true character of our government. To enlarge its limits is to extend the dominions of peace [and freedom]' (quoted in Perkins, 1993, p.178). Similarly the Monroe Doctrine, the Open Door policy and the 'preclusive imperialism' of the late nineteenth century display evidence of an imperial temptation. William Appelman Williams argues that since the founding of the republic the USA has courted an imperial vision although one which is quite removed from the European imperial tradition. This attachment to 'empire as a way of life', according to Williams, has permeated the entire history of post-war American diplomacy since the days of NSC-68, '...unquestionably ... one of the truly impressive imperial documents' (Williams, 1980, p.193).

Williams' argument is an important reminder of the 'weight of history' and diplomatic tradition in accounting for the current attachment to preponderant power. This is not to assert either that the USA is an 'imperialist state' or to proclaim the existence of an American 'Empire' in the traditional meaning of the word — controversies with which the Introduction has engaged more fully. Rather it is simply to acknowledge, as Raymond Aron stated in his classic study of American foreign policy *The Imperial Republic*, that throughout history all great powers have sought to shape the international order to their own purposes such that there is '...only a difference of degree between an "imperial" diplomacy and a great power diplomacy' (Aron, 1973, p.256). As a great power the USA is not exceptional in this respect and so is subject to the same 'imperial temptation'. But is there any evidence that post-Cold War US foreign policy manifests such a 'temptation'?

4.2 A POST-IMPERIAL FOREIGN POLICY?

In explaining to the American public the rationale for US military intervention in the Gulf in 1991, President Bush declared that the USA remained '...the only nation on this earth that could assemble the forces of peace' (Bush, 1991).

This rhetoric placed a rather different construction on the 'new world order' than that which had been evident some months earlier. This interpretation highlighted America's preponderant power and, by implication, portrayed the 'new world order' as one which was 'made in America' — in Schurmann's words 'a novum imperium Americanum' (Schurmann, 1993, p.210).

Even the most favourable reading of the diplomacy and rhetoric of the 'new world order' project could not fail to ignore its central reaffirmation of the primacy of American global power. Events since 1991 appear to confirm this drift 'back to the future'. Critical assessments of the new world order project view it primarily as a vehicle for legitimizing, both at home and abroad, a 'new' global mission for the USA in the post-Cold War era. That mission has expanded over several years to embrace humanitarian intervention, as in Operation Restore Hope in Somalia in 1992, unilateral intervention in Panama (Operation Just Cause, 1991), the threatened use of military intervention to restore democracy in Haiti (1993), air strikes (with NATO partners) in Bosnia to support UN peace-keeping objectives, and air strikes on Iraq in 1998. Although it has not acted unilaterally on all these occasions the USA has been a key proponent of political and military intervention where its interests appear to require it.

President Bush addressing the American people from the Oval Office on 16 January 1991 after US forces began military action against Iraq

Alongside this determined commitment to combat the forces of international instability there has also been an extremely vigorous reaffirmation of its alliance commitments, both with Europe and Japan. A new global 'partnership' with Japan was enshrined in the Tokyo Declaration of February 1992, whilst in early 1994 President Clinton proposed a revitalization of the United States 'partnership' with Europe '...to define a new security at a time of historic change' (Clinton, 1994). In celebrating 50 years of the NATO alliance, a new 'strategic concept' was unveiled that reaffirmed US commitments to Europe. Underlying these initiatives is an attempt to lock Japan and Germany more firmly into the American security order so preventing any resurgence of independent military power and any potential future challenge to US global primacy.

Within the economic arena successive administrations have expended enormous diplomatic energy, throughout the early 1990s, in securing global agreement on the Uruguay Round of the GATT negotiations. Their objective was to safeguard the American inspired liberal international trading order against the centripetal forces of growing regionalism and protectionism. The Clinton Administration in particular adopted an aggressive posture with respect to trade relations with Japan invoking a return to 'managed trade'. Threats of a trade war were exploited to force Japan into liberalizing its domestic markets while the East Asian economic crisis of 1997–98 was used to further the cause of liberalization and deregulation throughout the region. But the most conspicuous evidence of renewed emphasis on a strategy of primacy has been in the defence domain.

Describing the challenges confronting the US military in the post-Cold War environment General Colin Powell, at the time Chairman of the Joint Chiefs of Staff, declared that 'America is still the last best hope of earth, and we still hold the power and bear the responsibility for it remaining so' (Powell, 1993). As Kurth notes one of the key challenges to American primacy and security is the potential fragmentation of the world into regional (economic or political) blocs — such as MittleEuropa and Greater Asia — dominated by regional powers (Kurth, 1993). Acknowledging this potential development, the draft *Defense Planning Guidance for the Fiscal Years 1994–99* proposed that a primary objective of US post-Cold War national security strategy should be to prevent other states '...from challenging our leadership or seeking to overturn the established political and economic order'. To achieve this goal the USA '...therefore must maintain the mechanisms for deterring potential competitors from even aspiring to a large regional or global role' (quoted in Layne and Schwarz, 1993). This draft guidance (later withdrawn because of its controversial 'tone' rather than its substance) was clearly directed, not simply at obvious military threats, such as a revitalized Russia, but also towards Germany and Japan as potential rival centres of economic and political power. Similar sentiments were expressed throughout the 1990s in growing public animosity towards Japan since, as one observer commented, 'Japan's first misfortune is that it is now the only possible candidate for the role of America's Chief Enemy' (Luttwak, 1993, p.60).

Whilst some recent developments suggest a renewed commitment to a strategy of global primacy other evidence suggests a certain caution in reading into contemporary policy a firmly defined pattern in respect of post-Cold War national security strategy. In fact there are many ambiguities. Detectable shifts in strategic thinking specifically in respect of the focus, agenda, and conduct of foreign policy are equally evident.

There is a pronounced shift in the focus of American foreign policy, away from its post-war Eurocentrism, towards a progressive emphasis on relations with Pacific Rim states. In 1996, over 40 per cent of total American trade was with the Pacific region and by the year 2000 trade and investment flows across the Pacific are predicted to be twice the volume of those across the Atlantic (Gibney, 1993). But this gradual refocusing of American foreign policy is not simply a reflection of changing patterns of trade but also shifting patterns of security, political and cultural relations. Migration from the Asia Pacific region to the USA far outstrips that from Europe. There are also increasing pressures on the USA, from a number of Asian countries, to develop a more pronounced role in regional security affairs because of their fears of a resurgence of Japanese power and a revisionist China (Buscynski, 1992). President Clinton has welcomed the emergence of a 'new Pacific community' stressing to European leaders that '...without question, Europe is not the only focus of our engagement...' (Clinton, 1994). In more forthright language a senior State Department official acknowledged that 'Europe is still very important but, in relative terms, we believe Asia has become more significant for America' (Nicoll and Graham, 1993, p.15).

In respect of the foreign policy agenda the traditional distinction between high policy (military security) and low policy (economic and welfare issues) has been discarded. In practice economic security is displacing the conventional emphasis upon military security. During testimony on Capitol Hill, Secretary of State Warren Christopher acknowledged that revitalizing the economy was a primary goal of the Clinton administration's foreign policy (Christopher, 1993). Moreover, as the fortunes of the advanced capitalist economies become increasingly interwoven, and global economic competition intensifies, the traditional separation of foreign from domestic policy is becoming less tenable. Securing the future of Boeing workers in Seattle, for example, demands an active economic diplomacy. Some have referred to this development as the end of 'foreign policy'. Domestic concerns are therefore becoming increasingly inseparable from the conduct of the nation's foreign affairs. As President Clinton has observed, 'everything, from the strength of our economy to the safety of our cities, to the health of our people, depends on events not only within our borders but half a world away' (Clinton, 1999). The conduct of foreign policy too is changing.

Even though politicians and the foreign policy bureaucracy may aspire to American hegemony there is a deepening awareness that the accelerating diffusion of economic and political power in the global system enormously complicates the conduct and management of foreign policy. More specifically the achievement of national goals increasingly demands international co-operation. On a whole range of issues, from trade matters to defence issues, unilateral action is more and more likely to prove counterproductive. Even the very strategy of hegemony or preponderance is brought into question since, as Nye argues, in conditions of complex interdependence, acting unilaterally '...may lead to occasional foreign-policy triumphs, but it is an inadequate answer to the host of problems that can be addressed only through international co-operation' (Nye, 1990, p.254). Greater emphasis upon the necessity of international institutions, multilateral diplomacy and collective security mechanisms to the realization of American goals has therefore become a distinguishing feature of foreign policy in the 1990s. From the expansion of NATO and the establishment of APEC to the creation of a new international trade organization to police the GATT trade arrangements, the bias towards multilateralism, as opposed to unilateralism or bilateralism, is becoming a dominant theme in the conduct of foreign policy. Responding to Congressional questions concerning the contemporary conduct of foreign policy a State Department official explained 'We cannot do all of this alone — our biggest single task is to make the multilateral institutions stronger and stronger' (Wirk, 1993). This is likely to be the recurrent refrain of subsequent administrations well into the twenty-first century.

Undoubtedly the more visible consequences of the end of the Cold War are manifest in the defence domain. Successive reviews in the early 1990s have pared the defence budget by over 30 per cent, significantly reduced military capabilities from the highpoint of the Reagan era, involved the closure of scores of bases at home and abroad, and brought the most significant cut back in defence procurement since the end of the Vietnam War. American society and its economy are experiencing a process of significant demilitarization. Whilst official rhetoric may allude to the maintenance of military supremacy the planned reductions in military capability, combined with the abandonment of forward deployment of US forces and the shift towards a regional defence strategy, suggest a restructuring of America's global power projection capacity.

Seeking a national basis for planning this restructuring the Clinton Administration, in one of its first initiatives upon taking office, established 'the bottom-up review' of national defence. This aimed at a fundamental reassessment of national security strategy since, as the review report noted,

> ...it has become clear that the framework that guided our security policy during the Cold War is inadequate for the future ... We cannot, as we did for the past several decades, premise this year's forces, programs, and budgets on incremental shifts from last year's efforts. We must rebuild our defense strategy, forces, and defense programs and budgets from the bottom up.
>
> (Department of Defense, 1993, p.1)

The report's conclusions identified further reductions in defence capability. Defence spending too is to be reduced from its highpoint of 6.5 per cent GNP in the mid-1980s to around 3 per cent in the 1990s, with some increase from 1999 onwards. Since the Quadrennial Defense Review in 1997, the prime aim of the Clinton Administration has been to ensure US global military supremacy and military-technological primacy.

As the USA confronts the demands of the twenty-first century it has to refine its post-imperial foreign policy for a new historical epoch. In fact that process is already underway, being conspicuously evident in the tensions, inconsistencies and clashing visions which characterize the current foreign policy 'posture'. Foreign policy is in flux: with no 'clear or present danger' it has been robbed of the fixed point of perspective which informs consistent and coherent policy making. Buffeted by forces of continuity and change, trapped between existing commitments and idealistic aspirations, and pressured by public fickleness and turbulent international conditions, foreign policy no longer displays, as it arguably did in the Cold War era, a consistency of purpose, or coherent logic, but rather exhibits a kind of 'disjointed incrementalism' (Haas, 1976). 'Disjointed' in the sense that foreign policy lacks a coherent or consistent project and 'incremental' in the sense that adaptation to the dynamic conditions of the post-Cold War world is predominantly (although not exclusively) effected through a cautious process of marginal adjustments to existing policies and programmes. As a strategy for muddling through 'disjointed incrementalism' has distinct advantages but in the realm of foreign policy it also carries great dangers. Avoiding these dangers demands a sense of conviction, direction and national purpose. The most critical issue confronting the architects of post-imperial American foreign policy is therefore located in the realm of ideas and values rather than the realm of praxis. Many years ago Morgenthau concluded that: 'The main handicaps that American foreign policy must overcome ... are not to be found in the challenges confronting it from the outside. They lie in certain deeply ingrained habits of thought, and preconceptions as to the nature of foreign policy' (Morgenthau, 1951, p.91).

> *SUMMARY*
>
> Contemporary US foreign policy is argued by some to represent a continuing attachment to preponderant power driven by the habits of great power, or an imperial temptation.
>
> Evidence for this attachment to primacy is to be found in the conduct of defence and economic diplomacy particularly.
>
> But there is also evidence of a transformation of foreign policy in the shift towards the Pacific, the emphasis upon economic affairs, the stress on multilateralism and the reductions in defence capabilities and spending.
>
> A more accurate description of contemporary US foreign policy is reflected in the concept of 'disjointed incrementalism'.

5 STRUGGLE FOR THE TURF

For almost three decades after the end of the Second World War, American foreign policy was underwritten by a robust domestic consensus. Exceptional circumstances brought forth an exceptional domestic response as political and mass opinion was mobilized, by all available means, behind the strategy of containment. By the 1970s, in the aftermath of the Vietnam War, that domestic consensus and its associated bipartisan approach to foreign affairs had collapsed. The spirit of internationalism, which had been the primary ingredient in the post-war foreign policy consensus, was laid to rest in Saigon. Although a sense of national purpose and identity remained intact, there arose profound disagreements within the polity about how to conduct America's global role. The end of the Cold War has compounded subsequent decades of self-doubt, and political struggles to construct a new consensus, by eliminating the very rationale for that global role itself: the Soviet threat. Paradoxically, the demise of the Soviet Union has posed a more profound political challenge to the United States than the continuation of the Cold War since it has '…deprived Washington of its intellectual and conceptual moorings, provoking what is, in effect, a major identity crisis for the US' (Williams et al., 1993).

Coming to terms with this 'identity crisis' has involved revisiting the intellectual traditions which have guided American diplomacy since the founding of the Republic. This is an instinctively American reaction to crisis and one rooted in the culture of exceptionalism which compels political leaders and elites to justify foreign policy in the abstract language of moral codes and the Republic's eternal political principles. Think tanks and policy makers across Washington, and the nation, remain busily engaged in reinventing these traditions to match the new circumstances of the post-Cold War world. A serious and well-informed national debate has ensued but has yet to be successfully resolved. The conversation between competing social and political constituencies, each hoping to achieve intellectual hegemony in the reconstruction of foreign policy, remains intense. For the issues are profoundly controversial and the stakes formidable: the very possibility of a second American century is in the balance.

There are essentially three distinct, but in some ways overlapping, positions in this great national dialogue: the 'preponderants'; the 'neo-isolationists'; and the 'globalists'. Each of these positions articulates, rather than directly expresses, the interests, aspirations, beliefs and values of a particular constellation of social, political and economic forces in American society. Each position too reflects a specific cluster of public beliefs about foreign affairs — a belief system — which connect to significant political cleavages in American society. These three positions also exhibit strong allegiances to the powerful historical narratives which have informed and legitimated American foreign policy in the twentieth century, '…the realistic — thinking and acting in terms of power — represented by Alexander Hamilton; the ideological — thinking in terms of moral principles but acting in terms of power — represented by Thomas Jefferson and John Quincy Adams; and the moralistic — thinking and acting in terms of moral principles — represented by Woodrow Wilson' (Morgenthau, 1951, p.13). In the following pages each of the three positions will be briefly explored in respect of its core prescriptions and socio-political bases of support.

5.1   PRIMACY

In an essay entitled 'Why international primacy matters' Samuel Huntingdon, an influential conservative political scientist, presents a rigorous defence of the case for a post-Cold War strategy of preponderance. Simply put, his argument is that, 'States pursue primacy in order to be able to insure their security, promote their interests, and shape the international environment in ways that will reflect their interests and values. Primacy is desirable not primarily to achieve victory in war but to achieve the states' goals without recourse to war' (Huntingdon, 1993). As the earlier discussion has suggested, the attachment to primacy is linked to a distinctly 'realist' or power politics view of international affairs. A view in which the struggle for power and national security are the critical arbiters of foreign policy. But for Huntingdon, primacy is not simply about ensuring military supremacy, 'keeping the barracks 'manned' and the powder dry', but is much more to do with achieving, and sustaining, economic pre-eminence. This is because, '…in a world in which military conflict between major states is unlikely, economic power will be increasingly important in determining the primacy or subordination of states' (Huntingdon, 1993). Since the industrialization of warfare, economic power has been absolutely crucial to the coercive power of the state. Without preponderant power the future for the USA, suggests this line of reasoning, is as a 'power among powers' unable to shape its own destiny, or that of the planet, and increasingly vulnerable to international conditions and forces. Such a predicament would involve the effective abandonment of the national mission to promote global freedom and democracy and create a power vacuum encouraging the return of international instability and conflict. Primacy, or as Krauthammer refers to it 'the unipolar moment', must be maintained since,

> A world without US primacy will be a world with more violence and disorder and less democracy and economic growth … The sustained international primacy of the US is central to the welfare and security of Americans and to the future of freedom, democracy, open economies and international order in the world.
>
> (Huntingdon, 1993)

Ignoring the hyperbole, this sanctification of primacy, in part, issues from the ideology of American exceptionalism. Although dressed up in the language of realpolitik, there is a strong utopian undercurrent which asserts itself in the implication that without primacy the nation would be robbed of its national purpose and also the means to achieve it. Similarly, the notion of exceptionalism is embedded in the belief that without a world configured to American interests the very future of the American democratic 'experiment', will be placed in jeopardy. This has been a recurring theme in American diplomatic history since the era of Hamilton and Jefferson. It was most cogently articulated in the strategy of containment which, as Leffler explains, sought preponderant power for the USA because officials were driven 'by an ideological conviction that their own political economy of freedom would be jeopardized if a totalitarian foe became too powerful … the US would have to protect itself by increasing military spending or regimenting its domestic economy. And if such contingencies materialized, domestic freedoms would be imperiled' (Leffler, 1992, pp.13–14). The reaffirmation of this same strategy of preponderance in the 1990s, excepting that economic rivalry replaces superpower rivalry, emanates from important sectors of American society which desire continuity in foreign policy: a continuity in terms of both the national purpose and the means to achieve it.

Amongst the military, the defence industry, sections of corporate America, traditional conservatives, the New Right, and segments of liberal opinion, the appeal of preponderance is extremely strong. This is not explicable simply in terms of material or self-interest, but is related to ideological convictions and socially constructed belief systems (Holsti and Rosenau, 1984). Beyond elite opinion primacy also resonates with nationalist sentiment and the patriotic spirit which permeates all aspects of American cultural and social life. Despite this patriotic appeal and the powerful social interests mobilizing behind it, the reaffirmation of preponderance is received sceptically by those many Americans who are more concerned with jobs, health care and crime than events abroad, let alone any further costly global entanglements. This America is much more comfortable with the ultra-conservative Patrick Buchanan's plea 'Come home, America' (quoted in Harries, 1993, p.52).

5.2 NEO-ISOLATIONISM

Isolationist sentiment has been a feature of the domestic politics of American foreign policy since the eighteenth century. In some eras it has acted as a powerful constraint upon, or even determinant of, foreign policy, for instance in the inter-war period. In other periods it has been a marginal force, an irritant in the policy process, as in the Cold War era. But throughout the 1990s perceptions of economic vulnerability to global competition, especially following the East Asian crisis of 1997–98, created the conditions for a dramatic resurgence of isolationist opinion. The end of the Cold War was also an important catalyst, in so far as the absence of a real external threat strengthened the case for an 'America first' foreign policy.

Neo-isolationism emphasizes selective engagement with the world, on the USA's terms, rather than the political and diplomatic disengagement which characterized the isolationism of the 1920s and 1930s. It remains grounded philosophically in the kinds of concerns which Hamilton originally expressed over two hundred years ago in respect of the dangers foreign entanglement poses to liberty and democracy at home (McGrew, 1989). Neo-isolationists consider that the end of the Cold War is a historic moment of opportunity since the burdens of Empire have been lifted freeing the USA to concentrate upon domestic priorities. As Admiral Crowe, former Chairman of the Joint Chiefs of Staff, commented, there is no longer any rationale for '...looking overseas when our biggest long term threats are at home' (Williams *et al.*, 1993). This view has found a receptive audience across America and in the 1992 Presidential election contributed to the defeat of an incumbent president whose campaign had attempted to make foreign affairs a decisive issue amongst the electorate. Ironically it did prove decisive, but only in that it was dismissed by voters as of secondary importance to the 'economy, stupid!'.

In his study of American public opinion, Schneider notes that somewhere approaching 50 per cent of the public never really shared in the elite enthusiasm for a Cold War internationalist foreign policy (Schneider, 1984, p.17). Whilst not all the 50 per cent were isolationists, a sizeable segment of this opinion remains ill-disposed to an activist foreign policy. This antipathy towards the world beyond American shores grew decidedly more vociferous throughout the 1980s, partly as a response to intense international economic competition which brought about the destruction of entire industries and communities. The de-industrialization of the USA, corporate restructuring and the internationalization of American business were perceived as a direct consequence of growing vulnerability to Japanese and Third World economic competition. The USA was undoubtedly becoming more dependent on international trade and global economic markets. Blue-collar Americans, together with the more vulnerable sectors of corporate America, sought greater protection from what was considered unfair international competition. The consistent failure of the Federal government to act, but instead to preach the virtues of a global free trade order, merely contributed to strengthening isolationist sentiment providing the traditional core of isolationist support with new allies in the march on Washington.

With the end of the Cold War a curious coalition of neo-isolationist forces, embracing traditional conservatives, nationalists, farmers, protectionist campaigners, fundamentalist religious groups, and the representatives of labour and corporations threatened by foreign competition have sought to direct the reconstruction of American foreign policy. Initially, their vigorous campaigns, for instance in respect of the North American Free Trade Agreement, failed. But consistent political pressure has transformed the domestic political debate, creating a political environment strongly resistant to a moralistic interventionalist or internationalist foreign policy. Moreover, as the foreign policy agenda shifts towards economic security issues, the influence of neo-isolationist forces becomes measurably greater as is evident from recent trends towards a more unilateral and aggressive American trade diplomacy and the 1998 failure of Congress to give the President negotiating authority for a new round of global trade talks.

Although a broad coalition of social and economic interests, the neo-isolationist 'movement' promotes a fairly coherent post-Cold War foreign policy strategy for the USA. It is based around two key principles: 'selective engagement' and the primacy of national economic security. Goldberg argues that a return to 'selective engagement' is principally to rediscover the nation's traditional diplomatic practise — the posture adopted by the Founding Fathers and operationalized during the first one hundred years of the Republic (Goldberg, 1992). Today this translates into a pragmatic approach to foreign affairs, reducing permanent alliance commitments, bringing the troops home, and eschewing grand world visions for a more circumscribed role. Foreign and defence policy, it is argued, must be determined purely by a rational assessment of American interests abroad, rather than in relation to abstract ideological or moral principles. It must also be combined with a realistic acknowledgement of the limits to American power. Former US Ambassador to the UN (during the Reagan administration) Jean Kirkpatrick, somewhat surprisingly for a former Cold War warrior, echoes this view in suggesting that '...the United States should not try to manage the balance of power in Europe — we should neither seek to prevent nor assist Germany in re-establishing a dominant position in Europe or Central Europe. We could not control these matters if we tried and there is no reason to try' (quoted in Harries, 1993, p.51).

Associated with this commitment to selective engagement is the primacy attached to economic security. This reversal of traditional priorities arises, according to Luttwak, because 'geo-economics' has come to replace the traditional game of 'geo-politics' (Luttwak, 1993, p.35). In the twenty-first century world of 'geo-economics' the struggle for power has been replaced by a struggle for industrial and economic supremacy. To ensure its success in this 'new world order' the USA is therefore called upon to adopt a more unilateral and aggressive foreign economic strategy, even if this provokes conflict with its established 'allies'. Resources presently directed towards defence, particularly alliance commitments, would, it is argued, be better expended in developing America's own economic and industrial infrastructure so giving it a competitive edge in the global market. As Luttwak argues, in this emerging neo-mercantalist system, in which the competition for national (or even regional) economic and industrial supremacy is the sole driving force, '…the choice that remains for the US is between the successful negotiation of sweeping geo-economic disarmament, and the waging of the geo-economic struggle in full force' (Luttwak, 1993, p.323). For neo-isolationists this transformation of global politics demands a radically different approach to foreign affairs: one which begins at home with domestic economic renewal and one which sanctions '…post hegemonic America … not to care about what goes on over there' (Burnham, 1993).

5.3 GLOBALISTS

This isolationist rhetoric is complete anathema to the globalists who sympathize with its underlying concerns but reject completely its prescriptions (Chace, 1992). Disengaging from the world, for the globalists, is not a realistic option. On the contrary, they argue that because of the intensification of globalization over the last five decades the USA can no longer assert its independence nor so readily impose its will on others. In short they believe global politics has been transformed and consequently so have the options for US policy makers. Isolationism in an interdependent world is no longer a serious option, nor, in a global system in which power is increasingly fragmented, is the reassertion of primacy likely either to be sustainable in the long run, or an effective strategy for achieving national goals. In an interdependent world domestic and foreign policy are so intertwined that a vibrant domestic economy requires a successful foreign economic policy and a successful foreign policy demands a strong economy. Paul Nitze, the architect of containment, has written in a 'Postscript to NSC-68' that 'It is now more difficult than ever for the US to separate itself from an active role in world affairs [because] economic vulnerability has become a security issue, something upon which we can no longer act independently' (Nitze, 1993).

In decisively rejecting the prescriptions of the 'preponderants' and the 'neo-isolationists' the globalists accept some of their basic assumptions concerning the nation's post Cold War predicament. The dominant position of the

USA militarily, and as the world's single largest economy, is a shared assumption. The emphasis upon economic security and the need to concentrate upon domestic economic renewal are other shared assumptions. But the globalists reject primacy because they believe it is no longer effective in the transformed global political context and reject the isolationist assertion that selective engagement or neo-mercantalism are the only appropriate responses to the post-Cold War international environment.

By discounting these prescriptions the globalists refute the specific interpretations — the lessons of the past — which both the 'preponderants' and the 'neo-isolationists' impose upon post-war American diplomatic history. In particular they refute the notion that American hegemony, in the early post-war period, simply permitted the USA to impose its vision of world order on other states. Rather, they point to the common ideological bonds between Western governments and the common desire to defend the capitalist order as critical elements in the acquiescence of allied nations to the USA's post-war plans. Similarly they refute the New Right's argument that the reassertion of American hegemony during the 'New Cold War' phase of the Reagan period was the sole cause of the collapse of the Soviet Empire. On the contrary, they view Reagan's policy with disdain, emphasizing how it cost the Americans dear, weakened the economy and diluted American power, whilst all the time the internal contradictions of communism were unravelling the socialist experiment and doing the administration's work for it. Accordingly they reject the simple equation of American hegemony with ultimate control over global political events or outcomes. Nor do they accept that hegemony can be reasserted or even sustained since the historical evidence, as Paul Kennedy demonstrates, is unambiguous in that, '...the only answer to the question increasingly debated by the public of whether the US can preserve its existing position, is "no"' (Kennedy, 1988, p.533).

In similar vein the globalists refute the neo-isolationist argument that a return to the kind of selective engagement and unilateralism of the first one hundred years of the Republic, or the autarky of the inter-war period, will deliver either international stability or national prosperity. For the USA in the twenty-first century is a post-industrial economy, not an eighteenth century agricultural state. Moreover, the American experience of the post-war period is that global engagement, not disengagement, is the foundation of sustained peace, at least within the Northern hemisphere, whilst national prosperity depends upon an international regime of free trade, not protectionism. On purely historical grounds, the globalists therefore consider there is no politically feasible option for the USA in the post-Cold War era other than to develop a more sophisticated internationalist foreign policy strategy. But what exactly does this involve?

One of the most vigorous proponents of this 'new internationalism' is James Chace, a former editor of *Foreign Affairs*, the journal of the liberal foreign policy establishment. In his monograph, *The Consequences of the Peace*, a rigorous argument is made '...for embracing a new American internationalism' (Chace, 1992, p.192). This 'new internationalism' proffers an essentially liberal vision but attuned to the historical predicament of the United

States at the end of the twentieth century. It involves a commitment to collective defence, international co-operation and multilateral diplomacy, and an emphasis upon US global leadership (as opposed to hegemony) in the management of the new global order. Rather than a world fragmented into competing economic or political blocs it envisages a global order in which co-operation, multilateral diplomacy and mechanisms of global governance, such as the United Nations, provide the basis for global stability. Such an order '…would require the United States to abandon any pretence to being the only superpower, yet it would preclude a withdrawal into ourselves' (Chace, 1992, p.192).

Underlying this liberal vision is an implicit thesis namely that military (hard) power is no longer the main currency of power in international relations. At least amongst the developed states, military power has ceased to be the dominant instrument of foreign policy in part, because of the existence of nuclear weapons and in part because of the dire implications of military conflict. As Mueller suggests, major 'war in the developed world is becoming, like duelling and slavery, subrationally unthinkable and therefore obsolescent' (Mueller, 1988, p.219). Instead, economic power (soft power) is gaining ascendancy. But economic power is more widely diffused in the world, amongst states and even private actors, such as multinational corpor-

President Clinton addressing the 48th session of the United Nations General Assembly, 27 September 1993

ations. In this highly interdependent world even the most powerful states cannot control events unilaterally, so that the '...problem for US power in the twenty-first century will not be new challengers for hegemony but the new challenges of transnational interdependence' (Nye, 1990, p.260). To confront these challenges, the USA '...should recognize the need for international co-operation. We cannot act alone, but we must take the lead in meeting these challenges' (Nitze, 1993). Thus for the globalists multilateral diplomacy and international institutions are absolutely central to the achievement of American goals and to the welfare of its citizens. For this reason Coll proposes the '...integrating of multilateral institutions and practices more thoroughly into the fabric of US foreign and defence policy' (Coll, 1993).

This commitment to the collective management of the world order, in which the USA deploys its capacities for leadership rather than hegemony, is also applicable to the security domain. Thus the globalists propose an expanded role for the UN and a kind of global Concert of Powers to preserve the peace — a system of co-operative security. Rather than the role of 'globocop' the USA would share the responsibility for 'policing' the peace with other powers, either through NATO or the UN, and only act jointly with others where there was international support for such action. As Chace observes, 'At this moment in history and probably for some time to come, the great powers share a common interest in preserving the peace, and to the extent that this characterizes the international system, limited collective security is possible' (Chace, 1992, p.14). Global security will also be enhanced by '...anchoring German and Japanese security in a broader multinational security community, the Atlantic and Pacific alliances respectively play a key role in discouraging what has been described as the "renationalization" of both countries security policies' (Coll, 1993).

For the globalists the US role in the post-Cold War world is conceived in terms of leadership rather than dominance or disengagement. It is a role which fits with Jeffersonian principles in its emphasis upon constructing the preconditions for democracy and freedom rather than imposing them on others. It is also a vision, which as Chace reminds Americans, is closely linked to that of Roosevelt's original post-war 'new world order'. Roosevelt's conception was of 'a world of democratic nations, united in a 'permanent system of general security' and in a freely trading international economy — a vision, if we recognize it, that we can now hope to achieve as a consequence of the peace' (Chace, 1992, p.192).

Some four decades after authoring NSC-68, Paul Nitze contends that in the post-Cold War era, the primary purpose of the USA lies in '...protecting diversity within a general framework of world order. We should seek a global climate in which a large array of political groupings can exist, each with its own, perhaps eccentric, ways. We should seek to eliminate force and intimidation as an acceptable means of resolving disputes' (Nitze, 1993). This new order is one of complex interdependence and will require the United States to adopt a foreign policy strategy which involves '...investing its resources in the maintenance of the geopolitical balance, in an open attitude to the rest of the world, in the development of new international institutions, and in major reforms to restore the domestic sources of US strength' (Nye, 1990, p.261).

This strategy and vision for the post-Cold War era elicits considerable support from the bastions of the American liberal foreign policy establishment. Corporate America, in particular high technology sectors and internationally oriented business, find this liberal and pragmatic vision consonant with their interests. Not surprisingly it also attracts the allegiance of many Democrats, the more liberal elements of the military establishment, and those neo-conservatives who are uneasy with 'utopian' and 'sentimental' visions of America's global role. Beyond elite opinion there is significant public sympathy for a vision which recognizes existing commitments, but whilst pragmatic, is not devoid, of a moral basis. Post-Cold War internationalism may therefore provide the foundations for a new domestic consensus on *'fin de siècle'* foreign policy.

Over the coming years these three competing, but in some degree overlapping, visions will be frequently called upon in the deepening ideological 'struggle for the (foreign policy) turf'. But only a real international crisis will force a choice of visions. This 'struggle' is of profound national and international importance. Internationally, the outcome to this 'struggle' will be of supreme historical significance since, as Paul Kennedy concludes, the United States '…has so much power for good or evil, and because it is the linchpin of the Western alliance system and the centre of the existing global economy, what it does, or does not do, is so much more important that what any of the other powers decides to do' (Kennedy, 1988, p.535). Nationally, the outcome will be absolutely critical to America's sense of national purpose since it will define a new national 'covenant with power', a covenant for the twenty-first century.

SUMMARY

There are three dominant positions in the national debate on post-Cold War national security strategy: the preponderants; the neo-isolationists; and the globalists.

Preponderants believe in US primacy and effective economic supremacy as the means to a stable world order.

Neo-isolationists emphasize selective engagement and the primacy of national economic security in the determination of US foreign policy.

Globalists stress co-operative security, US leadership, multilateral diplomacy, economic renewal and collective management of global affairs as the basis for a new national foreign policy strategy.

6 A NEW COVENANT WITH POWER

Since the Founding of the Republic Americans have displayed a fundamental ambivalence towards the accrual of power. This may appear somewhat surprising since the accretion of wealth, itself a form of power, is such a dominant characteristic of American society. But in the political domain, and most especially in respect of foreign affairs, there remains a deep equivocalness towards power. Arising in part from a Colonial heritage and in part from a liberal political tradition this scepticism remains a significant burden upon the conduct of foreign affairs. Woodrow Wilson expressed this ambivalence in his attempts, in the early part of this century, to bring the United States, as an emerging global force, into a new 'covenant with power'. Wilson defined this new covenant in simple terms, 'Whenever we use our power, we must use it with this conception always in mind — that we are using it for the benefit of the persons who are chiefly interested, and not for our benefit' (quoted in Gardner, 1984, p.13). At the end of the century the nature of this liberal covenant is in question.

6.1 THE END OF THE AMERICAN CENTURY?

Henry Kissinger observed that, 'America entered the twentieth century largely unprepared for the part it would be called upon to play' (Kissinger, 1979, p.59). As it confronts the twenty-first century it appears prepared for all contingencies but has yet to define a convincing role for itself. This has serious consequences, for as Maynes convincingly argues, 'Now that the Cold War is over, Americans need a foreign policy that recognizes the new world before them. The path that America has followed since the fall of the Berlin Wall is understandable, but it is no longer constructive. A policy that tries to hang on to old privileges while pressing for greater economic advantage will inevitably give way to an approach that is increasingly nationalistic and narrow. That will not be the design, but it will be the result' (Maynes, 1993, p.20). Some perceive in this failure to reinvent foreign policy confirmation of the end of the American century.

The American century began, in the aftermath of the First World War, with the collapse of European domination of the global political economy. By the post-Second World War era the '…globalization of America was virtually complete' (Iriye, 1993, p.216). Since the apogee of its power in the early post-war years it might be argued that the American century has been converging upon its historic conclusion. In some respects the end of the Cold War may mark the end of the American century in that just as the First World War signalled the end of Europe's domination of the globe, the collapse of the Soviet Union brought the era of superpower rivalry, and with it the USA's role as a global superpower, to a historic close. Yet the American century, conceived primarily in terms of America's preponderant power, had begun to expire many years previously. In 1975 Kissinger had proclaimed already that '…the cold war division of the world into two rigid blocs has … broken down and major changes have taken place in the international economy … therefore it is time to go beyond the doctrines left over from a previous century that are made obsolete by modern reality' (quoted in Gardner, 1986, pp.202–3). This was the first official recognition of the arrival of a world of complex interdependence, a world order which the American century had brought into being.

A world of complex interdependence is a global order which no longer requires a hegemonic power to oversee its smooth functioning (Keohane, 1984). The very success of American policies of post-war reconstruction and liberal internationalism has created new centres of global power and in the process contributed to the erosion of America's global influence. By a cruel irony of history, the end of the American century in some senses may be conceived as epitomizing the ultimate realization of the ideology, aspirations and visions which sustained it.

To talk of the end of the American century is to do so in a very specific way — as the end of the era of American preponderant or 'imperial' power. This is far from suggesting that the USA no longer has a global role. On the contrary, its future global role is likely to be economically and strategically vital both for Americans and the world. Nevertheless, it will be significantly different from that of the past. As the United States enters the twenty-first century, the nation's leaders and the American people can no longer delay their response to that historic assignment so eloquently articulated by Woodrow Wilson as the American century commenced:

> We have never yet sufficiently formulated our programme for America with regard to the part she is going to play in the world, and it is imperative that we should formulate it at once … We are holding off, not because we do not feel concerned, but because when we exert the force of this Nation we want to know what we are exerting it for. We ought to have a touchstone. We want to have a test. We ought to know, whenever we act, what the purpose is, what the ultimate goal is.
>
> (Wilson, quoted in Niebuhr, 1959, p.18.)

6.2 WHO IS 'US'?

The matter of quite what this distinct end, or national purpose, might be is inseparable from the more complex and fraught issue of national identity. During the Cold War the answer to De Crèvecoueur's question 'What is an American?' appeared uncomplicated and was delivered with great confidence. The ideology of American exceptionalism, the hegemony of the melting pot philosophy, and the prevailing power structure, manufactured a (false) sense of common identity and thereby a unity of national purpose. The Cold War also contributed to this apparent solidarity since it defined the fate of the entire nation in terms of a common external threat. But the counterculture movements of the 1960s and 1970s, the long campaign for civil rights, the crisis of political authority in the 1970s, the arrival of the politics of identity in the 1980s and 1990s, and the end of the Cold War have seriously undermined the dominant ideologies of 'Americanization' and American 'exceptionalism'. With that unravelling has developed an intensely sceptical attitude within American society towards any attempts to articulate a discrete national identity. As Citrin and Haas conclude:

> The emerging debate over America's national interest usually is attributed to the changes engendered by the collapse of communism. We suggest that the changing character of American society is another source of discord about the country's foreign policy. In our view, the dwindling of consensus about America's international role follows from the waning of agreement on what it means to be an American, on the very character of American nationalism.
>
> (Citrin *et al.*, 1994, pp.26–7)

New patterns of immigration are also transforming the ethnic mix within American society. The long-term consequences of this are little understood and largely speculative. But it is evident from the past that the pull of ethnic ties influences the general orientation of foreign policy. Thus as the USA becomes a society of 'minorities' the dominance of the European connection may well be eroded. As 'Asian-America' and 'Mexican-America' become more significant and more powerful within the domestic political arena it is likely that the focus of the nation's foreign policy will shift Southwards and Westwards.

Robert Reich has also pointed to the globalization of the American economy as a further factor contributing to the socio-economic fragmentation of the nation. Reich argues that the intensification of global economic relations has unleashed on all nations, '…forces which are reducing the interdependence of their citizens and separating them into global winners and losers … The question is whether the habits of citizenship are sufficiently strong to withstand the centrifugal forces of the new global economy' (Reich, 1991, p.304). This further polarization of American society compounds existing ethnic divisions creating deep fractures in the polity.

As in the Cold War era the riposte to the question, What is an American? will be a powerful determinant of the nation's future response to the grand questions concerning post Cold War foreign policy: namely, What should the USA be? and What should the USA do? Those segments of society which acquire hegemony in the ideological struggle over identity will also be in a strategic position to author the nation's key responses to these grand questions concerning America's future global role and national purpose.

6.3 A SECOND AMERICAN CENTURY?

In the 1990s Americans were more aware of their power, or lack of it, than at any time this century. The triumphs of the Cold War and Gulf War, and the longest period of sustained economic growth in modern times, have brought the question of national power to the forefront of the political agenda. The debate is no longer about managing 'imperial decline'; on the contrary, as Tucker argues, the problem is defined rather differently: 'The growth of the nation's power has given it pretensions it once shunned and provided it with temptations it seldom had to face in the past' (Tucker and

Hendrickson, 1992, p.165). The competing visions of American strategy for the post-Cold War era, discussed in the previous pages, are in effect both dinstinctive characterizations of American power at the end of the twentieth century whilst, at the same time, discrete prescriptions for a new covenant with power.

Within American society, and particularly amongst political elites, there remains considerable unease about the 'bound to lead' ideology which defined post-war American foreign policy. Even the proponents of preponderance are exercised more by the desire to sustain the status quo than a project to transform the global order. Unlike the post-war years there is little enthusiasm, except amongst the more eccentric and messianic sectors of political opinion, for engaging the USA in a mission to democratize the globe, or equally for exerting American power to actively transform the global political economy. As Perkins observes since the early period of the Republic, Americans have preferred '…to see themselves as torchbearers or guardians of the flame, not crusaders in causes' (Perkins, 1993, p.50).

As a new millennium begins, Americans remain ambivalent towards the demands of global leadership. Despite its unassailable position, and its unparalleled economic and military dominance of the world order, the US lacks a coherent public philosophy to guide its foreign policy. Compared with the first two decades of the post-Second World War period, when Americans were prepared to 'pay any price and bear any burden', the first decade of the twenty-first century confronts an America that is uneasy with its own power and deeply uncertain about its national purpose. What is required is not simply a new strategy for the post-Cold War world, but a new covenant with power; a covenant that provides a more confident assertion of the national purpose and one that legitimizes, in the public conscience, the nation's power, 'not in terms of power itself, but of some quite separate end' (Gaddis, 1992, p.10). If this covenant is forthcoming, the twenty-first century may well turn out to be a second American century.

REFERENCES

Acheson, D. (1969) *Present at the Creation: My Years in the State Department*, New York, Norton.

Aron, R. (1973) *The Imperial Republic*, London, Weidenfeld and Nicholson.

Burnham, W. (1993) 'Beyond Afghanistanism', *New Perspectives Quarterly*, Summer 1992, pp.40–2.

Buscynski, L. (1992) 'ASEAN, security dilemmas', *Survival*, vol.34, no.4, pp.90–108.

Bush, President G. (1990) *Address to Special Joint Session of Congress*, Washington, DC, United States Information Service.

Bush, President G. (1991) *The State of the Union Address*, (January), Washington, DC, United States Information Service.

Bush, President G. (1992) *Address at Texas A&M Convocation*, Washington, DC, United States Information Service.

Chace, J. (1992) *The Consequences of the Peace*, Oxford, Oxford University Press.

Christopher, W. (1993) *Address*, Washington, DC, United States Information Service.

Citrin, J., Haas, E.B., Muste, C. and Reingold, B. (1994) 'Is American nationalism changing? Implications for foreign policy', *International Studies Quarterly*, vol.38, no.1, pp.1–31.

Clinton, President W. (1994) *Brussels Address*, (January 9), Washington, DC, United States Information Service.

Clinton, President W. (1999) *Remarks on US Foreign Policy*, (March 1), Washington, DC, United States Information Service.

Coll, A.R. (1993) 'Power, principles and prospects for a co-operative international order' in Roberts, B. (1993) pp.13–23 .

Conference on Security and Co-operation in Europe (1990) 'Joint declaration', Washington, DC, United States Information Service.

Department of Defense (1993) *The Bottom-up Review*, Washington, DC, Secretary of Defense.

Gaddis, J. (1988) *The Long Peace: Inquiries into the History of the Cold War*, New York, Oxford University Press.

Gaddis, J. (1992) *The United States and the End of the Cold War*, Oxford, Oxford University Press.

Gaddis, J. (1992) 'International relations theory and the end of the Cold War', *International Security*, vol.17, no.3, pp.5–58.

Gardner, L. (1984) *A Covenant with Power*, Oxford, Oxford University Press.

Gibney, F.B. (1993) 'Creating a Pacific community', *Foreign Affairs*, vol.72, no.5, November pp.5–25.

Goldberg, A.C. (1992) 'Selective engagement: US national security policy in the 1990s', *The Washington Quarterly*, Summer, pp.15–24.

Halliday, F. (1990) 'The ends of Cold War', *New Left Review*, no.180, March, pp.5–23.

Harries, O. (1993) 'The collapse of the West', *Foreign Affairs*, vol.72, Sept/Oct, pp.41–53.

Hass, E.B. (1976) 'Turbulent fields and the neo-functionalist theory of regional integration', *International Organization*, vol.30, no.2, pp.173–212.

Hoffman, S. (1980) *Primacy or World Order*, Boston, Little Brown.

Holsti, O.R. and Rosenau, J.N. (1984) *American Leadership in World Affairs — Vietnam and the Breakdown of Consensus*, London, Allen and Unwin.

Huntingdon, S.P. (1993) 'Why international primacy matters', *International Security*, vol.17, no.4, pp.68–83.

Hyland, W.G. (1990) 'America's new course', *Foreign Affairs*, vol.69, no.2, pp.1–12.

Iriye, A. (1993) *The Globalizing of America 1913–45, The Cambridge History of American Foreign Relations, Volume 3*, Cambridge, Cambridge University Press.

Kemp, B. (1993) 'The regionalization of conflict' in Roberts, B. (1993).

Kennedy, P. (1988) *The Rise and Fall of the Great Powers*, London, Unwin Hyman.

Keohane, R. (1984) *After Hegemony*, Princeton, Princeton University Press.

Kissinger, H. (1979) *The White House Years*, London, Weidenfeld and Nicholson and Michael Joseph.

Knock, T.J. (1993) *To End All Wars: Woodrow Wilson and the Quest for a New World Order*, Oxford, Oxford University Press.

Kurth, J. (1993) 'Mitteleuropa and East Asia' in Woo-Cummings, M. and Loriaux, M. (eds) (1993).

Layne, C. (1993) 'The unipolar illusion', *International Security*, vol.17, no.4, pp.5–51.

Layne, C. and Schwarz. B. (1993) 'American hegemony without an enemy', *Foreign Policy*, no.92 pp.5–23.

Leffler, M.P. (1992) *A Preponderance of Power*, Stanford, California, Stanford University Press.

Linder, S.B. (1986) *The Pacific Century*, Stanford, California, Stanford University Press.

Luttwak, E.N. (1993) *The Endangered American Dream*, New York, Simon and Schuster.

McGrew, A.G. (1989) 'Foreign policy and the constitution: an invitation to perpetual institutional struggle' in Maidment, R. and Zvesper, J. (eds), pp.172–98.

Maidment, R. and Zvesper, J. (eds.) (1989) *Reflections on the Constitution: The American Constitution after Two Hundred Years.*, Manchester, Manchester University Press.

Maynes, C.W. (1993) 'A workable Clinton doctrine', *Foreign Policy*, no.93, Winter, pp. 3–22.

Meirsheimer, J. (1990) 'Why we will soon miss the Cold War', *The Atlantic*, vol. CCLXVI, August, pp.35–50.

Morgenthau, H. (1951) *In Defence of the National Interest*, New York, Alfred A. Knopf.

Mueller, J. (1989) *Retreat from Domesday: the Obsolescence of Major War*, New York, Basic Books.

Naim, M. (1997) 'Clinton's foreign policy: a victim of globalization?', *Foreign Policy*, no.107, Winter, pp.34–45.

Nicoll, A. and Graham G. (1993) 'Hands across the water', *The Financial Times*, 15 November, p.15.

Niebuhr, R. (1959) *Nations and Empires*, London, Faber and Faber.

Nitze, P. (1993) *Postscript to NSC–68*, Mimeo, Washington DC.

Nordlinger, E. (1995) *Isolationism Reconfigured*, Princeton, Princeton University Press.

Nye, J. (ed) (1984) *The Making of America's Soviet Policy*, New Haven, Yale University Press.

Nye, J. (1990) *Bound to Lead*, New York, Basic Books.

Perkins B. (1993) *The Creation of a Republican Empire 1776–1865, The Cambridge History of Foreign Relations, Volume 1*, Cambridge, Cambridge University Press.

Powell, C. (1993) 'US Forces: challenges ahead', *Foreign Affairs*, vol.72, pp.32–45.

Reich, R. (1991) *The Work of Nations*, New York, Simon and Schuster.

Roberts, B. (1993) *US Security in an Uncertain Era*, Cambridge, MA, MIT Press.

Schlesinger, A.M. (1986) *The Cycles of American History*, Boston, Houghton Miflin.

Schlesinger, J, (1991) 'New instabilities and new priorities', *Foreign Policy*, no.85, pp. 3–25.

Schneider, W. (1984) 'Public opinion' in Nye, J. (ed.) (1984).

Schurmann, F. (1993) 'After Desert Storm: interests, ideology and history in American foreign policy' in Woo-Cummings, M. and Loriaux, M. (eds) (1993).

Segal, G. (1993) 'Managing new arms races in the Asian Pacific' in Roberts, B. (1993).

The White House (1991) *National Security Strategy of the United States*, Washington, DC.

The White House (1996) *A National Security Strategy of Engagement and Enlargement*, Washington, DC.

Tonelson, A. (1993) 'Superpower without a sword', *Foreign Affairs*, vol.72, no.3, pp. 166–80.

Treverton, G.F. (1992) 'America's stakes and choices in Europe', *Survival*, vol.34, no.3 pp.119–35.

Tucker, Robert W. and Hendrickson, D. C. (1992) *The Imperial Temptation — The New World Order and America's Purpose*, New York, Council on Foreign Relations.

Waltz, K.N. (1993) 'The emerging structure of international politics', *International Security*, vol.18, no.2, pp.44–79.

Williams, P. Hammond, P. and Brenner, M. (1993) 'Atlantis lost, paradise regained? The United States and Western Europe after the Cold War', *International Affairs*, vol. 69, pp.1–17.

Williams, W. A. (1980) *Empire as a Way of Life*, Oxford, Oxford University Press.

Wirk, T. (1993) State Department Counsellor, *Address* (June 11), Washington, DC, United States Information Service.

Wolfowitz, P.D. (1994) 'Clinton's first year', *Foreign Affairs*, vol.73, no.1, pp.28–43.

Woo-Cummings, M. and Loriaux, M. (eds) (1993) *Past as Prelude: History in the Making of a New World Order*, Bolder, Colorado, West View Press.

Ziemke, C.F. (1993) 'Military planning beyond the Cold War' in Roberts, B. (ed.) (1993), pp.45–60.

FURTHER READING

Chace, J. (1992) *The Consequences of the Peace*, Oxford, Oxford University Press.

Luttwak, E.N. (1993) *The Endangered American Dream*, New York, Simon and Schuster.

Nye, J. (1990) *Bound to Lead*, New York, Basic Books.

INDEX

A.E. Staley company, 153
accountability, 193, 197, 199, 201, 203
Acheson, Dean, 32, 37–8, 106, 217, 227
Adams, John Quincy, President, 235
Adenauer, Konrad, 31, 76
Adler, S., 8, 18
Afghanistan, 58, 59, 65, 121, 200
Africa, 58, 192, 204, 218
   South Africa, 154, 163, 214, 224
agencies, government, 147, 148, 158, 167, 168, 169
agriculture, 87, 119, 126, 133, 147, 149, 177
Aguinaldo, Emilio, 190
aircraft, 25, 224
airforces:
   America, 26, 63
   Soviet Union, 61
Allen, D., 118, 123, 125, 127
alliances, 9, 11, 23, 139–40
   Cold War, 51, 186
   post-Cold War, 222, 230, 238, 239, 243
   post-Second World War, 72, 75, 78, 82
   see also Atlantic alliance; NATO
Ambrose, S.E., 179
Ambrosius, L.E., 7, 11
America:
   'city upon a hill' image, 183, 187, 217
   founding of, 17
   idea of, 56
American Century, 39, 203, 211–47
American dream, 40, 59, 79
American empire see empire
American Indians, 189
'American way of life', 1, 33
Americanization, 79, 80, 82, 95, 96, 245
Anglo-American Trade Agreement (1938), 20
Anti-Ballistic Missile Treaty, 53
anti-communism, 34–8, 44, 55, 80, 82, 107
apartheid, 154
APEC (Asia-Pacific Economic Co-operation), 233
appeasement, 44
Arab–Israeli October War, 121
armies, 12, 105
   America, 16, 20, 23, 41, 63
   India, 223
   Iraq, 205
   Soviet Union, 26, 38, 109
arms control, 13, 114, 198
   arms embargoes, 8–9
   Nixon Administration, 52, 55, 117
   Reagan Administration, 62, 122, 127, 147
arms/munitions manufacturers, 9, 17
arms races, 9, 12, 62, 145, 220
   rearmament, 37, 39, 46, 109, 110
arms reductions, 11, 13, 17, 127
   disarmament, 5, 8, 9, 14
arms transfers, 61
Arnson, C., 191
Aron, Raymond, 1, 2, 229
Asia, 46, 119, 161, 190–91, 232
   East, 94, 98, 218, 223, 231, 237

South-Central, 214
South-East, 31, 44, 49, 57, 113, 147
Asia-Pacific region, 134, 171, 223, 224, 232
Asian Americans, 246
Asian-Pacific Americans, 156, 157
assassination of political leaders, 199
assembly lines, 79
Atlantic alliance, 51, 102–3, 113, 122, 242
Atlantic Charter, 26, 103, 211
   'new Atlantic Charter', 119
Atlantic Community, 115, 134
Atlantic system, 101–40
Atlanticism, 73, 78
atomic bombs, 26, 29, 31, 74
   see also nuclear weapons
Australia, 78
Austria, 80
autarky, 18, 28, 48, 75, 91, 95, 240
automobile industry, 14, 79, 80, 81
autonomy, 220, 221, 223, 226
Axis Powers, 26, 72, 73

Baggett, B., 203
Bain, D.H., 190
Baker, James, 126, 131–2
balance of payments, 83–4, 85, 91, 93, 98, 116, 124
balances of power, 177
   pre-Second World War, 6, 11, 21, 95, 185
   post-Second World War, 38, 42
   post-Cold War, 66, 221, 222, 227, 238
Baldwin, Stanley, 12
Baliles, Gerald, 167
'bancor', 84, 86
Bank for International Settlements (BIS), 14, 86, 90, 98
banking, 81, 82, 83, 94, 119, 186
   First World War, 9, 17
   inter-war years, 5, 8, 10, 15, 20
   Second World War (Swiss), 155, 163, 166, 167
Belgium, 14, 15, 80, 86
Benedick, R.E., 148
Bergner, J., 130
Bergsten, F.W., 123, 126, 134
Berlin, 31, 33, 53, 105
Berlin Wall, 43, 130, 132, 213, 214
Bevin, Ernest, 105
Bierce, Ambrose, 198
Bilder, R.B., 154
Bilderberg group, 78, 79, 81–2, 83
Billington, Ray Alan, 185
biological weapons, 224
bipolarity, 212, 219, 220, 226
BIS (Bank for International Settlements), 14, 86, 90, 98
black Americans, 35
Black Monday, 125
Block, F.L., 106, 114
Boland Amendments, 201, 202
Bolsheviks, 36
booms, 46, 86, 92, 94, 123
Boorstin, Daniel, 181
Borah, William, 18
Bosnia, 132, 133, 225, 230
Brandes, J., 16
Brazil, 52
Brenner, M., 172
Bretton Woods system, 20, 89, 109, 117

America/Europe relations, 108, 111, 112, 114, 115
economic multilateralism, 73, 83–6
world economy, 95, 104, 110
Brezhnev, Leonid, 53
Briand, Aristide, 12
Britain, 6, 14, 36, 189
   armed forces, 11–12, 16, 21, 26, 114, 176
   City of London, 81, 88, 89
   Cold War, 30, 37, 38, 104
   economic activity, 27, 76, 77, 91
   economic groupings, 79, 86, 111
   industry/trade, 25, 80, 153, 168
   League of Nations, 10
   NATO, 110, 122
   Second World War, 18, 77, 105
   sterling, 8, 18, 84, 85
   Tripartite Stabilization Agreement, 19–20
British Empire, 8, 25, 72, 178, 182, 227
Brittan, Leon, 94
Brzezinski, Zbigniew, 58, 227
Buchanan, Patrick, 237
budget deficits, 93, 214
   Nixon Administration, 116
   Reagan Administration, 62, 92, 123, 124, 125, 152, 158
Buenos Aires conference (1998), 147
Bulgaria, 42
Burk, Kathleen, 3, 5–21
Burma, 154, 155, 156, 163, 164
Burnham, James, 42
Burnham, W., 239
Buscynski, L., 232
Bush, George, President, 127, 205, 206, 224
   end of Cold War, 66–8, 158, 187–8, 211, 213–14
   Europe, 128–32
   new world order, 215–18, 229–30
business cycle, 46, 77
business interests, 106
businessmen, 5, 14, 15, 17
Butler, R.A., 76
Butskellism, 76, 80
Byrnes, James, 134

California, 157
California World Trade Commission, 166
Calleo, David, 85, 91, 116, 119
   America/Europe relations, 106, 108, 113, 114, 115, 123, 137
Campbell, David, 182
Canada, 79, 86, 160
   see also NAFTA
capital, 76, 82, 93, 228
   controls, 83, 84, 88
   corporate, 79–82
   movement, 77, 89, 92, 95
capitalism, 1, 27, 96, 220, 232, 240
   'democratic', 180
   reconstruction of, 42, 47
   and socialism/communism, 39, 43, 46, 50, 68, 79
capitalist economy, world, 25, 71, 74, 88, 109, 110
cartels, 20, 80
Carter, James E. (Jimmy), President, 24, 119, 121, 125, 159, 167, 228
   Cold War, 56–9, 62, 118
cash-and-carry arms sales, 9, 18
Castro, Fidel, 44

251

Center for Clean Air, 162
Central America, 1, 23, 154, 214
    Nicaragua, 58, 192, 200–02
Central Intelligence Agency (CIA), 31, 62, 66, 90, 198–200
Chace, J., 117, 187, 225, 239, 240–41, 242
Chamberlain, Neville, 17, 18, 21
Charter of Paris, 129, 211
checks and balances, 193, 197, 198, 199–200
chemical weapons, 223
Cheney, Dick, 66
child benefits, 76
China, 31, 33, 54, 58, 117
    communism, 46, 73, 74
    and Japan, 6, 12, 74
    post-Cold War, 221, 224, 232
    and Soviet Union, 43, 48, 52
cholorofluorocarbons (CFCs), 147–8
Chomsky, Noam, 60, 192
Christian Democrat parties, 76
Christopher, Warren, 134, 232
Churchill, Sir Winston, 27, 29, 30, 103, 105
CIA (Central Intelligence Agency), 31, 62, 66, 90, 198–200
Cingranelli, D.L., 191
'citizen diplomacy', 154
Citrin, J., 246
'city upon a hill' image, 183, 187, 217
civil rights, 36, 158, 245
civil society, global, 96
Civil War, American, 177
class divisions, 76, 176, 180
Clavin, P., 17
Clayton, J.L., 46
Clemenceau, Georges, 7
climate change negotiations, 147–8
Clinton, William (Bill), President, 145, 188, 232, 233, 241
    economic matters, 101, 158, 224
    Europe, 131, 132–5, 230–31
    NAFTA, 169
Cloud, S.W., 205
co-operation, competitive, 140
co-operation, international, 18, 221, 232, 241, 242
coal industry, 25, 177
Coker, C., 156–7
Cold War, 2, 23–68, 73, 79, 170, 217
    Carter Administration, 118
    and democracy, 186–8, 192, 196, 197, 198, 199
    Japan, 73–4, 78
    Reagan Administration, 122, 124, 158, 171
    Western Europe, 102, 104–5, 109–10, 111, 112, 113, 138
Cold War, end of, 5, 145, 147, 162, 204, 206
    new world order, 211–47
    Western Europe, 101, 128–9, 131, 134, 137
Cole, W., 8
Coll, A.R., 242
colonial rule, 39, 101, 176, 244
    decolonization, 73, 75
Commager, H.S., 176
Commerce Department, 160, 166
communism, 33, 42, 72, 76, 95, 204
    America, 36, 45
    anti-communism, 34–8, 44, 55, 80, 82, 107

and capitalism, 43, 50
China, 31, 46, 52–3, 73, 74
    collapse of, 67–8, 97, 213, 226, 228, 240, 246
    Europe, 107, 109, 111
    ideological antipathy, 40, 186, 187
    international/global threat, 56, 103, 158, 170
    Latin America, 200–01
    Soviet Union, 28, 30, 52–3, 74
Communist Information Bureau (Cominform), 31
competition, 47, 80, 140, 190, 222, 224, 238
    mercantilism, 77, 92, 160
competitive co-operation, 140
competitiveness, 57, 92, 113, 125, 130
computers, 80, 166
Conference on Security and Co-operation in Europe (CSCE), 129, 131, 132, 223
    Helsinki agreements, 53, 118
Congress, 15, 31, 73, 126, 152
    declaration of war, 7, 9
    foreign policy, 159–62, 233
    House of Representatives, 161
    isolationism, 8, 17, 18, 37
    lobbying groups, 149, 166, 168–70
    Senate, 10, 17, 18, 31, 161, 225
Congress and president, 26, 30, 151
    foreign policy, 49, 125, 147, 148, 198–203
    trade agreements, 19, 238
Conquest, R., 54
conservatism, 46, 51, 68, 76, 237
    neo-conservatism, 59, 60, 64, 90, 243
Constitution, 155, 156, 192
    presidency, 6, 194–5, 197, 198, 199
consumerism, 1, 82
consumption, 75, 79, 96
containment, 195, 214, 219, 226, 234, 236
    of communism, 46, 77, 158
    George F. Kennan, 32, 34, 211
    Paul Nitze, 32, 239
    and roll back, 40–42, 44
    of Soviet power, 51–2, 59–62
Contract with America, 161
Coolidge, Calvin, President, 6, 12, 13
corporations, 72, 80, 126, 130, 134, 168, 237
    multinational, 111, 148, 156, 241
    transnational, 89, 90
corporatism, 76, 82
Costigliola, Frank, 14, 20
Council on Foreign Relations, New York, 27, 72
'covenant with power', 3, 243, 244–7
Cox, Michael, 3, 23–68
Cox, R.W., 76
Crovitz, L.G., 201
Crowe, Admiral, 237
CSCE see Conference on Security and Co-operation in Europe
Cuba, 44, 46, 61, 162, 192
    Soviet involvement, 43, 48, 113
    Spanish–American War, 190
cultural democracy, 206
Cunliffe, M., 198
currencies, 17, 95
    Europe, 14, 15, 20, 101, 126
    international/single, 84, 86, 91, 134
    Japan, 85

sterling, 8, 18, 72, 84, 85
    see also dollar
currencies, convertible, 82, 84, 98
    inter-war years, 5, 8, 14, 16, 19, 20
Czech Republic, 134
Czechoslovakia, 17, 30, 31, 33, 42, 105, 113

Dawes, Charles Gates, 8, 15, 16
Dawes Plan, 8, 14
Dayton Accords, 133
De Cecco, M., 83, 85
De Crèvecoeur, St John, 176, 245
De Gaulle, Charles, 85, 114, 138, 139
De Tocqueville, Alexis, 180, 193, 197, 203, 206
debts:
    America, 92, 93, 125, 152, 158
    Mexico, 91, 94
    Russia, 94
    Third World, 92
    war debts, 14, 15
Declaration of Independence, 176
'Declaration of Interdependence', 115
decline, American, 24, 25, 218, 228, 246
    Carter Administration, 200
    economic, 152, 157, 170, 171–2, 205, 211, 225
    Nixon Administration, 51
    Reagan Administration, 60, 213, 215
defence, 109, 146, 153, 159, 223, 231, 241
defence spending see military spending
Defense, Department of, 31, 66, 72, 233
    Pentagon, 55, 80, 81, 219
defense treaties, 61
democracy, 26–7, 31, 35, 107, 175–207
    post-Cold War, 129, 211, 218, 227, 236, 237, 242
    see also liberal democracy
Democratic Party, 36, 46, 54, 90
    foreign policy, 17, 41, 55, 169, 243
demographic changes, 156, 157
dependence, 145
    on America, 42, 120, 137
    technological, 125
DePorte, Anton, 42, 104, 105
Depression, Great:
    America, 17, 19, 23, 25, 27, 71, 94
    Britain, 77
    East Asia, 94–5
depressions, 93, 95
derivatives, 95
destiny, manifest, 183–5, 188, 189, 211, 229
Destler, I.M., 116, 152, 153, 161, 200
détente, 51–2, 54, 55, 158, 159, 171, 228
    Europe, 62, 113, 117, 118, 120
diplomacy, 2, 9–11, 105, 185, 220, 228
    'citizen', 154
    coercive, 34
    economic, 226, 234
    multilateral, 221, 233, 241, 242
    private sector, 8, 15, 78–9
    Soviet, 127
disarmament, 5, 8, 9, 14
'disjointed incrementalism', 234
division of labour, 78, 115, 132
division of powers, 151, 162
dollar, 93, 104, 134, 186
    and gold, 84, 85, 89

INDEX

value, 91, 114, 116, 119, 152, 160
  see also Eurodollar
domestic policy, 17, 145–72, 196, 212, 217, 232
Doyle, M.W., 1
Driver, B., 162
drug addiction, 158, 205
Drummond, I., 20
Dulles, John Foster, 41, 110, 204
Dumbrell, J., 154, 157

Eagleburger, Lawrence, 124
East Asia: economic crisis, 94, 134, 231, 237
Eastern Europe *see* Europe, Eastern
EC *see* European Community
Economic and Monetary Union, 131, 134
economic power, 16, 21, 25, 160, 186, 232, 241
economic security, 118, 171, 224–5, 232, 238, 239, 240
economic supremacy, 3, 11, 16, 138, 152, 171, 186
  post-Cold War, 236, 241, 247
economic world/global order, 47, 71–99, 113, 145, 148, 151–3
  Europe, 108, 110, 113, 125, 129–30, 133, 140
  inter-war years, 5, 8, 23, 185
  open, 27, 28, 39, 40, 103, 104
  post-Cold War, 135, 138, 225, 232, 243
  states, 164, 166–7
economies: transatlantic relations, 102, 104, 106–7, 118–19, 127, 130–31, 138
economy, American, 25, 27, 49, 72, 122, 159
  dominance, 47, 222, 240
  globalization, 151–3, 224, 246
  see also economic supremacy
economy, 'real', 83, 88, 91
economy, Soviet, 29, 57
  planned, 39, 48, 66–7, 76
economy, world *see* economic world/global order
ECSC (European Coal and Steel Community), 81, 110, 111
EDC (European Defence Community), 109, 110, 122
education, 76, 158
EEC *see* European Economic Community
Egerton, G., 9
Egypt, 57
Eichenberg, R.C., 122
Eisenhower, Dwight D., President, 41, 42, 44, 45, 46, 109
Eizenstat, Stuart, 134
Ekirch, Arthur, 189
electronics industry, 80, 166
embedded liberalism, 83
emigration controls, 77
Emperor system: Japan, 74
empire, 136, 137–8, 227–34
  American, 1–2, 24, 31, 35, 37, 45–8
  burdens of, 51, 211, 237
  'by invitation', 2, 191
  see also imperialism
employers, 36, 76
employment, 46
enlightenment, 181–2, 184, 185, 190

environment, 145, 147–8, 150, 153, 162, 169
Environmental Protection Agency, 148
equality, 179, 181, 191
ethnic groups, 35, 156–7, 176, 246
Euro, 134
Euro-American system, 101–40
Eurodollar market, 89, 91, 152
Euromarkets, 88–9, 92
Europe, 3, 93, 246
  American history, 17–18, 176, 178, 180
  Cold War, 30, 38, 48, 52
  empires, 189, 229
  inter-war years, 6, 11, 14–16, 20–21, 23, 179, 244
  post-Cold War, 220, 222, 238–9
  Second World War, 25, 186
  security, 223, 224–5, 230–32
Europe, Eastern, 45, 48, 123
  roll back, 40, 41, 42
  post-Cold War, 66–7, 95, 133, 212, 213, 218
  and Soviet Union, 29, 38, 52, 57, 105, 214
Europe, Western, 78, 101–40, 151
  American economic involvement, 75, 77, 80–81, 84, 93
  Cold War, 38, 46, 58, 60, 62
European Coal and Steel Community (ECSC), 81, 110, 111
European Community (EC), 102, 110, 129–30, 131, 132, 138, 171
  Common Agricultural Policy, 126
  Single Market Programme, 126, 162, 167
European Defence Community (EDC), 109, 110, 122
European Economic Community (EEC), 86, 110–11
  1960–71, 113, 114, 115
  1971–81, 117, 118, 119, 120, 121
  Reagan Administration, 126
European Free Trade Association, 86
European Monetary System, 91
European Union, 99, 135, 149, 155, 156, 166, 223
  Common Foreign and Security Policy (CFSP), 133
exceptionalism, American, 1, 175, 179–83, 217
  Cold War, 35–6
  and imperialism, 189, 191
  post-Cold War, 235, 236, 245
exchange rates, 84, 85, 89, 98, 119, 126
executive branch, 7, 151, 159, 198, 201, 203
  see also presidency
executive prerogative, 192, 195, 197, 200, 201
expansionism, 58, 215
  American, 1, 73, 177–8, 183–5, 188, 189–91

'factor price equalization', 91
Far East, 46, 179
fascism, 36, 72, 95, 106
FBI (Federal Bureau of Investigation), 36
FDI (foreign direct investment), 77, 92, 152
Federal Reserve, 91, 92
federalism, 162, 184, 196

Ferrell, R.H., 6, 12
Ferris, J., 12
films, 44, 45
Fink, C., 15
First World War, 221, 244
  American intervention, 23, 178, 185
  causes of, 9, 13, 17
  period following, 6, 75, 102, 219
'flexible response', 113, 114, 115
Foggy Bottom, 219, 226
Foley, Michael, 3, 175–207
Ford, Gerald, President, 159
Ford, Henry, 81
Fordism, 79–82, 83, 92, 96
foreign direct investment (FDI), 77, 92, 152
foreign interest lobbying, 168–70
foreign policy, American, 1, 4
  Cold War, 23–68
  and democratic values, 175–207
  and domestic policy, 2, 3, 145–72
  economic multilateralism, 71–99
  inter-war years, 5–21
  post-Cold War, 211–47
  Western Europe, 101–40
Forrestal, James, 29–30
'fortress Europe', 126, 130
Fosler, R.S., 167
Founding Fathers, 238
Fourteen Points address (President Wilson), 9, 13, 216
France, 36, 80, 91, 107, 138, 139
  agriculture, 133, 149
  economic groupings, 79, 86
  European Defence Community, 109–10
  inter-war years, 12–13, 15, 19–20
  NATO, 48, 114
  post-Second World War, 38, 47, 75
Franck, T.M., 198, 200
free trade, 78, 86, 160, 238, 240
  Cold War, 28, 39
  inter-war years, 5, 8, 14, 16, 20, 185
  see also NAFTA
Free Trade Agreement, 161
free world, 185, 195
  Cold War, 24, 31, 34, 45, 50, 79
  transatlantic relationship, 102, 109, 127
Freedman, L., 110
freedom, 9, 27, 79
  Cold War, 33, 186, 211
  democratic values, 187, 188, 191
  expansionism, 184
  post-Cold War, 216, 227, 236, 242
'freedom fighters', 62, 201
Frieden, Jeff, 88, 89
frontier, 177
Fry, E.H., 151, 152, 164
Fukuyama, Francis, 204
Fulton, Missouri, 30
Fursdon, E., 110

Gaddis, John, 211, 212, 220, 247
Gaitskell, Hugh, 76
Gardner, L., 244, 245
Gardner, R.N., 86
Garthoff, R.L., 59
gas, natural, 25
Gates, Robert, 66
GATT (General Agreement on Tariffs and Trade), 20, 73, 75, 86, 87–8, 160, 233

253

GATT (cont.)
  American/Europe relations, 114, 117, 119, 132, 138
  Uruguay round, 94, 126, 130, 131, 133, 148, 166, 231
Gaulle, Charles de, 85, 114, 138, 139
Gaullism, 114
Gay, Peter, 181
Gelb, L.H., 116
General Motors company, 14
Geneva 'Big Four' conference, (1955), 41
Geneva Conference (1927), 12
Geneva summit conference (1985), 64
Genoa Conference (1922), 15
genocide, 74
George, L.N., 200
Georgia, 165
Germany, 79, 80, 81, 86
  First World War, 9, 178
  Gulf War, 218
  inter-war years, 10, 18, 23
  post-Cold War, 221, 222, 227, 231, 238, 242
  post-Second World War, 21, 28, 31, 47, 73, 74, 105
  reparation payments, 8, 14, 15, 75
  Second World War, 25, 26, 38, 39, 44
  unification, 128, 134, 213, 223
Germany, East, 42, 53, 54, 213
Germany, West, 42, 54, 110, 113, 122, 127
Gibney, F.B., 232
Gill, Stephen, 3, 71–99
Gillingham, J.R., 105, 106
Gilpin, Robert, 90
Gilpin, William, 184
Glickman, N.J., 152, 164
global warming, 162
globalism, 72, 78, 235, 239–43
globalization, 2–3, 32, 94, 145–72, 224, 244, 246
  resistance to, 95, 133, 139
'globocop' role, 204, 218, 242
GNP (gross national product), 25, 46, 151, 153, 186, 233
gold, 84, 85, 89, 177
gold standard, 8, 95
Goldberg, A.C., 238
Gompert, D., 134
Gorbachev, Mikhail, 62, 64–6, 67, 127, 211, 214
Gordon, L.W., 109
government, federal, 151, 158, 163, 198
  agriculture, 126
  environment, 162
  free trade, 238
  inter-war years, 5, 14–16, 106
Graham, G., 232
Gramsci, A., 74, 96
'grand alliance', 103
'Grand Area' strategy, 72–3
'grand design', 51–5
Great Britain see Britain
Great Depression see Depression, Great
great powers, 2, 11, 20, 221, 229, 234, 242
Great Society programme, 47
Greece, 30, 33, 37
greenhouse gases, 147
Greenstein, Fred, 205
Grey, Sir Edward, 10
gridlock, 171, 205

gross national product (GNP), 25, 46, 151, 153, 186, 233
Grosser, Alfred, 103, 104, 107, 114
Group of Seven (G7), 79, 86, 98, 132
Group of Ten (G10), 86, 98
Guatemala, 192
Gulf War, 158, 204–5, 225, 228–9
  American power, 129, 131, 223, 246
  new world order, 67, 68, 213–18, 219, 229–30

Haas, E.B., 234, 246
Haass, R.N., 157, 162
Haiti, 230
Halliday, F., 220
Hamilton, Alexander, 184, 235, 236, 237
Hammond, P., 172
Harding, Warren G., President, 6
Harmel Report, 117
Harries, O., 222, 227, 228, 237, 239
Hartz, Louis, 180, 181, 189, 204
Hata, Mr, 94
Hawley, J., 90
Hay, John, 13
healthcare, 76, 158
Heffner, R.D., 185, 187
hegemony, 2, 96, 145, 204
  Cold War, 171, 227
  economic order, 25, 27, 28, 47, 224, 228
  executive, 198
  Japan, 74
  post-Cold War, 172, 232, 235, 241, 242, 245
  Reagan Administration, 66, 214, 215, 240
  Soviet Union, 33
  transatlantic relationship, 73, 110
Helleiner, Eric, 83, 89, 90
Heller, F.H., 105, 106
Helms–Burton Act (1996), 162
Helsinki agreements, 53, 118
Hendrickson, D.C., 137, 218, 228–9, 246
Henkin, L., 195
Higham, J., 178
Hilsman, R., 109
Hiroshima, 74
Hirschfield, R.S., 194
Hispanic Americans, 156
history, 3, 204, 219–26
Hitler, Adolf, 81
Hocking, Brian, 3, 126, 145–72
Hodgson, G., 198
Hoffman, Paul, 81
Hoffman, S., 107, 117, 118
Hogan, M.J., 104, 106, 107, 110
Holocaust, 155
Holsti, O.R., 237
Hoover, Herbert, President, 7, 12, 15
Hoover, J. Edgar, 36
Hopkins, Harry, 28
hot-line, 44
House, E.M., 10
House of Representatives, 161
  see also Congress
Hufbauer, G.C., 126
Hull, Cordell, 8, 18–19, 20, 71, 72
human rights, 46, 103, 189, 198, 204
  Carter Administration, 56, 118
  Nixon Administration, 51
  Reagan Administration, 62
  social activism, 153–4

Hungary, 41, 43, 134, 213
Hunt, Michael H., 191, 192
Huntingdon, Samuel, 235–6
Hussein, Saddam, 67, 205
Hyland, W.G., 212
Hyster company, 164

identity see national identity
ideology, 49, 138, 191, 212, 235
  Cold War, 192, 216, 220
  Soviet, 65
IMF see International Monetary Fund
immigration, 17, 77, 177, 178, 232, 246
  illegal, 91
imperial overstretch, 137, 215
imperial power, 1, 2, 46, 138–40, 145, 189
Imperial (Sterling) Preference Area, 8, 18
imperial presidency, 49, 193–6, 197, 198, 199
imperial republic, 189–93
imperial temptation, 218, 228–9, 234, 246
imperialism, 50, 178–9
  economic, 72, 139–40, 185
  Soviet Union, 39
  see also empire
implied powers, 194
India, 97, 223, 224
individualism, 79, 180
Indo-China, 33, 170, 171
Indonesia, 94
Industrial Revolution, 25
industrialization, 177, 223, 238
industry, 11, 21, 80
  see also production
inequality, social, 97, 98
information technology, 93, 133, 148
inherent powers, 194–5
instrumental democracy, 206
intellectual property rights, 126
intelligence gathering, 78, 82, 104, 192, 198–200
interdependence, 3, 93
  America/Europe relations, 102, 114–15, 130, 139–40
  globalization, 149, 167, 171
  post-Cold War, 206, 214, 232, 239, 242, 245
interest groups, 11, 151, 157, 238
  agriculture, 149
  anti-'grand design', 54–5
  business, 14, 106
  internationalist, 37, 72, 78
  see also lobbying
international co-operation, 18, 221, 232, 241, 242
International Labour Organization, 87
International Monetary Fund, 20, 72, 73, 75, 88, 89
  international currency, 84, 86
  and national governments, 91, 161
  role, 83, 85, 87, 98
internationalism, 10, 72, 78, 111, 234, 240–41, 245
internationalization:
  American economy, 151, 153
  money capital, 88–91
  production, 83, 89, 95, 97, 153
  state activities, 93, 163
intolerance, 192
investment, 79, 92, 139
  foreign, 154, 164, 169, 186

INDEX

foreign direct, 77, 92, 152
　to states, 163–4
Iran, 29, 52, 59, 91, 154, 200
Iran-Contra affair, 65, 128, 200–03
Iraq, 67, 223, 224, 230
　see also Gulf War
Ireland, Northern, 154, 163
Ireland, T., 104, 105
Irish Americans, 154–5
Iriye, A., 244
iron curtain image, 30
iron industry, 177
Isaacson, W., 206
isolationism, 183, 189
　inter-war years, 8–9, 11, 13, 16, 17–20, 23, 179, 185
　neo-isolationism, 172, 217–18, 235, 237–9, 243
　post-Second World War, 27, 34, 37, 72, 103, 104, 217
　Vietnam War, 49
Israel, 55, 121
Italy, 14, 18, 75, 79, 86, 107

J.P.Morgan & Company, 10, 15
Jackson, Henry 'Scoop', 55
Jackson–Vanik amendment, 159
Japan, 78–9, 86, 99, 220, 222
　banking system, 94
　Gulf War, 218
　industry, 80, 168, 169–70
　inter-war years, 6, 12, 21
　investment to America, 92, 93, 152
　1970s, 117, 119, 120, 151, 171
　1980s, 125, 160, 238
　power balance, 130, 221, 224, 227, 231, 232, 242
　post-Second World War, 46, 72, 73–4, 75, 76, 85
　Second World War, 23, 25, 26
　states, 152, 155, 156
　Tokyo Declaration, 230
Jefferson, Thomas, President, 177, 184, 187, 228, 235, 236, 242
Jeffreys-Jones, R., 199
Jenkins, Simon, 204
Jewish emigration, 159
Jewish lobby, 55
JFK, 44
Joffe, J., 122
Johnson, Lyndon B., President, 24, 44, 89

Kaiser, K., 117, 120
Kanter, A., 127
Kantor, Mickey, 94, 169
Kaplan, L., 110, 113
keiretsu, 74
Kellogg, Frank, 6, 12
Kellogg–Briand Pact (1928), 6, 12
Kemp, B., 223
Kennan, George F., 29–30, 32, 34–5, 37, 72, 211
Kennedy, John F., President, 43–4, 45, 46, 49, 115, 119–20, 204
　Kennedy Round, 114
Kennedy, Paul, 137, 152, 215, 240, 243
Kentucky, 164
Kenya: embassy bombing, 145
Keohane, Robert, 2, 114, 119, 245
Keynes, John Maynard, 83, 84, 86
Keynesian economic policies, 76, 80, 91, 92, 93, 95, 125
Khrushchev, Nikita, 43

Kindleberger, C.P., 72
Kirkpatrick, Jean, 238–9
Kissinger, Henry, 47, 115, 159, 191, 204, 212
　'grand design'/détente, 51–5, 57, 62, 117, 221, 228
　post-Cold War, 227, 244–5
　'Year of Europe', 119–21
Knock, T.J., 9, 217
Koh, Harold, 195
Kohn, H., 184
Kolko, G., 106
Kolko, J., 106
Korea, 32, 33, 46, 52, 74, 220, 224
Korean War, 31, 40, 41, 49, 73, 74, 105, 109
Kosovo, 133
Kreider, C., 20
Kurth, J., 231
Kuwait, 67, 205, 213, 216
Kyoto conference (1997), 147

LaFeber, W., 191, 195
labour, 91, 92
　organized, 36, 55, 76, 82, 90, 93, 96
laissez faire economy, 177
Lake, A., 116
Lamont, Thomas, 10
land, 35, 177, 190
Larrabee, S., 134
Latin America, 7, 23, 92, 113, 178, 192, 200–01
Law, D., 77
law, rule of, 185, 197, 203, 216, 218
law and order, 158, 205
Layne, C., 226, 227, 228, 231
leadership, 54, 72, 228
　Europe, 108, 114, 124, 133, 134, 135
　free world, 127, 185, 186, 188
　and hegemony, 96, 241, 242
　and Japan/Germany, 99, 222, 231
　post-Cold War, 139, 220–21, 226, 227, 247
　post-Second World War, 73, 75, 151
League of Nations, 7, 9–10, 18, 95, 185, 225
Leffler, M.P., 8, 14, 226, 228, 236
legislative branch, 7, 198, 201, 203
　see also Congress
Lehman, J., 198
Lend-Lease, 20
Lenin, V.I., 79
Lerner, Max, 176, 192
less developed countries, 39
liberal democracy, 5, 23, 102
　American national identity, 175, 182
　communism, 186, 187, 204
　new world order, 216, 217
　post-Second World War, 28, 72, 73, 74
liberal internationalism, 10, 78
liberalism, 80, 83, 180, 193, 244
　Cold War, 36, 45, 51
　economic, 72, 73, 75, 77, 86
　neo-liberalism, 90, 93, 96, 97, 98
liberalization, economic, 83, 86–7, 92, 95, 98
liberty, 26, 79, 176, 178, 185, 237
　Cold War, 186, 192
　democratic values, 179, 181, 182
　expansionism, 184
Lichfield, J., 205
Linder, S.B., 224
Link, A.S., 11

Lippman, Walter, 72
Lipset, S.M., 176
living standards, 90
Lloyd George, David, 7
loans, 8, 91, 98
　inter-war years, 14, 15, 20
　post-Second World War, 82, 106
lobbying:
　foreign interest, 153, 168–70
　Jewish concerns, 55
　military/industrial, 45, 55
　states, 166
　see also interest groups
localization of foreign policy, 149–57, 158, 171
London Naval Conference (1930), 12
long boom, 86
'long peace', 220, 228
'Long Telegram', 30, 32
Louisiana, 184
Louvre Accord, 126
Love, J., 154
Luard, Evan, 150
Lundestad, G., 2, 140, 191
Luttwak, E.N., 231, 239
Luxembourg, 80
Lynch, A., 53

MacBride principles, 154–5
McCormick, T.J., 24
MacDonald, Ramsey, 12
McGrew, Anthony, 1–4, 211–47
McKenna, M.C., 18
McKinley, William, President, 190
Macnamara, Robert S., 81
Madison, James, President, 184, 228
Maier, C., 107
Malaysia, 33, 46
Mandelbaum, M., 109, 110
manifest destiny, 183–5, 188, 189, 211, 229
Mao Tse Tung, 53, 73
Marchetti, V., 198
market forces, 75, 98
markets, 5, 129
　free, 16, 59, 204
　overseas, 7, 14, 50, 185
　Soviet Union, 48, 57, 67
　world/global, 39, 47, 98, 152, 162
Marks, J.D., 198
Marks, S., 12
Marshall, George C., 31, 32, 107
Marshall Plan, 21, 73, 98
　anti-communist, 30, 31, 37, 40
　Europe, 85, 104, 107, 108, 110
　post-war reconstruction, 73, 76, 80, 81, 82
Marxism, 62, 67, 93, 95, 137
mass consumption, 75, 79
mass destruction, weapons of, 26, 98, 223–4, 226
mass media, 206
mass production, 75, 79–82, 110
Massachusetts, 154, 155, 156, 164
May, E.R., 195
Mayall, J., 53
Maynes, C.W., 244
media, 72, 78, 206, 213
Meirsheimer, J., 220
Melanson, R.A., 50
Melman, S., 80
melting pot image, 245
mercantilism, 77, 78, 92, 160, 239, 240
merchant shipping, 25

255

Mexican Americans, 246
Mexico, 91, 94, 161, 167, 169, 189
Michigan, 154, 164
Middle East, 77, 113, 117, 129, 214, 223
Midwest region, 18, 133
militarism (Japan/Germany), 74, 75
military aid, 37, 52
military balance, 48, 58
military bases, 63, 82, 214, 233
military build-up, 34, 40, 75, 195, 220, 223
    Kennedy Administration, 44
    Reagan Administration, 62, 64, 122, 124, 214, 216
military–industrial complex, 45–6, 80, 192, 236–7
'military Keynesianism', 125
military power/strength, 177
    inter-war period, 11, 20
    post-Cold War, 215, 222, 229, 231, 241
    post-Second World War, 25–6, 27, 138
    Reagan Administration, 63, 158
    Soviet, 51, 60, 61, 113
    see also balances of power
military security, 82, 118, 140, 147, 163, 224–5, 232
military/defence spending, 45–6, 52, 225, 233, 234
    budget, 23, 58
    Bush Administration, 214
    Eisenhower Administration, 41, 45, 85
    Reagan Administration, 62, 65, 92, 123, 125
military supremacy/primacy, 3, 28, 51, 185–6, 233, 236, 239–40, 247
Milward, A., 104, 108, 110, 111
missiles, 58, 113, 122, 123, 127, 224
mission *see* national mission
Mitterand, Francois, 91
monetary system, international, 84, 88–91, 98, 114, 117, 134
Monroe Doctrine, 229
Montreal Protocol on ozone depletion (1987), 148, 150
moral aspects of foreign policy, 34, 49, 56, 179, 183, 185–8, 192, 204
    post-Cold War, 212, 235, 238, 243
Morgenthau, Hans, 217, 234, 235
Morgenthau, Henry, 8, 19, 20, 28, 71
Morgenthau Plan, 75
most-favoured-nation principle, 86
Mueller, J., 241
multiculturalism, 205
multilateralism:
    free trade system, 39
    global economic system, 18–20, 71–99
    post-Cold War, 221, 233, 234, 241, 242
    transatlantic system, 110, 112, 117, 135
multinational corporations, 111, 148, 156, 241
    see also corporations
multipolarity, 219, 222, 226, 227
Muravchik, J., 187

NAFTA (North American Free Trade Agreement), 131, 161, 162, 167, 169, 224, 238

Nagasaki, 74
Naim, M., 226
Nathan, J.A., 194
National Association of State Development Agencies, 164
National Foreign Trade Council, 156
National Governors' Association, 152, 164, 166
national identity: America, 212, 245–6
    liberal democratic values, 175, 181, 182
    uniqueness, 176, 205
    Vietnam War, 235
national identity: France, 139
national mission/purpose, 33, 191, 217, 220
    Gulf War, 215
    manifest destiny, 189
    post-Cold War, 227, 230, 236, 245
    Vietnam War, 235
National Security Act (1947), 31, 195
National Security Council, 31
    order number 68 *see* NSC-68
nationalism, 42, 95, 219
    America, 17, 19, 205, 237, 246
    economic, 27, 106, 119
    Europe, 108, 114
    hyper-nationalism, 223
    welfare-nationalism, 76–82, 83, 87, 92
Native Americans, 189
NATO *see* North Atlantic Treaty Organization
natural rights, 185, 189, 191
Nau, H., 123
Navari, C., 53
navies:
    America, 11–12, 16, 20–21, 23, 26, 63, 190
    Britain, 11–12, 16, 20–21
    Germany, 9
    India, 223
    Japan, 12
    Soviet Union, 26, 61
Nazi Party, 44, 81, 95
neo-conservatism, 59, 60, 64, 90, 243
neo-Darwinism, 97
neo-isolationism, 172, 217–18, 235, 237–9, 243
neo-liberalism, 90, 93, 96, 97, 98
Netherlands, 80, 86, 122
neutrality, political, 23
Neutrality Acts (1935, 1936, 1937, 1939), 8–9, 17, 18, 20
New Deal, 36, 72, 83, 87, 90, 95
'new diplomacy', 9–11
'New Federalism', 167
New Jersey, 166, 167
New Right, 122, 216, 237, 240
New Transatlantic Agenda, 134
new world order, 177
    inter-war years, 5–21
    post-Cold War, 2, 67, 68, 211–47
    post-Second World War, 71–99
New York City, 155
New York money market, 15, 83–4
    see also Wall Street
Newhouse, J., 134
newspapers, 11
Nicaragua, 58, 192, 200–02
Nicholl, A., 232
Niebuhr, R., 1, 227, 245
Nitze, Paul, 32, 186–7, 192, 239, 242
Nixon, E., 162

Nixon, Richard M., President, 24, 46, 93, 119, 204, 221
    'grand design', 51–5, 57, 62, 117
    Watergate, 54, 116, 147, 159
Nixon Doctrine, 51, 52, 55
Nixon Shock, 85, 89, 116, 118, 120, 121, 139
Nogee, J., 198
Non-Aligned Movement, 73
non-conformity, 45
non-governmental organizations, 147, 168
non-tariff barriers to trade (NTBs), 160, 166
Nordlinger, E., 225
North, Oliver, 202–3
North American Free Trade Agreement (NAFTA), 131, 161, 162, 167, 169, 238, 224
North Atlantic Treaty (1949), 104, 105, 106, 107, 108
North Atlantic Treaty Organization (NATO), 81, 131, 138, 231
    alliance/security structures, 72, 82, 102, 222, 225, 242
    Bosnia, 225, 230
    formation, 21, 31, 37, 40, 107
    France, 48, 114, 139
    1950s, 109, 110, 111, 112
    1960s, 113, 114, 115
    1970s, 117, 120, 121
    Reagan Administration, 62, 122, 123, 127
    reform/enlargement, 101, 132–3, 134, 223, 233
    and Soviet Union, 38, 42
North Korea, 31, 41, 105, 220, 224
Northern Ireland, 154, 163
NSC-68, 229
    early Cold War, 32–4, 40, 44, 192
    later developments, 48, 60, 239, 242
NTBs (non-tariff barriers to trade), 160, 166
nuclear-free zones, 154
nuclear test ban treaty, 44
nuclear weapons:
    America–Europe relations, 58, 109, 114, 115, 120, 132
    American monopoly, 28, 185, 195
    atomic bombs, 26, 29, 31, 74
    Cold War, 212, 220
    Cuba missile crisis, 44, 48, 113
    NATO, 62, 110, 112, 122, 123, 127
    post-Cold War, 97, 101, 223–4, 241
    reductions, 81, 127
    Soviet Union, 26, 48, 67, 105, 113, 127
    state policies, 154, 163
    weapons of mass destruction, 26, 98, 223–4, 226
Nye, Jnr., J.S., 152, 232, 242, 243
Nye Committee, 17

OECD (Organization for Economic Co-operation and Development), 86, 89
offshore markets, 89, 90
oil, 25, 77, 80, 89, 119, 121
    price rises, 90, 91, 117
Okinawa, 74
oligopolies, 80
Oliver, J.K., 194
Olson, W.C., 200

INDEX

OPEC (Organization of Petroleum Exporting Countries), 90, 121
Open Door policy, 13, 72, 77, 229
openness: political/social systems, 145, 151, 153, 182
Operation Desert Shield/Desert Storm, 213, 215, 218
  see also Gulf War
Orde, A., 15
organized labour, 36, 55, 76, 82, 90, 93, 96
  see also trade unions
Orlando, Vittorio, 7
O'Sullivan, John, 184
Ottawa Agreements: Imperial Conference (1932), 8, 18
Organization for Economic Co-operation and Development (OECD), 86, 89
Organization for European Economic Co-operation, 107
Oye, K.W., 125

Pacific region, 78, 222, 224–5, 226, 234, 242
  Asia-Pacific region, 134, 171, 223, 224, 232
  Pacific Rim, 124, 126, 232
Pacific War, 74
Paine, Tom, 176
Pakistan, 97, 224
Panama, 230
patriotism, 205, 237
Pax Americana, 71–99, 216
peace, 14, 27–8, 45, 60, 64, 185, 226–34
  'long peace', 220, 228
'peace dividend', 101, 214
peace groups, 6, 12, 62
Pearce, J., 191
Pearl Harbor, 23
Pentagon see Defense, Department of
perestroika, 64
Perkins, B., 229, 247
Peterson, J., 111, 133
Peterson, M., 184
Pfaltzgraff, R., 115
Philippines, 33, 46, 190–91
Pipes, Richard, 62
planes see aircraft
planned economy, 39, 48, 66–7, 76
Plaza Agreement, 126
Poland, 21, 30, 42, 58, 123, 134, 213
Polanyi, K., 95
policing the world, 47, 204, 218, 242
policy process, 158–70
Policy Planning Staff, 31–2, 228
political economy, global, 92, 93, 102, 103
political system, American, 145, 153, 154, 158, 186, 193, 194
politics, international, 8, 60, 146, 157
  post-Cold War, 231, 232
  post-Second World War, 71, 78, 96
  transatlantic relationship, 102, 113, 118, 121, 125
Polk, James, President, 229
popular culture, 133, 139
Portugal, 126
Powell, Colin, 223, 231
power, American, 74, 75, 96, 203, 216
  'covenant with', 3, 244–7
  economic, 16, 21, 25, 160, 186, 232, 241
  post-Cold War, 228, 230, 235

  see also balances of power; military power; superpowers
powers, division of (state/federal governments), 151, 162
powers, separation of (executive/legislature/judiciary), 151, 198
preponderance, 24, 25, 77, 96, 211, 244
  Cold War status quo, 226, 227, 228, 229, 247
  post-Cold War foreign policy, 230, 232, 234
  and primacy, 235, 237, 239, 243
presidency:
  confidence in, 170, 171, 203
  imperial, 49, 193–6, 197, 198, 199
  use of power, 147, 159
  see also executive branch
presidential elections, 194
  Cold War, 36, 41, 45
  domestic/foreign policy, 101, 205, 237
  Vietnam War, 24
presidents:
  Commander-in-Chief, 81
  and Congress, 7, 151, 198, 201
  foreign affairs, 6, 45, 49
pressure groups see interest groups
primacy, 51–2, 92–6, 203–7, 231, 235–7, 240
private sector, 5, 8, 9, 15, 111
production, 77, 151, 152
  internationalization, 83, 89, 95, 97, 153
  mass production, 75, 79–82, 96, 110
  and transatlantic relationship, 130, 139
'Project Democracy', 202–3
property, 7, 180
protectionism, economic, 23, 71, 122, 160, 161, 166
  post-Cold War, 225, 231, 240
  post-Second World War, 74, 77, 78, 83, 87
public opinion, 201, 203, 206, 243
  Cold War, 55, 58–9, 237
  domestic/foreign policy, 172, 205
  inter-war years 8, 9, 11, 12
  social acitivism, 153–7

quotas, 86–7

racial hierarchy, 191
Ravenal, E., 117
Reagan, Ronald, President, 92, 93, 167, 213
  American hegemony, 214, 215, 228, 240
  Cold War, 59–66, 68, 158, 171, 187, 216, 233
  Europe, 122–8, 139
  foreign policy, 24, 145, 148, 154, 159
  Iran-Contra affair, 65, 128, 200–03
'Reaganomics', 123, 124
'real' economy, 83, 88, 91
realism, 219, 235, 236
rearmament, 37, 39, 46, 109, 110
recessions, 46, 90, 92, 95
Red Army, 38, 109
regionalization, 95, 223, 231
Reich, Robert, 130, 153, 164, 246
religion, 35, 36, 148, 176
reparation payments, 8, 14, 15, 75
Republican Party, 14, 15, 16–17, 161, 169
  Cold War, 36, 41, 42, 60

republicanism, 183, 184, 189, 235
retirement pensions, 76
Reykjavik superpower summit (1986), 65, 127
Rieff, D., 205
Riste, O.W., 106, 109, 110
Rock, W., 18
Rockefeller, David, 79, 81, 82
roll back of communism, 40–42, 44, 60, 77
Roman Catholic church, 36
Romania, 42
Roosevelt, Franklin D., President, 7, 160, 217, 242
  inter-war years, 17, 18, 36
  Second World War, 26, 29, 71, 103, 104, 211
Rosenau, J.N., 237
Rossiter, Clinton, 197
Rowland, B.C., 106, 113, 115
Ruggie, John, 83
rule of law, 185, 197, 203, 216, 218
Rummel, R., 118
Russia:
  inter-war years, 95
  Russian revolution, 10, 36, 79
  see also Soviet Union
Russia: post-Cold War, 101, 132, 218, 231
  economy, 94, 98, 131
  nuclear weapons, 97, 212
'rustbelt' states, 164

sanctions, 123, 126, 154, 155, 162, 164
Sandinista government, 200–02
Saudi Arabia, 218
Savings and Loan Associations, 94
Schacht, Hjalmar, 81
Schlesinger, Arthur, 1, 198
Schlesinger, James, 219, 227
Schmidt, Helmut, 123, 127
Schneider, W., 237
Schuker, S.A., 8, 15
Schultz, George, 148
Schuman Plan, 81
Schurmann, F., 219, 230
Schwartze, H.P., 117
Schwarz, B., 228, 231
Scowcroft, Brent, 66
Second World War, 25–8, 151
  American involvement, 18, 23, 71, 185, 244
  Holocaust, 155
  Soviet Union, 36, 44, 186
  transatlantic system, 102, 103, 105
secrecy, 9, 11, 192, 193, 197, 198–9
security:
  collective, 10, 11, 185, 214, 216, 242
  CSCE, 53, 118, 129, 131, 132, 223
  Europe, 120, 126–7, 129, 133
  North Atlantic Treaty, 104, 105, 106
  see also NATO
  post-Cold War, 97–8, 138, 223, 232
security: America, 8, 77, 125, 130, 145, 158, 168
  Cold War, 52, 55, 57, 58, 122, 195
  foreign policy, 188, 191, 192
  national strategy, 222–6, 231, 233
  post-Cold War, 212, 214, 220, 221, 227
  role of president, 194–5, 196, 198–200
  see also economic security; military security; NSC-68

257

segregation, 36
selective engagement, 238–9, 240
self-determination, national, 26, 72, 73, 185, 190, 191, 219
Senate, 10, 17, 18, 31, 161, 225
  see also Congress
separation of powers, 151, 198
Serfaty, S., 107, 117, 120
'Seven Sisters' corporations, 80
Shanghai communique, 53
Sharpe, K.E., 202
Shulman, Marshall, 57
Shultz, G., 66
Shuman, M.H., 154
Silva, M., 130
Sjogren, B., 130
Smith, H.N., 184
Smith, Michael, 3, 101–40, 167
Smith, T., 2
Smoot Hawley Act (1930), 160
social activism, 153–7, 163
Social Democrat parties, 76
socialism, 35–6, 39, 43, 79
Somalia, 204, 206, 230
South, the, 18, 36, 124, 177
South Africa, 154, 163, 214, 224
South Korea, 31, 46, 52, 105
South Vietnam, 58, 192
sovereign states, 2, 71
sovereignty, 1, 72, 146, 152, 194, 204
Soviet Union, 10, 15, 151, 154, 228
  Cold War, 2, 23–68, 102, 113, 186, 221
  Cold War, end of, 5, 128–9, 244
  collapse of, 147, 212–14, 216
  New Cold War, 122, 123, 124, 127, 187, 240
  post-Second World War, 73, 75, 95, 158
  and transatlantic system, 103, 105, 107, 109, 117
Spain, 105, 126, 189, 190
Spanier, J., 198
Spanish–American War, 190–91
Spero, Joan, 86, 151
spheres of influence, 71, 185, 220
Stalin, Joseph, 27, 29–30, 38, 43, 67
State Department, 104, 111, 147, 148, 166
  inter-war years, 8, 18, 20
  post-Cold War, 219, 226
  post-Second World War, 27, 28, 72, 228
states, 151, 158, 162–7, 168, 177
steel industry, 25, 80, 81, 111, 177
Steichen, Rene, 94
sterling, 18, 72, 84, 85
Stimson, Henry L., 6
stock market see Wall Street
Stone, Oliver, 44
Strange, Susan, 89
Strategic Arms Limitation Talks (SALT) Treaty, 53
Strategic Defence Initiative ('Star Wars'), 127, 145
Strauss, Robert, 168
Suez Canal Zone, 112
suffrage, adult, 76
Suharto, Raden, 94, 192
Sullivan principles, 154
Sunbelt region, 157
superpower, America as, 147, 185–8, 193, 204, 241

and Europe, 129, 137, 138
post-Cold War, 97, 145
post-Second World War, 23–4, 25–8, 37, 101, 151
and presidential power, 159, 194
superpowers, 223
  Britain, 25, 176
  conflict/rivalry, 49, 212, 214, 220, 244
  détente 54, 55, 159
  and Europe, 115, 118, 122, 127
  Japan, 74
  Soviet Union, 56–7, 66, 67
  summit conferences, 64–5
Supreme Court, 194
Sweden, 86
Switzerland: banks, 155, 163, 166, 167

Taft, William Howard, President, 10
Tanzania: embassy bombing, 145
tariffs, 8, 14, 18, 19, 20, 160, 166
Tate & Lyle company, 153
taxation, 77, 92, 123, 168–9, 214
Taylorism, 80
technological dependence, 125, 126, 130
technology, 178, 182, 223, 233
  high technology, 164, 225, 243
Teheran hostage crisis, 59
television, 207, 213, 218
Tennessee, 152, 167
territorial expansion, 177, 183–4, 189–90
TEU (Treaty on European Union), 133, 134
Thailand, 94
Third World, 81, 122
  American foreign policy, 46, 60, 62
  debt, 92
  finance/investment, 77, 113, 151, 224, 238
  Non-Aligned Movement, 73
  and Soviet Union, 48, 52, 57, 58, 65
Third World similarities: America, 91, 205
Thorne, C., 205
Thurow, L., 90, 91, 126, 130
Tibet, 33
Tocqueville, Alexis de, 180, 193, 197, 203, 206
Tokyo, 74
Tokyo Declaration, 230
Toshiba company, 169–70
totalitarianism, 24, 30, 33, 43, 60, 62, 79
Toyota company, 164
trade, 55, 154
  Europe, 52, 119, 123, 139
  inter-war years, 7–8, 12, 19
  international order, 86–8, 231
  states, 163–4, 167
  see also free trade
trade barriers, 9, 13, 18, 160
trade deficits, 85, 152, 158, 160
trade negotiations, global, 101, 114, 115, 151, 160, 161, 167
trade unions, 45, 80, 107, 153, 169
  International Labour Organization, 87
  multinational interests, 72, 78, 148
  see also organized labour
Transatlantic Agenda, New, 134
Transatlantic Business Dialogue, 134
Transatlantic Declaration, 132
transatlantic system, 101–40
transnational corporations, 89, 90
  see also corporations

transnational networks, 78–9
Treasury Department, 8, 18, 20, 72, 83, 168
Treaty of Rapallo, 15
Treaty of Versailles, 7, 10, 75
Treaty on European Union (TEU), 133, 134
Treverton, G.F., 122, 127, 223
Trilateral Commission, 79, 81
Tripartite Stabilization Agreement, 19–20
Truman, Harry S., President, 24, 131, 158, 226, 228
  Cold War, 40, 41, 44
  post-Second World War, 29, 36, 45, 105
Truman Doctrine, 30, 31, 46
Tsoukalis, L., 123, 125
Tucker, Robert W., 137, 218, 227, 228–9, 246
Turkey, 30, 37
'two presidencies' concept, 196, 203

un-American activities, 36, 45, 178, 182
unemployment, 76, 77, 98, 154, 164
unions see trade unions
uniqueness, American, 180–83, 187, 205
United Kingdom see Britain
United Nations, 103, 131, 230, 241, 242
  collective security, 214, 216, 225
  Soviet Union, 65, 67
United Nations Charter, 71, 72
United States of America (USA) see America
united states of Europe, 107, 108
United States v. Curtiss-Wright Export Corporation, 194–5
universality, 180–83, 187
universities, 45
urban decay, 158
urbanization, 177
Uruguay Round see GATT
USSR (Union of Soviet Socialist Republics) see Soviet Union
utopianism, 217, 236, 243

Valladao, A., 2
Van de Pijl, Kees, 80, 81, 137
Vance, Cyrus, 58
Vandenberg, Arthur, 161
Vauxhall Motors company, 14
Versailles Peace Conference, 9, 18, 211
Versailles Treaty, 7, 10, 75
Vietnam, 46, 52, 58, 73, 113, 192
Vietnam War, 44, 81, 117, 218
  effect on America, 24, 47, 49–51, 56, 116, 218
  Japan, 74
  presidency, 49, 159, 197
Volkman, E., 203
voting, 76
vulnerability, 171
  foreign investment, 152
  free society, 192
  internation economic competition, 125, 153, 170, 221, 238, 239
  national security, 113, 145, 227

wages, 79, 80, 90
Walker, M., 206
Wall Street, New York, 15, 17, 81, 83–4
  1929 Crash, 71, 94
  1987 Crash, 94, 125

INDEX

Wallace, Henry, 19
Walsh, J., 204
Walter, A., 93
Waltz, K.N., 222
war debts, 14, 15
War Powers Act (1974), 159
Warsaw Pact, 65, 214
Washington, George, President, 145
Washington Conference (1921–2), 11–12
Washington superpower summit (1988), 64
Watergate, 54, 56, 117, 128
   effect on presidency, 116, 147, 159, 170, 171
Watson, Thomas, 81
weapons of mass destruction, 26, 98, 223–4, 226
   see also nuclear weapons
Weinberg, A.K., 184
Weisband, E., 198, 200
welfare-nationalism, 76–82, 83, 87, 92
welfare state provision, 47, 91, 123, 232

Wessels, W., 118
Western Economic Summits, 119
Western Europe *see* Europe, Western
Western European Union (WEU), 110
White, Harry Dexter, 83
Wicker, T., 199
Wildavsky, Aaron, 196
Williams, P., 131, 172, 235, 237
Williams, William Appleman, 1, 191, 229
Wills, G., 199
Wilson, Woodrow, President, 79, 191, 217, 235, 244, 245
   Fourteen Points address, 9, 13, 216
   new world order, 5, 7, 9–11, 185
Wirk, T., 233
Wolfowitz, P.D., 226
women: voting, 76
Woods, R.B., 20
Woodward, D.P., 152, 164
Woolcock, S., 123, 126, 128, 131, 133
work force, 46, 76, 79, 152
working class, 35, 80
World Bank, 72, 73, 75, 81, 85, 87, 88, 98

World Economic and Monetary Conference (1933), 17, 20
world economy *see* economic world order
world order, 56, 62, 75, 115, 242
   see also economic world order; new world order
World Trade Center, New York, 145
World Trade Organization (WTO), 73, 87, 133, 135, 155, 156
World War I *see* First World War
World War II *see* Second World War

Yalta Accords, 40, 211
Yalta summit conference, 29
'Year of Europe', 119–21
Yeltsin, Boris, 132
yen, 85
Young Plan, 14
Yugoslavia, 101, 129, 131, 133, 138, 204, 218

zaibatsu, 74
Zucconi, M., 133
Zuckerman, M., 2

259

ACKNOWLEDGEMENTS

Grateful acknowledgement is made to the following sources for permission to reproduce material in this book.

CHAPTER 1

Photographs: pp.7, 10, 13, 16, 19: AP/Wide World Photos.

CHAPTER 2

Photographs/illustrations: pp.26, 29, 30, 32, 35, 41, 43, 53, 65: AP/Wide World Photos; p.33: Kegley, C.W. Jr and Wittkopf, E.R. (1993) *World Politics: Trend and Transformation*, © 1993 by St Martin's Press, Inc; p.50: Associated Press.

CHAPTER 3

Photographs: p.84: Courtesy of the International Monetary Fund; p.87: AP/Wide World Photos; p.94: AP-Jacques Collet/Wide World Photos.

CHAPTER 4

Photographs: pp.102, 120, 129: AP/Wide World Photos.

CHAPTER 5

Text: p.155 Authers, J. (1998) 'Swiss banks expect sanctions this week', *Financial Times*, 29 June 1998; p.156 Buckley, N. (1998) 'WTO drawn into row over anti-Burma law', *Financial Times*, 10 September 1998; p.169 Dunne, N. and Bransten, L. (1993) 'Mexico "spending $30m" to boost Nafta in US', *Financial Times*, 28 May 1993.

CHAPTER 6

Photographs/illustrations: p.170: Mansell Collection; p.202: AP/Wide World Photos.

CHAPTER 7

Photographs/illustrations: p.215: AP-Greg Gibson/Wide World Photos; pp.230, 241: AP/Wide World Photos.